GO!
with Microsoft®

PowerPoint 2007
Volume 1

Shelley Gaskin and Alicia Vargas

PEARSON

Prentice
Hall

Upper Saddle River, New Jersey

This book is dedicated to my students, who inspire me every day, and to my husband, Fred Gaskin.
—Shelley Gaskin

This book is dedicated with all my love to my husband Vic, who makes everything possible;
and to my children Victor, Phil, and Emmy, who are an unending source of inspiration
and who make everything worthwhile.
—Alicia Vargas

Library of Congress Cataloging-in-Publication Data

Gaskin, Shelley.
  Go! with. PowerPoint / Shelley Gaskin and Alicia Vargas. -- 1st ed.
    p. cm.
  Includes index.
  ISBN 0-13-244798-3
  1. Presentation graphics software. 2. Microsoft PowerPoint (Computer file) I. Vargas, Alicia.
II. Title.
  T385.G37877 2007
  005.5'8--dc22

                                        2007023983

Vice President and Publisher: Natalie E. Anderson
Associate VP/Executive Acquisitions Editor,
  Print: Stephanie Wall
Executive Acquisitions Editor, Media: Richard Keaveny
Product Development Manager: Eileen Bien Calabro
Editorial Project Manager: Laura Burgess
Development Editor: Ginny Munroe
Editorial Assistant: Becky Knauer
Executive Producer: Lisa Strite
Content Development Manager: Cathi Profitko
Media Project Manager: Alana Myers
Production Media Project Manager: Lorena Cerisano
Director of Marketing: Margaret Waples
Senior Marketing Manager: Jason Sakos
Marketing Assistants: Angela Frey, Kathryn Ferranti
Senior Sales Associate: Rebecca Scott

Senior Managing Editor: Cynthia Zonneveld
Managing Editor: Camille Trentacoste
Production Project Manager: Wanda Rockwell
Production Editor: GGS Book Services
Photo Researcher: GGS Book Services
Manufacturing Buyer: Natacha Moore
Production/Editorial Assistant: Sandra K. Bernales
Design Director: Maria Lange
Art Director/Interior Design: Blair Brown
Cover Photo: Courtesy of Getty Images, Inc./Marvin
  Mattelson
Composition: GGS Book Services
Project Management: GGS Book Services
Cover Printer: Phoenix Color
Printer/Binder: RR Donnelley/Willard

Microsoft, Windows, Word, PowerPoint, Outlook, FrontPage, Visual Basic, MSN, The Microsoft Network, and/or other Microsoft products referenced herein are either trademarks or registered trademarks of Microsoft Corporation in the U.S.A. and other countries. Screen shots and icons reprinted with permission from the Microsoft Corporation. This book is not sponsored or endorsed by or affiliated with Microsoft Corporation.

Credits and acknowledgments borrowed from other sources and reproduced, with permission, in this textbook are as follows or on the appropriate page within the text.

    Page 2: Rough Guides Dorling Kindersley; page 80: AGE Fotostock America, Inc.; page 162: The Stock Connection; page 236: Omni-Photo Communications, Inc.; page 316: PhotoEdit, Inc.; and page 384: Doris Kindersley Media Library.

10 9 8 7 6 5 4 3 2
ISBN 10: 0-13-244798-3
ISBN 13: 978-0-13-244798-0

Contents in Brief

Table of Contents

Letter from the Editor

Dear Instructors and Students,

The primary goal of the *GO!* Series is two-fold. The first goal is to help instructors teach the course they want in less time. The second goal is to provide students with the skills to solve business problems using the computer as a tool, for both themselves and the organization for which they might be employed.

The *GO!* Series was originally created by Series Editor Shelley Gaskin and published with the release of Microsoft Office 2003. Her ideas came from years of using textbooks that didn't meet all the needs of today's diverse classroom and that were too confusing for students. Shelley continues to enhance the series by ensuring we stay true to our vision of developing quality instruction and useful classroom tools.

But we also need your input and ideas.

Over time, the *GO!* Series has evolved based on direct feedback from instructors and students using the series. *We are the publisher that listens.* To publish a textbook that works for you, it's critical that we continue to listen to this feedback. It's important to me to talk with you and hear your stories about using *GO!* Your voice can make a difference.

My hope is that this letter will inspire you to write me an e-mail and share your thoughts on using the *GO!* Series.

Stephanie Wall
Executive Editor, *GO!* Series
stephanie_wall@prenhall.com

GO! System Contributors

We thank the following people for their hard work and support in making the *GO!* System all that it is!

Additional Author Support

Coyle, Diane	Montgomery County Community College
Fry, Susan	Boise State
Townsend, Kris	Spokane Falls Community College
Stroup, Tracey	Amgen Corporation

Instructor Resource Authors

Amer, Beverly	Northern Arizona University	Paterson, Jim	Paradise Valley Community College
Boito, Nancy	Harrisburg Area Community College	Prince, Lisa	Missouri State
Coyle, Diane	Montgomery County Community College	Rodgers, Gwen	Southern Nazarene University
Dawson, Tamara	Southern Nazarene University	Ruymann, Amy	Burlington Community College
Driskel, Loretta	Niagara County Community College	Ryan, Bob	Montgomery County Community College
Elliott, Melissa	Odessa College		
Fry, Susan	Boise State	Smith, Diane	Henry Ford Community College
Geoghan, Debra	Bucks County Community College	Spangler, Candice	Columbus State Community College
Hearn, Barbara	Community College of Philadelphia	Thompson, Joyce	Lehigh Carbon Community College
Jones, Stephanie	South Plains College	Tiffany, Janine	Reading Area Community College
Madsen, Donna	Kirkwood Community College	Watt, Adrienne	Douglas College
Meck, Kari	Harrisburg Area Community College	Weaver, Paul	Bossier Parish Community College
Miller, Cindy	Ivy Tech	Weber, Sandy	Gateway Technical College
Nowakowski, Tony	Buffalo State	Wood, Dawn	
Pace, Phyllis	Queensborough Community College	Weissman, Jonathan	Finger Lakes Community College

Super Reviewers

Brotherton, Cathy	Riverside Community College	Maurer, Trina	Odessa College
Cates, Wally	Central New Mexico Community College	Meck, Kari	Harrisburg Area Community College
		Miller, Cindy	Ivy Tech Community College
Cone, Bill	Northern Arizona University	Nielson, Phil	Salt Lake Community College
Coverdale, John	Riverside Community College	Rodgers, Gwen	Southern Nazarene University
Foster, Nancy	Baker College	Smolenski, Robert	Delaware Community College
Helfand, Terri	Chaffey College	Spangler, Candice	Columbus State Community College
Hibbert, Marilyn	Salt Lake Community College	Thompson, Joyce	Lehigh Carbon Community College
Holliday, Mardi	Community College of Philadelphia	Weber, Sandy	Gateway Technical College
Jerry, Gina	Santa Monica College	Wells, Lorna	Salt Lake Community College
Martin, Carol	Harrisburg Area Community College	Zaboski, Maureen	University of Scranton

Technical Editors

Janice Snyder
Joyce Nielsen
Colette Eisele
Janet Pickard
Mara Zebest
Lindsey Allen
William Daley
LeeAnn Bates

Student Reviewers

Allen, John	Asheville-Buncombe Tech Community College	Erickson, Mike	Ball State University
		Gadomski, Amanda	Northern Michigan University
Alexander, Steven	St. Johns River Community College	Gyselinck, Craig	Central Washington University
Alexander, Melissa	Tulsa Community College	Harrison, Margo	Central Washington University
Bolz, Stephanie	Northern Michigan University	Heacox, Kate	Central Washington University
Berner, Ashley	Central Washington University	Hill, Cheretta	Northwestern State University
Boomer, Michelle	Northern Michigan University	Innis, Tim	Tulsa Community College
Busse, Brennan	Northern Michigan University	Jarboe, Aaron	Central Washington University
Butkey, Maura	Central Washington University	Klein, Colleen	Northern Michigan University
Christensen, Kaylie	Northern Michigan University	Moeller, Jeffrey	Northern Michigan University
Connally, Brianna	Central Washington University	Nicholson, Regina	Athens Tech College
Davis, Brandon	Northern Michigan University	Niehaus, Kristina	Northern Michigan University
Davis, Christen	Central Washington University	Nisa, Zaibun	Santa Rosa Community College
Den Boer, Lance	Central Washington University	Nunez, Nohelia	Santa Rosa Community College
Dix, Jessica	Central Washington University	Oak, Samantha	Central Washington University
Moeller, Jeffrey	Northern Michigan University	Oertii, Monica	Central Washington University
Downs, Elizabeth	Central Washington University	Palenshus, Juliet	Central Washington University

Pohl, Amanda	Northern Michigan University	Shanahan, Megan	Northern Michigan University
Presnell, Randy	Central Washington University	Teska, Erika	Hawaii Pacific University
Ritner, April	Northern Michigan University	Traub, Amy	Northern Michigan University
Rodriguez, Flavia	Northwestern State University	Underwood, Katie	Central Washington University
Roberts, Corey	Tulsa Community College	Walters, Kim	Central Washington University
Rossi, Jessica Ann	Central Washington University	Wilson, Kelsie	Central Washington University
Shafapay, Natasha	Central Washington University	Wilson, Amanda	Green River Community College

Series Reviewers

Abraham, Reni	Houston Community College	Crawford, Thomasina	Miami-Dade College, Kendall Campus
Agatston, Ann	Agatston Consulting Technical College	Credico, Grace	Lethbridge Community College
Alexander, Melody	Ball Sate University	Crenshaw, Richard	Miami Dade Community College, North
Alejandro, Manuel	Southwest Texas Junior College	Crespo, Beverly	Mt. San Antonio College
Ali, Farha	Lander University	Crossley, Connie	Cincinnati State Technical Community College
Amici, Penny	Harrisburg Area Community College	Curik, Mary	Central New Mexico Community College
Anderson, Patty A.	Lake City Community College		
Andrews, Wilma	Virginia Commonwealth College, Nebraska University	De Arazoza, Ralph	Miami Dade Community College
Anik, Mazhar	Tiffin University	Danno, John	DeVry University/Keller Graduate School
Armstrong, Gary	Shippensburg University		
Atkins, Bonnie	Delaware Technical Community College	Davis, Phillip	Del Mar College
		DeHerrera, Laurie	Pikes Peak Community College
Bachand, LaDonna	Santa Rosa Community College	Delk, Dr. K. Kay	Seminole Community College
Bagui, Sikha	University of West Florida	Doroshow, Mike	Eastfield College
Beecroft, Anita	Kwantlen University College	Douglas, Gretchen	SUNYCortland
Bell, Paula	Lock Haven College	Dove, Carol	Community College of Allegheny
Belton, Linda	Springfield Tech. Community College	Driskel, Loretta	Niagara Community College
		Duckwiler, Carol	Wabaunsee Community College
Bennett, Judith	Sam Houston State University	Duncan, Mimi	University of Missouri-St. Louis
Bhatia, Sai	Riverside Community College	Duthie, Judy	Green River Community College
Bishop, Frances	DeVry Institute—Alpharetta (ATL)	Duvall, Annette	Central New Mexico Community College
Blaszkiewicz, Holly	Ivy Tech Community College/Region 1		
Branigan, Dave	DeVry University	Ecklund, Paula	Duke University
Bray, Patricia	Allegany College of Maryland	Eng, Bernice	Brookdale Community College
Brotherton, Cathy	Riverside Community College	Evans, Billie	Vance-Granville Community College
Buehler, Lesley	Ohlone College	Feuerbach, Lisa	Ivy Tech East Chicago
Buell, C	Central Oregon Community College	Fisher, Fred	Florida State University
Byars, Pat	Brookhaven College	Foster, Penny L.	Anne Arundel Community College
Byrd, Lynn	Delta State University, Cleveland, Mississippi	Foszcz, Russ	McHenry County College
		Fry, Susan	Boise State University
Cacace, Richard N.	Pensacola Junior College	Fustos, Janos	Metro State
Cadenhead, Charles	Brookhaven College	Gallup, Jeanette	Blinn College
Calhoun, Ric	Gordon College	Gelb, Janet	Grossmont College
Cameron, Eric	Passaic Community College	Gentry, Barb	Parkland College
Carriker, Sandra	North Shore Community College	Gerace, Karin	St. Angela Merici School
Cannamore, Madie	Kennedy King	Gerace, Tom	Tulane University
Carreon, Cleda	Indiana University—Purdue University, Indianapolis	Ghajar, Homa	Oklahoma State University
		Gifford, Steve	Northwest Iowa Community College
Chaffin, Catherine	Shawnee State University	Glazer, Ellen	Broward Community College
Chauvin, Marg	Palm Beach Community College, Boca Raton	Gordon, Robert	Hofstra University
		Gramlich, Steven	Pasco-Hernando Community College
Challa, Chandrashekar	Virginia State University	Graviett, Nancy M.	St. Charles Community College, St. Peters, Missouri
Chamlou, Afsaneh	NOVA Alexandria		
Chapman, Pam	Wabaunsee Community College	Greene, Rich	Community College of Allegheny County
Christensen, Dan	Iowa Western Community College		
Clay, Betty	Southeastern Oklahoma State University	Gregoryk, Kerry	Virginia Commonwealth State
		Griggs, Debra	Bellevue Community College
Collins, Linda D.	Mesa Community College	Grimm, Carol	Palm Beach Community College
Conroy-Link, Janet	Holy Family College	Hahn, Norm	Thomas Nelson Community College
Cosgrove, Janet	Northwestern CT Community	Hammerschlag, Dr. Bill	Brookhaven College
Courtney, Kevin	Hillsborough Community College	Hansen, Michelle	Davenport University
Cox, Rollie	Madison Area Technical College	Hayden, Nancy	Indiana University—Purdue University, Indianapolis
Crawford, Hiram	Olive Harvey College		

Hayes, Theresa — Broward Community College
Helfand, Terri — Chaffey College
Helms, Liz — Columbus State Community College
Hernandez, Leticia — TCI College of Technology
Hibbert, Marilyn — Salt Lake Community College
Hoffman, Joan — Milwaukee Area Technical College
Hogan, Pat — Cape Fear Community College
Holland, Susan — Southeast Community College
Hopson, Bonnie — Athens Technical College
Horvath, Carrie — Albertus Magnus College
Horwitz, Steve — Community College of Philadelphia
Hotta, Barbara — Leeward Community College
Howard, Bunny — St. Johns River Community
Howard, Chris — DeVry University
Huckabay, Jamie — Austin Community College
Hudgins, Susan — East Central University
Hulett, Michelle J. — Missouri State University
Hunt, Darla A. — Morehead State University, Morehead, Kentucky
Hunt, Laura — Tulsa Community College
Jacob, Sherry — Jefferson Community College
Jacobs, Duane — Salt Lake Community College
Jauken, Barb — Southeastern Community
Johnson, Kathy — Wright College
Johnson, Mary — Kingwood College
Johnson, Mary — Mt. San Antonio College
Jones, Stacey — Benedict College
Jones, Warren — University of Alabama, Birmingham
Jordan, Cheryl — San Juan College
Kapoor, Bhushan — California State University, Fullerton
Kasai, Susumu — Salt Lake Community College
Kates, Hazel — Miami Dade Community College, Kendall
Keen, Debby — University of Kentucky
Keeter, Sandy — Seminole Community College
Kern-Blystone, Dorothy Jean — Bowling Green State
Keskin, Ilknur — The University of South Dakota
Kirk, Colleen — Mercy College
Kleckner, Michelle — Elon University
Kliston, Linda — Broward Community College, North Campus
Kochis, Dennis — Suffolk County Community College
Kramer, Ed — Northern Virginia Community College
Laird, Jeff — Northeast State Community College
Lamoureaux, Jackie — Central New Mexico Community College
Lange, David — Grand Valley State
LaPointe, Deb — Central New Mexico Community College
Larson, Donna — Louisville Technical Institute
Laspina, Kathy — Vance-Granville Community College
Le Grand, Dr. Kate — Broward Community College
Lenhart, Sheryl — Terra Community College
Letavec, Chris — University of Cincinnati
Liefert, Jane — Everett Community College
Lindaman, Linda — Black Hawk Community College
Lindberg, Martha — Minnesota State University
Lightner, Renee — Broward Community College
Lindberg, Martha — Minnesota State University
Linge, Richard — Arizona Western College
Logan, Mary G. — Delgado Community College
Loizeaux, Barbara — Westchester Community College
Lopez, Don — Clovis-State Center Community College District

Lord, Alexandria — Asheville Buncombe Tech
Lowe, Rita — Harold Washington College
Low, Willy Hui — Joliet Junior College
Lucas, Vickie — Broward Community College
Lynam, Linda — Central Missouri State University
Lyon, Lynne — Durham College
Lyon, Pat Rajski — Tomball College
MacKinnon, Ruth — Georgia Southern University
Macon, Lisa — Valencia Community College, West Campus
Machuca, Wayne — College of the Sequoias
Madison, Dana — Clarion University
Maguire, Trish — Eastern New Mexico University
Malkan, Rajiv — Montgomery College
Manning, David — Northern Kentucky University
Marcus, Jacquie — Niagara Community College
Marghitu, Daniela — Auburn University
Marks, Suzanne — Bellevue Community College
Marquez, Juanita — El Centro College
Marquez, Juan — Mesa Community College
Martyn, Margie — Baldwin-Wallace College
Marucco, Toni — Lincoln Land Community College
Mason, Lynn — Lubbock Christian University
Matutis, Audrone — Houston Community College
Matkin, Marie — University of Lethbridge
McCain, Evelynn — Boise State University
McCannon, Melinda — Gordon College
McCarthy, Marguerite — Northwestern Business College
McCaskill, Matt L. — Brevard Community College
McClellan, Carolyn — Tidewater Community College
McClure, Darlean — College of Sequoias
McCrory, Sue A. — Missouri State University
McCue, Stacy — Harrisburg Area Community College
McEntire-Orbach, Teresa — Middlesex County College
McLeod, Todd — Fresno City College
McManus, Illyana — Grossmont College
McPherson, Dori — Schoolcraft College
Meiklejohn, Nancy — Pikes Peak Community College
Menking, Rick — Hardin-Simmons University
Meredith, Mary — University of Louisiana at Lafayette
Mermelstein, Lisa — Baruch College
Metos, Linda — Salt Lake Community College
Meurer, Daniel — University of Cincinnati
Meyer, Marian — Central New Mexico Community College
Miller, Cindy — Ivy Tech Community College, Lafayette, Indiana
Mitchell, Susan — Davenport University
Mohle, Dennis — Fresno Community College
Monk, Ellen — University of Delaware
Moore, Rodney — Holland College
Morris, Mike — Southeastern Oklahoma State University
Morris, Nancy — Hudson Valley Community College
Moseler, Dan — Harrisburg Area Community College
Nabors, Brent — Reedley College, Clovis Center
Nadas, Erika — Wright College
Nadelman, Cindi — New England College
Nademlynsky, Lisa — Johnson & Wales University
Ncube, Cathy — University of West Florida
Nagengast, Joseph — Florida Career College
Newsome, Eloise — Northern Virginia Community College Woodbridge
Nicholls, Doreen — Mohawk Valley Community College
Nunan, Karen — Northeast State Technical Community College

Odegard, Teri	Edmonds Community College
Ogle, Gregory	North Community College
Orr, Dr. Claudia	Northern Michigan University South
Otieno, Derek	DeVry University
Otton, Diana Hill	Chesapeake College
Oxendale, Lucia	West Virginia Institute of Technology
Paiano, Frank	Southwestern College
Patrick, Tanya	Clackamas Community College
Peairs, Deb	Clark State Community College
Prince, Lisa	Missouri State University-Springfield Campus
Proietti, Kathleen	Northern Essex Community College
Pusins, Delores	HCCC
Raghuraman, Ram	Joliet Junior College
Reasoner, Ted Allen	Indiana University—Purdue
Reeves, Karen	High Point University
Remillard, Debbie	New Hampshire Technical Institute
Rhue, Shelly	DeVry University
Richards, Karen	Maplewoods Community College
Richardson, Mary	Albany Technical College
Rodgers, Gwen	Southern Nazarene University
Roselli, Diane	Harrisburg Area Community College
Ross, Dianne	University of Louisiana in Lafayette
Rousseau, Mary	Broward Community College, South
Samson, Dolly	Hawaii Pacific University
Sams, Todd	University of Cincinnati
Sandoval, Everett	Reedley College
Sardone, Nancy	Seton Hall University
Scafide, Jean	Mississippi Gulf Coast Community College
Scheeren, Judy	Westmoreland County Community College
Schneider, Sol	Sam Houston State University
Scroggins, Michael	Southwest Missouri State University
Sever, Suzanne	Northwest Arkansas Community College
Sheridan, Rick	California State University-Chico
Silvers, Pamela	Asheville Buncombe Tech
Singer, Steven A.	University of Hawai'i, Kapi'olani Community College
Sinha, Atin	Albany State University
Skolnick, Martin	Florida Atlantic University
Smith, T. Michael	Austin Community College
Smith, Tammy	Tompkins Cortland Community Collge
Smolenski, Bob	Delaware County Community College
Spangler, Candice	Columbus State
Stedham, Vicki	St. Petersburg College, Clearwater
Stefanelli, Greg	Carroll Community College
Steiner, Ester	New Mexico State University
Stenlund, Neal	Northern Virginia Community College, Alexandria
St. John, Steve	Tulsa Community College
Sterling, Janet	Houston Community College
Stoughton, Catherine	Laramie County Community College
Sullivan, Angela	Joliet Junior College
Szurek, Joseph	University of Pittsburgh at Greensburg
Tarver, Mary Beth	Northwestern State University
Taylor, Michael	Seattle Central Community College
Thangiah, Sam	Slippery Rock University
Thompson-Sellers, Ingrid	Georgia Perimeter College
Tomasi, Erik	Baruch College
Toreson, Karen	Shoreline Community College
Trifiletti, John J.	Florida Community College at Jacksonville
Trivedi, Charulata	Quinsigamond Community College, Woodbridge
Tucker, William	Austin Community College
Turgeon, Cheryl	Asnuntuck Community College
Turpen, Linda	Central New Mexico Community College
Upshaw, Susan	Del Mar College
Unruh, Angela	Central Washington University
Vanderhoof, Dr. Glenna	Missouri State University-Springfield Campus
Vargas, Tony	El Paso Community College
Vicars, Mitzi	Hampton University
Villarreal, Kathleen	Fresno
Vitrano, Mary Ellen	Palm Beach Community College
Volker, Bonita	Tidewater Community College
Wahila, Lori (Mindy)	Tompkins Cortland Community College
Waswick, Kim	Southeast Community College, Nebraska
Wavle, Sharon	Tompkins Cortland Community College
Webb, Nancy	City College of San Francisco
Wells, Barbara E.	Central Carolina Technical College
Wells, Lorna	Salt Lake Community College
Welsh, Jean	Lansing Community College Nebraska
White, Bruce	Quinnipiac University
Willer, Ann	Solano Community College
Williams, Mark	Lane Community College
Wilson, Kit	Red River College
Wilson, Roger	Fairmont State University
Wimberly, Leanne	International Academy of Design and Technology
Worthington, Paula	Northern Virginia Community College
Yauney, Annette	Herkimer County Community College
Yip, Thomas	Passaic Community College
Zavala, Ben	Webster Tech
Zlotow, Mary Ann	College of DuPage
Zudeck, Steve	Broward Community College, North

About the Authors

Shelley Gaskin, Series Editor, is a professor of business and computer technology at Pasadena City College in Pasadena, California. She holds a master's degree in business education from Northern Illinois University and a doctorate in adult and community education from Ball State University. Dr. Gaskin has 15 years of experience in the computer industry with several Fortune 500 companies and has developed and written training materials for custom systems applications in both the public and private sector. She is also the author of books on Microsoft Outlook and word processing.

Alicia Vargas is a faculty member in Business Information Technology at Pasadena City College. She holds a master's and a bachelor's degree in business education from California State University, Los Angeles, and has authored several textbooks and training manuals on Microsoft Word, Microsoft Excel, and Microsoft PowerPoint.

Visual Walk-Through of the *GO!* System

The *GO!* System is designed for ease of implementation on the instructor side and ease of understanding on the student. It has been completely developed based on professor and student feedback.

The *GO!* System is divided into three categories that reflect how you might organize your course— **Prepare**, **Teach**, and **Assess**.

Prepare

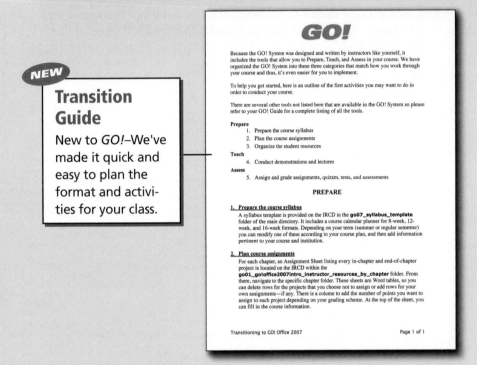

NEW

Transition Guide

New to *GO!*–We've made it quick and easy to plan the format and activities for your class.

Syllabus Template

Includes course calendar planner for 8-, 12-, and 16-week formats.

Assignment Sheet

One per chapter. Lists all possible assignments; add to and delete from this simple Word table according to your course plan.

GO! with Microsoft Office 2007 Introductory

Assignment Sheet for GO! with Microsoft Office 2007 Introductory
Chapter 5

Instructor Name: _____
Course Information: _____

Do This (✔ when done)	Then Hand in This Check each Project for the elements listed on the Assignment tag. Attach the tag to your Project.	Submit Printed Formulas	By This Date	Possible Points	Your Points
Study the text and perform the steps for Activities 5.1 – 5.11	Project 5A Application Letter				
Study the text and perform the steps for Activities 5.12 – 5.29	Project 5B Company Overview				
End-of-Chapter Assessments					
Complete the Matching and Fill-in-the-Blank questions	As directed by your instructor				
Complete Project 5C	Project 5C Receipt Letter				
Complete Project 5D	Project 5D Marketing				
Complete Project 5E	Project 5E School Tour				
Complete Project 5F	Project 5F Scouting Trip				
Complete Project 5G	Project 5G Contract				
Complete Project 5H	Project 5H Invitation				
Complete Project 5I	Project 5I Fax Cover				
Complete Project 5J	Project 5J Business Running Case				
Complete Project 5K	Project 5K Services				
Complete Project 5L	Project 5L Survey Form				
Complete Project 5M	Project 5M Press Release				

Copyright © 2008 Pearson Prentice Hall — Page 1 of 1

File Guide to the *GO!* Supplements

Tabular listing of all supplements and their file names.

Assignment Planning Guide

Description of *GO!* assignments with recommendations based on class size, delivery mode, and student needs. Includes examples from fellow instructors.

GO! with Microsoft Office 2007 Introductory
Assignment Planning Guide

Planning the Course Assignments

For each chapter in GO!, an Assignment Sheet listing every in-chapter and end-of-chapter project is located on the IRCD. These sheets are Word tables, so you can delete rows for the projects that you will not assign, and then add rows for any of your own assignments that you may have developed. There is a column to add the number of points you want to assign to each project—depending on your grading scheme. At the top of the sheet, you can fill in your course information.

Additionally, for each chapter, student Assignment Tags are provided for every project (including Problem Solving projects)—also located on the IRCD. These are small scoring checklists on which you can check off errors made by the student, and with which the student can verify that all project elements are complete. For campus classes, the student can attach the tags to his or her paper submissions. For online classes, many GO! instructors have the student include these with the electronic submission.

Deciding What to Assign

Front Portion of the Chapter—Instructional Projects: The projects in the front portion of the chapter, which are listed on the first page of each chapter, are the instructional projects. Most instructors assign all of these projects, because this is where the student receives the instruction and engages in the active learning.

End-of-Chapter—Practice and Critical Thinking Projects: In the back portion of the chapter (the gray pages), you can assign on a prescriptive basis; that is, for students who were challenged by the instructional projects, you might assign one or more projects from the two *Skills Reviews*, which provide maximum prompting and a thorough review of the entire chapter. For students who have previous software knowledge and who completed the instructional projects easily, you might assign only the *Mastery Projects*.

You can also assign prescriptively by Objective, because each end-of-chapter project indicates the Objectives covered. So you might assign, on a student-by-student basis, only the projects that cover the Objectives with which the student seemed to have difficulty in the instructional projects.

The five Problem Solving projects and the You and GO! project are the authentic assessments that pull together the student's learning. Here the student is presented with a "messy real-life situation" and then uses his or her knowledge and skill to solve a problem, produce a product, give a presentation, or demonstrate a procedure. You might assign one or more of the Problem

GO! Assignment Planning Guide — Page 1 of 1

Student Data Files

Music School Records discovers, launches, and and develops the careers of young artists in classical, jazz, and contemporary music. Our philosophy is to not only shape, distribute, and sell a music product, but to help artists create a career that can lats a lifetime. too often in the music industry, artists are forced to fit their music to a trend that is short-lived. Music School Records doesn't just follow trends, we take a long-term view of the music industry and help our artists develop a style and repertiore that is fluid and flexible and that will appeal to audiences for years and even decades.

The music industry is constantly changing, but over the last decade the changes have been enormous. New forms of entertainment such as DVDs, video games, and the Internet mean there are more competition for the leisure dollar in the market. New technologies give consomers more options for buying and listening to music, and they are demaning high quality recordings. Young consomers are comfortable with technology and want the music they love when and where they want it, no matter where they are or what they are doing.

Music School Records embraces new technologies and the sophisticated market of young music lovers. We believe that providing high quality recordings of truly talented artists make for more discerning listeners who will cherish the gift of music for the rest of their lives. The expertise of Music School Records includes:

- Insight into our target market and the ability to reach the desired audience
- The ability to access all current sources of music income
- A management team with years of experience in music commerce
- Innovative business strategies and artist development plans
- Investment in technology infrastructure for high quality recordings and business services
- Initiative and proactive management of artist careers

Online Study Guide for Students

Interactive objective-style questions based on chapter content.

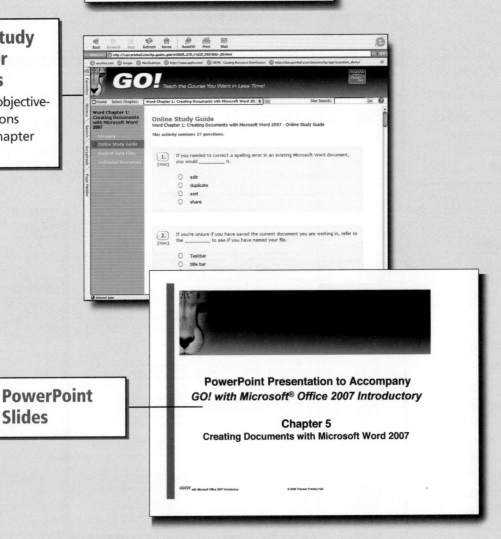

PowerPoint Slides

Teach

Student Textbook

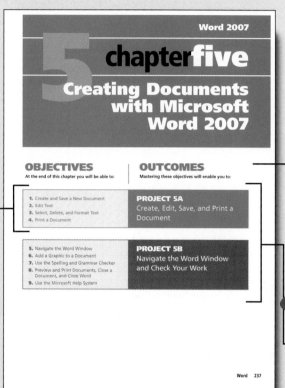

Learning Objectives and Student Outcomes

Objectives are clustered around projects that result in student outcomes. They help students learn how to solve problems, not just learn software features.

Project-Based Instruction

Students do not practice features of the application; they create real projects that they will need in the real world. Projects are color coded for easy reference and are named to reflect skills the students will be practicing.

A and B Projects

Each chapter contains two instructional projects—A and B.

Each chapter opens with a story that sets the stage for the projects the student will create; the instruction does not force the student to pretend to be someone or make up a scenario.

Each chapter has an introductory paragraph that briefs students on what is important.

Visual Summary

Shows students upfront what their projects will look like when they are done.

Objective

The skills the student will learn are clearly stated at the beginning of each project and color coded to match projects listed on the chapter opener page.

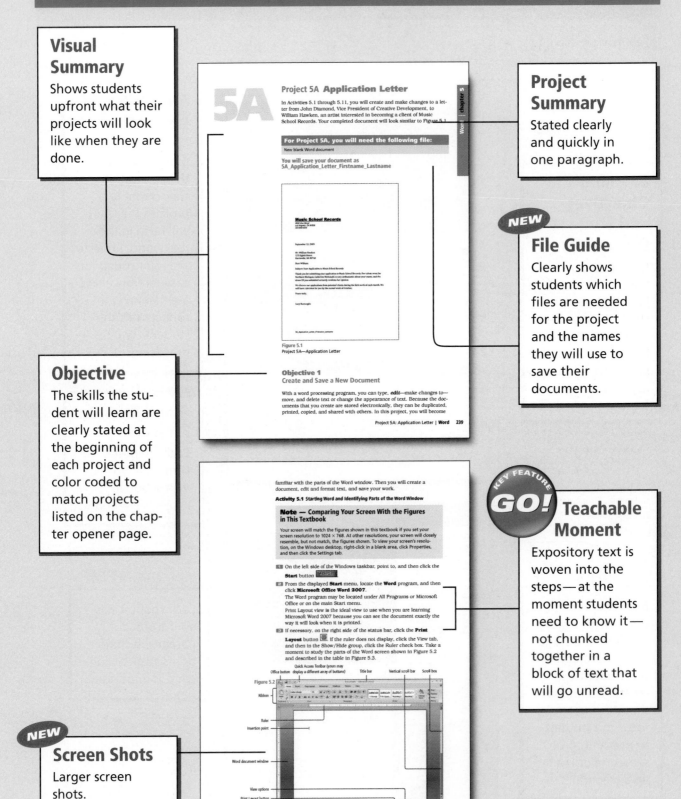

Project Summary

Stated clearly and quickly in one paragraph.

NEW

File Guide

Clearly shows students which files are needed for the project and the names they will use to save their documents.

Teachable Moment

Expository text is woven into the steps—at the moment students need to know it—not chunked together in a block of text that will go unread.

NEW

Screen Shots

Larger screen shots.

Steps

Color coded to the current project, easy to read, and not too many to confuse the student or too few to be meaningless.

Sequential Pagination

No more confusing letters and abbreviations.

End-of-Project Icon

All projects in the *GO! Series* have clearly identifiable end points, useful in self-paced or on-line environments.

Microsoft Procedural Syntax

All steps are written in Microsoft Procedural Syntax to put the student in the right place at the right time.

Press **Enter** two more times.

In a business letter, insert two blank lines between the date and the inside address, which is the same as the address you would use on an envelope.

Type **Mr. William Hawken** and then press **Enter**.

The wavy red line under the proper name *Hawken* indicates that the word has been flagged as misspelled because it is a word not contained in the Word dictionary.

On two lines, type the following address, but do not press **Enter** at the end of the second line:

123 Eighth Street
Harrisville, MI 48740

Note — Typing the Address

Include a comma after the city name in an inside address. However, for mailing addresses on envelopes, eliminate the comma after the city name.

On the **Home tab**, in the **Styles group**, click the **Normal** button.

The Normal style is applied to the text in the rest of the document. Recall that the Normal style adds extra space between paragraphs; it also adds slightly more space between lines in a paragraph.

Press **Enter**. Type **Dear William:** and then press **Enter**.

This salutation is the line that greets the person receiving the letter.

Type **Subject: Your Application to Music School Records** and press **Enter**. Notice the light dots between words, which indicate spaces and display when formatting marks are displayed. Also, notice the extra space after each paragraph, and then compare your screen with Figure 5.6.

The subject line is optional, but you should include a subject line in most letters to identify the topic. Depending on your Word settings, a wavy green line may display in the subject line, indicating a potential grammar error.

Note — Space Between Lines in Your Printed Document

The Cambria font, and many others, uses a slightly larger space between the lines than more traditional fonts like Times New Roman. As you progress in your study of Word, you will use many different fonts and also adjust the spacing between lines.

From the **Office** menu, click **Close**, saving any changes if prompted to do so. Leave Word open for the next project.

Another Way

To Print a Document

To Print a document:

• From the Office menu, click Print to display the Print dialog box (to be covered later), from which you can choose a variety of different options, such as printing multiple copies, printing on a different printer, and printing some but not all pages.

• Hold down **Ctrl** and then press **P**. This is an alternative to the Office menu command, and opens the Print dialog box.

• Hold down **Alt**, press **F**, and then press **P**. This opens the Print dialog box.

End You have completed Project 5A

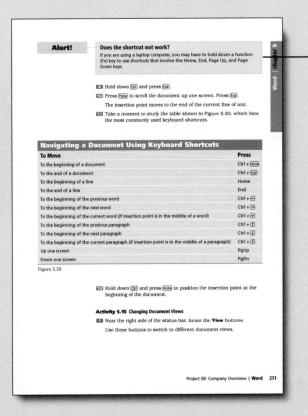

Alert box

Draws students' attention to make sure they aren't getting too far off course.

Another Way box

Shows students other ways of doing tasks.

More Knowledge box

Expands on a topic by going deeper into the material.

Note box

Points out important items to remember.

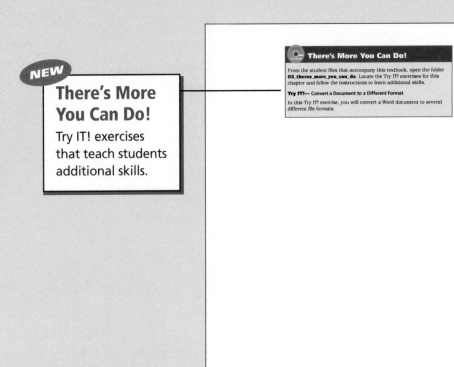

NEW

There's More You Can Do!

Try IT! exercises that teach students additional skills.

End-of-Chapter Material

Take your pick! Content-based or Outcomes-based projects to choose from. Below is a table outlining the various types of projects that fit into these two categories.

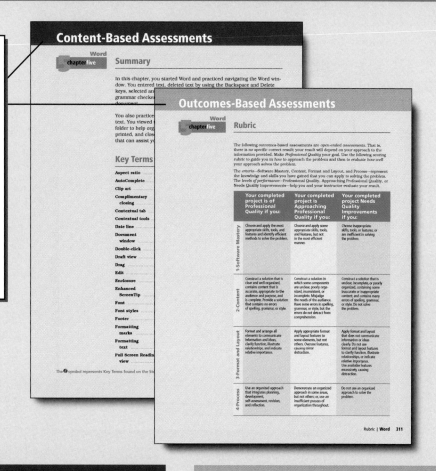

Content-Based Assessments
(Defined solutions with solution files provided for grading)

Project Letter	Name	Objectives Covered
N/A	Summary and Key Terms	
N/A	Multiple Choice	
N/A	Fill-in-the-blank	
C	Skills Review	Covers A Objectives
D	Skills Review	Covers B Objectives
E	Mastering Excel	Covers A Objectives
F	Mastering Excel	Covers B Objectives
G	Mastering Excel	Covers any combination of A and B Objectives
H	Mastering Excel	Covers any combination of A and B Objectives
I	Mastering Excel	Covers all A and B Objectives
J	Business Running Case	Covers all A and B Objectives

Outcomes-Based Assessments
(Open solutions that require a rubric for grading)

Project Letter	Name	Objectives Covered
N/A	Rubric	
K	Problem Solving	Covers as many Objectives from A and B as possible
L	Problem Solving	Covers as many Objectives from A and B as possible.
M	Problem Solving	Covers as many Objectives from A and B as possible.
N	Problem Solving	Covers as many Objectives from A and B as possible.
O	Problem Solving	Covers as many Objectives from A and B as possible.
P	You and GO!	Covers as many Objectives from A and B as possible
Q	GO! Help	Not tied to specific objectives
R	* Group Business Running Case	Covers A and B Objectives

* This project is provided only with the *GO! with Microsoft Office 2007 Introductory* book.

Teach (continued)

Objectives List

Most projects in the end-of-chapter section begin with a list of the objectives covered.

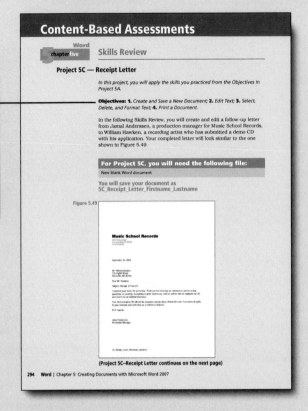

Content-Based Assessments

Word chapter five Skills Review

Project 5C — Receipt Letter

In this project, you will apply the skills you practiced from the Objectives in Project 5A.

Objectives: 1. Create and Save a New Document; **2.** Edit Text; **3.** Select, Delete, and Format Text; **4.** Print a Document.

In the following Skills Review, you will create and edit a follow-up letter from Jamal Anderssen, a production manager for Music School Records, to William Hawken, a recording artist who has submitted a demo CD with his application. Your completed letter will look similar to the one shown in Figure 5.49.

For Project 5C, you will need the following file:
New blank Word document

You will save your document as
5C_Receipt_Letter_Firstname_Lastname

Figure 5.49

Music School Records

September 22, 2009

Mr. William Hawken
123 Eighth Street
Knoxville, KY 40190

Dear Mr. Hawken:

Subject: Receipt of Your CD

(Project 5C–Receipt Letter continues on the next page)

294 **Word** | Chapter 5: Creating Documents with Microsoft Word 2007

Content-Based Assessments

Word chapter five Skills Review

(Project 5C–Receipt Letter continued)

14. **Save** the changes you have made to your document. Press Ctrl + A to select the entire document. On the **Home tab**, in the **Font group**, click the **Font button arrow**. Scroll as necessary, and watch Live Preview change the document font as you point to different font names. Click to choose **Tahoma**. Recall that you can type T in the Font box to move quickly to the fonts beginning with that letter. Click anywhere in the document to cancel the selection.

15. Select the entire first line of text—Music School Records. On the Mini toolbar, click the **Font button arrow**, and then click **Arial Black**. With the Mini toolbar still displayed, click the **Font Size button arrow**, and then click **20**. With the Mini toolbar still displayed, click the **Bold** button.

16. Select the second, third, and fourth lines of text, beginning with 2620 Vine Street and ending with the telephone number. On the Mini toolbar, click the **Font button arrow**, and then click **Arial**. With the Mini toolbar still displayed, click the **Font Size button arrow**, and then click **10**. With the Mini toolbar still displayed, click the **Italic** button.

17. In the paragraph beginning Your demonstration, select the text Music School Records. On the Mini toolbar, click the **Italic** button, and then click anywhere to deselect the text.

18. Click the **Insert tab**. In the **Header & Footer group**, click the **Footer** button,

and then click **Edit Footer**. On the **Design tab**, in the **Insert group**, click the **Quick Parts** button, and then click **Field**. In the **Field** dialog box, under **Field names**, scroll down and click to choose **FileName**, and then click **OK**. Double-click anywhere in the document to leave the footer area.

19. Click the **Page Layout tab**. In the **Page Setup group**, click the **Margins** button to display the Margins gallery. At the bottom of the **Margins gallery**, click **Custom Margins** to display the **Page Setup** dialog box. Near the top of the **Page Setup** dialog box, click the **Layout tab**. Under **Page**, click the **Vertical alignment arrow**, click **Center**, and then click **OK**.

20. From the **Office** menu, point to the **Print arrow**, and then click **Print Preview** to make a final check of your letter. Follow your instructor's directions for submitting this file. Check your Chapter Assignment Sheet or Course Syllabus or consult your instructor to determine if you are to submit your assignments on paper or electronically. To submit electronically, go to Step 22, and then follow the instructions provided by your instructor.

21. On the **Print Preview tab**, in the **Print group**, click the **Print** button. Collect your printout from the printer and submit it as directed.

22. From the **Office** menu, click **Exit Word**, saving any changes if prompted to do so.

End You have completed Project 5C

End of Each Project Clearly Marked

Clearly identified end points help separate the end-of-chapter projects.

296 **Word** | Chapter 5: Creating Documents with Microsoft Word 2007

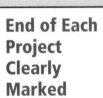

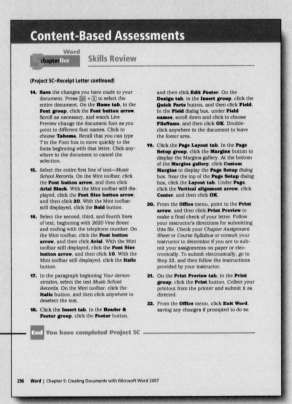

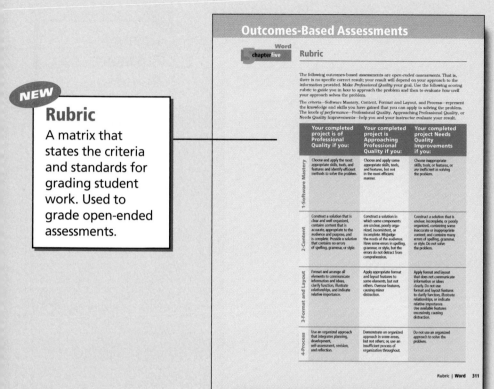

NEW

Rubric

A matrix that states the criteria and standards for grading student work. Used to grade open-ended assessments.

GO! with Help

Students practice using the Help feature of the Office application.

NEW

You and *GO!*

A project in which students use information from their own lives and apply the skills from the chapter to a personal task.

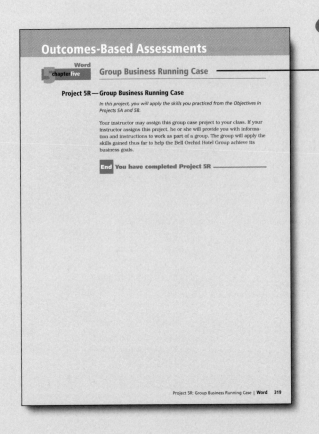

Group Business Running Case

A continuing project developed for groups that spans the chapters within each application.

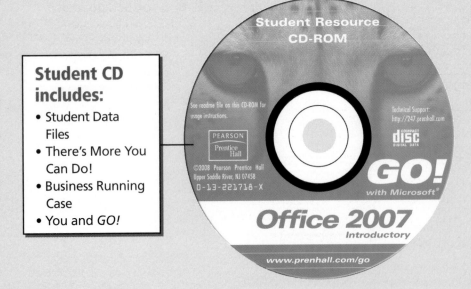

Student CD includes:

- Student Data Files
- There's More You Can Do!
- Business Running Case
- You and *GO!*

Companion Web site

An interactive Web site to further student leaning.

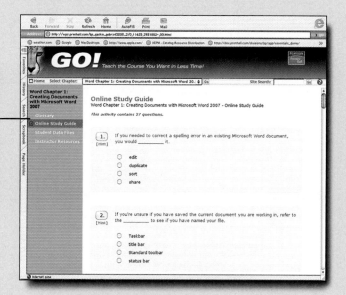

Online Study Guide

Interactive objective-style questions to help students study.

Annotated Instructor Edition

The Annotated Instructor Edition contains a full version of the student textbook that includes tips, supplement references, and pointers on teaching with the *GO!* instructional system.

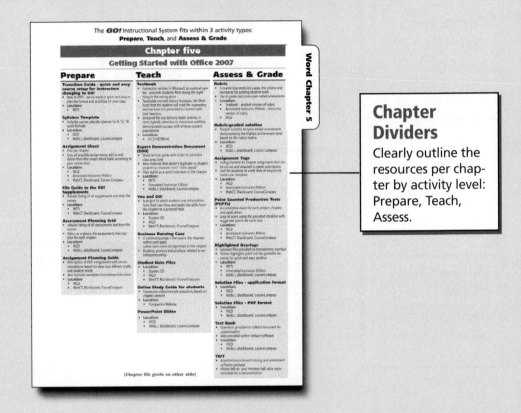

Chapter Dividers

Clearly outline the resources per chapter by activity level: Prepare, Teach, Assess.

Instructor File Guide

Complete list of all Student Data Files and instructor Solution Files needed for the chapter.

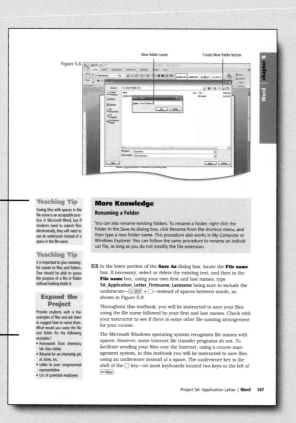

Helpful Hints, Teaching Tips, Expand the Project

References correspond to what is being taught in the student textbook.

NEW

Full-Size Textbook Pages

An instructor copy of the textbook with traditional Instructor Manual content incorporated.

End-of-Chapter Concepts Assessments contain the answers for quick reference.

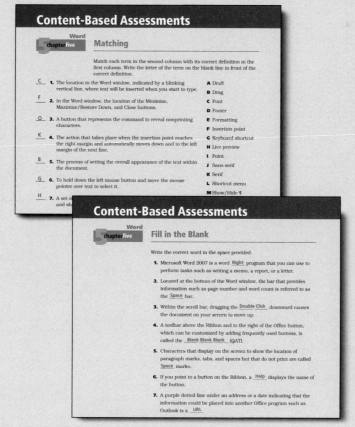

Rubric

A matrix to guide the student on how they will be assessed is reprinted in the Annotated Instructor Edition with suggested weights for each of the criteria and levels of performance. Instructors can modify the weights to suit their needs.

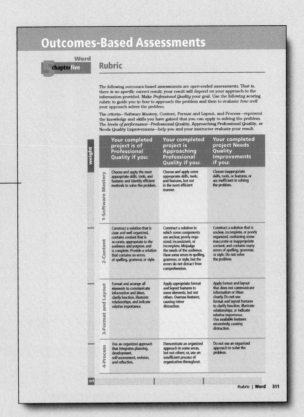

Assignment Tags

Scoring checklist for assignments. Now also available for Problem-Solving projects.

NEW

GO! with Microsoft® Office 2007

Assignment Tags for GO! with Office 2007
Word Chapter 5

Name:	Project:	**5A**
Professor:	Course:	

Task	Points	Your Score
Center text vertically on page	2	
Delete the word "really"	1	
Delete the words "try to"	1	
Replace "last" with "first"	1	
Insert the word "potential"	1	
Replace "John W. Diamond" with "Lucy Burrows"	2	
Change entire document to the Cambria font	2	
Change the first line of text to Arial Black 20 pt. font	2	
Bold the first line of text	2	
Change the 2nd through 4th lines to Arial 10 pt.	2	
Italicize the 2nd through 4th lines of text	2	
Correct/Add footer as instructed	2	
Circled information is incorrect or formatted incorrectly		
Total Points	**20**	**0**

Name:	Project:	**5B**
Professor:	Course:	

Task	Points	Your Score
Insert the file w05B_Music_School_Records	4	
Insert the Music Logo	4	
Remove duplicate "and"	2	
Change spelling and grammar errors (4)	8	
Correct/Add footer as instructed	2	
Circled information is incorrect or formatted incorrectly		
Total Points	**20**	**0**

Name:	Project:	**5C**
Professor:	Course:	

Task	Points	Your Score
Add four line letterhead	2	
Insert today's date	1	
Add address block, subject line, and greeting	2	
Add two-paragraph body of letter	2	
Add closing, name, and title	2	
In subject line, capitalize "receipt"	1	
Change "standards" to "guidelines"	1	
Insert "quite"	1	
Insert "all"	1	
Change the first line of text to Arial Black 20 pt. font	2	
Bold the first line of text	1	
Change the 2nd through 4th lines to Arial 10 pt.	1	
Italicize the 2nd through 4th lines of text	1	
Correct/add footer as instructed	2	
Circled information is incorrect or formatted incorrectly		
Total Points	**20**	**0**

Name:	Project:	**5D**
Professor:	Course:	

Task	Points	Your Score
Insert the file w05D_Marketing	4	
Bold the first two title lines	2	
Correct spelling of "Marketting"	2	
Correct spelling of "geners"	2	
Correct all misspellings of "allready"	2	
Correct grammar error "are" to "is"	2	
Insert the Piano image	4	
Correct/add footer as instructed	2	
Circled information is incorrect or formatted incorrectly		
Total Points	**20**	**0**

Highlighted Overlays

Solution files provided as transparency overlays. Yellow highlights point out the gradable elements for quick and easy grading.

Music School Records

20 point Arial Black, bold and underline

2620 Vine Street
Los Angeles, CA 90028
323-555-0028

10 point Arial, italic

September 12, 2009

Mr. William Hawken
123 Eighth Street
Harrisville, MI 48740

Text vertically centered on page

Body of document changed to Cambria font, 11 point

Dear William:

Subject: Your Application to Music School Records

Thank you for submitting your application to Music School Records. Our talent scout for Northern Michigan, Catherine McDonald, is very enthusiastic about your music, and the demo CD you submitted certainly confirms her opinion.

Word "really" deleted

We discuss our applications from potential clients during the first week of each month. We will have a decision for you by the second week of October.

Words "try to" deleted

Yours Truly,

Lucy Burroughs

Point-Counted Production Tests (PCPTs)

A cumulative exam for each **project**, **chapter**, and **application**. Easy to score using the provided checklist with suggested points for each task.

GO! with Microsoft® Office 2007 Introductory

Point-Counted Production Test—Project for GO! with Microsoft® Office 2007 Introductory Project 5A

Instructor Name: _____

Course Information: _____

1. Start Word 2007 to begin a new blank document. Save your document as 5A_Cover_Letter_Firstname_Lastname Remember to save your file frequently as you work.

2. If necessary, display the formatting marks. With the insertion point blinking in the upper left corner of the document to the left of the default first paragraph mark, type the current date (you can use AutoComplete).

3. Press Enter three times and type the inside address:

    Music School Records
    2620 Vine Street
    Los Angeles, CA 90028

4. Press Enter three times, and type Dear Ms. Burroughs:

    Press Enter twice, and type Subject: Application to Music School Records

    Press Enter twice, and type the following text (skipping one line between paragraphs):

    I read about Music School Records in Con Brio magazine and I would like to inquire about the possibility of being represented by your company.

    I am very interested in a career in jazz and am planning to relocate to the Los Angeles area in the very near future. I would be interested in learning more about the company and about available opportunities.

    I was a member of my high school jazz band for three years. In addition, I have been playing in the local coffee shop for the last two years. My demo CD, which is enclosed, contains three of my most requested songs.

    I would appreciate the opportunity to speak with you. Thank you for your time and consideration. I look forward to speaking with you about this exciting opportunity.

5. Press Enter three times, and type the closing Sincerely, Press enter four times, and type your name.

6. Insert a footer that contains the file name.

7. Delete the first instance of the word *very* in the second body paragraph, and insert the word modern in front of *jazz*.

Copyright © 2008 Pearson Prentice Hall   Page 1 of 1

Test Bank

Available as TestGen Software or as a Word document for customization.

Chapter 5: Creating Documents with Microsoft Word 2007

Multiple Choice:

1. With word processing programs, how are documents stored?

    A. On a network

    B. On the computer

    C. Electronically

    D. On the floppy disk

Answer: C   **Reference:** Objective 1: Create and Save a New Document   **Difficulty:** Moderate

2. Because you will see the document as it will print, _____ view is the ideal view to use when learning Microsoft Word 2007.

    A. Reading

    B. Normal

    C. Print Layout

    D. Outline

Answer: C   **Reference:** Objective 1: Create and Save a New Document   **Difficulty:** Moderate

3. The blinking vertical line where text or graphics will be inserted is called the:

    A. cursor.

    B. insertion point.

    C. blinking line.

    D. I-beam.

Answer: B   **Reference:** Objective 1: Create and Save a New Document   **Difficulty:** Easy

Solution Files– Application and PDF format

Music School Records

Music School Records discovers, launches, and develops the careers of young artists in classical, jazz, and contemporary music. Our philosophy is to not only shape, distribute, and sell a music product, but to help artists create a career that can last a lifetime. Too often in the music industry, artists are forced to fit their music to a trend that is short-lived. Music School Records does not just follow trends, we take a long-term view of the music industry and help our artists develop a style and repertoire that is fluid and flexible and that will appeal to audiences for years and even decades.

The music industry is constantly changing, but over the last decade, the changes have been enormous. New forms of entertainment such as DVDs, video games, and the Internet mean there is more competition for the leisure dollar in the market. New technologies give consumers more options for buying and listening to music, and they are demanding high quality recordings. Young consumers are comfortable with technology and want the music they love when and where they want it, no matter where they are or what they are doing.

Music School Records embraces new technologies and the sophisticated market of young music lovers. We believe that providing high quality recordings of truly talented artists make for more discerning listeners who will cherish the gift of music for the rest of their lives. The expertise of Music School Records includes:

- Insight into our target market and the ability to reach the desired audience
- The ability to access all current sources of music income
- A management team with years of experience in music commerce
- Innovative business strategies and artist development plans
- Investment in technology infrastructure for high quality recordings and business services

pagexxxix_top.docx

Online Assessment and Training

myitlab is Prentice Hall's new performance-based solution that allows you to easily deliver outcomes-based courses on Microsoft Office 2007, with customized training and defensible assessment. Key features of myitlab include:

A *true* "system" approach: myitlab content is the same as in your textbook.

Project-based *and* **skills-based:** Students complete real-life assignments.

Advanced reporting *and* **gradebook**: These include student click stream data.

No **installation required:** myitlab is completely Web-based. You just need an Internet connection, small plug-in, and Adobe Flash Player.

Ask your Prentice Hall sales representative for a demonstration or visit:

www.prenhall.com/myitlab

chapterone

Getting Started with Microsoft PowerPoint 2007

OBJECTIVES

At the end of this chapter you will be able to:

1. Open, View, and Save a Presentation
2. Edit a Presentation
3. Format a Presentation
4. Create Headers and Footers and Print a Presentation

5. Create a New Presentation
6. Use Slide Sorter View
7. Add Pictures to a Presentation
8. Use the Microsoft Help System

OUTCOMES

Mastering these objectives will enable you to:

PROJECT 1A
Open, Edit, Save, and Print a Presentation

PROJECT 1B
Create and Format a Presentation

Skyline Bakery and Cafe

Skyline Bakery and Cafe is a chain of casual dining restaurants and bakeries based in Boston. Each restaurant has its own in-house bakery, which produces a wide variety of high-quality specialty breads, breakfast sweets, and desserts. Breads and sweets are sold by counter service along with coffee drinks, gourmet teas, fresh juices, and sodas. The full-service restaurant area features a menu of sandwiches, salads, soups, and light entrees. Fresh, high-quality ingredients and a professional and courteous staff are the hallmarks of every Skyline Bakery and Cafe.

Getting Started with Microsoft Office PowerPoint 2007

Presentation skills are among the most important skills you will ever learn. Good presentation skills enhance all of your communications—written, electronic, and interpersonal. In our technology-enhanced world of e-mail and wireless phones, communicating ideas clearly and concisely is a critical personal skill. Microsoft Office PowerPoint 2007 is a presentation graphics software program used to create electronic slide presentations and black-and-white or color overhead transparencies that you can use to effectively present information to your audience.

Project 1A **Expansion**

In Activities 1.1 through 1.17, you will edit and format a presentation that Lucinda dePaolo, Chief Financial Officer, has created that details the Skyline Bakery and Cafe's expansion plan. Your completed presentation will look similar to Figure 1.1.

For Project 1A, you will need the following file:

p1A_Expansion

You will save your presentation as
1A_Expansion_Firstname_Lastname

Skyline Bakery and Cafe

Expansion Plans

Mission

To provide a nutritious, satisfying, and delicious meal experience for each of our customers in a relaxing and temptingly aromatic environment.

Company Information

- ▸ Founded in Boston by Samir Taheri in 1985
- ▸ Current locations in Massachusetts and Maine
- ▸ Expansion plans in 2009
  - ▫ Rhode Island
  - ▫ Virginia
- ▸ Awards received this year
  - ▫ Golden Bakery
  - ▫ Cuisine Excellence

Expansion Plans

- ▸ 2009
  - ▫ Rhode Island and Virginia
- ▸ 2010
  - ▫ New Hampshire and New Jersey
- ▸ 2011
  - ▫ West Virginia and Ohio
- ▸ 2012
  - ▫ New York and Connecticut

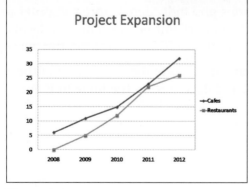

Figure 1.1
Project 1A—Expansion

Objective 1
Open, View, and Save a Presentation

Microsoft Office PowerPoint is a ***presentation graphics software*** program that you can use to effectively present information to your audience. The purpose of any presentation is to influence your audience. Whether you are presenting a new product to coworkers, making a speech at a conference, or expressing your opinion to your city council, you want to make a good impression and give your audience a reason to agree with your point of view. The way in which your audience reacts to your message depends on the information you present and how you present yourself. In the following activities, you will start Microsoft Office PowerPoint 2007, become familiar with the PowerPoint window, and then open, edit, and save an existing PowerPoint presentation.

Activity 1.1 Starting PowerPoint and Identifying Parts of the PowerPoint Window

In this activity, you will start PowerPoint and identify the parts of the PowerPoint window.

> ### Note — Comparing Your Screen with the Figures in This Textbook
>
> Your screen will match the figures shown in this textbook if you set your screen resolution to 1,024 × 768. At other resolutions, your screen will closely resemble, but not match, the figures shown. To view your screen's resolution, on the Windows desktop, right-click in a blank area, click Properties, and then click the Settings tab.

1 On the left side of the Windows taskbar, point to, and then click, the **Start** button.

2 From the displayed **Start** menu, locate the **PowerPoint** program, and then click **Microsoft Office PowerPoint 2007**.

Organizations and individuals store computer programs in a variety of ways. The PowerPoint program may be located under All Programs, or Microsoft Office, or from the main Start menu.

3 Take a moment to study the main parts of the screen as shown in Figure 1.2 and described in the table in Figure 1.3.

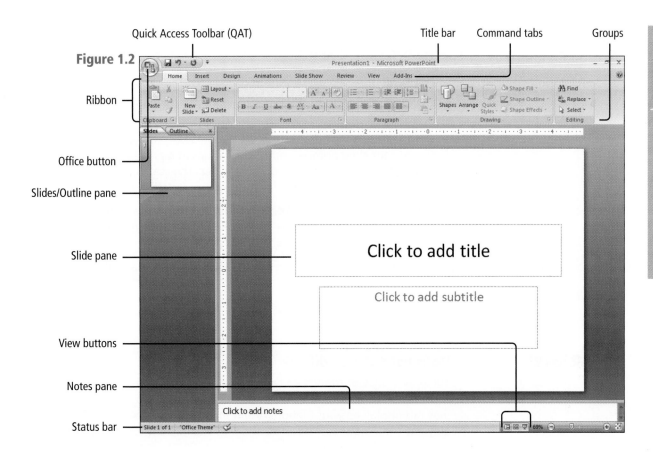

Figure 1.2

Microsoft PowerPoint Screen Elements

Screen Element	Description
Command tab	Displays the commands most relevant for a particular task area, such as inserting, designing, and animating.
Group	Related command buttons associated with the selected command tab.
Notes pane	Displays below the Slide pane and allows you to type notes regarding the active slide.
Office button	Displays a list of commands related to things you can do with a presentation, such as opening, saving, printing, or sharing.
Quick Access Toolbar (QAT)	Displays buttons to perform frequently used commands with a single click. Frequently used commands in PowerPoint include Save, Undo, and Repeat. For commands that you use frequently, you can add additional buttons to the Quick Access Toolbar.
Ribbon	Organizes commands on tabs, and then groups the commands by topic for performing related presentation tasks.
Slide pane	Displays a large image of the active slide.

(Continued)

(Continued)

Screen Element	Description
Slides/Outline pane	Displays either the presentation outline (Outline tab) or all of the slides in the presentation in the form of miniature images called *thumbnails* (Slides tab).
Status bar	A horizontal bar at the bottom of the presentation window that displays the current slide number, number of slides in a presentation, Design Template, View buttons, and Zoom slider. The status bar can be customized to include other information.
Title bar	Displays the name of the presentation and the name of the program. The Minimize, Maximize/Restore Down, and Close buttons are grouped on the right side of the title bar.
View buttons	A set of commands that control the look of the presentation window.

Figure 1.3

Alert!

Does your screen differ?

The appearance of the screen can vary, depending on settings that were established when the program was installed. For example, the Add-Ins tab may or may not display on your Ribbon. Additionally, the Quick Access Toolbar can display any combination of buttons, and may occupy its own row on the Ribbon.

Activity 1.2 Opening a Presentation

To open a presentation that has already been created in PowerPoint, use the Office button. As you work on a presentation, save your changes frequently.

1 In the upper left corner of the PowerPoint window, click the **Office**

button 🔲, and then click **Open** to display the Open dialog box.

2 In the **Open** dialog box, at the right edge of the **Look in** box, click the **Look in arrow** to view a list of the drives available on your system, as shown in Figure 1.4.

Your list of available drives may differ.

Figure 1.4

Your list of available drives will differ   Look in arrow

Look in box

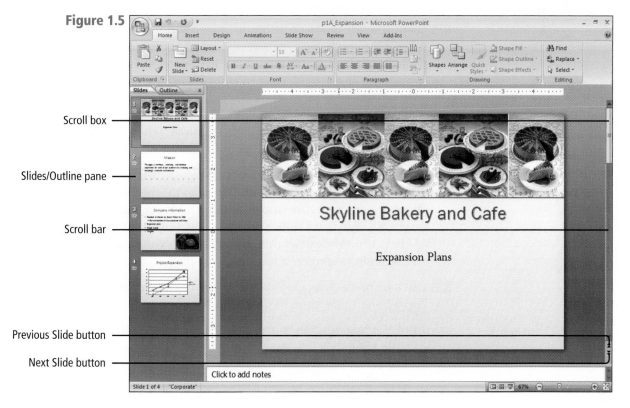

3 Navigate to the location where the student files for this textbook are stored. Click **p1A_Expansion**, and then click the **Open** button or press Enter to display Slide 1 of the presentation in the PowerPoint window.

PowerPoint displays the file name of the presentation in the title bar at the top of the screen.

4 Look at the **Slides/Outline pane** on the left side of the window and notice that the presentation contains four slides. Additionally, at the right side of the window, a scroll bar displays a scroll box and up and down pointing arrows for navigating through your presentation.

Below the scroll bar, the Previous Slide ⬆ and Next Slide ⬇ buttons display. See Figure 1.5.

Figure 1.5

Scroll box

Slides/Outline pane

Scroll bar

Previous Slide button

Next Slide button

5 In the scroll bar, click the **Next Slide** button ⊠ three times so that each slide in the presentation displays. Then click the **Previous Slide** button ⊠ three times until Slide 1 displays.

When you click the Next Slide or the Previous Slide button, you can scroll through your presentation one slide at a time.

Activity 1.3 Viewing a Slide Show

When a presentation is viewed as an electronic slide show, the entire slide fills the computer screen, and a large audience can view your presentation if your computer is connected to a projection system.

1 On the Ribbon, click the **Slide Show tab**. In the **Start Slide Show group**, click the **From Beginning** button.

The first slide fills the entire screen and animation effects display the picture, and then the title and subtitle. *Animation effects* introduce individual slide elements one element at a time. These effects add interest to your slides and draw attention to important features.

Another Way

To Start a Slide Show

On the right side of the status bar, from the View buttons, click the Slide Show button. You can also display the first slide that you want to show, and then press F5.

2 Click the left mouse button or press Spacebar to advance to the second slide, noticing the transition as Slide 1 moves off the screen and Slide 2 displays. An animation effect stretches the graphic images across the screen from left to right.

Transitions refer to the way that a slide appears or disappears during an onscreen slide show. For example, when one slide leaves the screen, it may fade or dissolve into another slide.

3 Click the left mouse button or press Spacebar and notice that the third slide displays and the slide title drops onto the screen from the top of the slide and a picture appears from the lower right corner. Click again or press Spacebar and notice that the first bullet point displays. Continue to click or press Spacebar until each bullet point displays on the slide and the next slide—*Project Expansion*—displays.

4 Click or press Spacebar to display the chart, and then click or press Spacebar one more time to display a black slide.

After the last slide in a presentation, a *black slide* with the text *End of slide show, click to exit.* displays. A black slide is inserted at the end of every slide show to indicate that the presentation is over.

5 On the black slide, click the left mouse button to exit the slide show and return to Slide 1.

Activity 1.4 Creating Folders and Saving a Presentation

In the same way that you use file folders to organize your paper documents, Windows uses a hierarchy of electronic folders to keep your electronic files organized. When you save a presentation file, the Windows operating system stores your presentation permanently on a storage medium. Changes that you make to existing presentations, such as changing text or typing in new text, are not permanently saved until you perform a Save operation.

1 In the upper left corner of the PowerPoint window, click the **Office**

button [🔲], and then click **Save As** to display the **Save As** dialog box.

2 In the **Save As** dialog box, at the right edge of the **Save in** box, click the **Save in arrow** to view a list of the drives available to you, as shown in Figure 1.6.

Your list of available drives will differ   Save in arrow

Figure 1.6

Save in box

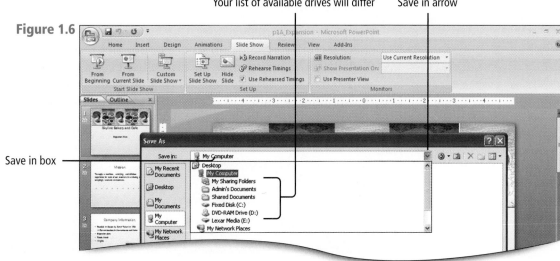

3 Navigate to the drive on which you will be storing your folders and projects for this chapter—for example, a USB flash drive that you have connected, a shared drive on a network, or the drive designated by your instructor or lab coordinator.

4 In the **Save As** dialog box, on the toolbar, click the **Create New**

Folder button [🗀]. In the displayed **New Folder** dialog box, in the **Name** box, type **PowerPoint Chapter 1** as shown in Figure 1.7, and then click **OK**.

The new folder name displays in the Save in box, indicating that the folder is open and ready to store your presentation.

Figure 1.7

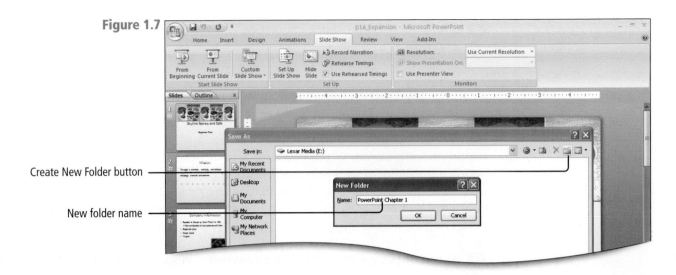

Create New Folder button

New folder name

5 In the lower portion of the **Save As** dialog box, locate the **File name** box. If necessary, select or delete the existing text, and then in the **File name** box, using your own first and last names, type **1A_Expansion_Firstname_Lastname** as shown in Figure 1.8.

Throughout this textbook, you will be instructed to save your files, using the file name followed by your first and last names. Check with your instructor to see if there is some other file-naming arrangement for your course.

The Microsoft Windows operating system recognizes file names with spaces. However, some Internet file transfer programs do not. To facilitate sending your files over the Internet if you are using a course management system, in this textbook you will be instructed to save files by using an underscore instead of a space.

Figure 1.8

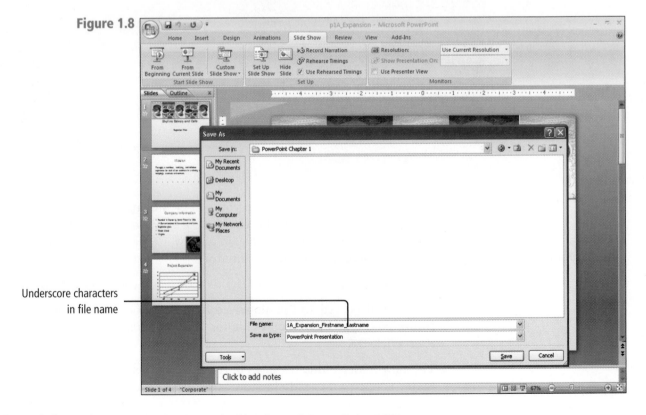

Underscore characters in file name

6 In the lower portion of the **Save As** dialog box, click the **Save** button, or press Enter.

Your presentation is saved on the storage device that you selected, and it is contained in the *PowerPoint Chapter 1* folder with the new file name. The new file name also displays in the title bar.

Objective 2
Edit a Presentation

In *Normal view*, the PowerPoint window is divided into three areas—the Slide pane, the Slides/Outline pane, and the Notes pane. When you make changes to the presentation in the Slides/Outline pane, the changes are reflected immediately in the Slide pane. Likewise, when you make changes in the Slide pane, the changes are reflected in the Slides/Outline pane.

Activity 1.5 Editing Slide Text

Editing is the process of adding, deleting, or changing the contents of a slide. When you click in the middle of a word or sentence and start typing, the existing text moves to the right to make space for your new keystrokes. In this activity, you will edit text in the Slide pane.

1 In the **Slides/Outline pane**, if necessary, click the **Slides tab** to display the slide thumbnails.

You can use the slide thumbnails to navigate in your presentation. When you click on a slide thumbnail, the slide displays in the Slide pane.

2 In the **Slides/Outline pane**, on the **Slides tab**, click **Slide 2** to display the company's mission statement. Move your pointer into the paragraph that contains the company's mission statement, and then click to the left of the word *experience* as shown in Figure 1.9.

On this slide a red wavy underline indicates that there is a misspelled word. Do not be concerned at this time with the misspelling—you will correct it in a later activity.

Figure 1.9

Click here

Slides tab

Slide 2

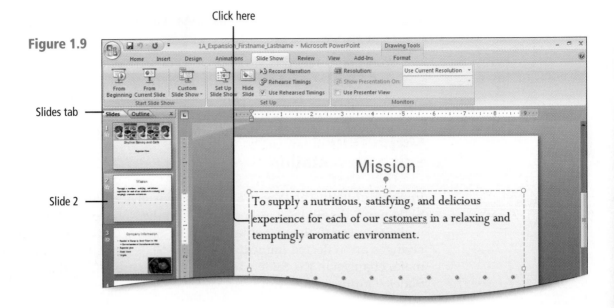

3 Type **meal** and notice that as you type, the existing text moves to the right to accommodate the text that you are inserting. Press Spacebar to insert a space between *meal* and *experience*.

After you type the space, the word *meal* moves to the first line of the paragraph because there is enough space in the first line to accommodate the text.

4 In the **Slides/Outline pane**, on the **Slides tab**, click **Slide 3**. In the bulleted list, in the third line, click to the right of the word *plans* and press Spacebar. Type **in 2009**

5 On the **Quick Access Toolbar**, click the **Save** button 🔲 to save the changes you have made to the presentation since your last save operation.

Activity 1.6 Inserting a New Slide

To insert a new slide in a presentation, display the slide that will come before the slide that you want to insert.

1 If necessary, display **Slide 3**. On the Ribbon, click the **Home tab**.

On the Home tab, the Slides group includes the New Slide button. The New Slide button is divided into two parts: the upper part contains the New Slide icon, which inserts a slide without displaying options; the lower part contains the words New Slide and a down-pointing arrow that when clicked, displays a gallery. The *gallery*—a visual representation of a command's options—displays slide layouts. *Layout* refers to the placement and arrangement of the text and graphic elements on a slide.

2 In the **Slides group**, click the lower part of the **New Slide** button to display the gallery.

Did you insert a slide without displaying the gallery?

The New Slide button is divided into two parts. If you click the upper part, a new slide is inserted, using the layout of the previous slide. To view the gallery, you must click the lower part of the New Slide button. Do not be concerned if the gallery did not display—the correct type of slide was inserted. Read Step 3, and then continue with Step 4.

3 Point to **Title and Text** as shown in Figure 1.10, and then click to insert a slide with the Title and Text layout. Notice that the new blank slide displays in the Slide pane and in the Slides/Outline pane.

The new slide contains two *placeholders*—one for the slide title and one for content. A placeholder reserves a portion of a slide and serves as a container for text or other content, including pictures, graphics, charts, tables, and diagrams.

Title and Text layout

Figure 1.10

Click New Slide

Gallery

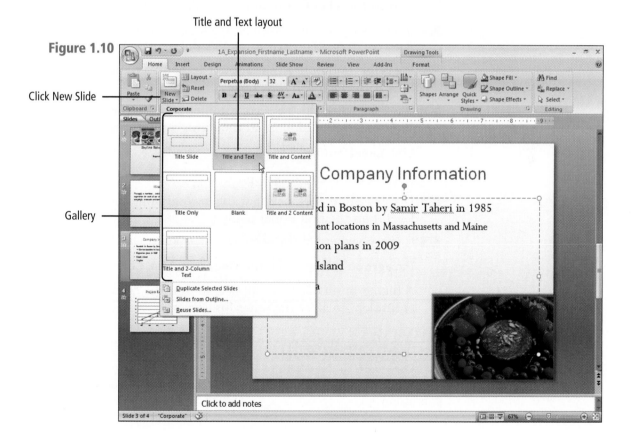

4 In the **Slide pane**, the title placeholder displays the text *Click to add title*. Click in the title placeholder. Type **Expansion Plans** and then click in the *Click to add text* content placeholder.

5 Type **2009** and then press Enter.

6 Type **Rhode Island and Virginia** and then press Enter.

7 Type **2010** and then on the **Quick Access Toolbar**, click the **Save** button 🖫 to save your presentation.

Activity 1.7 Increasing and Decreasing List Levels

Text in a PowerPoint presentation is organized according to outline levels, similar to the outline levels you might make for a book report. The highest level on an individual slide is the title. ***Bulleted levels***—outline levels represented by a bullet symbol—are identified in the slides by the indentation and the size of the text. Indented text in a smaller size indicates a lower outline level. It is easy to change the outline level of text to a higher or lower level. For example, you may create a presentation with four bullets on the same level. Then you may decide that one bulleted item relates to one of the other bullets, rather than to the slide title. In this case, a lower outline level should be applied. You can increase the list or indent level of text to apply a *lower* outline level, or decrease the list or indent level of text to apply a *higher* outline level.

1 If necessary, display **Slide 4**, click at the end of the last bullet point—*2010*—and then press Enter to create a new bullet.

2 Press Tab and notice that a lower level bullet point is created. Type **New Hampshire and New Jersey**

3 Click anywhere in the second bullet point—*Rhode Island and Virginia*. On the Ribbon, in the **Paragraph group**, click the **Increase List Level** button 📑.

A lower outline level is applied to the text.

4 Display **Slide 3**. Notice that the second bullet point is a lower outline level than the first bullet point.

5 Click anywhere in the second bullet point. On the Ribbon, in the **Paragraph group**, click the **Decrease List Level** button 📑.

A higher outline level is applied so that the second bullet point is equivalent to all of the other bullet points on the slide.

Another Way ─ **To Decrease List Level**

You can decrease the list level of a bullet point by holding down Shift and pressing Tab.

6 You can change the outline level of more than one bullet point by first selecting all of the text whose outline level you want to change. In the fourth bullet point, position the pointer to the left of *Rhode*, hold down the left mouse button, and then drag to the right and down to select the *Rhode Island* and the *Virginia* bullet points as shown in Figure 1.11. Release the mouse button.

Dragging is the technique of holding down the left mouse button and moving over an area of text so that it is selected. Selected text is indicated when the background changes to a different color than the slide background. When you select text, a ***Mini toolbar*** displays near the selection. The Mini toolbar displays buttons that are commonly used with the selected object, as shown in Figure 1.11. The Mini toolbar is semitransparent unless you move the pointer to it. When you move the pointer away from the Mini toolbar, it disappears. You will learn more about the Mini toolbar in a later activity.

Figure 1.11

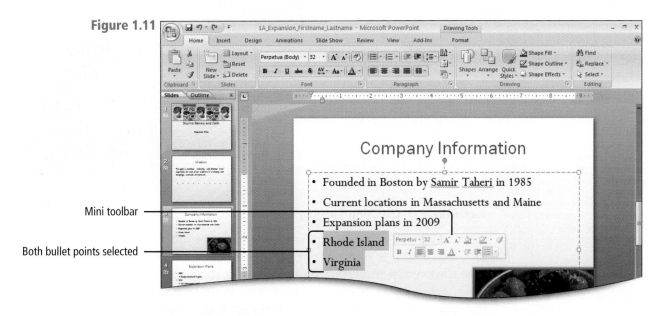

Mini toolbar

Both bullet points selected

Note — **Demoting and Promoting Text**

Increasing and decreasing the list level of a bullet point is sometimes referred to demoting and promoting text.

---

7 On the **Home** tab, in the **Paragraph group**, click the **Increase List Level** button.

Both bulleted items are demoted to lower levels.

8 Click at the end of the word *Virginia*. Press Enter to create a new bullet, and notice that the new bullet is indented at the same level as *Virginia*.

9 Click the **Decrease List Level** button to promote the new bullet. Type **Awards received this year** and then press Enter.

10 Click the **Increase List Level** button. Type **Golden Bakery** and press Enter. Type **Cuisine Excellence**

11 Compare your slide to Figure 1.12. **Save** your presentation.

Figure 1.12

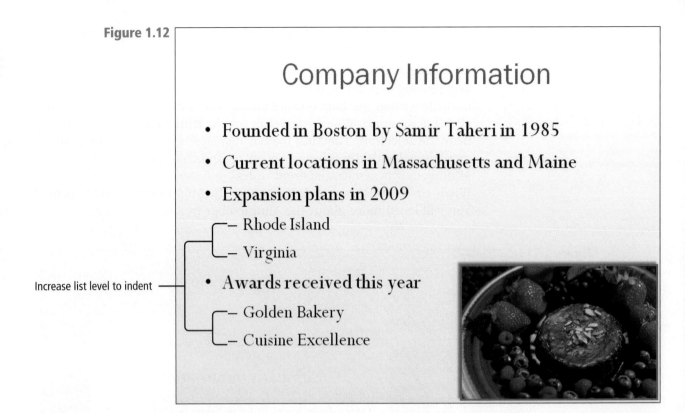

Increase list level to indent

Activity 1.8 Checking Spelling

As you type, PowerPoint compares your words to those in the PowerPoint dictionary. Words that are not in the PowerPoint dictionary are marked with a wavy red underline. Sometimes these words are correct. For example, a person's name may not be in the dictionary and may be flagged as misspelled even though it is correctly spelled. The red wavy underline does not display when the presentation is viewed as a slide show.

One way to check spelling errors flagged by PowerPoint is to right-click the flagged word or phrase and, from the displayed shortcut menu, select a suitable correction or instruction.

1 Display **Slide 2**. Notice that the word *cstomers* is flagged with a red wavy underline, indicating that it is misspelled.

2 Point to *cstomers* and click the right mouse button to display the **shortcut menu** with a suggested solution for correcting the misspelled word, and the Mini toolbar, as shown in Figure 1.13.

A shortcut menu is a context-sensitive menu that displays commands and options relevant to the selected object.

Mini toolbar

Figure 1.13

Misspelled word

Suggested solution

Shortcut menu

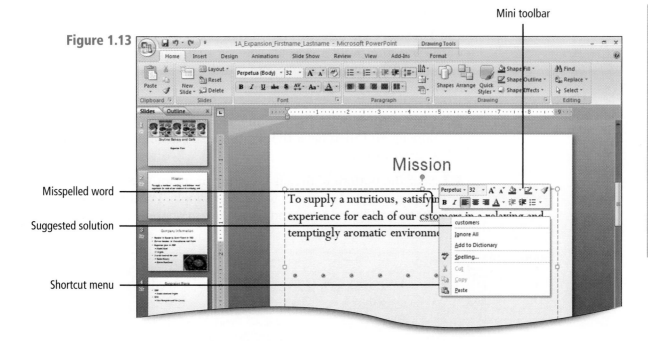

▣ From the shortcut menu, click **customers** to correct the spelling of the word.

▣ Display **Slide 3** and notice that the name *Samir Taheri* is flagged as misspelled, although it is spelled correctly.

▣ Right-click *Samir*, and from the shortcut menu, click **Ignore All** so that every time the name *Samir* displays in the presentation, it will not be flagged as a misspelled word. Repeat this procedure to ignore the flagged word *Taheri*.

More Knowledge

Spelling Correction Options

The Ignore All option is particularly useful when proper nouns are flagged as spelling errors even when they are spelled correctly. If you are using PowerPoint 2007 on a system that you can customize—such as your home computer—you can add frequently used names and proper nouns to the PowerPoint custom dictionary by clicking the Add to Dictionary option from the shortcut menu.

▣ Display each slide in the presentation and correct any spelling errors that you may have made when editing the slides.

▣ **Save** 💾 your presentation.

Another Way

To Check Spelling

You can check the spelling of the entire presentation at one time. On the Ribbon, click Review, and then click the Spelling button to display a dialog box that will select each spelling error in your presentation and provide options for correcting it.

Activity 1.9 Editing Text by Using the Thesaurus

The **Thesaurus** is a research tool that provides a list of **synonyms**—
words with the same meaning—for text that you select. You can access
synonyms by using either the shortcut menu or the Review tab on the
Ribbon.

1 Display **Slide 2**. In the first line of the paragraph, point to the word
supply, and then click the right mouse button to display the
shortcut menu.

2 Near the bottom of the shortcut menu, point to **Synonyms** to display
a list of suggested words to replace *supply*. Point to **provide** as
shown in Figure 1.14, and then click to change *supply* to *provide*.

Figure 1.14

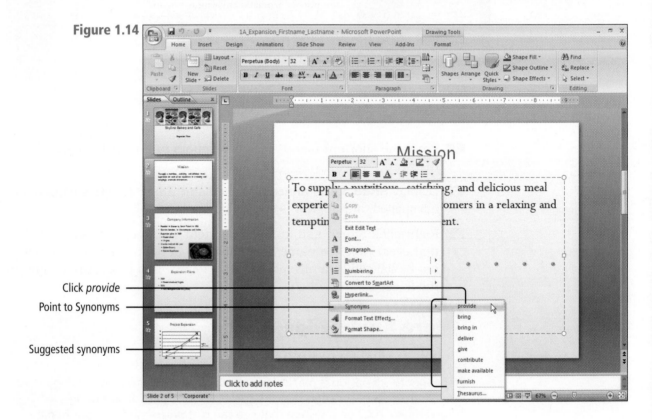

Click *provide*

Point to Synonyms

Suggested synonyms

3 **Save** the presentation.

Another Way ── To Access the Thesaurus

After you select the word that you want to replace, on the Ribbon, click
Review. Click Thesaurus to display the Research task pane, which contains a
more comprehensive list of suggested synonyms.

Activity 1.10 Adding Speaker's Notes to a Presentation

Recall that when a presentation is displayed in Normal view, the Notes pane displays below the Slide pane. The Notes pane is used to type speaker's notes that can be printed below a picture of each slide. You can refer to these printouts while making a presentation, thus reminding you of the important points that you want to make while running an electronic slide show.

1 Display **Slide 4**. Look at the PowerPoint window and notice the amount of space that is currently dedicated to each of the three panes—the Slides/Outline pane, the Slide pane, and the Notes pane. Locate the horizontal and vertical borders that separate the three panes.

These narrow borders are used to adjust the size of the panes. If you decide to type speaker notes, you may want to make the Notes pane larger.

2 Point to the border that separates the **Slide pane** from the **Notes pane**. The resize pointer displays as an equal sign with an upward-pointing and a downward-pointing arrow, as shown in Figure 1.15.

Figure 1.15

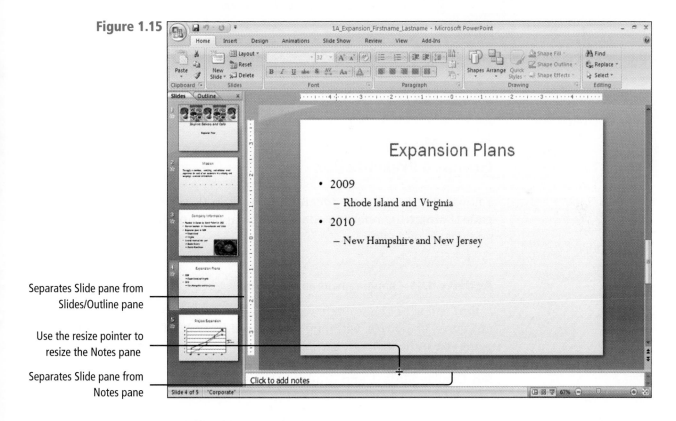

Separates Slide pane from Slides/Outline pane

Use the resize pointer to resize the Notes pane

Separates Slide pane from Notes pane

3 Press and hold down the left mouse button and drag the ⬍ pointer up approximately 1 inch, and then release the left mouse button to resize the pane.

4 With **Slide 4** displayed, click in the **Notes** pane and type **These expansion plans have been approved by the board of directors.** Compare your screen to Figure 1.16.

Figure 1.16

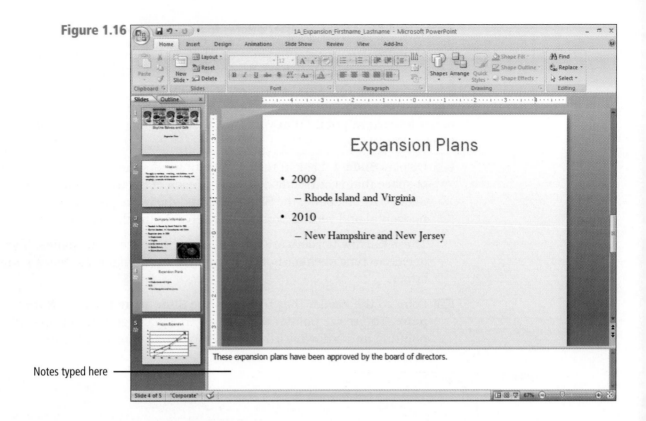

Notes typed here ——————

5 **Save** 💾 the presentation.

Objective 3
Format a Presentation

You will do most of your ***formatting*** work in PowerPoint in the Slide pane. Formatting refers to changing the appearance of the text, layout, and design of a slide.

Activity 1.11 Changing Font and Font Size

A ***font*** is a set of characters with the same design and shape. Fonts are measured in ***points***, with one point equal to 1/72 of an inch. A higher point size indicates a larger font size.

1 Display **Slide 1** and drag to select the title text—*Skyline Bakery and Cafe.*

2 Point to the Mini toolbar so that it is no longer semitransparent, and then click the **Font button arrow** Calibri (Headings) ▾ to display the available fonts, as shown in Figure 1.17.

The two fonts that display at the top of the list are the fonts currently used in the presentation.

Did the Mini toolbar disappear?

When you select text, the Mini toolbar displays. If you move your pointer away from the selection and into the slide area without pointing to the Mini toolbar, it may no longer display. If this happened to you, select the text again, and then point to the Mini toolbar, making sure that you do not point to another area of the slide.

Figure 1.17

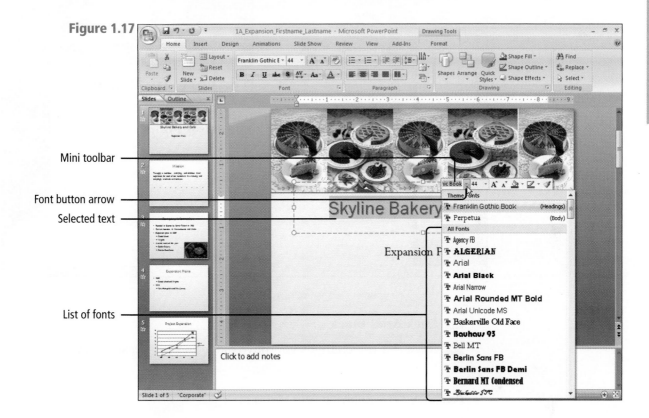

Mini toolbar

Font button arrow

Selected text

List of fonts

> **3** Scroll the displayed list as necessary, and then click **Book Antiqua**.

> **4** On the Ribbon, if necessary, click the **Home tab**. In the **Font group**, click the **Font Size button arrow** [44 ▾]. On the displayed list, click **48**.

> **5** Select the subtitle text—*Expansion Plans*. On the Ribbon, in the **Font group**, click the **Font button arrow** [Calibri (Headings) ▾]. In the displayed list, scroll as necessary, and then point to—but do not click—**Arial Black**. Compare your screen with Figure 1.18.

Live Preview is a feature that displays formatting in your presentation so that you can decide whether or not you would like to apply the formatting. In this case, Live Preview displays the selected text in the Arial Black font, even though you did not click the font name. The font will actually change when you click the font name.

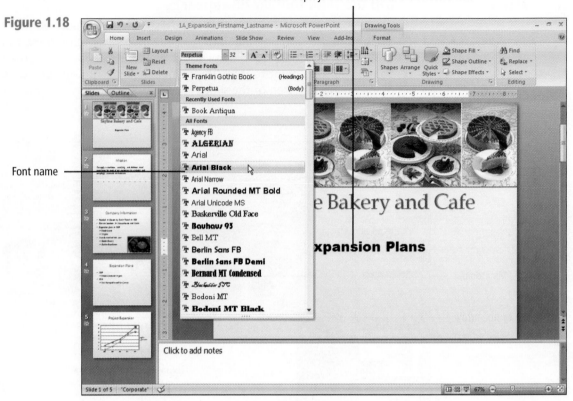

Live Preview displays the selection in the selected font

Figure 1.18

Font name

6 Click **Arial Black**.

7 **Save** the changes you have made to your presentation.

Activity 1.12 Applying Font Styles

Font styles emphasize text and are a visual cue to draw the reader's eye to important text. Font styles include bold, italic, and underline.

1 On **Slide 1**, drag to select the title—*Skyline Bakery and Cafe.* On the

Home tab, in the **Font group**, point to the **Bold** button **B** as shown in Figure 1.19, and then click to apply bold to the title.

Figure 1.19

Click the Bold button ———

Selected text ———

☑ Select the subtitle—*Expansion Plans.* On the Mini toolbar, click the

Bold button **B**, and then click the **Italic** button **I** to apply both bold and italic to the selection. Notice that on the **Home tab**, in the **Font group**, the **Bold** and **Italic** buttons are selected.

The Bold, Italic, and Underline buttons are *toggle buttons*; that is, you can click the button once to turn it on and click it again to turn it off.

☑ With the subtitle still selected, on the **Home tab**, in the **Font group**,

click the **Bold** button **B** to turn off the bold formatting.

☑ **Save** 🔲 your changes.

Another Way

To Apply Font Styles

There are four methods to apply font styles:

- On the Home tab, in the Font group, click the Bold, Italic, or Underline button.
- On the Mini toolbar, click the Bold or Italic button.
- From the keyboard, use the keyboard shortcuts of [Ctrl] + [B] for bold, [Ctrl] + [I] for italic, or [Ctrl] + [U] for underline.
- On the Home tab, in the Font group, click the Dialog Box Launcher to open the Font dialog box, and then click the font styles that you want to apply.

Activity 1.13 Aligning Text and Changing Line Spacing

Text alignment refers to the horizontal placement of text within a place-holder. Text can be aligned left, centered, aligned right, or justified. When text is justified, the left and right margins are even.

☑ Display **Slide 2** and click in the paragraph.

☑ On the **Home tab**, in the **Paragraph group**, click the **Center**

button 🔳 to center align the paragraph within the placeholder.

3 In the **Paragraph group**, click the **Line Spacing** button [icon]. In the displayed list, click **1.5** to change from single-spacing between lines to one and a half spaces between lines.

4 **Save** [icon] your changes.

Activity 1.14 Modifying Slide Layout

Recall that layout refers to the placement and arrangement of the text and graphic elements on a slide. PowerPoint includes a number of pre-defined layouts that you can apply to your slide for the purpose of arranging slide elements. For example, a Title Slide contains two place-holder elements—the title and the subtitle. Additional slide layouts include Title and Content, Title and 2 Content, Comparison, and Picture with Caption. When you design your slides, consider the content that you want to include, and then choose a layout that contains elements that best display the message that you want to convey.

1 Display **Slide 4.**

2 On the **Home tab**, in the **Slides group**, click the **Layout** button to display the **Slide Layout gallery**. The gallery displays an image of each layout and the name of each layout.

3 Point to each layout and notice that a ***ScreenTip*** also displays the name of the layout.

A ScreenTip is a small box, activated by holding the pointer over a button or other screen object, that displays information about a screen element.

4 Point to **Title and 2-Column Text**—as shown in Figure 1.20—and then click to change the slide layout.

The existing text displays in the placeholder on the left and a blank content placeholder is displayed on the right.

Figure 1.20

Slide Layout gallery —

Title and 2-Column Text layout —

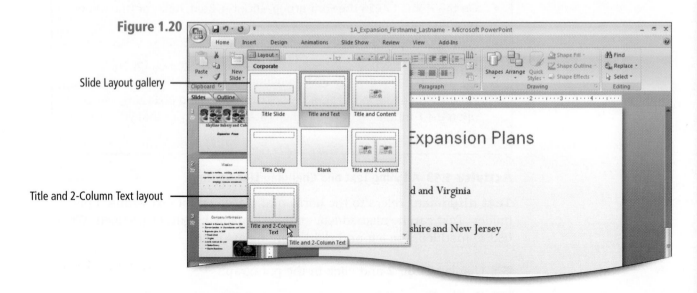

5 Click in the placeholder on the right. Type **2011** and then press Enter. Press Tab to increase the list level. Type **West Virginia and Ohio** and then press Enter.

6 Press ⇧ Shift + Tab to decrease the list level. Type **2012** and then press Enter. Press Tab to increase the list level. Type **New York and Connecticut**

7 Click outside of the placeholder so that it is not selected, and then compare your slide to Figure 1.21.

8 **Save** 💾 your changes.

Figure 1.21

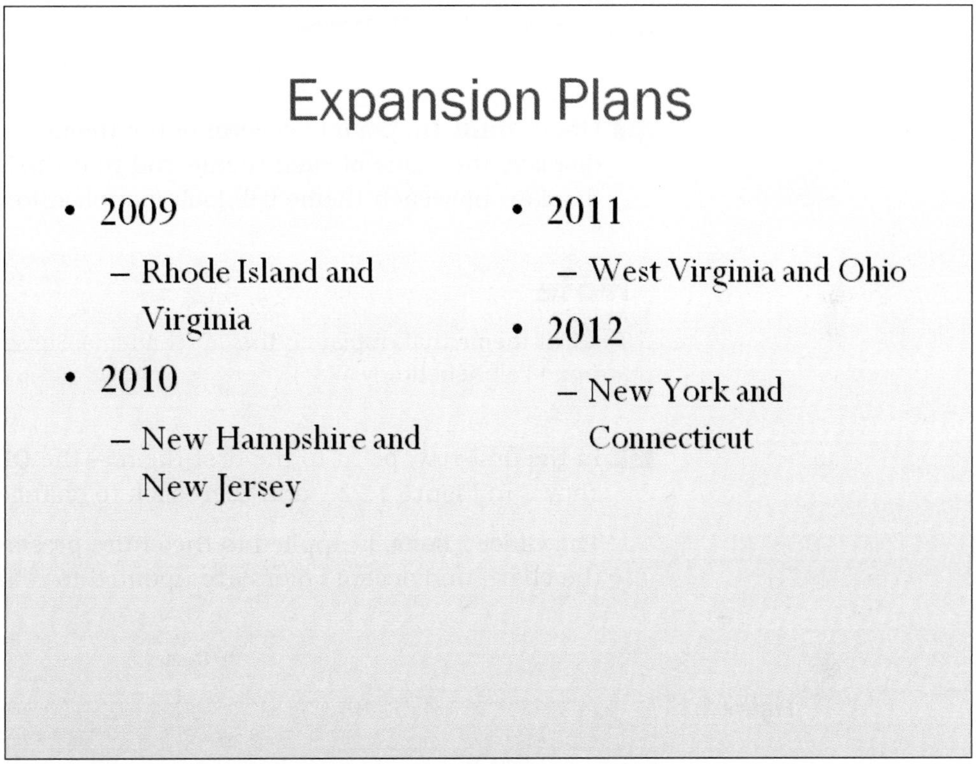

Expansion Plans

- 2009
  - Rhode Island and Virginia
- 2010
  - New Hampshire and New Jersey

- 2011
  - West Virginia and Ohio
- 2012
  - New York and Connecticut

Activity 1.15 Changing the Presentation Theme

A *theme* is a set of unified design elements that provides a look for your presentation by using color, fonts, and graphics. The overall *presentation theme* may include background designs, graphics, and objects that can be customized, using one of the three additional types of themes available in PowerPoint 2007. The color themes include sets of colors; the font themes include sets of heading and body text fonts; and the effect themes include sets of effects that can be applied to lines and other objects on your slides. Themes are found on the Design tab.

1 On the Ribbon, click the **Design tab**. In the **Themes group**, to the right of the last displayed theme, point to the **More** button ▼ as shown in Figure 1.22, and then click to display the **Themes gallery**.

Themes   More button

Figure 1.22

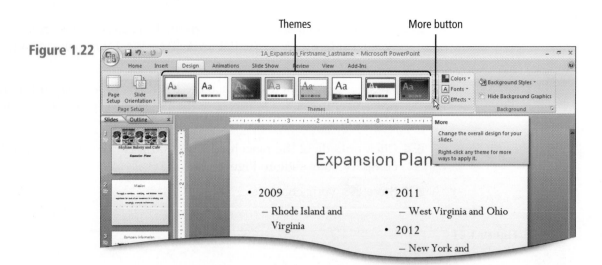

2 Under **Built-In**, *point* to several of the themes and notice a ScreenTip displays the name of each theme and that the Live Preview feature displays how each theme will look if applied to your presentation.

Note

The first theme that displays is the Office theme. Subsequent themes are arranged alphabetically.

3 In the first row, point to the first theme—the **Office Theme**, as shown in Figure 1.23—and then click to change the theme.

The Office Theme is applied to the entire presentation, and all text, the chart, and accent colors are updated to reflect the change.

Themes

Figure 1.23

Office Theme

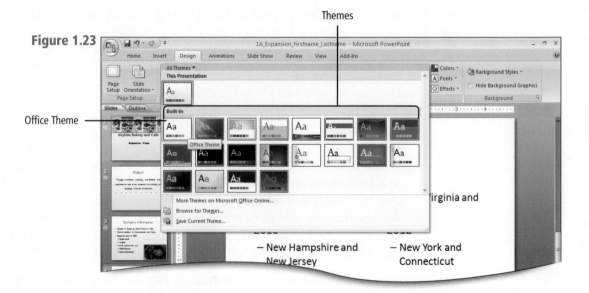

4 In the **Slides/Outline pane**, click to select **Slide 3**, and then press and hold down ⇧ Shift and click **Slide 4**. Compare your screen with Figure 1.24.

Both slides are selected as indicated by the contrasting colors that surround the slides in the Slides/Outline pane.

Figure 1.24

Selected slides

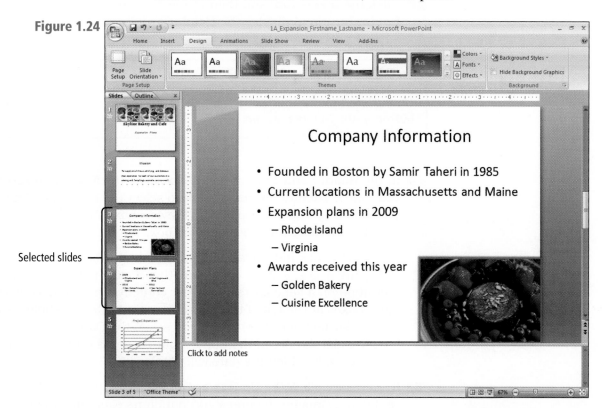

5 On the **Design tab**, in the **Themes group**, click the **More** button ⊽ to display the **Themes gallery**. In the first row, *point* to the fifth theme—**Concourse**—and then click the right mouse button to display the shortcut menu. Click **Apply to Selected Slides**.

The Concourse Theme is applied to Slides 3 and 4.

6 **Save** 🖫 your presentation.

Objective 4
Create Headers and Footers and Print a Presentation

A *header* is text that prints at the top of each sheet of *slide handouts* or *notes pages*. Slide handouts are printed images of multiple slides on a sheet of paper. Notes pages are printouts that contain the slide image in the top half of the page and notes that you have created in the Notes pane in the lower half of the page.

In addition to headers, you can create *footers*—text that displays at the bottom of every slide or that prints at the bottom of a sheet of slide handouts or notes pages.

Activity 1.16 Creating Headers and Footers

In this activity, you will add a header to the handouts and notes pages that includes the current date and a footer that includes the page number and the file name.

1 Click the **Insert tab**, and then in the **Text group**, click the **Header & Footer** button to display the **Header and Footer** dialog box.

Another Way

To Display the Header and Footer Dialog Box

On the Insert tab, in the Text group, you can click either the Date & Time button or the Number button.

2 In the **Header and Footer** dialog box, click the **Notes and Handouts tab**. Under **Include on page**, click to select the **Date and time** check box, and as you do so, watch the Preview box in the lower right corner of the Header and Footer dialog box.

The Preview box indicates the placeholders on the printed Notes and Handouts pages, similar to the way that a slide placeholder reserves a location on a slide for text or other content. The two narrow rectangular boxes at the top of the Preview box indicate placeholders for the header text and date. When you select the Date and time check box, the placeholder in the upper right corner is outlined, indicating the location in which the date will display.

3 If necessary, click the **Update automatically** button so that the current date prints on the notes and handouts each time the presentation is printed.

4 If necessary, click to *clear* the **Header** check box to omit this element. Notice that in the Preview box, the corresponding placeholder is no longer selected.

5 If necessary, click to select the **Page number** and **Footer** check boxes, noticing that when you do so, the insertion point displays in the Footer box. Using your own first and last names, type **1A_ Expansion_Firstname_Lastname** and then compare your dialog box with Figure 1.25.

6 Click **Apply to All**. On the Ribbon, click the **View tab**, and then in the **Presentation Views group**, click the **Handout Master** button. In the lower left corner of the Handout Master, select the file name, right-click, and then in the Mini toolbar, change the **Font Size** to **12**. Click the **View tab**, and then in the **Presentation Views group**, click the **Notes Master** button, and use a similar technique to change the **Font Size** of the file name to **12**. At the right end of the Ribbon, click **Close Master View**, and then **Save** your changes.

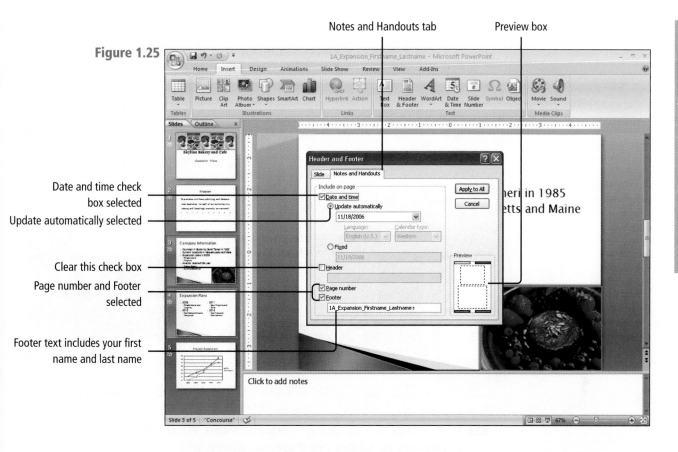

Figure 1.25

Notes and Handouts tab

Preview box

Date and time check box selected

Update automatically selected

Clear this check box

Page number and Footer selected

Footer text includes your first name and last name

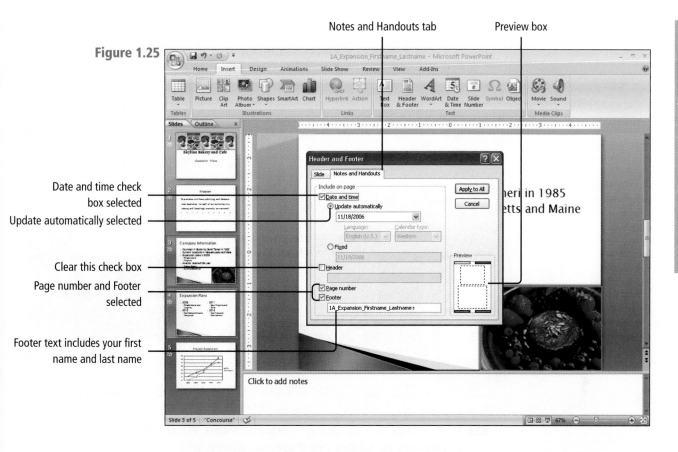

More Knowledge

Adding Footers to Slides

You can add footers to slides by using the Slide tab in the Header and Footer dialog box. Headers cannot be added to slides.

Activity 1.17 Previewing and Printing a Presentation and Closing PowerPoint

1 Click the **Office** button 🔳, point to the **Print arrow** as shown in Figure 1.26, and then click **Print Preview.**

Print Preview displays your presentation as it will print, based on the options that you choose. In the Print Preview window, you can change the direction on which the paper prints—landscape or portrait—you can choose whether you will print slides, handouts, note pages, or the presentation outline, and you can choose to print your presentation in color, grayscale, or black and white. By default, PowerPoint prints your presentation in grayscale.

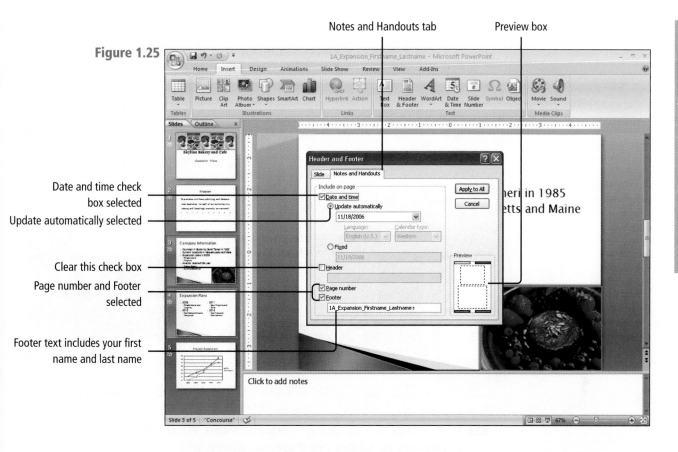

Figure 1.26

Office button

Print Preview

Print arrow

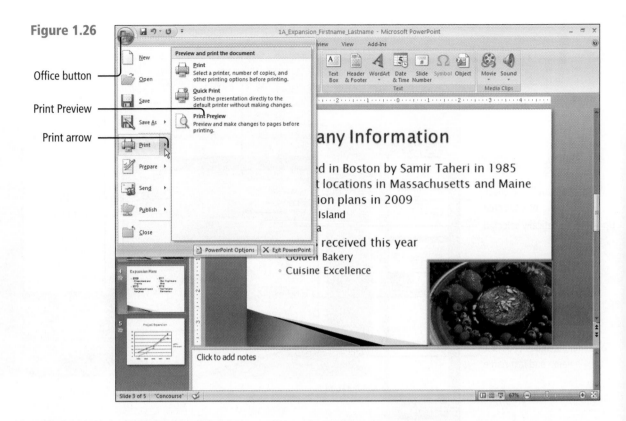

2 In the **Page Setup group**, click the **Print What arrow**, and then click **Handouts (6 Slides Per Page)** as shown in Figure 1.27. Notice that the preview of your printout changes to reflect your selection.

Note — Printing Slide Handouts

Printing a presentation as Slides uses a large amount of ink and toner. Thus, the majority of the projects in this textbook require that you print handouts, not slides.

Figure 1.27

Print What arrow

Click Handouts
(6 Slides Per Page)

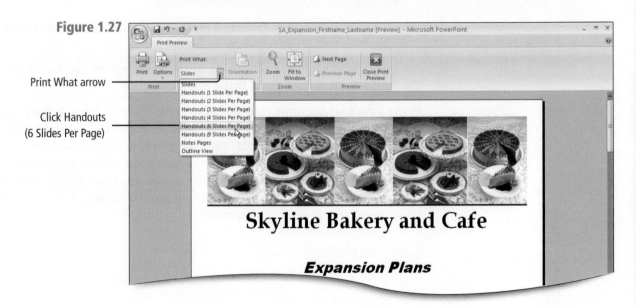

3 Check your *Chapter Assignment Sheet* or *Course Syllabus*, or consult your instructor, to determine if you are to submit your assignments on paper or electronically by using your college's course information management system. To submit electronically, go to Step 8, and then follow the instructions provided by your instructor.

4 In the **Print group**, click the **Print** button, and then in the **Print** dialog box, click **OK** to print your handouts.

5 In the **Page Setup group**, click the **Print What Arrow**, and then click **Notes Pages** to preview the presentation notes for Slide 1.

Recall that you created Notes for Slide 4.

6 At the right side of the **Print Preview** window, drag the scroll box down until **Slide 4** displays.

7 In the **Print group**, click the **Print** button. In the middle of the **Print** dialog box, under **Print range**, click **Current slide**, and then click **OK** to print the Notes pages for Slide 4.

8 Click **Close Print Preview** to close the Print Preview window and return to the presentation.

Another Way ── **To Print a Presentation**

Click the Office button, and then click Print to display the Print dialog box. The options that are available in Print Preview can be accessed and modified in the Print dialog box.

9 **Save** 🖫 your presentation. On the right edge of the title bar, click the **Close** button ☒ to close the presentation and **Close** PowerPoint.

Note — Changing Print Options

When you preview your presentation, check to be sure that the text displays against the slide background. If it does not, on the Print Preview tab in the Print group, click Options. Point to Color/Grayscale, and then click Color or Color (On Black and White Printer).

End **You have completed Project 1A** ─────────

Project 1B **Overview**

In Activities 1.18 through 1.25 you will create a presentation that provides details of the Skyline Bakery and Cafe projected expansion. You will add a graphic image to the presentation, insert slides from another PowerPoint presentation, and rearrange and delete slides. Your completed presentation will look similar to Figure 1.28.

For Project 1B, you will need the following files:

p1B_Skyline
p1B_Cake
p1B_Template

**You will save your presentation as
1B_Overview_Firstname_Lastname**

Figure 1.28
Project 1B—Overview

Objective 5
Create a New Presentation

Microsoft Office PowerPoint 2007 provides a variety of options for starting a new presentation. You can use a *template* that is saved on your system or that you access from Microsoft Online. A template is a file that contains the styles in a presentation, including the type and size of bullets and fonts, placeholder sizes and positions, background design and fill color schemes, and theme information. You can also start a blank presentation that has no text, background graphics, or colors that you can then customize yourself.

Activity 1.18 Starting a New Presentation

In this activity, you will create a new presentation based on a template from Microsoft Office Online.

1 **Start** PowerPoint. From the **Office** menu 🔳, click **New** to display the **New Presentation** window. See Figure 1.29.

At the left of the New Presentation window is a list of the Template categories installed on your system or available from Microsoft Office Online. The center section displays either subcategories or thumbnails of the slides in the category that you select. When you click on a template, the right section displays a larger view of the selected template and in some cases, additional information about the template.

New blank presentation

Figure 1.29

Template categories available from Microsoft Online

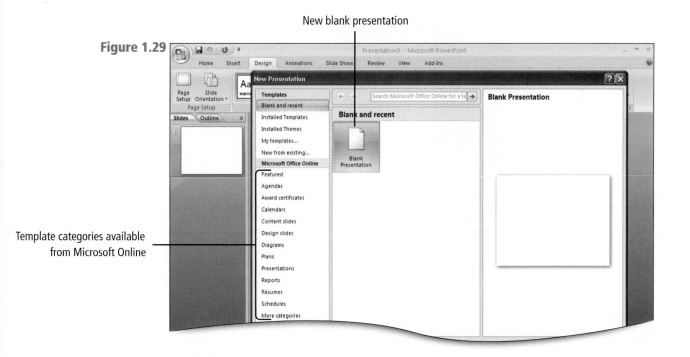

2 Under **Templates**, click **Installed Templates**, and then click each displayed template to preview it.

3 In the left panel under **Microsoft Office Online**, click several of the categories. Notice that as you do so, the title of the center panel changes to the name of the category that you have chosen, and in some instances, subcategories display.

Alert!

Are you unable to access the templates from Microsoft Office Online?

If you are unable to access the templates from Microsoft Office Online, the template for this project is available from your student data files. In the New Presentation window, click Cancel to close the New Presentation window. Click the Office button, and then click Open. Navigate to your student files and open the p1B_Template file. Then, skip to Step 6.

4 Under **Microsoft Office Online**, click **Presentations**, and then in the center panel, point to **Other presentations** to display the Link Select pointer [👆] as shown in Figure 1.30.

Figure 1.30

Other Presentations ———

Click Presentations ———

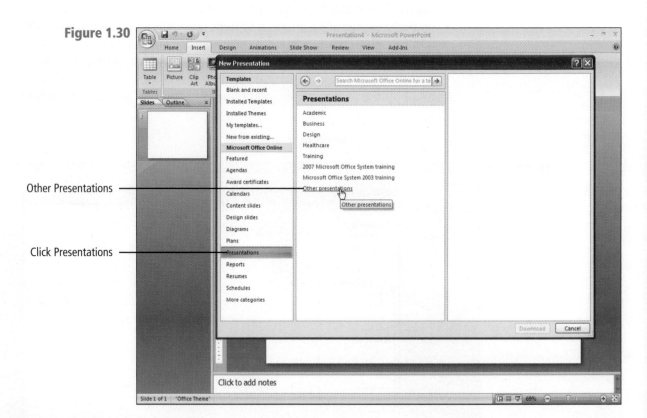

Another Way

To Locate Templates

In the New Presentation window, you can search for templates by using keywords. Click the Office button, and then click New. At the top center of the New Presentation Window, type the keyword and then press Enter to view the presentation templates with the keyword that you typed.

5 Click **Other Presentations**. In the center section of the New Presentation window, click **Project overview presentation**, and then in the lower right corner of the window, click **Download** to access the template from Microsoft Office Online.

Alert! — **Does a Microsoft window display?**

If a window displays regarding the validation of your software, click Continue. If you are unable to download the template, close all message windows and the New Presentation window. Click the Office button, and then click Open. Navigate to your student files, open the p1B_Template file, and then continue with Step 6.

6 If necessary, close any windows that display after the template is downloaded.

The new presentation includes 11 slides with ideas for content when making a project overview presentation. Scroll through the presentation to view the suggested content. Later, you will delete slides that are not relevant to the presentation and you will modify slide text so that the content is specific to this presentation topic.

7 On **Slide 1**, drag to select the text in the title placeholder—*Project Overview*—and then type **Skyline Bakery and Cafe** to replace it. Drag to select the three lines of text in the subtitle placeholder, and then type **Planning for the Future**

8 Display **Slide 2**. Select the text *Ultimate goal of project*, and then type **To develop a culinary presence throughout the East Coast**

9 Select the remaining two bullet points on the slide, and then type to replace them with the text **To expand operations in a manner that maximizes profit while providing outstanding service to customers**

10 Display **Slide 4**. In the bulleted list, select the *Competitors* bullet point and its second-level bullet point—*You may want to allocate one slide per competitor*—and then press Delete. Select *Your strengths relative to competitors*, and then type **Outstanding reputation for quality service** and then press Enter. Type **Nationally recognized chefs**

11 Replace the text *Your weaknesses relative to competitors* with **Inexperience in marketing in new locations**

12 In the scroll bar, click the **Next Slide** button ⬇ several times until **Slide 11** displays. Select and delete the *Post-mortem* and *Submit questions* bullet points and their subordinate bullet points. Under the *Marketing plan* bullet point, select *Location or contact name/phone*, and then type **Janet Liu/555-9012** Under the *Budget* bullet point, select *Location or contact name/phone*, and then type **Lucinda dePaolo/555-9019**

13 Click the **Office** button 🔘, and then click **Save As** to display the **Save As** dialog box. Click the **Save in arrow**, and then navigate to your *PowerPoint Chapter 1* folder.

14 In the **File name** box, delete any existing text, and then using your own first and last names type **1B_Overview_Firstname_Lastname** and then click **Save**.

Activity 1.19 Inserting Slides from an Existing Presentation

Teamwork is an important aspect of all organizations, and presentations are often shared among employees. Another employee may create several slides for a presentation that you are developing. Rather than re-creating the slides, you can insert slides from an existing presentation into the current presentation. In this activity, you will insert slides from an existing presentation into your 1B_Overview presentation.

1 Display **Slide 1**. Click the **Home tab**, and in the **Slides group**, click the **New Slide arrow** to display the **Slide Layout gallery** and additional options for inserting slides as shown in Figure 1.31.

Figure 1.31

New Slide arrow

Slide Layout gallery

Additional options for inserting slides

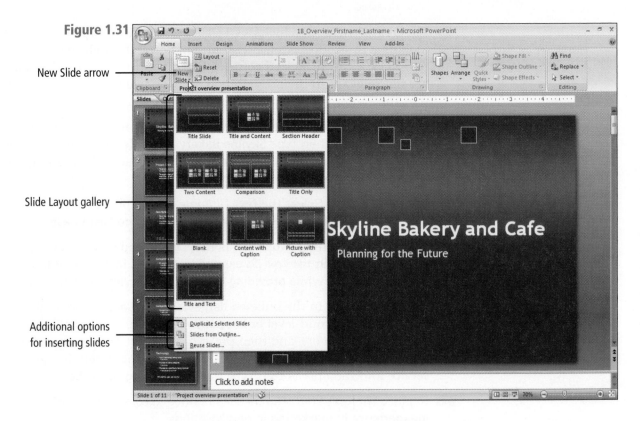

2 Below the gallery, click **Reuse Slides** to open the **Reuse Slides** task pane on the right side of the PowerPoint window.

A **task pane** enables you to enter options for completing a command.

3 In the **Reuse Slides** task pane, click the **Browse** button, and then click **Browse File**. In the **Browse** dialog box, navigate to where your student files are stored, and then double-click **p1B_ Skyline**.

The slides contained in the p1B_Skyline presentation display in the Reuse Slides task pane. The title of each slide displays to the right of the slide image.

4 In the **Reuse Slides** task pane, point to **Slide 2** and notice that a zoomed image is displayed, as is a ScreenTip with the presentation title and the slide title. See Figure 1.32.

Reuse Slides task pane

Figure 1.32

Zoomed image of slide

5 Click **Slide 2—Mission**—and notice that it is inserted into the current presentation after Slide 1.

The theme of the current presentation is applied to the slide that you inserted. If you want to retain the theme and other formatting from the slide that you insert, you can click to select the *Keep source formatting* check box at the bottom of the Reuse Slides task pane.

More Knowledge

Inserting All Slides

You can insert all of the slides from an existing presentation into the current presentation at one time. In the Reuse Slides task pane, right-click one of the slides that you want to insert, and then click Insert All Slides.

6 In your **1B_Overview** presentation, in the **Slides/Outline pane**, scroll the slide thumbnails to display **Slide 11**. Click **Slide 11** to display it in the **Slide** pane. In the **Reuse Slides** task pane, click **Slide 3—Company Information**, and then click **Slide 4—Expansion Plans** to insert both slides after Slide 11.

Your presentation contains 14 slides.

7 In the **Reuse Slides** task pane, click the **Close** button ☒. **Save** ▣ your presentation.

Note — Inserting Slides

You can insert slides in any order into your presentation. Just remember to display the slide that will precede the slide that you want to insert.

Objective 6
Use Slide Sorter View

Slide Sorter view displays all of the slides in your presentation in miniature. You can use Slide Sorter view to rearrange and delete slides, to apply formatting to multiple slides, and to get an overall impression of your presentation.

Activity 1.20 Selecting and Deleting Slides

To select more than one slide, click the first slide that you want to select, press and hold down ⇧Shift or Ctrl, and then click another slide. Using ⇧Shift enables you to select a group of slides that are adjacent. Using Ctrl enables you to select a group of slides that are nonadjacent (*not* next to each other). When multiple slides are selected, you can move or delete them as a group. These techniques can also be used when slide miniatures are displayed on the Slides tab.

1 Recall that the View buttons are located on the status bar in the lower right corner of the PowerPoint window. Locate the **View** buttons, and then click the **Slide Sorter** button ▦ to display all of the slide thumbnails. Alternatively, on the Ribbon, click the View tab, and then in the Presentation Views group, click Slide Sorter.

2 Click **Slide 4** and notice that a thick outline surrounds the slide, indicating that it is selected. On your keyboard, press Delete to delete the slide.

3 Click **Slide 5**, and then hold down ⇧Shift and click **Slide 10** so that slides 5 through 10 are selected. Compare your screen to Figure 1.33.

Selected slides

Figure 1.33

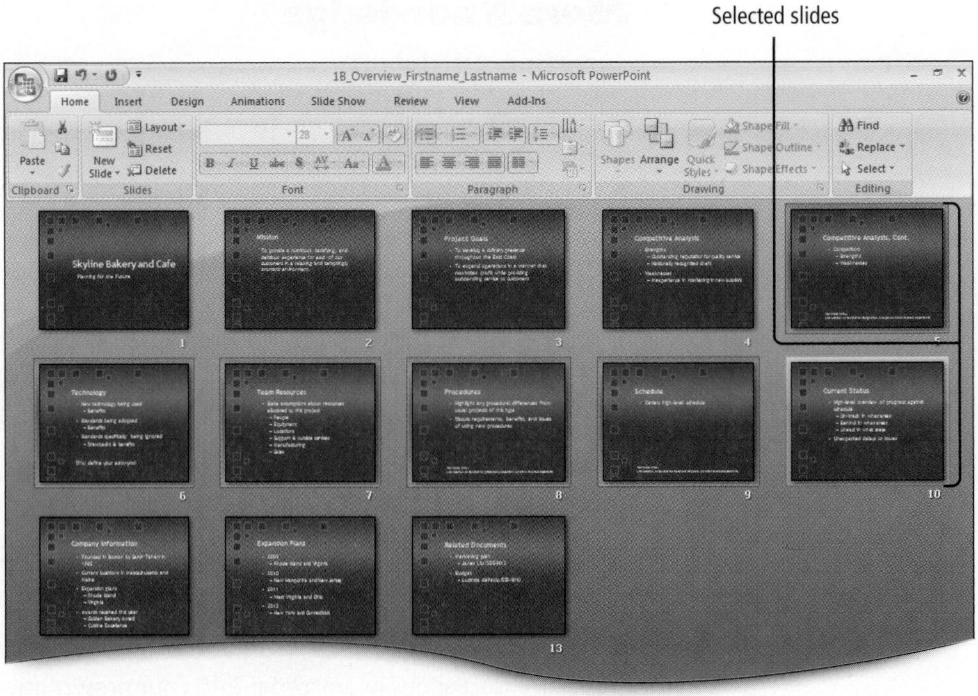

4 Press [Delete] to delete the selected slides.

Your presentation contains seven slides.

5 **Save** 🖫 your changes.

Activity 1.21 Moving Slides

1 Click **Slide 5** to select it.

2 While pointing to **Slide 5**, press and hold down the left mouse button, and then drag the slide to the left until the displayed vertical bar is positioned to the left of **Slide 2**, as shown in Figure 1.34. Release the left mouse button.

The slide that you moved becomes Slide 2.

Selected slide

Figure 1.34

Vertical bar positioned between Slides 1 and 2 to move slide to this position

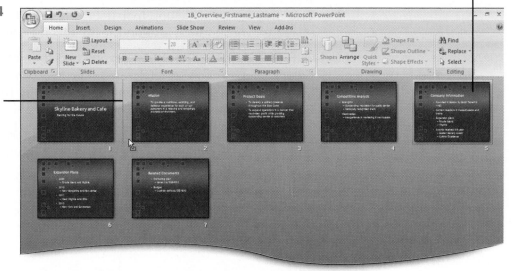

3 Select **Slide 6**. Using the same technique that you used in Step 2, drag to position the slide between **Slides 4** and **5**.

4 In the status bar, click the **Normal** button 🖳. **Save** 🖫 your presentation.

Objective 7
Add Pictures to a Presentation

Images can be inserted into a presentation from many sources. One type of image that you can insert is **_clip art_**. Clip art can include drawings, movies, sounds, or photographic images that are included with Microsoft Office or downloaded from the Web.

Activity 1.22 Inserting Clip Art

In this activity you will access Microsoft Office Online to insert a clip art image on the title slide.

1 Display **Slide 1**. On the Ribbon, click the **Insert tab**, and then in the **Illustrations group**, click **Clip Art** to display the **Clip Art** task pane.

2 In the **Clip Art** task pane, click in the **Search for** box and type **wedding cake** so that PowerPoint 2007 can search for images that contain the keywords *wedding cake*.

A message may display asking if you would like to include additional clip art images from Microsoft Office online. If this message displays, click Yes.

3 In the **Clip Art** task pane, click the **Search in arrow**, and if necessary, click to select the **Everywhere** check box. Click the **Search in** arrow again to collapse the search list.

When you click the Everywhere option, *All collections* displays in the Search in box. This action instructs PowerPoint to search for images stored on your system and on the Microsoft Office Online Web site.

4 Click the **Results should be arrow**, and then click as necessary to *deselect*—clear the selection by removing the check mark—the **Clip Art**, **Movies**, and **Sounds** check boxes so that only the **Photographs** check box is selected as shown in Figure 1.35.

With the Photographs check box selected, PowerPoint will search for images that were created with a digital camera or a scanner.

Type **wedding cake** to search for images

Figure 1.35

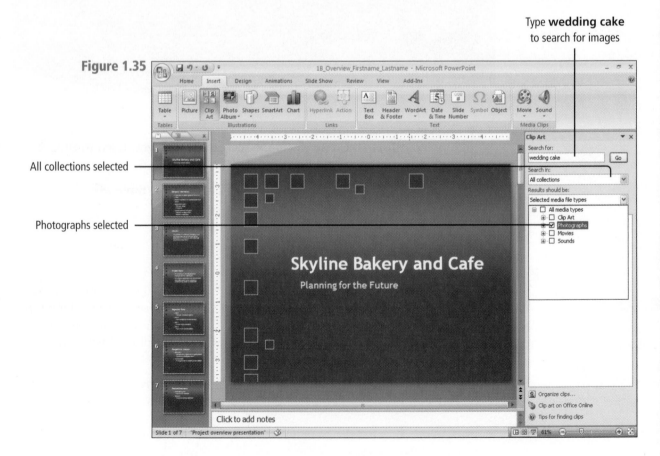

All collections selected

Photographs selected

5 In the **Clip Art** task pane, click **Go**. After a brief delay, several images display in the Clip Art task pane. Locate the image of the wedding cake shown in Figure 1.36.

Selected image

Figure 1.36

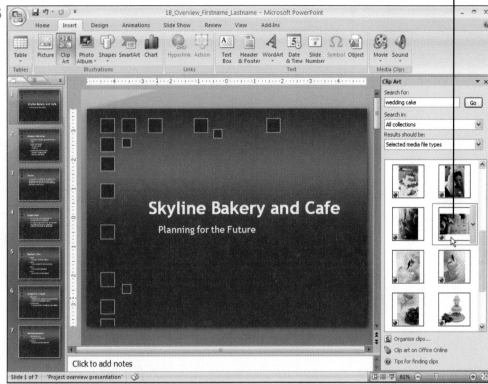

Was the wedding cake picture unavailable?

If you are unable to locate the picture for this project, it is available from your student data files. On the Insert tab, in the Illustrations group, click Picture. Navigate to your student files, and then double-click the p1B_Cake file.

6 Click the wedding cake picture to insert it in the center of Slide 1, and then notice that the Ribbon has changed and the picture is surrounded by white square and circular handles, indicating that it is selected.

Because the picture is selected, ***contextual tools*** named *Picture Tools* display and add a ***contextual tab***—*Format*—next to the standard tabs on the Ribbon as shown in Figure 1.37.

Contextual tools enable you to perform specific commands related to the selected object, and display one or more contextual tabs that contain related groups of commands that you will need when working with the type of object that is selected. Contextual tools display only when needed for a selected object; when you deselect the object,

Figure 1.37

Contextual tab

the contextual tools no longer display. In this case, the Format contextual tab contains four groups—Adjust, Picture Styles, Arrange, and Size. In a later activity, you will use the Picture Styles group to format the wedding cake picture.

7 **Close** ☒ the Clip Art task pane. **Save** 💾 your changes.

Activity 1.23 Moving and Sizing Images

When an image is selected, it is surrounded by white *sizing handles* that are used to size the image. In the corners of the image, the handles are circular. When you point to a circular sizing handle, a diagonal pointer displays, indicating that you can resize the image by dragging up or down. In the center of each side of the selected image, the handles are square. When you point to a square handle, a left- and right-pointing arrow or an up- and down-pointing arrow displays. These arrows indicate the direction in which you can size the image. When you point to an image without positioning the pointer over a handle, a four-headed arrow displays, indicating that you can move the image.

1 If necessary, click to select the picture of the wedding cake so that the handles display.

2 Position the pointer anywhere over the image to display the Move pointer ⊕. Drag down and to the right until the lower right corner of the picture is aligned with the lower right corner of the slide as shown in Figure 1.38. Release the mouse button.

3 If necessary, select the picture, and then point to the upper left circular handle to display the Diagonal Resize pointer ⬉.

Figure 1.38

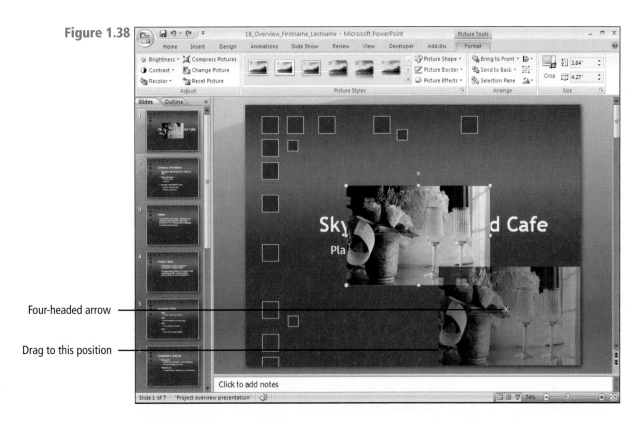

Four-headed arrow ———

Drag to this position ———

4 Drag down and to the right, noticing that as you do so, a semitransparent image displays the size of the picture. Continue to drag until the semitransparent image is approximately half the height and width of the original picture as shown in Figure 1.39. Release the mouse button to size the picture.

5 Save the presentation.

Figure 1.39

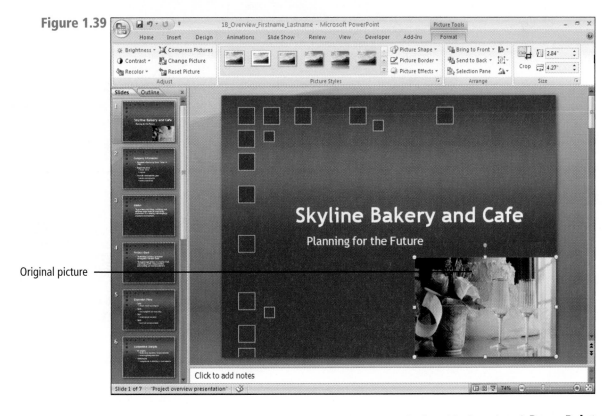

Original picture ———

Sizing a Picture

Using one of the corner sizing handles ensures that the original proportions of the image are maintained. When a top or side sizing handle is used, the picture is stretched either taller or wider, thus distorting the image.

Activity 1.24 Applying a Style to a Picture

Recall that when a picture is selected, the Picture Tools contextual tool and the Format contextual tab display on the Ribbon. You can use the Format tab to change the color and brightness of your picture; apply a shape, border, or effect; arrange multiple images; or size your picture.

1 If necessary, click the picture of the wedding cake to select it and notice that the Picture Tools are available.

2 On the **Format tab**, in the **Picture Styles group**, click the **More** button ⬇ to display the **Picture Styles gallery**.

3 In the displayed gallery, move your pointer over several of the picture styles to display the ScreenTip and to use Live Preview to see the effect of the style on your picture. Then, in the first row, click **Simple Frame, White**.

4 Click on a blank area of the slide so that the picture is not selected, and then compare your slide to Figure 1.40. Make any necessary adjustments to the size and position of the picture.

Figure 1.40

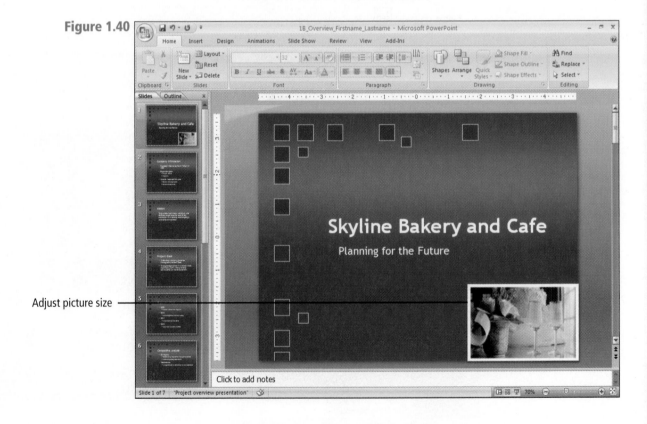

Adjust picture size

5 Click the **Insert tab**, and then, in the **Text group**, click the **Header & Footer** button to display the **Header and Footer** dialog box. Click the **Notes and Handouts tab**. Under **Include on page**, click to select the **Date and time** check box, and if necessary, click the **Update automatically** button so that the current date prints on the notes and handouts each time the presentation is printed. If necessary, *clear* the **Header** check box to omit this element from the header and footer. Click to select the **Page number** and **Footer** check boxes, noticing that when you do so, the insertion point displays in the Footer box. Using your own first and last names, type **1B_Overview_ Firstname_Lastname** and then click **Apply to All**.

6 Check your *Chapter Assignment Sheet* or *Course Syllabus* or consult your instructor to determine if you are to submit your assignments on paper or electronically. To submit electronically, go to Step 8, and then follow the instructions provided by your instructor.

7 From the **Office** menu, point to the **Print arrow**, and then click **Print Preview** to make a final check of your presentation. In the **Page Setup group**, click the **Print What arrow**, and then click **Handouts, (4 slides per page)**. Your presentation will print on two pages. Click the **Print** button, and then click **OK** to print the handouts. Click **Close** ☒ to close Print Preview.

8 **Save** 🖫 the changes to your presentation, and then from the **Office** menu, click **Exit PowerPoint**.

Objective 8
Use the Microsoft Help System

As you work with PowerPoint 2007, you can get assistance by using the Help feature. You can ask questions and Help will provide you with information and step-by-step instructions for performing tasks.

Activity 1.25 Accessing PowerPoint Help

In this activity, you will use the Microsoft Help feature to learn more about this feature.

1 **Start** PowerPoint. In the upper right corner of your screen, click the **Microsoft Office PowerPoint Help** button ⓘ. Alternatively, press F1.

You can browse the PowerPoint Help topics by clicking any of the listed items; or, near the top of the Help window, you can click in the search box and type a keyword to search for a specific item. If you have access to the Internet, PowerPoint will search Office Online for your help topic.

2 Near the upper left corner of the Help window, in the **Search** box, type **Printing Slides** as shown in Figure 1.41.

Search box

Figure 1.41

3 Press Enter or click **Search**. On the list of results, click **Print your slides** and then read the information that displays.

4 On the PowerPoint Help title bar, click the **Close** button ☒. On the right side of the title bar, click the **Close** button ☒ to close PowerPoint.

End **You have completed Project 1B**

There's More You Can Do!

From the student files that accompany this textbook, open the folder **02_theres_more_you_can_do**. Locate the Try IT! exercises for this chapter and follow the instructions to learn additional skills.

Try IT!—Set Slide Orientation and Size

In this Try IT! exercise, you will change the size and orientation of a slide.

Content-Based Assessments

Summary

In this chapter, you started PowerPoint and opened a PowerPoint presentation. You entered, edited, and formatted text in Normal view and worked with slides in Slide Sorter view; you added speaker notes; and you viewed the presentation as a slide show. The spelling checker tool was demonstrated, and you practiced how to change font style and size and add emphasis to text.

You created a new presentation, added content and clip art, and moved and deleted slides. You also added a footer to the notes and handouts pages and created a chapter folder to help organize your files. Each presentation was saved, previewed, printed, and closed. Finally, the Help program was introduced as a tool that can assist you in using PowerPoint.

Key Terms

Animation effects	8	**Header**	27	**Sizing handles**	42
Black slide	8	**Layout**	12	**Slide handouts**	27
Bulleted levels	14	**Live Preview**	21	**Slide Sorter view**	38
Clip art	39	**Mini toolbar**	15	**Synonym**	18
Contextual tabs	41	**Normal view**	11	**Task pane**	36
Contextual tools	41	**Notes pages**	27	**Template**	33
Deselect	40	**Placeholder**	13	**Text alignment**	23
Dragging	15	**Points**	20	**Theme**	25
Editing	11	**Presentation graphics software**	4	**Thesaurus**	18
Font	20			**Thumbnails**	6
Font styles	22			**Toggle buttons**	23
Footers	27	**Print Preview**	29	**Transitions**	8
Formatting	20	**ScreenTip**	24		
Gallery	12	**Shortcut menu**	16		

Content-Based Assessments

Matching

Match each term in the second column with its correct definition in the first column. Write the letter of the term on the blank line in front of the correct definition.

_____ **1.** A feature that introduces individual slide elements one element at a time.

_____ **2.** The PowerPoint view in which the window is divided into three panes—the Slide pane, the Slides/Outline pane, and the Notes pane.

_____ **3.** Outline levels represented by a symbol that are identified in the slides by the indentation and the size of the text.

_____ **4.** A feature that displays buttons that are commonly used with the selected object.

_____ **5.** A context-sensitive menu that displays commands and options relevant to the selected object.

_____ **6.** The action of holding down the left mouse button and moving the mouse pointer over text to select it.

_____ **7.** A set of characters (letters and numbers) with the same design and shape.

_____ **8.** A unit of measure to describe the size of a font.

_____ **9.** A container that reserves a portion of a slide for text, graphics, and other slide elements.

_____ **10.** A slide that is inserted at the end of every slide show to indicate that the presentation is over.

_____ **11.** The changing of the appearance of the text, layout, and design of a slide.

_____ **12.** A feature that displays formatting in your presentation so that you can decide whether or not you would like to apply the formatting.

_____ **13.** A feature that changes the horizontal placement of text within a placeholder.

_____ **14.** Printouts that contain the slide image in the top half of the page and notes that you have created in the Notes pane in the lower half of the page.

_____ **15.** A feature that displays your presentation as it will print, based on the options that you select.

A Animation

B Black slide

C Bulleted levels

D Dragging

E Font

F Formatting

G Live Preview

H Mini toolbar

I Normal view

J Notes pages

K Placeholder

L Point

M Print Preview

N Shortcut menu

O Text alignment

Content-Based Assessments

Fill in the Blank

Write the correct word in the space provided.

1. Microsoft Office PowerPoint 2007 is a presentation _____ pro-gram that you can use to effectively present information to your audience.

2. Miniature images of slides are known as _____.

3. A slide _____ controls the way in which a slide appears or disap-pears during an onscreen slide show.

4. The process of adding, deleting, or changing the contents of a slide is known as _____.

5. A _____ is a visual representation of a command's options.

6. The placement and arrangement of the text and graphic elements on a slide refer to its _____.

7. Tools that enable you to perform specific commands related to the selected object are _____ tools.

8. A file that contains the styles in a presentation, including the type and size of bullets and fonts, placeholder sizes and positions, back-ground design and fill color schemes, and theme information, is known as a _____.

9. The _____ is a research tool that provides a list of synonyms for a selection.

10. Words with the same meaning are known as _____.

11. Font _____ add emphasis to text, and may include bold, italic, and underline.

12. A _____ button is one in which you can click the button once to turn it on and click it again to turn it off.

13. Text that prints at the top of a sheet of slide handouts or notes pages is known as a _____.

14. Text that displays at the bottom of every slide or that prints at the bottom of a sheet of slide handouts or notes is known as a _____.

15. The view in which all of the slides in your presentation display in miniature is _____ _____ view.

Content-Based Assessments

Skills Review

Project 1C — Hospitality

In this project, you will apply the skills you practiced from the Objectives in Project 1A.

Objectives: 1. *Open, View, and Save a Presentation;* **2.** *Edit a Presentation;* **3.** *Format a Presentation;* **4.** *Create Headers and Footers and Print a Presentation.*

In the following Skills Review, you will edit a presentation created by Shawna Andreasyan, the Human Resources Director, for new Skyline Bakery and Cafe employees. Your completed presentation will look similar to the one shown in Figure 1.42.

For Project 1C, you will need the following file:

p1C_Hospitality

You will save your presentation as 1C_Hospitality_Firstname_Lastname

Figure 1.42

(Project 1C–Hospitality continues on the next page)

(Project 1C–Hospitality continued)

1. **Start** PowerPoint. Click the **Office** button, and then click **Open.** Navigate to the location where your student files are stored and open the file **p1C_Hospitality**. Click the **Office** button, and then click **Save As**. Navigate to your **PowerPoint Chapter 1** folder and using your own first and last name, save the file as 1C_Hospitality_Firstname_Lastname.

2. Click the **Design tab**. In the **Themes group**, to the right of the last displayed theme, click the **More** button to display the **Themes gallery**. Recall that after the first theme—Office—the remaining themes display alphabetically. Under **Built-in**, locate and click the **Flow** theme to apply the theme to the entire presentation.

3. Display **Slide 2**, and then click in the paragraph. Click the **Home tab**, and then, in the **Paragraph group**, click the **Center** button to center align the paragraph within the placeholder. In the **Paragraph group**, click the **Line Spacing** button, and then click **2.0** to apply double-spacing to the paragraph. Then, click in the slide title, and click the **Center** button to center align the title.

4. On **Slide 2**, drag to select all of the text in the paragraph. Point to the Mini toolbar, and then click **Bold** and **Italic** to apply both font styles to the paragraph.

5. Display **Slide 4** and notice the red wavy underline under the last word of the last bullet. Point to *atmoshere*, and then click the right mouse button to display the shortcut menu. Click **atmosphere** to correct the spelling of the word.

6. On **Slide 4**, in the third bullet point, right-click the word *good* to display the shortcut menu. Near the bottom of the menu, point to **Synonyms**, and then in the synonyms list, click **excellent** to use the Thesaurus to change *good* to *excellent*.

7. With **Slide 4** still displayed, on the **Home tab**, in the **Slides group**, click **Layout** to display the **Slide Layout gallery**. Click the **Two Content** layout.

8. Click in the placeholder on the right. Type **Do you** and then press Enter. Press Tab to increase the list level. Type **Greet every guest** and then press Enter. Type **Make every guest feel welcome**

9. In the placeholder at the left of **Slide 4**, drag to select the last three bulleted items. On the **Home tab**, in the **Paragraph group**, click the **Increase List Level** button to demote the three bulleted items one level below the first bulleted item.

10. With **Slide 4** still displayed, on the **Home tab**, in the **Slides group**, click the **New Slide arrow**, and then in the gallery, click **Title and Content** to create a new Slide 5.

11. On **Slide 5**, click in the title placeholder, type **Why Our Customers Return** and then click in the content placeholder. Type the following five bulleted items, pressing Enter at the end of each line to create a new bullet. Do not press Enter after the last item.

    We exceed their expectations

    They enjoy our relaxing atmosphere

    They feel comfortable in their surroundings

    We ensure fresh, high-quality food

    Our customer service is outstanding

12. With **Slide 5** displayed, click in the **Notes** pane and type **Remember that every single one of our customers is a VIP!** Make spelling corrections as necessary on the slide and in the notes.

(Project 1C–Hospitality continues on the next page)

Content-Based Assessments

(Project 1C–Hospitality continued)

13. Display **Slide 1** and drag to select the sub-title text—*New Employee Training*. On the Mini toolbar, click the **Font size button arrow**, and then change the font size to **44**.

14. Click the **Insert tab**, and then, in the **Text group**, click **Header & Footer** to display the **Header and Footer** dialog box.

15. Click the **Notes and Handouts tab**. Under **Include on page**, click to select the **Date and time** check box and, if necessary, click the **Update automatically** button so that the current date prints on the notes and handouts each time the presentation is printed. If necessary, clear the **Header** check box to omit this element from the header and footer. If necessary, click to select the **Page number** and **Footer** check boxes, noticing that when you do so, the insertion point displays in the Footer box. Using your own first and last names, in the Footer box type **1C_Hospitality_ Firstname_Lastname** and then click **Apply to All**.

16. On the Ribbon, click the **Slide Show tab**, and then in the **Start Slide Show group**, click **From Beginning**. Press [Spacebar] or click the left mouse button to advance through the presentation and view the slide show.

17. Check your *Chapter Assignment Sheet* or *Course Syllabus* or consult your instructor to determine if you are to submit your assignments on paper or electronically. To submit electronically, go to Step 20, and then follow the instructions provided by your instructor.

18. From the **Office** menu, point to the **Print arrow**, and then click **Print Preview** to make a final check of your presentation. In the **Page Setup group**, click the **Print What arrow**, and then click **Handouts, (6 slides per page)**. Click the **Print** button, and then click **OK** to print the handouts.

19. In the **Page Setup group**, click the **Print What arrow**, and then click **Notes Pages**. Click the **Print** button, and in the **Print** dialog box, under **Print range**, click the **Slides** option button. In the **Slides** box, type **5** to instruct PowerPoint to print the notes pages for Slide 5. Click **OK**, and then close Print Preview.

20. **Save** changes to your presentation, and then from the **Office** menu, click **Exit PowerPoint**.

 You have completed Project 1C ———————————————

Content-Based Assessments

Skills Review

Project 1D — Funding

In this project, you will apply the skills you practiced from the Objectives found in Project 1B.

Objectives: 5. *Create a New Presentation;* **6.** *Use Slide Sorter View;* **7.** *Add Pictures to a Presentation.*

In the following Skills Review, you will create the preliminary slides for a presentation that Lucinda dePaolo, Chief Financial Officer for Skyline Bakery and Cafe, will use to provide an overview of financial plans to a group of investors. Your completed presentation will look similar to the one shown in Figure 1.43.

For Project 1D, you will need the following files:

p1D_Background

p1D_Proposal_Template

p1D_Calculator

You will save your presentation as
1D_Funding_Firstname_Lastname

Figure 1.43

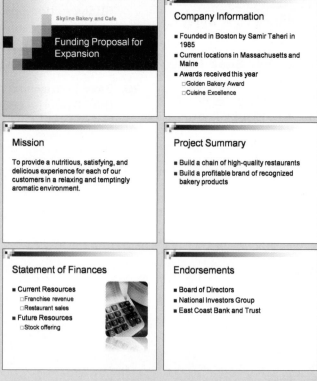

(Project 1D–Funding continues on the next page)

(Project 1D–Funding continued)

1. **Start** PowerPoint. From the **Office** menu, click **New** to display the **New Presentation** window. Under **Microsoft Office Online**, click **More Categories**, and then under **More categories**, click **Proposals**. Click the **Grant proposal** template, and then in the lower right corner of the **New Presentation** window, click **Download** to access the template from Microsoft Office Online. If a Microsoft Office window displays, click Continue. Alternatively, if you are unable to access the templates from Microsoft Office Online, the template for this project is available from your student data files. Click the Office button, and then click Open. Navigate to your student files and open the p1D_Proposal_Template presentation.

2. On **Slide 1**, drag to select the text *Organization Name*, and type **Skyline Bakery and Cafe** to replace it. Select the text that you just typed, and on the Mini toolbar, click the **Font Size button arrow**, and then click **24**. Drag to select the text in the title placeholder, and then type **Funding Proposal for Expansion**

3. Click the **Office** button, and then click **Save As**. In the **Save As** dialog box, click the **Save in** arrow, and then navigate to the location where you are storing your files for this chapter. In the **File name** box, delete any existing text, and then using your own first and last names type **1D_Funding_Firstname_Lastname** and then click **Save**.

4. Scroll through the presentation to view the content suggested for a funding proposal. Notice that in Slide 2, an introduction and mission statement are suggested. This content exists in another presentation and can be inserted without retyping the slides.

5. Display **Slide 1**. On the **Home tab**, in the **Slides group**, click the **New Slide arrow** to display the **Slide Layout gallery** and additional options for inserting slides. At the bottom of the gallery, click **Reuse Slides** to open the **Reuse Slides** task pane.

6. In the **Reuse Slides** task pane, click the **Browse** button, and then click **Browse File**. In the **Browse** dialog box, navigate to where your student files are stored and double-click **p1D_Background**. In the **Reuse Slides** task pane, point to either of the two slides that display and click the right-mouse button. From the shortcut menu, click **Insert All Slides** to insert both slides into the presentation. **Close** the **Reuse Slides** task pane.

7. On the status bar, locate the **View** buttons, and then click the **Slide Sorter** button to display the 15 slides in the presentation. Click to select **Slide 4**, and then press Delete to delete the slide. Click **Slide 5**, hold down ⬆Shift and click **Slide 7** so that slides 5 through 7 are selected. Press Delete to delete the selected slides.

8. Click **Slide 6**, hold down ⬆Shift and click **Slide 9** so that slides 6 through 9 are selected. With the four slides still selected, hold down Ctrl, and then click **Slide 11**. Press Delete to delete the selected slides. Six slides remain in the presentation.

9. Click **Slide 3** to select it. While pointing to **Slide 3**, press and hold down the left mouse button, and then drag the slide to the left until the displayed vertical bar is positioned to the left of **Slide 2**. Release the left mouse button to move the slide.

10. In the status bar, click the **Normal** button, and then **Save** your presentation. Display **Slide 4**, and then select the text in the

(Project 1D–Funding continues on the next page)

(Project 1D–Funding continued)

content placeholder. Replace the selected text with the following two bullets:

Build a chain of high-quality restaurants

Build a profitable brand of recognized bakery products

11. Display **Slide 5,** change the title to **Statement of Finances** and then select the text in the content placeholder. Replace the selected text with the following bullet points, increasing and decreasing the list level as indicated:

Current Resources

    Franchise revenue

    Restaurant sales

Future Resources

    Stock offering

12. Click the **Insert tab**, and then in the **Illustrations group**, click **Clip Art** to display the **Clip Art** task pane. In the **Clip Art** task pane, click in the **Search for** box, and then type **calculator**

13. In the **Clip Art** task pane, click the **Search in arrow**, and if necessary, click the **Everywhere** check box so that it is selected. Click the **Results should be arrow**, and then click as necessary to *clear* the **Clip Art**, **Movies**, and **Sounds** check boxes so that only **Photographs** is selected. Click **Go** to display the photographs of calculators. Click the picture of the white calculator with an adding machine tape on a blue background. Check Figure 1.43 at the beginning of this project if you are unsure of the picture that you should insert. **Close** the **Clip Art** task pane. (Note: If you cannot locate the picture, on the Insert tab, in the Illustrations group, click Picture. Navigate to your student files and then double-click p1D_Calculator.)

14. Position the pointer anywhere over the picture to display the ⊕ pointer. Drag to the right so that the picture is positioned approximately one-half inch from the right edge of the slide.

15. If necessary, click the picture of the calculator to select it and to activate the Picture Tools. On the Ribbon, click the **Format tab**, and then in the **Picture Styles group**, in the first row, click **Reflected Rounded Rectangle**.

16. Display **Slide 6**. Select the bulleted list text, and then replace it with the following bulleted items:

Board of Directors

National Investors Group

East Coast Bank and Trust

17. Click the **Insert tab**, and then in the **Text group**, click **Header & Footer** to display the **Header and Footer** dialog box.

18. Click the **Notes and Handouts tab**. Under **Include on page**, click to select the **Date and time** check box and, if necessary, click the **Update automatically** button so that the current date prints on the notes and handouts each time the presentation is printed. If necessary, clear the **Header** check box to omit this element from the header and footer. Click to select the **Page number** and **Footer** check boxes. Using your own first and last names, in the Footer box, type **1D_Funding_Firstname_ Lastname** and then click **Apply to All**.

19. Check your *Chapter Assignment Sheet* or *Course Syllabus* or consult your instructor to determine if you are to submit your assignments on paper or electronically. To submit electronically, go to Step 21, and then follow the instructions provided by your instructor.

(Project 1D–Funding continues on the next page)

Content-Based Assessments

Skills Review

(Project 1D–Funding continued)

20. From the **Office** menu, point to **Print**, and then click **Print Preview** to make a final check of your presentation. In the **Page Setup group**, click the **Print What arrow**, and then click **Handouts, (6 slides per page)**. Click the **Print** button, and then

click **OK** to print the handouts. **Close** Print Preview.

21. **Save** changes to your presentation, and then from the **Office** menu, click **Exit PowerPoint**.

 You have completed Project 1D ——————————————————————

Content-Based Assessments

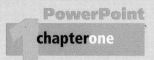
Mastering PowerPoint

Project 1E—Recruitment

In this project, you will apply the skills you practiced from the Objectives found in Project 1A.

Objectives: 1. *Open, View, and Save a Presentation;* **2.** *Edit a Presentation;* **3.** *Format a Presentation;* **4.** *Create Headers and Footers and Print a Presentation.*

In the following Mastering PowerPoint project, you will edit a presentation created by Shawna Andreasyan regarding the new online recruiting program at Skyline Bakery and Cafe. Your completed presentation will look similar to Figure 1.44.

For Project 1E, you will need the following file:

p1E_Recruitment

You will save your presentation as
1E_Recruitment_Firstname_Lastname

Figure 1.44

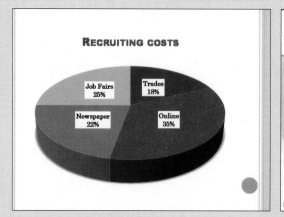

(Project 1E–Recruitment continues on the next page)

(Project 1E–Recruitment continued)

1. **Start** PowerPoint and **Open** the file **p1E_Recruitment**. Save the presentation as **1E_Recruitment_Firstname_Lastname**

2. On **Slide 1**, change the **Font Size** for the title to **48** so that the entire title fits on one line. Add the subtitle **Online Recruiting Plan** and then apply **Italic** to the subtitle.

3. Add a **New Slide** to the presentation with the **Title and Content** layout. The slide title is **Need for Online Recruiting** In the content placeholder, type the following bullet points and correct any spelling errors that you make while typing:

   Expansion into new geographic locations

   Cost savings over traditional methods

   New graduates search online for jobs

   Reach a more diverse applicant pool

4. On **Slide 3**, **Center** the slide title, and then change the **Font** to **Arial Black**. Add the following speaker's notes, correcting spelling errors as necessary. **We currently use three major recruiting methods. This chart indicates the amount that will be spent on each method once online recruiting is established.**

5. Add a **New Slide** to the presentation with the **Title and Content** layout. The slide title is **Online Recruiting Advantages** In the content placeholder, type the following bullet points, and then correct any spelling errors that you make while typing. After you type the text, increase the list level of the fourth bullet point—*Automated database.*

Access to more qualified applicants

Streamlined application process

Improved manageability

Automated database

Easily maintained and updated

6. Display **Slide 3**, and then on the Ribbon, click the **Design tab**. Using the **More** button, display the **Themes gallery**. Under **Built-In**, apply the **Oriel** theme to **Slide 3** only. (Hint: Right-click the theme, and then click **Apply to Selected Slides.**)

7. Display **Slide 1** and view the slide show, pressing Spacebar to advance through the presentation. When the black slide displays, press Spacebar one more time return to the presentation.

8. Create a **Header and Footer** for the **Notes and Handouts**. Include only the **Date and time updated automatically**, the **Page number**, and a **Footer** with the filename **1E_Recruitment_Firstname_Lastname** using your own first and last names.

9. Check your *Chapter Assignment Sheet* or *Course Syllabus* or consult your instructor to determine if you are to submit your assignments on paper or electronically. To submit electronically, go to Step 11, and then follow the instructions provided by your instructor.

10. **Print Preview** your presentation, and then print **Handouts, (4 slides per page)** and the **Notes Pages** for **Slide 3**.

11. **Save** changes to your presentation, and then **Close** the presentation.

End You have completed Project 1E

Content-Based Assessments

Mastering PowerPoint

Project 1F — Kitchen

In this project, you will apply the skills you practiced from Objectives in Project 1B.

Objectives: 5. *Create a New Presentation;* **6.** *Use Slide Sorter View;* **7.** *Add Pictures to a Presentation.*

In the following Mastering PowerPoint project, you will create a presentation that Peter Wing, Executive Chef for Skyline Bakery and Cafe, will use to describe the different types of chefs employed by the restaurant. Your completed presentation will look similar to Figure 1.45.

For Project 1F, you will need the following files:

p1F_Chefs
p1F_Tools
p1F_Nutrition_Template

**You will save your presentation as
1F_Kitchen_Firstname_Lastname**

Figure 1.45

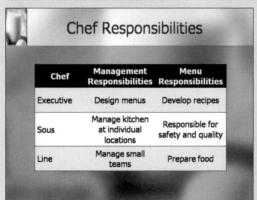

(Project 1F– Kitchen continues on the next page)

Content-Based Assessments

Mastering PowerPoint

(Project 1F–Kitchen continued)

1. **Start** PowerPoint and begin a new presentation based on the **Nutrition** design template. You may search by using the keyword *Nutrition* or you may find the template in the **Design slides, Academic** category. If you do not have access to the online templates, open **p1F_Nutrition_Template** from your student files. **Save** the presentation as **1F_Kitchen_Firstname_Lastname**

2. The title for the first slide is **The Kitchen is Open!** and the subtitle is **Skyline Bakery and Cafe**

3. From your student files, add all of the slides in the **p1F_Chefs** presentation into the current presentation. Then, display the presentation in **Slide Sorter view** and rearrange the slides so that the *Kitchen Organization* slide is the second slide, and the *Director of Kitchen Operations* slide is the fourth slide.

4. Display **Slide 2** in **Normal** view and insert a clip art image by searching for **Photographs** in **All collections**, using the keyword **skillet** Insert the picture that contains a chef's hat, skillet, wooden spoon,

knife, and guest check. If you cannot find the picture, insert the picture found in your student files, p1F_Tools.

5. Drag the picture to the lower right corner of the slide, and then apply a **Picture Style—Bevel Rectangle**. (Hint: Picture Styles are found in the Format tab of the Picture Tools contextual tool.)

6. Create a **Header and Footer** for the **Notes and Handouts**. Include only the **Date and time updated automatically**, the **Page number**, and a **Footer** with the filename **1F_Kitchen_Firstname_Lastname** using your own first and last names.

7. Check your *Chapter Assignment Sheet* or *Course Syllabus* or consult your instructor to determine if you are to submit your assignments on paper or electronically. To submit electronically, go to Step 9, and then follow the instructions provided by your instructor.

8. **Print Preview** your presentation, and then print **Handouts, (4 slides per page)**.

9. **Save** changes to your presentation, and then **Close** the file.

End You have completed Project 1F

Content-Based Assessments

Mastering PowerPoint

Project 1G—Flyer

In this project, you will apply the skills you practiced from the Objectives found in Projects 1A and 1B.

Objectives: 2. *Edit a Presentation;* **3.** *Format a Presentation;* **4.** *Create Headers and Footers and Print a Presentation;* **5.** *Create a New Presentation;* **7.** *Add Pictures to a Presentation.*

In the following Mastering PowerPoint project, you will create a single slide to be used as a flyer for the annual employee baking contest. Your completed presentation will look similar to Figure 1.46.

For Project 1G, you will need the following files:

New blank PowerPoint presentation
p1G_Cookies

You will save your presentation as
1G_Flyer_Firstname_Lastname

Figure 1.46

(Project 1G–Flyer continues on the next page)

(Project 1G–Flyer continued)

1. **Start** PowerPoint and begin a new blank presentation. Change the **Layout** of the title slide to the **Comparison** layout. Change the **Design** of the presentation by applying the **Oriel** theme. **Save** your presentation as **1G_Flyer_Firstname_ Lastname**

2. The title of the slide is **Annual Employee Baking Contest** Change the **Font** to **Bradley Hand ITC** and the **Font Size** to **36**. Apply **Bold**, and then **Center** the title.

3. In the orange box on the left side of the slide, type **How do you participate and join the fun?** In the orange box on the right side of the slide, type **Bring your favorite yummy dessert! Center** the text in both boxes.

4. In the content placeholder on the left side of the slide, type the following bullet points:

   Bake your favorite secret recipe!

   Bring it to work on December 15!

   Our chefs will be judging all day!

   Great prizes in lots of different categories!

5. Click in the content placeholder on the right side of the slide and insert a clip art by using the keyword **cookies** Search for **Photographs** in **All collections**. Click the picture with the star-shaped cookies on the brown background. If you cannot find the picture, insert the picture found in your student files, **p1G_Cookies**.

6. Move the picture so that it is centered below the *Bring your favorite yummy dessert!* text. Then, apply **Picture Style— Drop Shadow Rectangle**.

7. Insert a **Footer** on the Slide (*not* the Notes and Handouts), that includes the file name **1G_Flyer_Firstname_Lastname** Because of the layout of this slide, the footer will display vertically on the right side of the slide.

8. Check your *Chapter Assignment Sheet* or *Course Syllabus* or consult your instructor to determine if you are to submit your assignments on paper or electronically. To submit electronically, go to Step 10, and then follow the instructions provided by your instructor.

9. **Print Preview** your presentation. There is only one slide in the presentation, so print **Slides**.

10. **Save** and **Close** your presentation.

End **You have completed Project 1G**

Content-Based Assessments

Mastering PowerPoint

Project 1H—Fresh

In this project, you will apply the skills you practiced from the Objectives found in Projects 1A and 1B.

Objectives: 2. *Edit a Presentation;* **3.** *Format a Presentation;* **4.** *Create Headers and Footers and Print a Presentation;* **5.** *Create a New Presentation;* **6.** *Use Slide Sorter View;* **7.** *Add Pictures to a Presentation.*

In the following Mastering PowerPoint project, you will create a presentation that describes some of the steps taken by Skyline Bakery and Cafe to ensure that their food is fresh. Your completed presentation will look similar to Figure 1.47.

For Project 1H, you will need the following files:
New blank PowerPoint presentation
p1H_Text
p1H_Apple_Template
p1H_Vegetables
p1H_Tomato

You will save your presentation as
1H_Fresh_Firstname_Lastname

Figure 1.47

(Project 1H–Fresh continues on the next page)

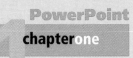

(Project 1H–Fresh continued)

1. **Start** PowerPoint and begin a new presentation by searching for a template with the keyword **Apple** Click the template with the three green apples. If the template is not available, from your student files, open **p1H_Apple_Template**.

2. The title of this presentation is **Keeping It Fresh!** and the subtitle is **Skyline Bakery and Cafe Save** the presentation as **1H_Fresh_Firstname_Lastname**

3. Add the two slides from the **p1H_Text** presentation. Display **Slide 3**, and then in the left bulleted list placeholder, increase the list level of the *Patisserie chef*, *Executive chef*, and *Line chef* bullet points. In the right bulleted list placeholder, increase the list level of the *Federally regulated* bullet point.

4. Add a **New Slide** with the **Title and Content** layout, and in the title placeholder, type **Our Commitment** In the bulleted list placeholder, type the following bullet points:

   Fresh food, unforgettable taste, served in a clean and cozy setting

   Quality ingredients picked by our discerning staff of chefs

   Cooked to perfection at all times

5. In **Slide Sorter** view, switch **Slides 2 and 4** so that **Slide 2** becomes the last slide and the **Our Commitment** slide becomes the second slide. Return the presentation to **Normal** view.

6. On **Slide 2**, in the second bullet point, use the shortcut menu to view **Synonyms** for the word *picked*. Change the word *picked* to **selected**.

7. Display **Slide 4**. Insert a clip art image by using the keyword **cabbage** Search for

Photographs in **All collections**. Click the picture with many different types and colors of vegetables. Move the picture down and to the left so that it covers the apples and is positioned in the lower left corner of the slide. If you cannot locate the picture, it is available in your student files. The filename is **p1H_Vegetables**.

8. Insert the vegetable picture again so that there are two copies of the same pictures on the slide. Move the picture down and to the right so that it is positioned in the lower right corner of the slide.

9. Insert another clip art image, this time by using the keywords **cherry tomato** Search for **Photographs** in **All collections**. Click the picture with tomatoes that look like they are spilling out of a bowl as shown in the figure at the beginning of this project. If you cannot locate the picture, it is available in your student files. The filename is **p1H_Tomato**. Drag the tomato picture straight down so that it overlaps the two vegetable pictures and its bottom edge aligns with the bottom edge of the slide. Apply **Picture Style—Simple Frame, Black**.

10. Create a **Header and Footer** for the **Notes and Handouts**. Include only the **Date and time updated automatically**, the **Page number**, and a **Footer** with the file name **1H_Fresh_Firstname_Lastname** and then view the slide show.

11. Check your *Chapter Assignment Sheet* or *Course Syllabus* or consult your instructor to determine if you are to submit your assignments on paper or electronically. To submit electronically, go to Step 13, and then follow the instructions provided by your instructor.

(Project 1H–Fresh continues on the next page)

Content-Based Assessments

(Project 1H–Fresh continued)

12. **Print Preview** your presentation, and then print **Handouts, (4 slides per page)**. If the text or pictures do not display, on the Print Preview tab, in the Print group click Options, point to Color/Grayscale, and

then click Color or Color (On Black and White Printer).

13. **Save** changes to your presentation. **Close** the presentation.

 You have completed Project 1H

PowerPoint
chapterone

Mastering PowerPoint

Project 1I—Holiday

In this project, you will apply the skills you practiced from Objectives found in Projects 1A and 1B.

Objectives: 1. *Open, View, and Save a Presentation;* **2.** *Edit a Presentation;* **3.** *Format a Presentation;* **4.** *Create Headers and Footers and Print a Presentation;* **5.** *Create a New Presentation;* **6.** *Use Slide Sorter View;* **7.** *Add Pictures to a Presentation;* **8.** *Use the Microsoft Help System.*

In the following Mastering PowerPoint project, you will create a presentation that details the holiday activities at Skyline Bakery and Cafe. Your completed presentation will look similar to Figure 1.48.

For Project 1I, you will need the following files:

New blank PowerPoint presentation
p1I_December
p1I_Green_Template
p1I_Coffee
p1I_Ornaments

You will save your presentation as
1I_Holiday_ Firstname_Lastname

Figure 1.48

(Project 1I–Holiday continues on the next page)

Content-Based Assessments

(Project 1I–Holiday continued)

1. **Start** PowerPoint and begin a new presentation by searching for the green and gold holiday template. If the template is not available, from your student files, open **p1I_Green_Template**. The title of the presentation is **Holiday Happenings** and the subtitle is **With Skyline Bakery and Cafe** Insert all of the slides from the presentation **p1I_December**. **Save** the presentation as **1I_Holiday_Firstname_Lastname**

2. On **Slide 2**, increase the list level for bullet points 2, 3, and 4 and for the last two bullet points. Change the **Layout** to **Two Content**, and then in the right placeholder insert a clip art photograph of a white coffee mug on a green background. If you cannot find the image, it is located with your student files—**p1I_Coffee**. Size the picture so that it is approximately as wide as the word *December* and as tall as the text in the left placeholder. Apply **Picture Style—Compound Frame, Black** and position the picture, using Figure 1.48 at the beginning of this project as your guide.

3. Display **Slide 3** and change the **Layout** to **Comparison**. In the *Click to add text* box on the left side of the slide, type **Traditional Elegance** and then in the box on the right side of the slide type **Bountiful Buffet Center** and **Underline** the text in both boxes, and then change the **Font Size** to **28**.

4. Insert a **New Slide** with the **Content with Caption** layout. In the *Click to add title* box, type **Luncheon** and then change the **Font Size** to **36**. In the text placeholder on the left side of the slide, type the following paragraph:

   Luncheons during December are reminiscent of years gone by. Join us for a pleasing array

of old-fashioned festive delights, served by candlelight while holiday music plays.

5. Select the paragraph, and then change the **Font** to **Constantia** and the **Font Size** to **20**. Apply **Bold** and **Italic**, and then change the **Line Spacing** to **1.5**.

6. In the content placeholder on the right side of the slide, insert a clip art of five, brightly colored glass ornaments. Apply **Picture Style—Reflected Bevel, Black** and use Figure 1.48 at the beginning of this project as your guide for sizing and positioning the picture. If you cannot locate the picture, the file name in your student files is **p1I_Ornaments**.

7. Insert a **New Slide** with the **Title Slide** layout. In the title placeholder, type **Savor the Holidays** and in the subtitle placeholder type **Skyline Bakery and Cafe**

8. Move **Slide 4** so that it is between **Slides 2** and **3**. Add the **Date and time updated automatically**, the **Page number**, and the file name **1I_Holiday_Firstname_Lastname** to the **Notes and Handouts Footer.** Check the presentation for spelling errors, and then view the slide show from the beginning.

9. Check your *Chapter Assignment Sheet* or *Course Syllabus* or consult your instructor to determine if you are to submit your assignments on paper or electronically. To submit electronically, go to Step 11, and then follow the instructions provided by your instructor.

10. **Print Preview** your presentation, and then print **Handouts, (6 slides per page)**.

11. **Save** changes to your presentation, and then **close** the file.

End **You have completed Project 1I**

Content-Based Assessments

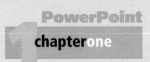
Project 1J—Business Running Case

In this project, you will apply the skills you practiced in Projects 1A and 1B.

From the student files that accompany this textbook, open the folder
03_business_running_case. Locate the Business Running Case project
for this chapter. Follow the instructions and use the skills you have
gained thus far to assist Jennifer Nelson in meeting the challenges of
owning and running her business.

Rubric

The following outcomes-based assessments are *open-ended assessments*. That is, there is no specific correct result; your result will depend on your approach to the information provided. Make *Professional Quality* your goal. Use the following scoring rubric to guide you in *how* to approach the problem, and then to evaluate *how well* your approach solves the problem.

The *criteria*—Software Mastery, Content, Format and Layout, and Process—represent the knowledge and skills you have gained that you can apply to solving the problem. The *levels of performance*—Professional Quality, Approaching Professional Quality, or Needs Quality Improvements—help you and your instructor evaluate your result.

	Your completed project is of Professional Quality if you:	Your completed project is Approaching Professional Quality if you:	Your completed project Needs Quality Improvements if you:
1-Software Mastery	Choose and apply the most appropriate skills, tools, and features and identify efficient methods to solve the problem.	Choose and apply some appropriate skills, tools, and features, but not in the most efficient manner.	Choose inappropriate skills, tools, or features, or are inefficient in solving the problem.
2-Content	Construct a solution that is clear and well organized, contains content that is accurate, appropriate to the audience and purpose, and is complete. Provide a solution that contains no errors of spelling, grammar, or style.	Construct a solution in which some components are unclear, poorly organized, inconsistent, or incomplete. Misjudge the needs of the audience. Have some errors in spelling, grammar, or style, but the errors do not detract from comprehension.	Construct a solution that is unclear, incomplete, or poorly organized, containing some inaccurate or inappropriate content; and contains many errors of spelling, grammar, or style. Do not solve the problem.
3-Format and Layout	Format and arrange all elements to communicate information and ideas, clarify function, illustrate relationships, and indicate relative importance.	Apply appropriate format and layout features to some elements, but not others. Overuse features, causing minor distraction.	Apply format and layout that does not communicate information or ideas clearly. Do not use format and layout features to clarify function, illustrate relationships, or indicate relative importance. Use available features excessively, causing distraction.
4-Process	Use an organized approach that integrates planning, development, self-assessment, revision, and reflection.	Demonstrate an organized approach in some areas, but not others; or, use an insufficient process of organization throughout.	Do not use an organized approach to solve the problem.

Outcomes-Based Assessments

Problem Solving

Project 1K — Catering

In this project, you will construct a solution by applying any combination of the Objectives found in Projects 1A and 1B.

For Project 1K, you will need the following file:

New blank PowerPoint presentation

You will save your presentation as
1K_Catering_Firstname_Lastname

Using the information provided, create a presentation that contains four to six slides that Nancy Goldman, Chief Baker, can use to describe the catering services offered by Skyline Bakery and Cafe. The presentation will be used at a business expo attended by representatives of many companies that frequently host business luncheons and dinners for their clients. The presentation should include a title slide, a slide that describes why customers would be interested in Skyline Bakery and Cafe's catering services, at least two slides with sample menus, and an ending slide that summarizes the presentation. The tone of the presentation should be positive and sales oriented so that the audience is encouraged to try Skyline's catering service.

The presentation should include a theme or template that is creative and is appropriate to the upbeat tone of the presentation. Use at least two different slide layouts to vary the way in which the presentation text is displayed. Search for clip art that visually represents the types of menu items described. Add the file name to the Notes and Handouts footer and check the presentation for spelling errors. Save the presentation as **1K_Catering_Firstname_Lastname** and submit it as directed.

End **You have completed Project 1K**

Problem Solving

Project 1L — Picnic

In this project, you will construct a solution by applying any combination of the Objectives found in Projects 1A and 1B.

For Project 1L, you will need the following file:

New blank PowerPoint presentation

**You will save your presentation as
1L_Picnic_Firstname_Lastname**

In this project, you will create a one-slide flyer to be distributed to employees of Skyline Bakery and Cafe advertising the upcoming employee picnic. The picnic is held every summer at a large, regional park. The tone of the flyer is fun! Use two fonts that are informal and inviting and large enough to easily read if the flyer were posted on a bulletin board. Include in the flyer a slide title that will make the employees feel welcome and excited about attending. Choose a content layout that includes multiple placeholders for the information that you need to provide. The flyer should include information on location, date, time, and types of activities. Include a picture that is reminiscent of a picnic or large outdoor gathering. Refer to Project 1G for ideas on how to lay out the flyer.

Add the file name to the footer and check the presentation for spelling errors. Save the presentation as **1L_Picnic_Firstname_Lastname** and submit it as directed.

 You have completed Project 1L ——————————

Problem Solving

Project 1M—Customer Service

In this project, you will construct a solution by applying any combination of the Objectives found in Projects 1A and 1B.

> ### For Project 1M, you will need the following files:
>
> New blank PowerPoint presentation
> p1M_Mission_Statement

**You will save your presentation as
1M_Customer_Service_Firstname_Lastname**

In this project, you will create a six-slide customer service presentation to be used by Shawna Andreasyan, Director of Human Resources for Skyline Bakery and Cafe. All employees will be attending customer service training seminars and this presentation is a brief introduction to the overall topic of customer service.

Good customer service is grounded in the Skyline Bakery and Cafe's mission statement. The mission statement has been provided for you in presentation p1M_Mission_Statement and should be inserted early in the presentation. Think about the mission statement, and then in the next slide, use a title slide layout to make a brief statement that summarizes how the mission statement is tied to customer service. Then consider some of the following principles of good customer service. A company should make a commitment to customer service so that every employee believes in it and is rewarded by it. Employees should also understand that everyone is involved in good customer service. The company is not just about the product; people are critically important to the success of any business and good customer service ensures that success. Furthermore, employees who are rewarded for good customer service will likely continue to work with good practices, perhaps leading to increased sales.

Using the information in the previous paragraph and other information that you may gather by researching the topic of "restaurant customer service," create at least two additional slides that Shawna Andreasyan can use to describe the importance of good customer service and how it is rewarded at Skyline Bakery and Cafe. When creating the design template, search Microsoft Online for customer service or training templates; there are several available. The tone of this presentation is informative and serious. Keep this in mind when choosing a template, theme, fonts, and clip art. Add the date and file name to the Notes and Handouts footer and check the presentation for spelling errors. Save the presentation as **1M_Customer_Service_Firstname_Lastname** and submit it as directed.

End You have completed Project 1M

Outcomes-Based Assessments

Problem Solving

Project 1N—Menus

In this project, you will construct a solution by applying any combination of the Objectives found in Projects 1A and 1B.

For Project 1N, you will need the following file:

New blank PowerPoint presentation

You will save your presentation as 1N_Menus_Firstname_Lastname

In this exercise, you will create a presentation that contains special menus that are used for different holidays. Recognizing that holiday menus are frequently used in a number of presentations throughout the year, Peter Wang, Executive Chef, has decided to create sample menus in one presentation so that the menus are available when the marketing staff need to insert them into PowerPoint presentations.

Choose five holidays and create slides that include one holiday menu per slide. You may research holiday menus on the Internet, visit local restaurants to find out if they have special holiday menus, or you may use your own experience with family traditions in creating these menus. The slide title should identify the holiday and every slide should include a picture that portrays the holiday meal or represents the holiday in some way. Alternatively, consider using a Two Content layout in which the menu is in one column and a quote describing why the menu is special is in the other column. Keep your theme simple so that it does not interfere with the pictures that you have selected. Because these slides will likely be used in different presentations throughout the year, you may choose different fonts and font styles that characterize each holiday.

Add the date and file name to the Notes and Handouts footer and check the presentation for spelling errors. Save the presentation as **1N_Menus_Firstname_Lastname** and submit it as directed.

 You have completed Project 1N —————

PowerPoint

chapterone

Problem Solving

Project 1O — Opening

In this project, you will construct a solution by applying any combination of the Objectives found in Projects 1A and 1B.

For Project 1O, you will need the following file:

New blank PowerPoint presentation

You will save your presentation as 1O_Opening_Firstname_Lastname

In this project, you will create a presentation to be shown by Skyline Bakery and Cafe's Chief Executive Officer, Samir Taheri, at a Chamber of Commerce meeting. The presentation will explain the details of the company's grand opening of two new locations in Rhode Island taking place in June. The presentation should contain six to eight slides and the first two to three slides should include background information that may be taken from the following paragraph that describes the company and the new restaurant's location.

Skyline Bakery and Cafe is a chain of casual dining restaurants and bakeries based in Boston. Each restaurant has its own in-house bakery, which produces a wide variety of high-quality specialty breads, breakfast sweets, and desserts. Breads and sweets are sold by counter service along with coffee drinks, gourmet teas, fresh juices, and sodas. The full-service restaurant area features a menu of sandwiches, salads, soups, and light entrees. Fresh, high-quality ingredients and a professional and courteous staff are the hallmarks of every Skyline Bakery and Cafe.

The new restaurant is located in an outdoor lifestyle center where many residents gather in the evening to socialize. The restaurants are opening in June, so consider a summer theme as you develop ideas about the kinds of events that the owners may host during the grand opening. Include in the presentation four slides representing four different days of events—two at each of the new locations. The Comparison and Two Content slide layouts may be very effective for these four slides. Use fonts and clip art to enhance your presentation but do not clutter the presentation with excess images or many different types of fonts. Add the date and file name to the Notes and Handouts footer and check the presentation for spelling errors. Save the presentation as **1O_Opening_Firstname_Lastname** and submit it as directed.

End **You have completed Project 1O**

Outcomes-Based Assessments

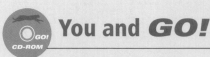 You and *GO!*

Project 1P—You and *GO!*

In this project, you will construct a solution by applying any combination of the Objectives found in Projects 1A and 1B.

From the student files that accompany this textbook, open the folder **04_you_and_go**. Locate the You and *GO!* project for this chapter and follow the instructions to create a presentation about a place to which you have traveled or would like to travel.

 End You have completed Project 1P ————————

GO! with Help

Project 1Q—*GO!* with Help

The PowerPoint Help system is extensive and can help you as you work. In this project, you will view information about getting help as you work in PowerPoint.

1 **Start** PowerPoint. At the right end of the Ribbon, click the **Microsoft Office PowerPoint Help** button to display the **PowerPoint Help** dialog box. In the **Search** box, type **keyboard shortcuts** and then press [Enter].

2 In the displayed search results, click **Keyboard shortcuts for PowerPoint 2007**. Maximize the displayed window and read how you can use keyboard shortcuts in PowerPoint.

3 If you want, print a copy of the information by clicking the **Print** button at the top of the **Microsoft Office PowerPoint Help** window.

4 **Close** the Help window, and then **Close** PowerPoint.

 End You have completed Project 1Q ————————

Outcomes-Based Assessments

Group Business Running Case

Project 1R—Group Business Running Case

In this project, you will apply the skills you practiced from the Objectives in Projects 1A and 1B.

Your instructor may assign this group case project to your class. If your instructor assigns this project, he or she will provide you with information and instructions to work as part of a group. The group will apply the skills gained thus far to help the Bell Orchid Hotel Group achieve its business goals.

End You have completed Project 1R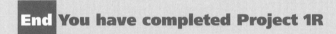

chapter two

Designing a PowerPoint Presentation

OBJECTIVES

At the end of this chapter you will be able to:

1. Format Slide Elements
2. Insert and Format Pictures and Shapes
3. Apply Slide Transitions

4. Reorganize Presentation Text and Clear Formats
5. Create and Format a SmartArt Graphic

OUTCOMES

Mastering these objectives will enable you to:

PROJECT 2A
Format a Presentation

PROJECT 2B
Enhance a Presentation with SmartArt Graphics

Montagna del Pattino

Montagna del Pattino was founded and built by the Blardone family in the 1950s. It has grown from one ski run and a small lodge to 50 trails, 6 lifts, a 300-room lodge, and a renowned ski and snowboard school. Luxurious condominiums on the property have ski in/ski out access. A resort store offers rental and sale of gear for enthusiasts who want the latest advances in ski and snowboard technology. A variety of quick service, casually elegant, and fine dining restaurants complete the scene for a perfect ski-enthusiast getaway.

Designing a PowerPoint Presentation

A PowerPoint presentation is a visual aid in which well-designed slides help the audience understand complex information, while keeping them focused on the message. Color is an important element that provides uniformity and visual interest. When used correctly, color enhances your slides and draws the audience's interest by creating focus. When designing the background and element colors for your presentation, use a consistent look throughout the presentation and be sure that the colors you use provide contrast so that the text is visible on the background.

Project 2A **Welcome**

In Activities 2.1 through 2.13, you will edit and format a presentation that Kirsten McCarty, Director of Marketing, has created for a travel fair that introduces potential resort visitors to the types of activities available at Montagna del Pattino. Your completed presentation will look similar to Figure 2.1.

For Project 2A, you will need the following files:

p2A_Snow
p2A_Snowboard
p2A_Welcome
p2A_Winter

**You will save your presentation as
2A_Welcome_Firstname_Lastname**

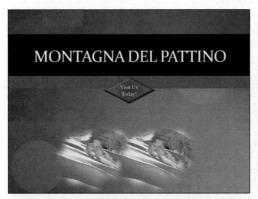

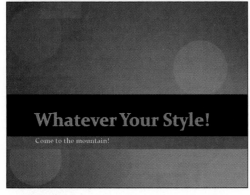

Figure 2.1
Project 2A—Welcome

Objective 1
Format Slide Elements

Recall that formatting is the process of changing the appearance of the text, layout, and design of a slide. You have practiced formatting text by changing the font and font size, and by applying bold and italic text styles. Other slide elements can be formatted, such as bulleted and numbered lists, and there are other methods that you can use to enhance text, including WordArt and the Format Painter.

Note — Comparing Your Screen with the Figures in This Textbook

Your screen will match the figures shown in this textbook if you set your screen resolution to 1024 × 768. At other resolutions, your screen will closely resemble, but not match, the figures shown. To view your screen's resolution, on the Windows desktop, right-click in a blank area, click Properties, and then click the Settings tab.

Activity 2.1 Selecting Placeholder Text and Using the Repeat Key

1 **Start** PowerPoint. From your student files, **Open** the file **p2A_Welcome**. From the **Office** menu 🔲, click **Save As**, and then click the **Create New Folder** button 🔲. Navigate to the location where you are saving your solution files, create a folder with the name **PowerPoint Chapter 2** and then click **OK**. In the **File name** box, type 2A_Welcome_Firstname_Lastname and then click **Save** to save your file.

2 Display **Slide 2**. Click anywhere in the bulleted list on the left side of the slide and notice that the placeholder is surrounded by a dashed border, as shown in Figure 2.2.

The dashed border indicates that you can make editing changes to the placeholder text.

Figure 2.2

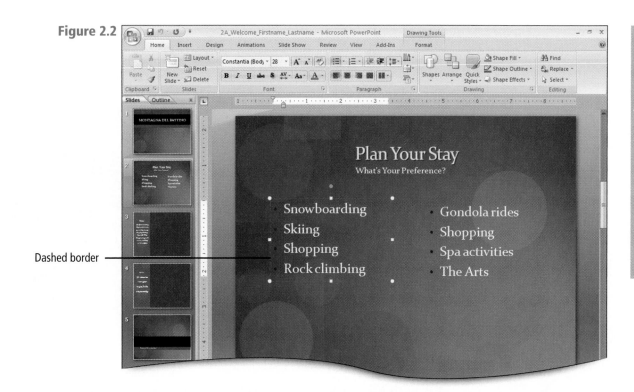

Dashed border

> **3** Point to the dashed border to display the ⊕ pointer, as shown in Figure 2.3.

Figure 2.3

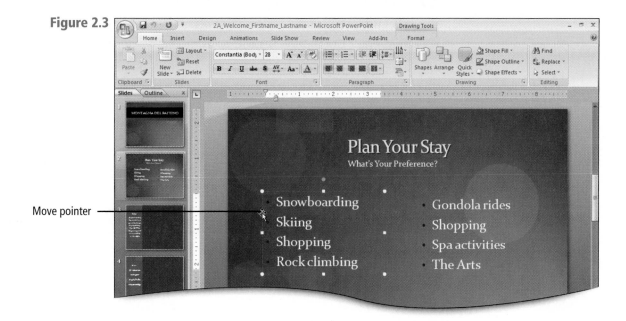

Move pointer

> **4** With the ⊕ pointer displayed, click the mouse button to display the border as a solid line as shown in Figure 2.4.
>
> When a placeholder's border displays as a solid line, all of the text in the placeholder is selected and can be formatted at one time. Thus, any formatting changes that you make will be applied to all of the text in the placeholder.

Figure 2.4

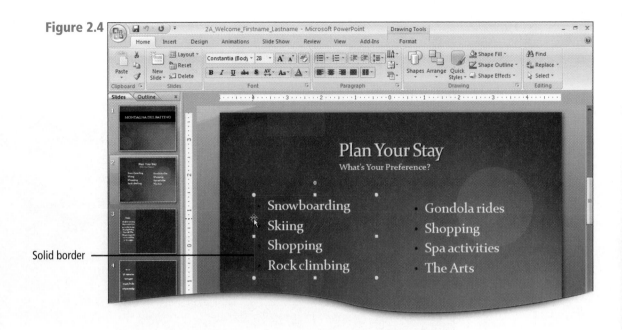

Solid border —

▐5▐ With the border of the placeholder displaying as a solid line, on the **Home tab**, in the **Font group**, click the **Font button arrow**, and then click **Arial**.

All of the text in the placeholder is changed to Arial.

▐6▐ Click in the text in the bulleted list placeholder on the right side of the slide. Point to the dashed border to display the ⊕ pointer, and then click the mouse button so that the border is solid.

▐7▐ Press F4, which repeats the last command or keystroke that you entered.

All of the text in the placeholder on the right is formatted in Arial.

▐8▐ **Save** 🖫 your changes.

Another Way ── **To Repeat a Command**

On the Quick Access Toolbar, click the Repeat button ◎ to repeat the last command or keystroke that you entered.

Activity 2.2 Changing a Bulleted List to a Numbered List

1 With **Slide 2** still displayed, click anywhere in the bulleted list on the left side of the slide, and then point to its dashed border to display the ⊕ pointer. Click the dashed border so that it displays as a solid line, indicating that all of the text is selected.

2 On the **Home tab**, in the **Paragraph group**, click the **Numbering** button ▤.

All of the bullets are converted to numbers. The color of the numbers is determined by the presentation theme.

Alert!

Did you display the Numbering gallery?

If you clicked the Numbering button arrow instead of the Numbering button, the Numbering gallery displays. Click the Numbering button arrow again to close the gallery, and then click the Numbering button to convert the bullets to numbers.

---

3 Select the bulleted list placeholder on the right side of the slide so that the border displays as a solid line. In the **Paragraph group**, click the **Numbering** button ▤.

4 **Save** ▤ the presentation.

Activity 2.3 Modifying the Bulleted List Style

The theme that is applied to your presentation includes default styles for the bulleted points in content placeholders. In this presentation, the default bullet is a blue circle. You can customize a bullet by changing its style, color, and size.

1 With **Slide 2** still displayed, click anywhere in the numbered list on the left side of the slide, and then point to its dashed border. Click the dashed border so that it displays as a solid line, indicating that all of the text is selected.

2 On the **Home tab**, in the **Paragraph group**, click the **Bullets button arrow** ▤ to display the **Bullets gallery**, as shown in Figure 2.5. If your bullets gallery looks different, at the bottom of the Bullets and Numbering dialog box, click the Reset button.

The gallery displays several bullet characters that you can apply to the selection. Below the gallery, the Bullets and Numbering option, when clicked, displays the Bullets and Numbering dialog box.

Bullets button arrow   Bullets gallery

Figure 2.5

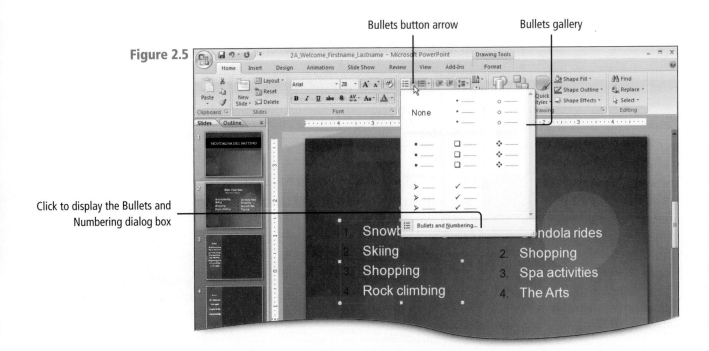

Click to display the Bullets and
Numbering dialog box

Alert!   **Did you replace the numbers with bullets?**

If you replaced the numbers with bullets, then you clicked the Bullets *button* instead of the Bullets *arrow*. Click the Bullets arrow, and then continue with Step 3.

3 At the bottom of the **Bullets gallery**, click **Bullets and Numbering**. In the displayed **Bullets and Numbering** dialog box, point to each bullet style to display its ScreenTip. Then, in the second row, click **Star Bullets**. Below the gallery, click the **Color** button. Under **Theme Colors**, in the first row, click the first color—**Black, Background 1**. Click **OK** to apply the bullet style.

4 Click in the text in the numbered list placeholder on the right side of the slide. Point to the dashed border to display the ⊕ pointer, and then click the mouse button so that the placeholder border is solid, indicating that all of the text in the placeholder can be formatted at one time.

5 Press F4 to repeat the bullet formatting, and then compare your slide with Figure 2.6.

Figure 2.6

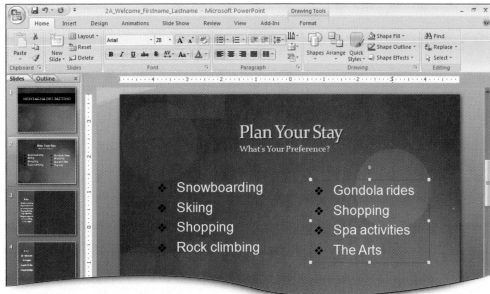

6 Save  your changes.

More Knowledge

Using Other Symbols as Bullet Characters

Many bullets styles are available for you to insert in your presentation. In the Bullets and Numbering dialog box, click the Customize button to view additional bullet styles.

Activity 2.4 Applying WordArt Styles to Text

WordArt is a feature that applies combinations of decorative formatting to text, including shadows, reflections, and 3-D effects, as well as changing the line and *fill color* of text. A fill color is the inside color of text or of an object. You can choose from a gallery of WordArt styles to insert a new WordArt object or you can customize existing text by applying WordArt formatting.

1 Display **Slide 3**, and then drag to select the word *Relax*. On the **Format tab**, in the **WordArt Styles group**, click the **More** button

to display the **WordArt Styles gallery.**

The WordArt gallery is divided into two sections. If you choose a WordArt style in the *Applies to Selected Text* section, you must first select all of the text to which you want to apply the WordArt. If you choose a WordArt style in the *Applies to All Text in the Shape* section, the WordArt style is applied to all of the text in the placeholder.

2 Move your pointer over several of the WordArt styles and notice that Live Preview displays the formatting effects.

3 Under **Applies to Selected Text**, in the first row, click the second style—**Fill – None, Outline – Accent 2**.

The word *Relax* displays outlined in blue.

4 With the word *Relax* still selected, in the **Word Art Styles group**, click the **Text Fill button arrow** 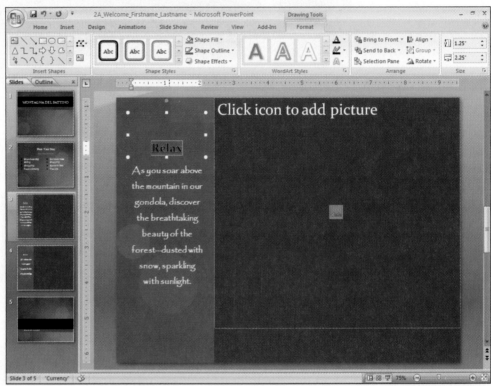. Under **Theme Colors**, in the first row, click the first color—**Black, Background 1**, and then compare your slide with Figure 2.7.

Figure 2.7

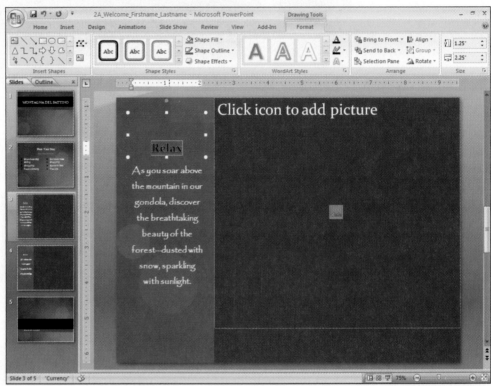

5 Display **Slide 5**. Click the **Insert tab**, and then in the **Text group**, click the **WordArt** button. In the gallery, click the first WordArt style in the first row—**Fill – Text 2, Outline – Background 2**.

In the center of your slide, a WordArt placeholder displays *Your Text Here*. When you type, your keystrokes will replace this text and fill the placeholder with wide letters. The placeholder will expand to accommodate the text. The WordArt is surrounded by sizing handles that are used to adjust its size by using the same technique that you learned when sizing clip art.

6 Type **Whatever Your Style!** to replace the WordArt placeholder text.

7 Look at the Slide pane and verify that the horizontal ruler displays above the slide and that the vertical ruler displays to the left of the slide. If the rulers do not display, on the Ribbon, click the View tab. In the Show/Hide group, click to select the Ruler check box.

8 Point to the WordArt border to display the ⊕ pointer. Using Figure 2.8 as a guide, drag down and to the left approximately 1 inch to move the WordArt.

Figure 2.8

Position WordArt here —

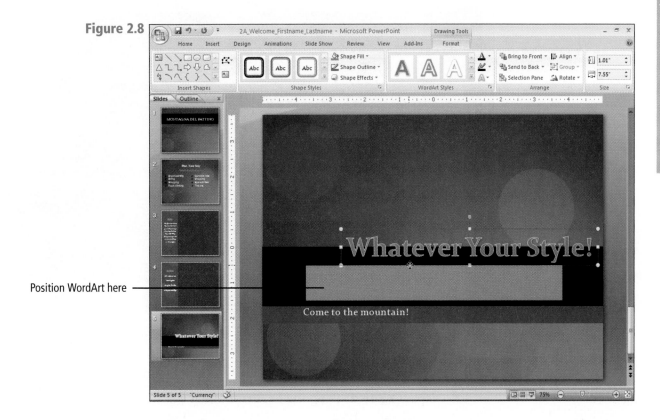

9 Save 🖫 the presentation.

Activity 2.5 Using Format Painter

Format Painter copies *formatting* from one selection of text to another, thus ensuring formatting consistency in your presentation.

1 Display **Slide 3**, and then select the word *Relax*. On the **Home tab**, in the **Clipboard group**, double-click the **Format Painter** button 🖌, and then move your pointer anywhere into the Slide pane.

The pointer displays with a small paintbrush attached to it, indicating that Format Painter is active, as shown in Figure 2.9.

Figure 2.9

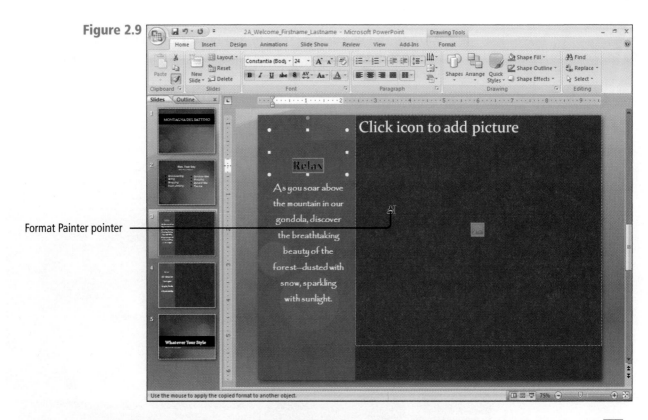

Format Painter pointer

2 In the **Slides/Outline** pane, click **Slide 4** to display it. Drag the pointer over the slide title—**Or Not!**

The WordArt formatting is applied to the title on Slide 4.

3 Display **Slide 2**. Drag the Format Painter pointer over the text **What's Your Preference?**, and then click the **Format Painter** button again to turn it off.

4 **Save** the presentation.

Alert!

Were you unable to use Format Painter more than one time?

When the Format Painter button is clicked one time instead of double-clicked, you can only use it to apply formatting to one selection. If you were only able to use Format Painter once, repeat Steps 1, 3, and 4.

Objective 2
Insert and Format Pictures and Shapes

PowerPoint 2007 provides a number of options for adding pictures and shapes to your presentation. You can draw lines, arrows, stars and banners, and a number of other basic shapes including ovals and rectangles. You can add text to a shape that you create and position it anywhere on a slide, and you can fill a shape with a picture. After you create a shape, you can add 3-D, glow, bevel effects, and shadows, or you can apply a predefined **Shape Style** that includes a combination of formatting effects.

Activity 2.6 Inserting a Picture Using a Content Layout

Many of the slide layouts in PowerPoint 2007 are designed to accommodate digital pictures that you have stored on your system or on a portable storage device.

1 Display **Slide 3**, which is formatted with the Content and Caption layout.

In the center of the large Content placeholder on the right side of the slide, the *Insert Picture* button displays.

2 In the center of the content placeholder, click the **Insert Picture from File** button to open the **Insert Picture** dialog box. Navigate to the location in which your student files are stored, and then double-click **p2A_Winter**. Alternatively, click p2A_Winter, and then click Insert.

The picture fills the entire placeholder.

3 Display **Slide 4**. Using the technique that you practiced in **Step 2**, insert the picture **p2A_Snowboard**, and then compare your slide with Figure 2.10.

Figure 2.10

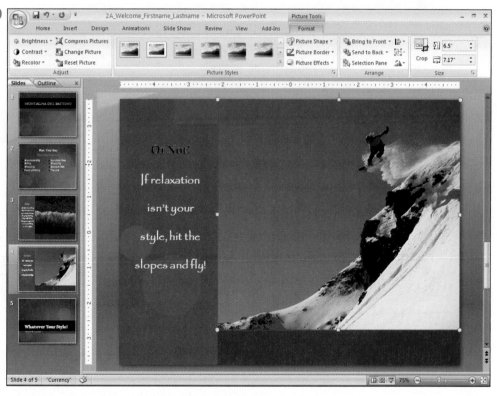

4 **Save** the presentation.

Workshop

Using Pictures Effectively in a Presentation

Large photographic images add impact to a presentation and help the audience visualize the message that you are trying to convey.

Activity 2.7 Changing the Size and Shape of a Picture

Recall that you can resize a picture by dragging the sizing handles. Alternatively, you can use the Picture contextual tools to specify a picture's height and width. You can also modify a picture by changing its shape.

1 Display **Slide 1**. Click the **Insert tab**, and then in the **Illustrations group**, click **Picture**. Navigate to the location where your student files are stored, and then double-click **p2A_Snow**.

The picture is inserted in the center of your slide and the Picture contextual tools tab displays on the Ribbon.

2 On the **Format tab**, in the **Size group**, notice that the height of the picture is 5.34 inches and the width of the picture is 6.68 inches, as shown in Figure 2.11.

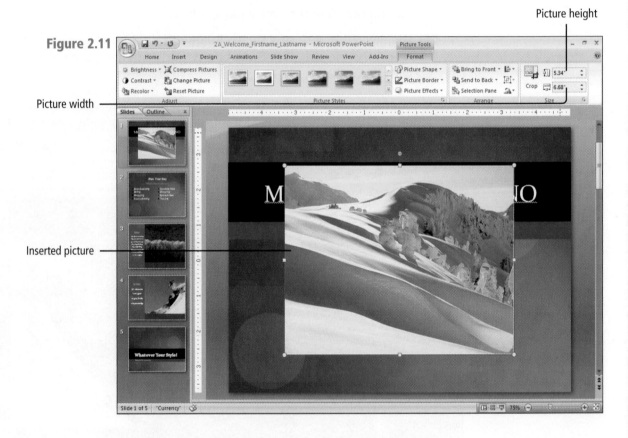

Figure 2.11

Picture height

Picture width

Inserted picture

3 On the **Format tab**, in the **Size group**, click in the **Shape Height box** so that 5.34 is selected. Type **3** and then press Enter. Notice that the height of the picture is resized to 3 inches and the width is also resized. When you change the height of a picture, the width is adjusted proportionately unless you type a new size in the Width box.

4 If necessary, select the picture. On the **Format tab**, in the **Picture Styles group**, click the **Picture Shape** button to display a gallery of shapes that you can apply to the picture. Under **Basic Shapes**, in the third row, click the third to last shape—**Cloud**.

5 Point to the picture to display the ⊕ pointer and then drag straight down so that the bottom edge of the cloud touches the bottom of the slide. Compare your slide with Figure 2.12.

Figure 2.12

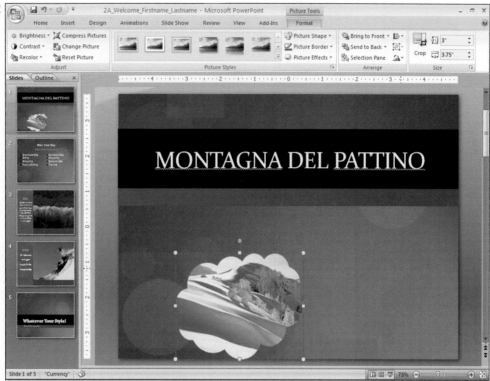

6 Save 💾 your presentation.

More Knowledge

Moving an Object by Using the Arrow Keys

You can use the directional arrow keys on your keyboard to move a picture, shape, or other object in small increments. Select the object so that its outside border displays as a solid line. Then, on your keyboard, press the directional arrow keys to precisely move the selected object.

Activity 2.8 Inserting and Positioning a Text Box

The slide layouts in PowerPoint 2007 are versatile and provide a variety of options for positioning text and objects on the slide. One way that you can customize a slide layout is by adding a **text box**. A text box is an object that is used to position text anywhere on the slide. When you create a text box, the **insertion point**—a blinking vertical line that indicates where text will be inserted—displays inside the text box, indicating that you can begin to type.

1 Display **Slide 4**. Click the **Insert tab**, and then in the **Text group**, click the **Text Box** button. Move the pointer into the slide to position the pointer below the picture as shown in Figure 2.13.

Figure 2.13

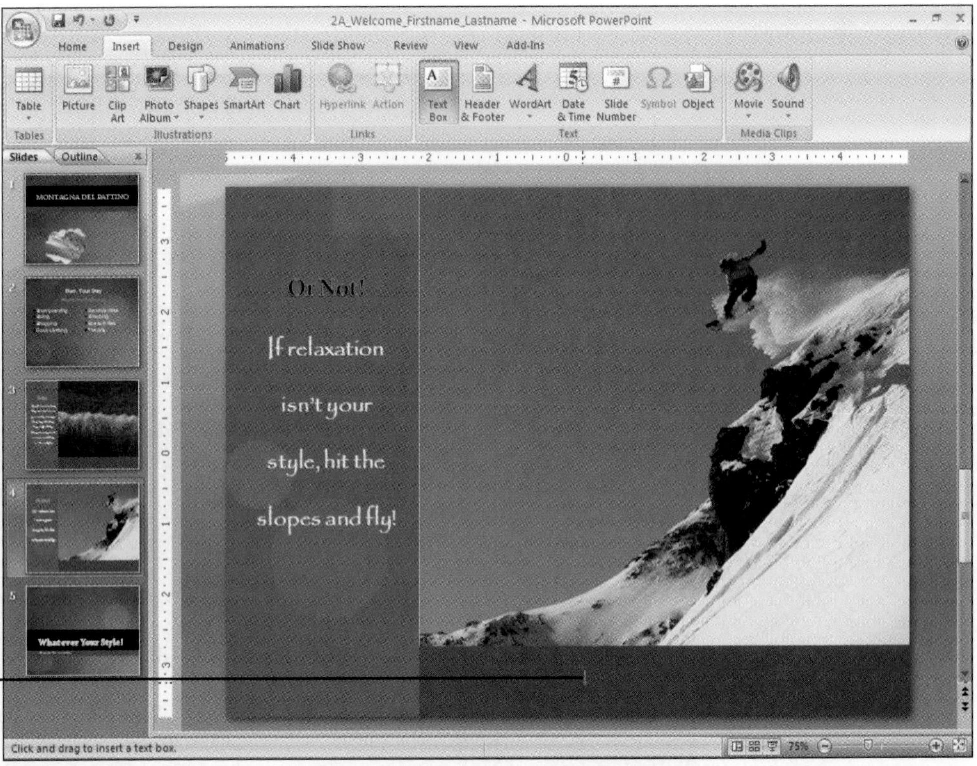

Position pointer here

2 Click to create a narrow rectangular text box. Type **Another View From Above** and notice that as you type, the width of the text box expands to accommodate the text.

<table>
<tr><td>**Alert!**</td><td>**Does the text that you type in the text box display vertically, one character at a time?**

If you move the pointer when you click to create the text box, PowerPoint sets the width of the text box and does not widen to accommodate the text. If this happened to you, your text may display vertically instead of horizontally or it may display on two lines. Point to the center right sizing handle and drag to the right so that the text box is approximately 3 inches wide. When you finish typing the text, adjust the width of the text box as necessary so that all of the text displays on one line.</td></tr>
</table>

3 Compare your slide with Figure 2.14 and if necessary, use the 🔁 pointer to adjust the size and position of the text box.

Do not be concerned if your text box does not match Figure 2.14 exactly. In a later Activity, you will practice using the Align tools to position slide elements precisely.

Position text box here

Figure 2.14

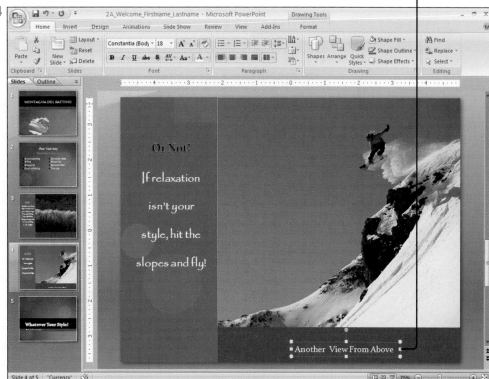

4 Display **Slide 3**. On the **Insert tab**, in the **Text group,** click the **Text Box** button. Click to create a text box in approximately the same position as the one that you created on Slide 4. Type **Spectacular Morning Vistas** and then click in a blank area of the slide.

5 Compare your slide with Figure 2.15, and if necessary, use the ⊕ pointer to adjust the position of the text box.

Figure 2.15

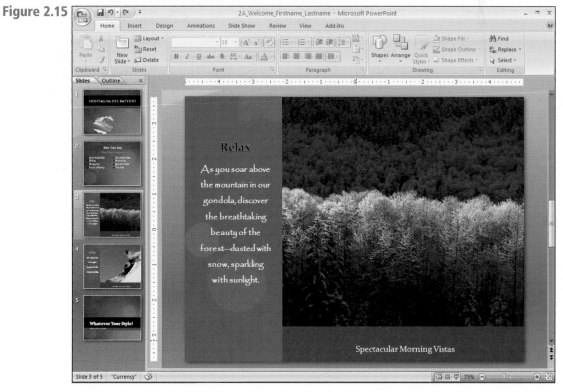

6 **Save** 🖫 the presentation.

More Knowledge
Formatting a Text Box

You can format the text in a text box by using the same techniques that you use to format text in any other placeholder. For example, you can change fonts, font styles, and font sizes, and you can apply WordArt styles to the text in a text box.

Activity 2.9 Inserting, Sizing, and Positioning Shapes

Shapes can be used to help convey your message by illustrating an idea, a process, or a workflow. You can draw lines, arrows, stars and banners, and a number of other basic shapes including ovals and rectangles. Shapes can be sized and moved by using the same techniques that you used to size and move clip art images.

1 Display **Slide 1**, and then verify that the rulers display. If the rulers do not display, on the View tab, in the Show/Hide group, select the Ruler check box.

2 Click the **Insert tab**, and then in the **Illustrations group**, click the **Shapes button** to display the **Shapes gallery**. Under **Basic Shapes**, in the first row, click the seventh shape—**Diamond**.

3 Move the pointer into the slide until the ⊞ pointer—called the *crosshair pointer*—displays, indicating that you can draw a shape. Notice that when you move the ⊞ pointer into the slide, *guides*—vertical and horizontal lines—display in the rulers to give you a visual indication of where the pointer is positioned so that you can draw a shape.

4 Move the ⊞ pointer so that the guides are positioned at approximately **1 inch to the left of zero** on the **horizontal ruler** and **1 inch above zero** on the **vertical ruler**, as shown in Figure 2.16.

Figure 2.16

Guide on horizontal ruler

Guide on vertical ruler —

Crosshair pointer —

5 Hold down the left mouse button, and then drag down and to the right so that the guide displays at **1 inch to the right of zero** on the **horizontal ruler** and displays at **zero** on **the vertical ruler**. Release the mouse button to draw the diamond.

The Drawing Tools contextual tab displays on the Ribbon.

6 On the **Format tab**, in the **Size group**, look at the **Shape Height** [⊡ 2″ ⊡] and **Shape Width** [⊡ 2.67″ ⊡] boxes. If necessary, change the **Height** to **1** and the **Width** to **2** and then click on the diamond to change its size and to keep the diamond selected. Compare your slide with Figure 2.17. If necessary, move the diamond so that it is positioned correctly.

Figure 2.17

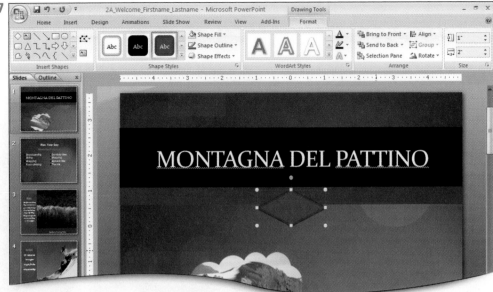

7 **Save** 🖫 your presentation.

Another Way

To Insert a Shape

On the Home tab, in the Drawing group, click the Shapes button.

Activity 2.10 Adding Text to Shapes

Shapes can be used as containers for text. After you add text to a shape, you can change the font and font size, apply font styles, and change text alignment.

1 On **Slide 1**, if necessary, click the diamond so that it is selected.

Text can be typed in a shape when the shape is selected.

2 Type **Visit Today!** Notice that the text wraps to two lines and is centered.

3 Point to the left of the word *Today*, and then click so that the insertion point displays to the left of the word. Type **Us** and press Spacebar, and then click outside of the shape.

The text wraps to three lines and extends slightly outside of the diamond. The diamond shape is not large enough to accommodate the amount of text that you have typed.

4 Select the text *Visit Us Today!* On the **Home tab**, in the **Font group**, click the **Decrease Font Size** button to change the font size to **16**. Click outside of the shape.

The text displays on two lines and fits within the diamond shape.

5 Compare your slide with Figure 2.18. **Save** the presentation.

Figure 2.18

Text displays on two lines ————

Activity 2.11 Applying Shape and Picture Styles

Shapes and pictures can be formatted using a variety of effects, including 3-D, glow, bevel, and shadows. These effects soften the outer edges of a shape or image. Shapes can also be formatted by changing the inside fill color and the outside line color. Predefined combinations of these styles are available in the Shape Styles, Quick Styles, and Picture Styles galleries.

1 On **Slide 1**, click to select the diamond, and then click the **Format tab**. In the **Shape Styles group**, click the **Shape Fill** button, and then point to several of the theme colors and watch as Live Preview changes the inside color of the diamond.

2 Point to **Gradient** to display the **Gradient Fill** gallery. A *gradient fill* is a color combination in which one color fades into another. Under **Dark Variations**, in the second row, click the second variant—**From Center**.

The diamond is filled with a blue gradient in which the outer points of the diamond are light and the center of the diamond is a darker color.

3 In the **Shape Styles group**, click the **Shape Outline** button, and then point to **Weight**. Click **6 pt** and notice that a thick outline surrounds the diamond.

4 With the diamond still selected, in the **Shape Styles group**, click the **Shape Effects** button. Point to **Bevel**, and then under **Bevel**, in the first row, click the last bevel—**Cool Slant**.

The Cool Slant bevel applies a 3-dimensional effect to the diamond.

5 Select the snow picture in the shape of a cloud. Click the **Format tab**, and then in the **Picture Styles group**, click **Picture Effects**. Point to **Soft Edges**, and then click the second to last effect—**25 Point** to blur and soften the edges of the picture, giving it a more cloudlike effect.

6 Click on a blank part of the slide so that none of the objects are selected, and then compare your slide with Figure 2.19.

Figure 2.19

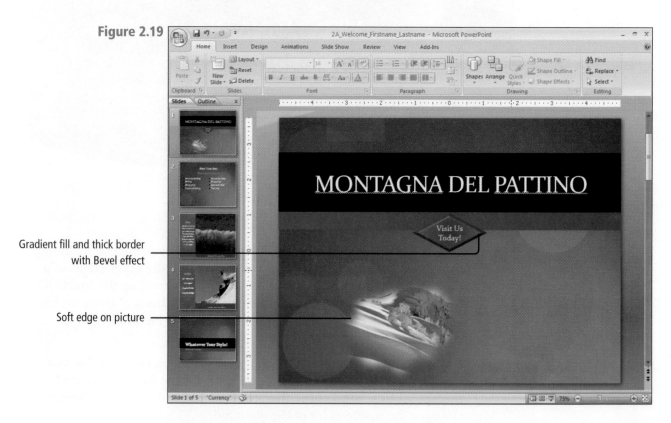

Gradient fill and thick border with Bevel effect

Soft edge on picture

7 **Save** your presentation.

More Knowledge

Applying a Quick Style or Shape Style to a Shape or Placeholder

You can quickly format an object such as a shape, text box, or placeholder by using one of the predefined Quick Styles or Shape Styles. Quick Styles and Shape Styles apply combinations of edges, shadows, line styles, gradients, and 3-D effects to the selected object. To apply a Quick Style, select the object, and then on the Home tab, click Quick Styles to display the gallery. To apply a Shape Style, select the object, and then on the Format Tab, in the Shape Styles group, click the More button to display the gallery.

Activity 2.12 Duplicating and Aligning Objects

You can duplicate an object by using a keyboard shortcut. You can align objects by dragging the object to another position on the slide or by using the Ribbon.

1 On **Slide 1**, click to select the picture. Press and hold down Ctrl, and then press D one time. Release Ctrl.

A duplicate of the picture overlaps the original picture and the duplicated image is selected.

2 Point to the duplicated image to display the ⊕ pointer. Drag the duplicated image to the right so that its left edge overlaps the right edge of the picture, using Figure 2.20 as a guide.

Figure 2.20

Duplicated picture overlaps
original picture

3 Display **Slide 2**. Click the **Insert tab**, and then in the **Illustrations group**, click the **Shapes** button to display the **Shapes gallery**.

4 Under **Block Arrows**, in the first row, click the fourth arrow—**Down Arrow**. Position the ⊞ pointer at approximately **3 inches to the left of zero** on the **horizontal ruler** and at **1 inch below zero** on the **vertical ruler**, as shown in Figure 2.21.

Horizontal guide

Figure 2.21

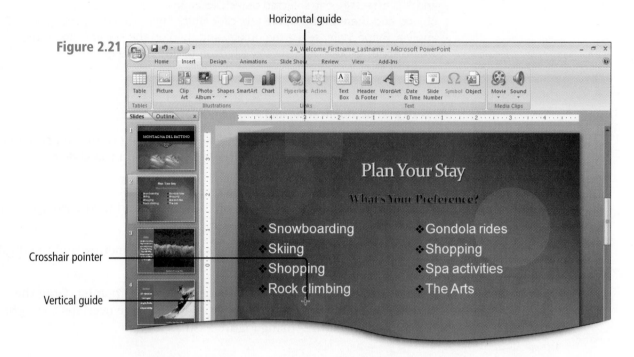

Crosshair pointer

Vertical guide

5 Drag approximately **1/2 inch to the right** and **1 inch down** to create the arrow and to display the Drawing Tools contextual tab. Check the size of the shape by looking at the **Format tab** in the **Size group**. If necessary, adjust the size of the arrow to a Height of 1 inch and a Width of 0.5 inch.

6 With the arrow selected, on the **Format tab**, in the **Shape Styles group**, click the **More** button ⏷. In the last row, click the second effect—**Intense Effect – Accent 1**.

7 With the arrow still selected, hold down Ctrl, and then press D to duplicate the arrow. Drag the arrow to the right so that the arrow is positioned below the text on the right of the slide at approximately **2 inches to the right of zero** on the **horizontal ruler**.

8 With the arrow on the right selected, press ⇧ Shift, and then click the arrow on the left so that both arrows are selected. Click the **Format tab**, and then in the **Arrange group**, click the **Align** button. Click **Align Selected Objects**.

The Align Selected Objects option enables you to align the objects that you select relative to each other. The Align to Slide option enables you to align objects with the edges of the slide determining placement.

9 On the **Format tab**, in the **Arrange group**, click the **Align** button 📄 ▾, and then click **Align Top**.

With the two arrows selected, the lower arrow moves up so that its top edge is aligned with the top edge of the higher arrow. Thus, the tops of the two arrows are positioned at the same location on the vertical ruler. Compare your slide with Figure 2.22.

Figure 2.22

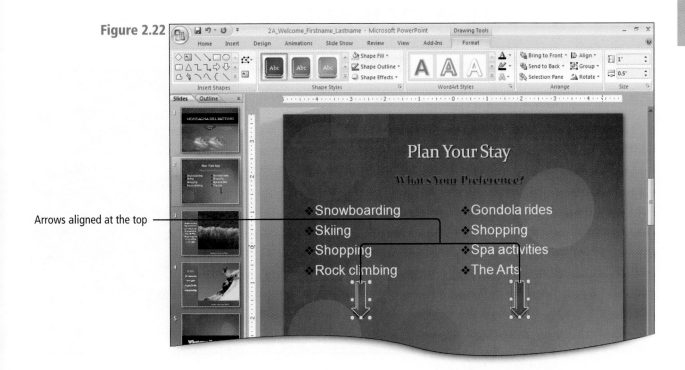

Arrows aligned at the top

10 Click the **Insert tab**, and then in the **Text group**, click **Text Box**. Position the pointer at approximately **4 inches to the left of zero** on the **horizontal ruler** and at **2.5 inches below zero** on the **vertical ruler.** Click to create a text box, type **High Energy** and then select the text that you typed. On the Mini toolbar, click the **Font Size button arrow** 44 ▾ and then click **32**. Click the **Center** button ▤. If the text box does not expand to accommodate the text, use the center right sizing handle to widen the text box.

11 Click the **Format tab**, and then in the **Shape Styles group**, click the **More** button ▾. In the last row, click the first style—**Intense Effect – Dark 1**.

12 Point to the outer edge of the text box to display the ✛ pointer and then click to select the text box. Hold down Ctrl, and then press D to duplicate the text box. Drag the duplicated textbox to the right so that it is positioned below the arrow on the right side of the slide. Select the text **High Energy**, and then type **Relaxation** to replace the text.

13 Use the ⇧Shift key to select the two text boxes—**High Energy** and **Relaxation**. On the **Format tab**, in the **Arrange group**, click the **Align** button. Click **Align Top** to align the top edges of the two text boxes, and then click anywhere on the slide so that none of the objects are selected.

14 Click the bulleted list placeholder on the left side of the slide. Press ⇧Shift and click the arrow on the left and the **High Energy** text box so that all three objects are selected, as shown in Figure 2.23.

Figure 2.23

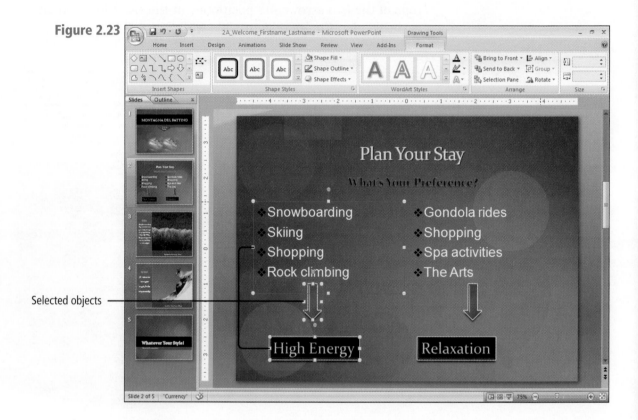

Selected objects ——

15 On the **Format tab**, in the **Arrange group**, click the **Align** button. Click **Align Selected Objects**. Click the **Align** button again, and then click **Align Center**.

The three objects are aligned at their center points.

16 Using the same procedure that you used in Steps 14 and 15, **Align Center** the placeholder, arrow, and text box on the right side of the slide.

17 **Save** 🖫 the presentation.

Objective 3
Apply Slide Transitions

Recall that a slide transition controls the way that a slide appears or disappears during an onscreen slide show. For example, when one slide leaves the screen, it may fade or dissolve into another slide. You can choose from a variety of transitions, and you can control the speed and method with which the slides advance during a presentation.

Activity 2.13 Applying Slide Transitions to a Presentation

In this activity, you will add slide transitions to all of the slides in the presentation.

1 If necessary, in the **Slides/Outline pane**, click the **Slides tab** so that the slide thumbnails display. Display **Slide 1**.

2 Click the **Animations tab**. In the **Transition to This Slide group**, click the **More** button ⬇ to display the **Transitions gallery** as shown in Figure 2.24.

The slide transitions are categorized in six groups—No Transition, Fades and Dissolves, Wipes, Push and Cover, Stripes and Bars, and Random. You may need to scroll the gallery in order to view all of the transitions. The pictures illustrate the type of transition and the arrows indicate the direction in which the slide moves.

Figure 2.24

Transitions gallery ——

3 Point to several of the transitions to Live Preview the transition effects and to display the ScreenTip with the transition name. Under **Wipes**, locate and then click the **Box Out** transition.

4 In the **Transition to This Slide group**, click the **Transition Speed arrow**, and then click **Medium**.

5 In the **Transition to This Slide group** verify that under **Advance Slide**, **On Mouse Click** is selected. If it is not, click the On Mouse Click check box, as shown in Figure 2.25.

The On Mouse Click option enables you to control when the slide will advance to the next slide. During the slide show, you can click the mouse button or press [Spacebar] to advance the presentation.

On Mouse Click selected

Figure 2.25

Medium speed

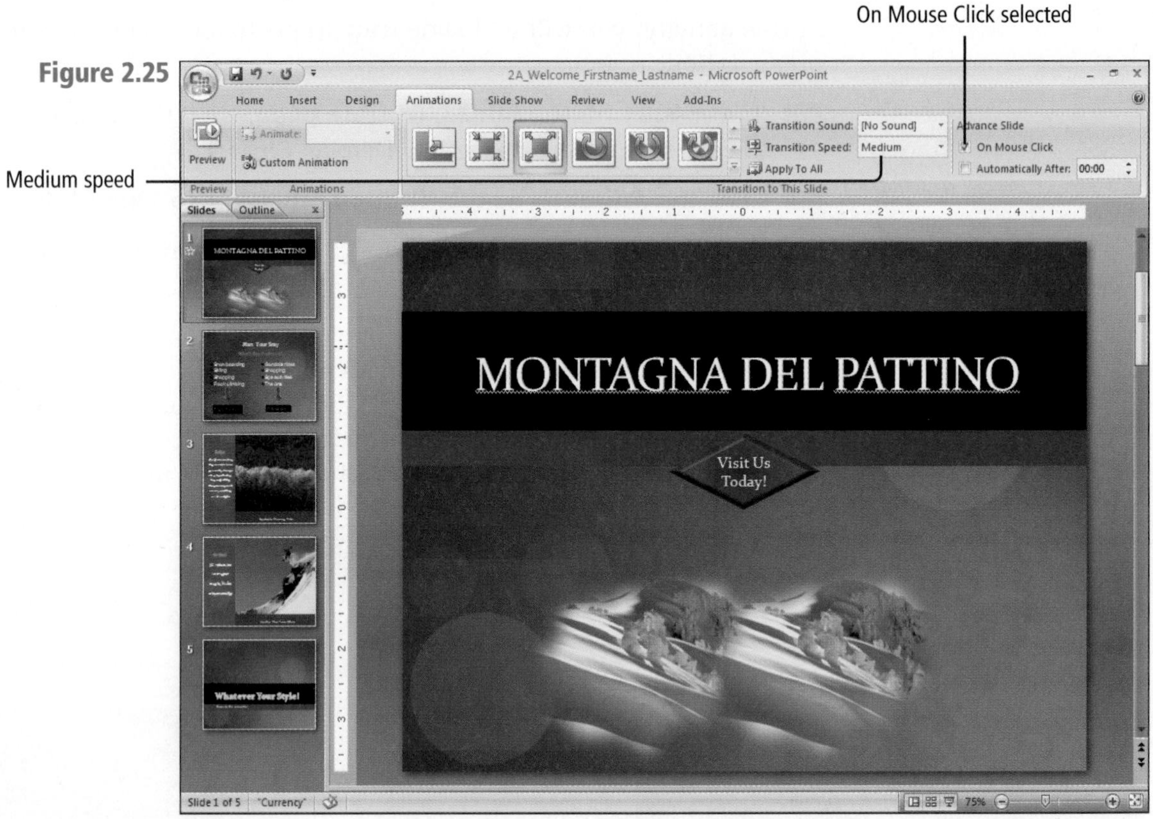

6 In the **Transition to This Slide group**, click the **Apply To All** button so that the medium speed Box Out transition is applied to all of the slides in the presentation. Notice that in the Slides/Outline pane, a star displays below each slide number, indicating that a transition has been applied.

Workshop

Applying Transitions

You can apply more than one type of transition in your presentation by displaying the slides one at a time, and then clicking the transition that you want to apply instead of clicking the Apply To All button. However, using too many different transitions in your presentation may distract the audience. Choose one basic transition to use on most of the slides in your presentation, and use one or two additional transitions if you feel that a particular slide would display effectively with a different transition.

7 Click the **Slide Show tab**. In the **Start Slide Show group**, click the **From Beginning** button, and then view your presentation, clicking the mouse button to advance through the slides. When the black slide displays, click the mouse button one more time to display the presentation in Normal view.

8 Create a **Header and Footer** for the **Notes and Handouts**. Include only the **Date and time updated automatically**, the **Page number**, and a **Footer** with the file name **2A_Welcome_Firstname_Lastname**

9 Check your *Chapter Assignment Sheet* or *Course Syllabus* or consult your instructor to determine if you are to submit your assignments on paper or electronically. To submit electronically, go to Step 11, and then follow the instructions provided by your instructor.

10 **Print Preview** your presentation, and then print **Handouts, (6 slides per page)**.

11 **Save** changes to your presentation. **Close** the presentation.

End **You have completed Project 2A** ————————————

Project 2B **Itinerary**

In Activities 2.14 through 2.22, you will edit a presentation that Kirstin McCarty, Director of Marketing, has created that includes itineraries and contact information for resort guests. You will move and copy text, and you will create diagrams that will illustrate different types of itineraries. Your completed presentation will look similar to Figure 2.26.

For Project 2B, you will need the following files:

p2B_Itinerary
p2B_Reservations_Director
p2B_Ski_Lodge_Director
p2B_Spa_Director
p2B_Tour_Director

**You will save your presentation as
2B_Itinerary_Firstname_Lastname**

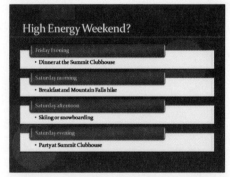

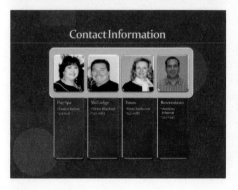

Figure 2.26
Project 2B—Itinerary

Objective 4
Reorganize Presentation Text and Clear Formats

When you select text or objects and then perform the Copy command or the Cut command, the selection is placed on the *Office Clipboard*—a temporary storage area maintained by your Microsoft Office program. From the Office Clipboard storage area, the object is available to *paste* into other locations, including other Office programs.

Activity 2.14 Moving and Copying Text

The *Cut* command removes selected text or graphics from your presentation and moves the selection to the Office Clipboard. From the Office Clipboard, the selection can be pasted to a new location. The *Copy* command duplicates a selection and places it on the Office Clipboard.

1 **Start** PowerPoint and from your student files, open **p2B_Itinerary**. **Save** the file in your **PowerPoint Chapter 2** folder as 2B_Itinerary_Firstname_Lastname

2 Display **Slide 2**, and on the **Home tab**, in the **Slides group**, click the **New Slide arrow**. In the displayed gallery, click **Title and Content**. If you inserted a slide without displaying the gallery, on the Home tab, in the Slides group, click Layout, and then click Title and Content. In the title placeholder, type **High Energy Weekend?**

3 Display **Slide 4,** and then select all of the text in the bulleted list placeholder. On the **Home tab**, in the **Clipboard group**, click the

Copy button ⬚. Alternatively, hold down Ctrl and then press C.

4 Display **Slide 3**, and then click in the content placeholder. In the **Clipboard group**, click the **Paste** button to copy the selection to Slide 3. Alternatively, hold down Ctrl and then press V.

Below the pasted text an additional bullet may display and notice that a button displays, as shown in Figure 2.27. This is the Paste Options button that provides three options for formatting pasted text.

Figure 2.27

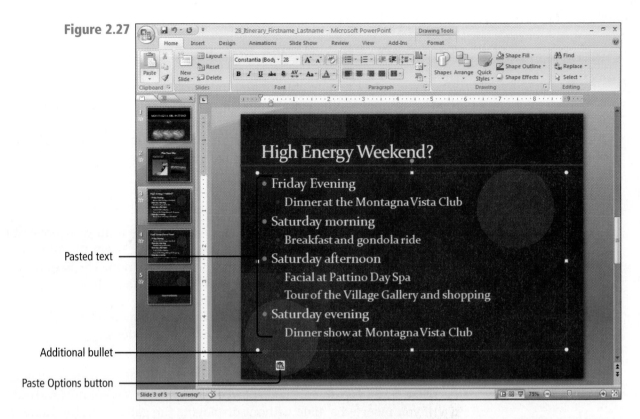

Pasted text —

Additional bullet —

Paste Options button —

5 Pause your pointer over the Paste Options button so that a down arrow displays to its right, and then click the arrow to display the formatting options. Be sure that **Use Destination Theme** is selected so that the formatting of Slide 3 is applied to the pasted text.

Use Destination Theme applies the format of the slide to which you pasted the text to the selection, and *Keep Text Only* removes all formatting from the selection.

Note — Removing the Paste Options Button

You do not need to click the Paste Options button arrow every time you paste a selection. The default setting is *Use Destination Theme*. Thus, you need only click the arrow if you want to apply a different option. The Paste Options button will remain on the screen until you perform another action.

---

6 If necessary, use ⟨←Bksp⟩ or ⟨Delete⟩ to delete any extra bullets at the bottom of the pasted text. In the second bullet point, replace the text *Montagna Vista Club* with **Summit Clubhouse** In the fourth bullet point, replace *gondola ride* with **2-mile hike** Under *Saturday afternoon*, select both of the subordinate level bullet points, and then type **Skiing or snowboarding** to replace both of the selected bullet points. Select the last bullet point on the slide, and then replace it with **Party at Summit Clubhouse**

7 Click outside the content placeholder, and then compare your slide with Figure 2.28. Make spelling and layout corrections as necessary.

Figure 2.28

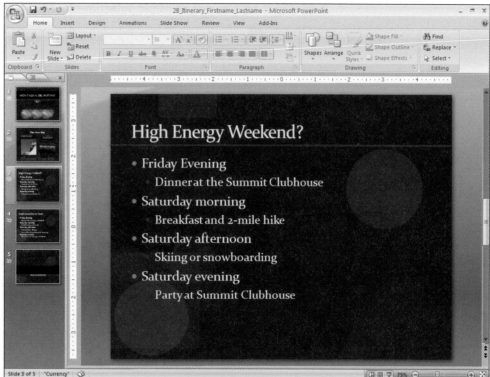

8 Display **Slide 2**. Click the WordArt text at the bottom of the slide—*Whatever Your Style*, and then click its dashed boundary box so that it displays as a solid line, indicating that all of the text is selected.

9 In the **Clipboard group**, click the **Cut** button. Alternatively, hold down Ctrl and then press X.

The text is removed from the slide and is stored on the Clipboard.

10 Display **Slide 5**. In the **Clipboard group**, click the **Paste** button to move the selection to the bottom of the last slide. Point to the edge of the pasted text to display the ⊕ pointer, and then drag up to position the text in the center of the black rectangle.

11 **Save** the presentation.

More Knowledge
Using Drag-and-Drop Text Editing

Another method of moving text is the *drag-and-drop* technique, which uses the mouse to drag selected text from one location to another. To use drag-and-drop text editing, select the text you want to move, and then position the pointer over the selected text to display the pointer. Drag the text to the new location. A vertical line attached to the pointer enables you to see exactly where the text will be pasted.

Activity 2.15 Copying Multiple Selections by Using the Office Clipboard

The Office Clipboard can store up to 24 selections that you have cut or copied, and each one can be pasted multiple times. Additionally, groups of items on the Office Clipboard can be pasted all at one time.

1 Display **Slide 1**. On the **Home tab**, in the lower right corner of the **Clipboard group**, click the **Dialog Box Launcher** ⟐ to display the Clipboard task pane on the left side of the PowerPoint window.

2 In the **Clipboard** task pane, check to see if any items display. Compare your screen with Figure 2.29.

When the Office Clipboard is empty, *Clipboard empty* displays in the task pane. If items have been cut or copied, they will display on the Office Clipboard. In Figure 2.29, the WordArt text that was cut in the previous Activity displays. You may or may not have items displayed on the Office Clipboard, depending upon its last use.

Figure 2.29

Dialog Box Launcher button

tems on Clipboard display here

Clipboard task pane

3 At the top of the **Clipboard** task pane, click the **Clear All** button to delete any items that are stored on the Office Clipboard.

4 Click in the slide title, and then click its dashed border so that it displays as a solid line. In the **Clipboard group**, click the **Copy** button 📋, and then notice that a boxed object displays in the Clipboard task pane.

The box appears to be empty, because the text is white, and the Clipboard task pane uses a white background. Even though the letters are not visible, they are still there.

5 At the bottom of the slide, three copies of the same picture display. Click any one of the three pictures to select it. In the **Clipboard**

group, click the **Copy** button, and then notice that the object displays in the Office Clipboard as the first item, and the previous item that you copied moves down.

You have collected two objects for copying.

6 Display **Slide 5**. In the **Clipboard** task pane, click **Paste All** to paste both objects to Slide 5.

The objects are pasted in the same location from which they were copied.

7 Drag the picture to the upper right corner of the slide.

8 Click the pasted text so that its dashed border displays. Point to the dashed border to display the ⊕ pointer. Using Figure 2.30 as a guide, hold down ⇧ Shift, and then drag the pasted text down approximately one inch.

Pressing ⇧ Shift while dragging constrains the textbox from moving off center, allowing for precision placement.

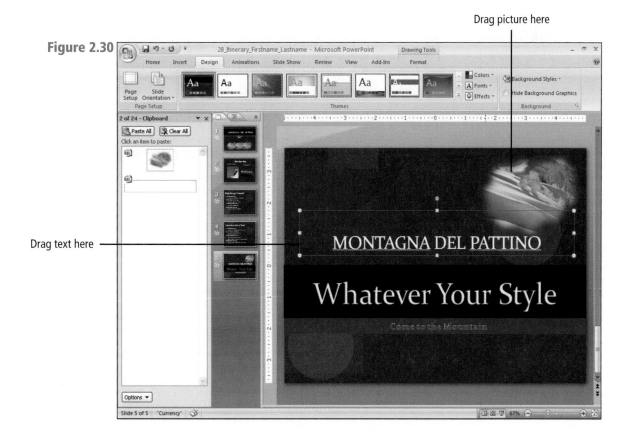

Figure 2.30

9 In the **Clipboard** task pane, click the **Clear All** button to delete the two selections from the Office Clipboard. **Close** ✕ the task pane.

10 **Save** the presentation.

More Knowledge

Pasting and Deleting Single Items from the Office Clipboard

When you point to an item on the Office Clipboard, a down arrow displays to its right. Click the arrow to display a menu with two options—Paste and Delete. You can paste and delete individual items from the Office Clipboard using this menu.

Activity 2.16 Undoing and Redoing Changes

PowerPoint remembers each change that you make so that you can undo them if you change your mind or perform an action by mistake. You can change your mind again and reverse an undo by using the Redo command.

1 Display **Slide 3**. In the fourth bullet point, select the words *2-mile*, and then type **Mountain Falls** to replace the selected words.

2 On the **Quick Access toolbar**, click the **Undo** button.

2-mile displays on the slide.

3 On the **Quick Access Toolbar**, click the **Redo** button.

Mountain Falls displays in the slide.

4 **Save** the presentation.

Alert!

Did you repeat an action instead of redo an action?

The Redo button is context-sensitive—it changes depending upon the action that you have performed. Before you click Undo, the Redo button displays as the Repeat button. Recall that the Repeat button repeats the last command or keystroke. In order to activate the Redo button, you must first Undo a command.

Activity 2.17 Clearing Formatting from a Selection

After applying multiple formats to a selection of text, you may decide that the selection is best displayed without the formats that you applied. You can clear formatting from a selection and return it to its default font and font size, and remove styles that have been applied.

1 Display **Slide 5** and notice that the text *Come to the Mountain* does not display well against the background.

2 Select *Come to the Mountain*, and then on the **Home tab**, in the **Font group**, click the **Clear All Formatting** button, and then click in a blank area of the slide.

The text is restored to its original formatting and contrasts with the background, making it easier to read.

3 **Save** the presentation.

Creating Contrast on a Slide

Contrast is an important element of slide design because it helps in distinguishing text and objects from the slide background. Be sure that the font color that you choose contrasts with the background so that your audience can easily read the text. For example, if your background is dark, choose a light-colored font. If your background is light, choose a dark-colored font.

Objective 5
Create and Format a SmartArt Graphic

A **SmartArt graphic** is a designer-quality visual representation of information that you can create by choosing from among many different layouts to effectively communicate your message or ideas. SmartArt graphics can illustrate processes, hierarchies, cycles, lists, and relationships. You can include text and pictures in a SmartArt graphic, and you can apply colors, effects, and styles that coordinate with the presentation theme.

Activity 2.18 Creating a SmartArt Diagram by Using a Content Layout

When you create a SmartArt graphic, it is a good idea when choosing a layout to consider the message that you are trying to convey. Large amounts of text can make some types of SmartArt graphics difficult to read so keep that in mind when choosing a layout. The table in Figure 2.31 describes types of SmartArt layouts and suggested purposes.

Microsoft PowerPoint SmartArt Graphic Types	
Graphic Type	**Purpose of Graphic**
List	Show nonsequential information.
Process	Show steps in a process or timeline.
Cycle	Show a continual process.
Hierarchy	Show a decision tree or create an organization chart.
Relationship	Illustrate connections.
Matrix	Show how parts relate to a whole.
Pyramid	Show proportional relationships with the largest component on the top or bottom.

Figure 2.31

1 Display **Slide 4**, and then on the **Home tab**, in the **Slides group**, click the **New Slide** button to add a slide with the **Title and Content** layout. In the title placeholder, type **Contact Information** and then **Center** ▤ the title. Notice that in addition to adding text to this slide, you can insert a SmartArt graphic by clicking the Insert SmartArt Graphic button ▥ in the center of the slide, as shown in Figure 2.32.

Figure 2.32

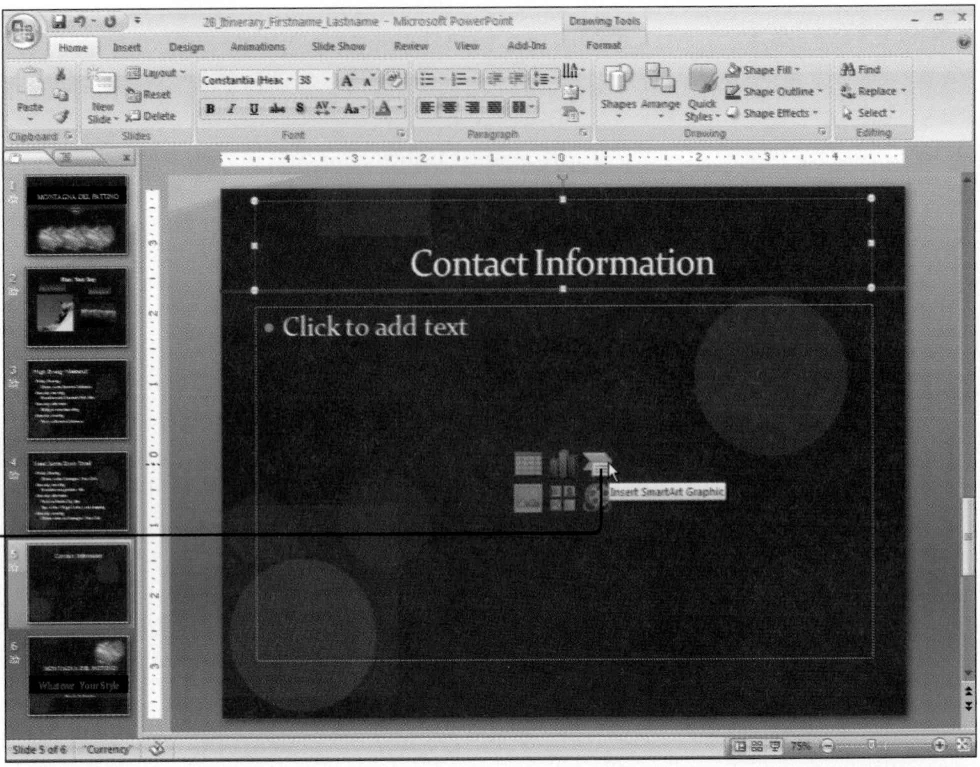

Insert SmartArt Graphic button

2 In the center of the slide, click the **Insert SmartArt Graphic** button ▦ to open the **Choose a SmartArt Graphic** dialog box.

The dialog box is divided into three sections. The left section lists the diagram types. The center section displays the diagrams according to type. The third section displays the selected diagram, its name, and a description of its purpose and how text displays.

Another Way

To Insert a SmartArt Graphic

On the Insert tab, in the Illustrations group, click the SmartArt button.

3 Explore the types of diagrams available by clicking on several and reading their descriptions. Then, on the left side of the **Choose a SmartArt Graphic** dialog box, click **Hierarchy**. In the center section in the second row, click the last diagram—**Hierarchy List**—and then click **OK** to create a hierarchical diagram surrounded by a thick border, indicating the area that the diagram will cover on the slide. Notice that on the Ribbon, the SmartArt contextual tool displays two tabs—Design and Format, as shown in Figure 2.33.

The hierarchical diagram displays with two upper level shapes and two subordinate level shapes under each upper level shape. You will use the upper level shapes to enter the resort areas that customers frequently call, and the lower level shapes to enter the contact person's name and phone number. You can type text directly into the shapes or you can type text in the Text pane. The Text pane is displayed by clicking the Text pane tab on the left side of the SmartArt graphic border.

Figure 2.33

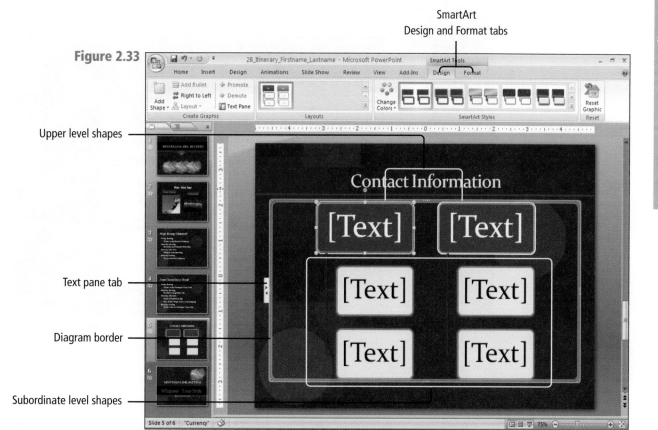

SmartArt
Design and Format tabs

Upper level shapes

Text pane tab

Diagram border

Subordinate level shapes

Note — Displaying and Closing the Text Pane

On the Ribbon, in the SmartArt Tools group, click the Design tab. In the Create Graphic group, click the Text pane button to toggle the Text pane on and off.

4 In the diagram, click in the dark red box on the left, and then type **Day Spa** Click in the box below it, and then type **Patricia Reeves** Click in the box below Patricia's name, and then type **555-0921**

The text is resized and when necessary, wraps to two lines in order to fit into each shape. When text is typed into additional shapes, the text in all shapes at the same level adjusts to the same size.

5 On the right side of the diagram, enter the following information in the boxes, and then click in a blank area of the slide. Compare your slide with Figure 2.34.

Ski Lodge

Victor Blardone

555-0563

Figure 2.34

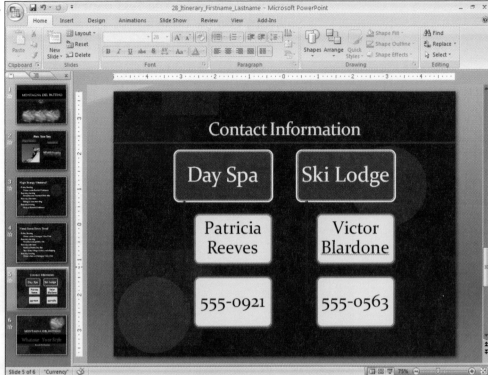

6 **Save** 🔲 the presentation.

Activity 2.19 Adding and Removing Shapes in a Diagram

If a diagram does not have enough shapes to illustrate a concept or display the relationships, you can add more shapes.

1 Click in the shape that contains the text *Ski Lodge*. Click the **Design tab**. In the **Create Graphic group**, click the **Add Shape arrow**, and then click **Add Shape After** to insert an upper level shape to the right of the *Ski Lodge* shape. Type **Tours**

Alert!   Did you add a shape below the Ski Lodge shape?

If you clicked the Add Shape button instead of the arrow, the new shape displays below the phone number shape. Click Undo to delete the shape, and then repeat Step 1, being sure to click the Add Shape arrow.

2 On the **Design tab**, in the **Create Graphic group**, click the **Add Shape** button.

When an upper level shape is selected and the Add Shape button is clicked, a lower level shape is added.

3 Type **Terry Anderson** and then click the **Add Shape** button. Type **555-0987** and then click the **Add Shape** button.

An additional shape is added below the phone number. You can promote the shape so that it is at the same level as the Day Spa, Ski lodge, and Tours shapes.

4 On the **Design tab**, in the **Create Graphic group**, click the **Promote** button to create a fourth, upper level shape. Type **Reservations** and notice that the text in all of the upper level shapes is resized. Add a shape, type **Anthony Johnson** and then add one more shape, and then type **555-0547**

5 On the **Design tab**, in the **Create Graphic group**, click the **Add Shape** button to create an extra shape below Anthony Johnson's phone number.

6 Press Delete to delete the shape, and then click on a blank area of the slide. Compare your slide with Figure 2.35.

Figure 2.35

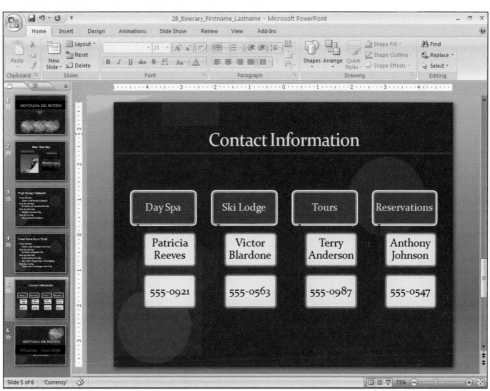

7 Save the presentation.

More Knowledge

Deleting Shapes That Contain Text

To delete a shape that contains text, you must click its border. If you click the shape without clicking the border, you will delete text instead of the shape. When you delete an upper level shape that has subordinate shapes with text, the first subordinate shape is promoted to an upper level shape.

Activity 2.20 Changing the Diagram Type and Size

When you are creating a diagram, remember that it is important to choose the layout and type that provides the best visual representation of your information. In this Activity, you will change the diagram type to one that includes placeholders for pictures of each contact person.

1 Click anywhere in the diagram. Click the **Design tab**. In the **Layouts group**, click the **More** button ⬇, and then click **More Layouts** to display the **Choose a SmartArt Graphic** dialog box.

2 On the left side of the dialog box, click **List**, and then click **Horizontal Picture List**, as shown in Figure 2.36. Click **OK**.

The diagram is converted and contains shapes at the top of each group to insert pictures.

Figure 2.36

Horizontal Picture List

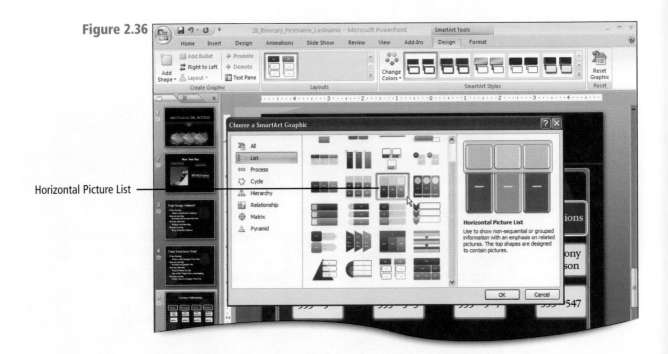

3 In the shape above the *Day Spa* information, click the **Insert Picture From File** button 🖼. Navigate to the location where your student files are stored, and then double-click **p2B_Spa_Director** to insert the picture of Patricia Reeves. Repeat this process in each of the three remaining shapes by inserting the files **p2B_Ski_Lodge_ Director**, **p2B_Tour_Director**, and **p2B_Reservations_Director**.

Alert! | **Did you move a shape when inserting a picture?**
If you move the mouse when you click the Insert Picture from File button in one of the diagram shapes, the shape may move. If this happens, click the Undo button to reposition the shape. Then, click the Picture button, making sure that you hold the mouse steady.

4 Notice that the shapes of that contain the pictures are wider than they are long, and thus distort the pictures. You can adjust the size of all of the pictures at one time by sizing the SmartArt graphic.

5 The border surrounding a diagram contains sizing handles in the shape of three small circles in the corners and at the center of each side. You can use these sizing handles to size the diagram. Point to the center-right sizing handle to display the ↔ pointer, as shown in Figure 2.37.

Figure 2.37

Pointer positioned over sizing handle

6 Hold down the mouse button and drag to the left, noticing that as you do so the ⊞ pointer displays, as does a semitransparent rectangle that indicates the size of the SmartArt graphic. Continue to drag to the left until the pointer and semitransparent rectangle display between the Tours and Reservations shapes, as shown in Figure 2.38. Release the mouse button to size the diagram.

Figure 2.38

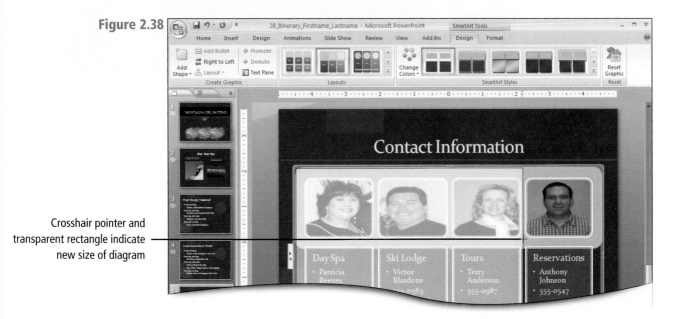

Crosshair pointer and transparent rectangle indicate new size of diagram

7 Point to the border surrounding the diagram to display the ⊕ pointer, and then drag to the right to center the diagram.

8 Compare your slide with Figure 2.39, and then **Save** 🖫 your presentation.

<table>
<tr><td>**Alert!**</td><td>**Did only a part of the diagram move?**

Individual parts of a SmartArt diagram, such as text and picture shapes, can be moved. Be sure that when you move the diagram that you are pointing to the border that surrounds the SmartArt graphic and not an individual element. If you inadvertently moved a portion of the diagram instead of the entire diagram, click the Undo button, and then repeat step 7.</td></tr>
</table>

Figure 2.39

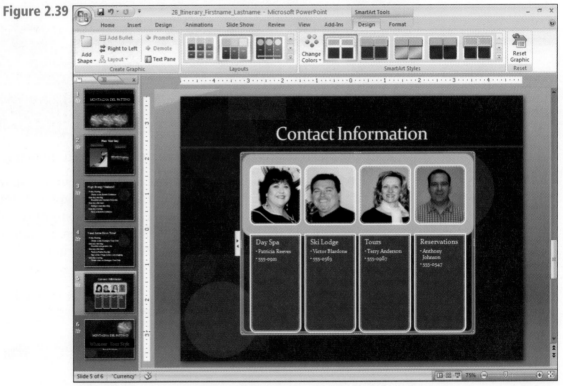

Activity 2.21 Creating a SmartArt Diagram from Bullet Points

You can convert an existing bulleted list into a SmartArt diagram. In this Activity, you will convert the bulleted lists on Slides 3 and 4 to list diagrams.

1 Display **Slide 3**. Right-click anywhere in the bulleted list placeholder to display the shortcut menu. Point to **Convert to SmartArt**, and at the bottom of the gallery, click **More SmartArt Graphics**.

2 In the **Choose a SmartArt Graphic** dialog box, click **List**, and then in the first row, point to each SmartArt graphic so that the ScreenTips display, and then click **Vertical Box List**. Click **OK**.

The entire bulleted list is converted to a diagram. It is not necessary to select all of the text in the bulleted list. By clicking in the list, PowerPoint converts all of the bullet points to the selected diagram.

3 Display **Slide 4**. Right-click anywhere in the bulleted list placeholder to display the shortcut menu. Point to **Convert to SmartArt**, and then at the bottom of the gallery, click **More SmartArt Graphics**. In the **Choose a SmartArt Graphic** dialog box, click **List**, and then use the ScreenTips to locate **Vertical Block List**. Click **Vertical Block List**, and then click **OK**.

4 Save ![save icon] the presentation.

Activity 2.22 Changing the Color and Style of a Diagram

SmartArt Styles are combinations of formatting effects that you can apply to diagrams. If you change the layout of a diagram, the SmartArt Style is applied to the new layout, as are any color changes that you have made.

1 Display **Slide 5** and click on the diagram. Click the **Design tab**. In the **SmartArt Styles group**, click the **Change Colors** button to display the color gallery.

The colors that display are coordinated with the presentation theme.

2 Under **Accent 1**, click the last style—**Transparent Gradient Range - Accent 1**—to change the color scheme of the diagram.

3 On the **Design tab**, in the **SmartArt Styles group**, click the **More** button ![More button] to display the **SmartArt Styles gallery**. Point to several of the styles to Live Preview their effects on the diagram. Then, under **3-D**, in the first row, click the first style—**Polished**. Click in a blank area of the slide, and then compare your slide with Figure 2.40.

4 Display **Slide 3** and click on the diagram. Click the **Design tab**.

In the **SmartArt Styles group**, click the **More** button ![More button] to display the **SmartArt Styles gallery**. Under **3-D**, in the first row, click the second style—**Inset**.

5 Display **Slide 4**. Using the same technique that you used in Step 4, under **Best Match for Document** apply the last style—**Intense Effect**.

Figure 2.40

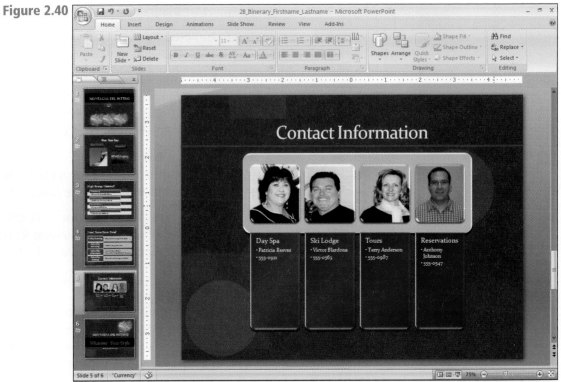

6 Click the **Slide Show tab**. In the **Start Slide Show group**, click **From Beginning**, and then view your presentation, clicking the mouse button to advance through the slides. When the black slide displays, click the mouse button one more time to display the presentation in Normal view.

7 Create a **Header and Footer** for the **Notes and Handouts**. Include only the **Date and time updated automatically**, the **Page number**, and a **Footer** with the file name **2B_Intinerary_Firstname_Lastname**

8 Check your *Chapter Assignment Sheet* or *Course Syllabus* or consult your instructor to determine if you are to submit your assignments on paper or electronically. To submit electronically, go to Step 10, and then follow the instructions provided by your instructor.

9 **Print Preview** your presentation, and then print **Handouts, (6 slides per page)**.

10 **Save** the changes to your presentation, and then **Close** the presentation.

End **You have completed Project 2B**

There's More You Can Do!

From My Computer, navigate to the student files that accompany this textbook. In the folder **02_theres_more_you_can_do_pg1_36**, locate and open the folder for this chapter. Open and print the instructions for this project, which are provided to you in Adobe PDF format.

Try IT! 1—Prepare a Presentation for Remote Delivery

In this Try IT! exercise, you will prepare a presentation for remote delivery by compressing images and packaging the presentation for CD.

Content-Based Assessments

Summary

In this chapter, you formatted a presentation by changing the bullet style and by applying WordArt styles to text. You copied formatting by using Format Painter and you also copied text and objects by using drag-and-drop and the Office Clipboard. You enhanced your presentations by inserting, sizing, and formatting shapes, pictures, and SmartArt diagrams. You gave your presentation a finished look by applying transitions to your slides, resulting in a professional-looking presentation.

Key Terms

Content-Based Assessments

Matching

Match each term in the second column with its correct definition in the first column. Write the letter of the term on the blank line in front of the correct definition.

_____ **1.** A feature that applies combinations of decorative formatting to text, including shadows, reflections, and 3-D effects, and that changes the line and fill color of text.

_____ **2.** The inside color of text or an object.

_____ **3.** A feature that copies formatting from one selection of text to another, ensuring formatting consistency in your presentation.

_____ **4.** A combination of formatting effects that includes 3-D, glow, and bevel effects and shadows that can be applied to shapes.

_____ **5.** An object that is used to position text anywhere on the slide.

_____ **6.** The pointer that indicates that you can draw a shape.

_____ **7.** Vertical and horizontal lines that display in the rulers to give you a visual indication of the pointer position so that you can draw a shape.

_____ **8.** A blinking vertical line that indicates where text will be inserted.

_____ **9.** A color combination in which one color fades into another.

_____ **10.** The way a slide appears or disappears during an onscreen slide show.

_____ **11.** The action of placing text or objects that have been copied or moved from one location to another location.

_____ **12.** A temporary storage area maintained by your Microsoft Office program.

_____ **13.** The action of moving a selection by dragging it to a new location.

_____ **14.** A designer-quality visual representation of your information that you can create by choosing from among many different layouts to effectively communicate your message or ideas.

_____ **15.** Combinations of formatting effects that are applied to diagrams.

A Crosshair pointer

B Drag-and-drop

C Fill color

D Format Painter

E Gradient fill

F Guides

G Insertion point

H Office Clipboard

I Paste

J Shape Styles

K SmartArt graphic

L SmartArt Styles

M Text box

N Transition

O WordArt

Content-Based Assessments

Fill in the Blank

Write the correct word in the space provided.

1. When you click the dashed border of a placeholder, it displays as a _____ line.

2. To repeat the last command or text that you entered, press the _____ function key.

3. To copy formatting to multiple selections, _____-_____ Format Painter.

4. To horizontally or vertically position selected objects on a slide relative to each other, use the _____ tools.

5. When you apply slide transitions, you can control the _____ and the method with which the slides advance during the presentation.

6. The Clipboard can store up to _____ selections that you have cut or copied.

7. You can reverse an Undo by using the _____ command.

8. To show nonsequential information, use a _____ diagram.

9. To show steps in a process or timeline, use a _____ diagram.

10. To show a continual process, use a _____ diagram.

11. To show a decision tree or create an organization chart, use a _____ diagram.

12. To illustrate connections, use a _____ diagram.

13. To show how parts relate to a whole, use a _____ diagram.

14. To show proportional relationships with the largest component on the top or bottom, use a _____ diagram.

15. When you are creating a diagram, remember that it is important to choose the layout and type that provides the best _____ representation of your information.

Content-Based Assessments

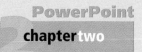
Skills Review

Project 2C—Snowboarding

In this project, you will apply the skills you practiced from the Objectives in Project 2A.

Objectives: 1. *Format Slide Elements;* **2.** *Insert and Format Pictures and Shapes;* **3.** *Apply Slide Transitions.*

In the following Skills Review, you will edit a presentation created by Dane Richardson, the Director of Ski and Snowboarding Instruction, that describes the snowboarding events and services available at Montagna del Pattino. Your completed presentation will look similar to the one shown in Figure 2.41.

For Project 2C, you will need the following files:

p2C_Board
p2C_Hillside
p2C_Silhouette
p2C_Snowboarding

You will save your presentation as
2C_Snowboarding_Firstname_Lastname

Figure 2.41

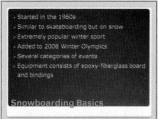

(Project 2C–Snowboarding continues on the next page)

Content-Based Assessments

(Project 2C–Snowboarding continued)

1. **Start** PowerPoint, and then from your student data files, open **p2C_Snowboarding**. Click the **Office** button, and then click **Save As**. Navigate to your *PowerPoint Chapter 2* folder and using your own first and last name, save the file as **2C_Snowboarding_Firstname_Lastname**

2. Display **Slide 1** and drag to select the title text. On the **Format tab**, in the **WordArt Styles group**, click the **More** button to display the **WordArt gallery**. Under **Applies to All Text in the Shape**, in the last row, click the last style—**Fill – Accent 1, Metal Bevel, Reflection**.

3. Click the **Insert tab**, and then in the **Illustrations group**, click **Picture**. Navigate to the location where your student files are stored, and then double-click **p2C_Silhouette** to insert the picture in the middle of the slide.

4. With the picture selected, click the **Format tab**. In the **Size group**, click in the **Height** box, and then type **4** Click on the picture to change its size, and then point to the picture to display the ⊕ pointer. Drag the picture up and to the left so that its upper left corner aligns with the upper left corner of the white rounded rectangle.

5. With the picture still selected, in the **Picture Styles group**, click **Picture Effects**. Point to **Soft Edges**, and then click **50 Point** to blur the edges of the image.

6. Display **Slide 2**, and then click in the bulleted list placeholder. Point to the dashed border so that the ⊕ pointer displays, and then click so that the border displays as a solid line, indicating that all of the text in the placeholder is selected. On the **Home tab**, in the **Paragraph group**, click the

Bullets button arrow to display the **Bullets gallery**, and then click **Arrow Bullets**.

7. Display **Slide 3**, and then select the bulleted list placeholder on the right side of the slide so that its solid border displays. Press F4 to repeat the bullet formatting that you applied in the previous step. If you have entered another action before pressing F4 and the bullet formatting does not repeat, click the Bullets button arrow, and then apply the Arrow Bullets style.

8. On **Slide 3**, in the placeholder on the left of the slide click the first button in the second row of buttons—**Insert Picture from File**. From your student files, double-click **p2C_Hillside**. In the **Picture Styles group**, click the **Picture Shape** button. Under **Basic Shapes**, in the third row, click the fourth shape —**Folded Corner**. In the **Picture Styles group**, click the **Picture Effects** button, point to **Glow**, and then under **Glow Variations**, in the third row, click the first effect—**Accent color 1, 11 pt glow**.

9. Click in the bulleted list placeholder on the right, and then click its border so that it displays as a solid line, indicating that all of the text is selected. On the **Home tab**, in the **Font group**, apply **Italic**, and then, in the **Paragraph group**, click the **Line Spacing** button. Click **2.0**. **Save** your presentation.

10. Display **Slide 4** and verify that the rulers display. If the rulers do not display, on the View tab, in the Show/Hide group, select the Ruler check box. Click the **Insert tab**, and then in the **Illustrations group**, click the **Shapes** button to display the **Shapes gallery**.

(Project 2C–Snowboarding continues on the next page)

Content-Based Assessments

(Project 2C–Snowboarding continued)

11. Under **Block Arrows**, in the first row, click the fourth arrow—**Down Arrow**. Position the crosshair pointer at approximately **2.5 inches to the left of zero** on the **horizontal ruler** and at **2 inches above zero** on the **vertical ruler**.

12. Drag approximately 0.5 inch to the right and 1 inch down to create the arrow. Check the size of the shape by looking at the **Format tab** in the **Size group**. If necessary, adjust the size of the arrow to a Height of **1** and a Width of **0.5**.

13. With the arrow selected, on the **Format tab**, in the **Shape Styles group**, click the **More** button. In the last row, click the second style—**Intense Effect – Accent 1**.

14. With the arrow still selected, hold down [Ctrl], and then press [D] to duplicate the arrow. Point to the arrow, and then drag to the right so that the arrow is positioned above the text on the right of the slide at approximately **2 inches to the right of zero** on the **horizontal ruler**.

15. With the arrow on the right selected, press [⇧ Shift], and then click the arrow on the left so that both arrows are selected. On the **Format tab**, in the **Arrange group**, click the **Align** button. Click **Align Selected Objects** to align the objects that you select relative to each other. On the **Format tab**, in the **Arrange group**, click the **Align** button, and then click **Align Top**.

16. Click the **Insert tab**, and then in the **Text group**, click **Text Box**. Position the pointer at approximately **3 inches to the left of zero** on the **horizontal ruler** and at **3 inches above zero** on the **vertical ruler**. Click to create a text box, and then type **Gear** Select the text that you typed, and then on the **Home tab**, in the **Font group**,

click the **Font Color arrow** and then click **White, Background 1**. Change the **Font Size** to **24**, and then click on a blank area of the slide.

17. Click the **Insert tab**, and then in the **Text group**, click **Text Box**. Position the pointer at approximately **1 inch to the right of zero** on the **horizontal ruler** and at **3 inches above zero** on the **vertical ruler**. Click to create a text box, and then type **Accessories** Select the text that you typed, and then on the **Home tab**, in the **Font group**, click the **Font Color button arrow** and then click **White, Background 1**. Change the **Font Size** to **24**.

18. Use the [⇧ Shift] key to select the two text boxes—*Gear* and *Accessories*. Click the **Format tab**, and then in the **Arrange group**, click the **Align** button. Click **Align Top** to align the top edges of the two text boxes, and then click anywhere on the slide so that none of the objects are selected. **Save** your presentation.

19. Click the bulleted list placeholder on the left side of the slide. Press [⇧ Shift], and then click the arrow on the left, and then press [⇧ Shift] and click the *Gear* text box so that all three objects are selected. On the **Format tab**, in the **Arrange group**, click the **Align** button. Click **Align Selected Objects**. Click the **Align** button again, and then click **Align Center**.

20. Using the same process that you used in Step 19, align center the placeholder, arrow, and text box on the right side of the slide. **Save** your presentation.

21. Display **Slide 5**. In the placeholder on the left side of the slide, click the **Insert Picture from File** button, and then navigate to your student files. Double-click

(Project 2C–Snowboarding continues on the next page)

Content-Based Assessments

(Project 2C–Snowboarding continued)

p2C_Board. On the **Format tab**, in the **Picture Styles group**, click the **Picture Effects** button, and then point to **Glow**. In the last row, click the first glow effect—**Accent color 1, 18 pt glow**.

22. On **Slide 5**, select the slide title. On the **Home tab**, in the **Clipboard group**, click the **Format Painter** button. Display **Slide 3**, and then drag the ⬓I pointer over the title to apply the font, font size, and shadow effects from the title on **Slide 5** to the title on **Slide 3**.

23. Click the **Animations tab**. In the **Transition to This Slide group**, click the **More** button, and then under **Wipes**, in the first row, click the third transition—**Wipe Right**. In the **Transition to This Slide group**, click the **Apply To All** button. Click the **Slide Show tab**. In the **Start Slide Show group**, click **From Beginning** and then view your presentation, clicking the mouse button to advance from slide to slide.

24. Create a **Header and Footer** for the **Notes and Handouts**. Include only the **Date and time updated automatically**, the **Page number**, and a **Footer** with the file name 2C_Snowboarding_Firstname_Lastname

25. Check your *Chapter Assignment Sheet* or *Course Syllabus* or consult your instructor to determine if you are to submit your assignments on paper or electronically. To submit electronically, go to Step 27, and then follow the instructions provided by your instructor.

26. From the **Office** menu, point to the **Print arrow**, and then click **Print Preview** to make a final check of your presentation. In the **Page Setup group**, click the **Print What arrow**, and then click **Handouts, (6 slides per page)**. Click the **Print** button, and then click **OK** to print the handouts.

27. **Save** the changes to your presentation, and then close the file.

End   **You have completed Project 2C**

Content-Based Assessments

Project 2D — Lessons

In this project, you will apply the skills you practiced from the Objectives in Project 2B.

Objectives: 4. *Reorganize Presentation Text and Clear Formats;* **5.** *Create and Format a SmartArt Graphic.*

In the following Skills Review, you will edit a presentation created by Dane Richardson, the Director of Ski and Snowboarding Instruction, that describes the ski and snowboarding lessons for children at Montagna del Pattino. Your completed presentation will look similar to the one shown in Figure 2.42.

For Project 2D, you will need the following files:

p2D_Cara
p2D_Dane
p2D_Lessons
p2D_Marty

You will save your presentation as
2D_Lessons_Firstname_Lastname

Figure 2.42

(Project 2D–Lessons continues on the next page)

(Project 2D–Lessons continued)

1. **Start** PowerPoint, and then from your student files, open **p2D_Lessons**. Click the **Office** button, and then click **Save As**. Navigate to your **PowerPoint Chapter 2** folder, and then using your own first and last name, save the file as **2D_Lessons_Firstname_Lastname**

2. Display **Slide 3**. On the **Home tab**, in the **Clipboard group**, click the **Dialog Box Launcher** to display the Clipboard task pane. In the **Clipboard** task pane, click the **Clear All** button. Drag to select the slide title—**Private Lessons**. In the **Clipboard group**, click the **Cut** button to move the title to the Office Clipboard.

3. Display **Slide 4**. Drag to select the title and on the **Home tab**, in the **Clipboard group**, click the **Cut** button to move the title to the Office Clipboard.

4. With **Slide 4** still displayed and the insertion point blinking in the title placeholder, in the **Clipboard** task pane, click **Private Lessons** to paste the item to the title placeholder.

5. Display **Slide 3**, and then click in the title placeholder. In the **Clipboard** task pane, click **Group Lesson for Beginners** to paste the item to the title placeholder. In the **Clipboard** task pane, click **Clear All**, and then **Close** the Clipboard task pane.

6. On **Slide 3**, right-click in the bulleted list placeholder to display the shortcut menu, and then point to **Convert to SmartArt**. In the first row, click the second graphic—**Vertical Block List**.

7. Click in the blank, fourth shape, and then press Delete to delete the extra shape. **Save** your presentation.

8. Click the **Design tab**. In the **SmartArt Styles group**, click the **Change Colors** button. Under **Primary Theme Colors**,

click the third color set—**Dark 2 Fill**. In the **SmartArt Styles group**, click the **More** button. Under **3-D**, in the first row, click the third style—**Cartoon**.

9. Display **Slide 4**. Right-click in the bulleted list placeholder to display the shortcut menu. Point to **Convert to SmartArt**, and then click **More SmartArt Graphics**. Click **List**, and then in the fifth row, click **Trapezoid List**. Click **OK** to create a diagram with four shapes. Click in the blank, fourth shape, and then press Delete to delete the extra shape. In the **SmartArt tools Design tab**, click the **Change Colors** button. and then under **Primary Theme Colors**, click the third color—**Dark 2 Fill**.

10. Click the **Home tab**. In the **Slides group**, click the **New Slide** button to insert a slide with the **Title and Content** layout. Click in the title placeholder, and then type **Meet the Team Leaders**

11. In the content placeholder, click the **Insert SmartArt Graphic** button. In the fourth row, click the second graphic—**Vertical Picture Accent List**, and then click **OK**. Click in the first **Text** shape, type **Cara Nielsen** and then press Enter. Type **Specializes in 3–5 year olds**

12. In the second shape type **Dane Richardson** and then press Enter. Type **Specializes in 6-9 year olds**

13. In the third shape type **Marty Blair** and then press Enter. Type **Specializes in 10-15 year olds** and then **Save** your presentation.

14. Click the **Design tab**. In the **SmartArt Styles group**, click the **Change Colors** button. Scroll the color list, and then under **Accent 4**, click the second color set—**Colored Fill - Accent 4**. In the **SmartArt Styles group**, click the **More**

(Project 2D–Lessons continues on the next page)

Content-Based Assessments

(Project 2D–Lessons continued)

button. Under **Best Match for Document**, click the last style—**Intense Effect**.

15. To the left of Cara Nielsen's information, in the circle shape, click the **Insert Picture From File** button. Navigate to your student files, and then double-click **p2D_Cara** to insert the picture. Repeat this process for the remaining two circles, inserting the files **p2D_Dane**, and **p2D_Marty**.

16. Click the **Slide Show tab**. In the **Start Slide Show group**, click **From Beginning**, and then view your presentation, clicking the mouse button to advance from slide to slide. Create a **Header and Footer** for the **Notes and Handouts**. Include only the **Date and time updated automatically**, the **Page number**, and a **Footer** with the file name **2D_Lessons_Firstname_Lastname**

17. Check your *Chapter Assignment Sheet* or *Course Syllabus* or consult your instructor to determine if you are to submit your assignments on paper or electronically. To submit electronically, go to Step 19, and then follow the instructions provided by your instructor.

18. From the **Office** menu, point to the **Print arrow**, and then click **Print Preview** to make a final check of your presentation. In the **Page Setup group**, click the **Print What arrow**, and then click **Handouts, (6 slides per page)**. Click the **Print** button, and then click **OK** to print the handouts. **Close** Print Preview.

19. **Save** changes to your presentation, and then from the **Office** menu, click **Exit PowerPoint**.

End **You have completed Project 2D**

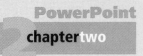

Mastering PowerPoint

Project 2E — Condos

In this project, you will apply the skills you practiced from the Objectives in Project 2A.

Objectives: 1. *Format Slide Elements;* **2.** *Insert and Format Pictures and Shapes;* **3.** *Apply Slide Transitions.*

In the following Mastering PowerPoint project, you will create a presentation that Kirsten McCarty, Director of Marketing will use to showcase the new timeshare condos at Montagna del Pattino. Your completed presentation will look similar to Figure 2.43.

> **For Project 2E, you will need the following files:**
>
> New blank PowerPoint presentation
> p2E_Condominiums
> p2E_Timeshare

**You will save your presentation as
2E_Condos_Firstname_Lastname**

Figure 2.43

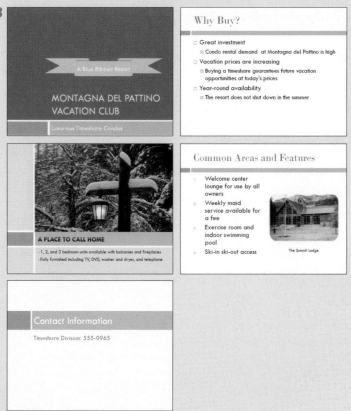

(Project 2E–Condos continues on the next page)

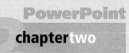
(Project 2E–Condos continued)

1. **Start** PowerPoint, and then begin a new blank presentation. On the **Design tab**, display the **Themes gallery**, and then under **Built-In**, apply the **Median** theme. The title of the presentation is **Montagna del Pattino Vacation Club** and the subtitle is **Luxurious Timeshare Condos Save** the presentation as **2E_Condos_Firstname_Lastname**

2. On the **Insert tab**, display the **Shapes gallery**. Under **Stars and Banners**, in the second row, click the second shape—**Down Ribbon**. Position the crosshair pointer at **1 inch above zero on the vertical ruler** and aligned with the **M** in *Montagna*. Drag down approximately 1 inch and to the right so that the ribbon shape extends to the **o** in *Pattino*. In the **Format tab**, verify the **Size** of the shape and if necessary, change the **Height** to **1** and the **Width** to **6**

3. In the shape, type **A Blue Ribbon Resort** and then apply a **Shadow Shape Effect**, using **Inner** style—**Inside Center**. Select the text, and then change the **Font Size** to **24**.

4. Add a new slide to the presentation with the **Title and Content** layout. The slide title is **Why Buy?** Type the following bullet points, increasing and decreasing the list levels as indicated. Correct any spelling errors that you make while typing.

   Great investment

       More affordable than buying a vacation home

   Vacation prices are increasing

       Buying a timeshare guarantees future vacation opportunities at today's prices

   Year-round availability

       The resort does not shut down during summer

(Project 2E–Condos continues on the next page)

5. Add a **New Slide** to the presentation with the **Picture with Caption** layout. The slide title is **A Place to Call Home** Select the title text. On the **Format tab**, display the **WordArt Styles gallery**, and then apply the **Fill – White**, **Warm Matte Bevel** style—the first style under **Applies to All Text in the Shape**. In the text placeholder, type the following two bullet points, increase the **Font Size** to **20**, and then apply the **Star Bullets** bullet style.

   1-, 2-, and 3-bedroom units available with balconies and fireplaces

   Fully furnished including TV, DVD, washer and dryer, and telephone

6. From your student files, insert the picture **p2E_Condominiums** in the picture placeholder.

7. Add a **New Slide** to the presentation with the **Two Content** layout. The slide title is **Common Areas and Features** Type the following bullet points in the placeholder on the left, and then correct any spelling errors that you make while typing.

   Welcome center lounge for use by all owners

   Weekly cleaning service available for a fee

   Exercise room and indoor swimming pool

   Ski-in and ski-out access

8. Apply **Numbering** to the list. On the right side of the slide, from your student files, insert the picture **p2E_Timeshare**. On the **Format tab**, display the **Picture Shape** gallery, and then under **Rectangles**, apply the second shape—**Rounded Rectangle**. Apply a **5 Point**, **Soft Edges Picture Effect**.

9. Insert a **Text Box** approximately 0.5 inch below the picture, and then type **The Summit Lodge** Use ⇧Shift to select the picture and the text box. Using the **Drawing Tools Format tab** (Note: Be sure to use

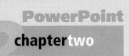

(Project 2E–Condos continued)

the *Drawing Tools*, not the Picture Tools), **Align Center** the picture and the text box.

10. Add a **New Slide** to the presentation with the **Section Header** layout. The title of the slide is **Contact Information** and the subtitle is **Timeshare Division: 555-0965**

11. Display **Slide 2** and change the title **Font** to **Bodoni MT**. Use **Format Painter** to copy the formatting to the slide title on **Slide 4**. Apply the **Wipe Down Transition**, and then change the **Transition Speed** to **Medium** for all of the slides in the presentation. View the slide show from the beginning.

12. Create a **Header and Footer** for the **Notes and Handouts**. Include only the **Date and time updated automatically**, the **Page**

number, and a **Footer** with the file name **2E_Condos_Firstname_Lastname** using your own first and last name.

13. Check your *Chapter Assignment Sheet* or *Course Syllabus* or consult your instructor to determine if you are to submit your assignments on paper or electronically. To submit electronically, go to Step 15, and then follow the instructions provided by your instructor.

14. **Print Preview** your presentation, and then print **Handouts, (6 slides per page)**.

15. **Save** changes to your presentation, and then **Close** the presentation.

End **You have completed Project 2E** —————————————————

Content-Based Assessments

Project 2F—Job Listings

In this project, you will apply the skills you practiced from the Objectives in Project 2B.

Objectives: 4. *Reorganize Presentation Text and Clear Formats;* **5.** *Create and Format a SmartArt Graphic.*

In the following Mastering PowerPoint Assessment, you will create a presentation that Leah Huynh, Director of Human Resources will use to describe some of the seasonal employment opportunities available at Montagna del Pattino. Your completed presentation will look similar to Figure 2.44.

For Project 2F, you will need the following files:

New blank PowerPoint presentation
p2F_Employment
p2F_Snowflake_Template

You will save your presentation as
2F_Job_Listings_Firstname_Lastname

Figure 2.44

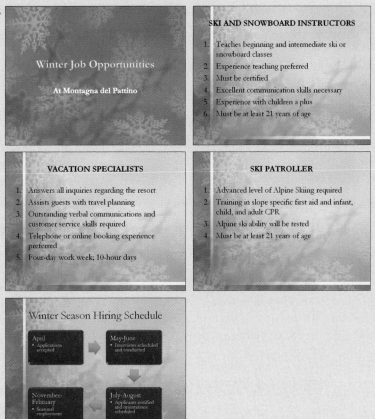

(Project 2F–Job Listings continues on the next page)

(Project 2F–Job Listings continued)

1. **Start** PowerPoint, and then open **p2F_Snowflake_Template** from your student files. **Save** the file as **2F_Job_Listings_Firstname_Lastname**

2. The title for the first slide is **Winter Job Opportunities** The subtitle is **At Montagna del Pattino**

3. Several slides for this presentation are contained in a file that lists summer and winter seasonal employment opportunities. From the file **p2F_Employment**, reuse **Slides 2—Ski and Snowboard Instructors**; **3—Vacation Specialists**; and **4—Ski Patroller**. (Hint: In the New Slide gallery, click Reuse Slides).

4. Display **Slide 2**, and then select and **Copy** the last bullet point—*Must be at least 21 years of age.* **Paste** the selection to **Slide 4** so that it is the fifth bullet point. On **Slide 4**, **Cut** the second to last bullet point—*Four-day work week; 10-hour days*, and then paste it to **Slide 3** so that it is the fifth bullet point.

5. Display **Slide 2**, and then select the bullet list placeholder so that its border displays as a solid line. Apply **Numbering** to the list and then use F4 to repeat the numbering for the bulleted lists on **Slides 3 and 4**.

6. Display **Slide 4**, and then add a new slide with the **Title and Content** layout. The title of the new slide is **Winter Season Hiring Schedule**

7. In the content placeholder, insert the second **Process** type **SmartArt Graphic—Accent Process**. In the first blue box, type **April** and then in its attached white

box, type **Applications accepted** In the second blue box, type **May-June** and then in its attached white box, type **Interviews scheduled and conducted** In the third blue box, type **July-August** and then in its attached white box, type **Applicants notified and orientations scheduled**

8. Click in the third blue box, and then in the **SmartArt Tools** click the **Design tab**. Add a shape at the same level, and then in the blue box, type **November-February** In its attached white box, type **Seasonal employment** Notice that this diagram does not use the slide space efficiently and the font size of the text is small and difficult to read. Change the **Layout** of the **SmartArt** to a **Process** layout—**Basic Bending Process** and its color to the second **Accent 2** scheme—**Colored Fill - Accent 2**. Apply **3-D Style Cartoon**.

9. Create a **Header and Footer** for the **Notes and Handouts**. Include only the **Date and time updated automatically**, the **Page number**, and a **Footer** with the file name **2F_Job_Listings_Firstname_Lastname** using your own first and last name.

10. Check your *Chapter Assignment Sheet* or *Course Syllabus* or consult your instructor to determine if you are to submit your assignments on paper or electronically. To submit electronically, go to Step 12, and then follow the instructions provided by your instructor.

11. **Print Preview** your presentation, and then print **Handouts, (6 slides per page)**.

12. **Save** changes to your presentation, and then **Close** the presentation.

End **You have completed Project 2F**

Content-Based Assessments

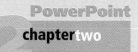
Mastering PowerPoint

Project 2G—Packages

In this project, you will apply the skills you practiced from the Objectives in Projects 2A and 2B.

Objectives: 1. *Format Slide Elements;* **2.** *Insert and Format Pictures and Shapes;* **3.** *Apply Slide Transitions;* **5.** *Create and Format a SmartArt Graphic.*

In the following Mastering PowerPoint project, you will edit a presentation that Kirsten McCarty, Director of Marketing, will be showing at a travel fair to highlight the vacation packages offered at Montagna del Pattino. Your completed presentation will look similar to Figure 2.45.

For Project 2G, you will need the following files:

p2G_Fireworks
p2G_Mountain
p2G_Packages
p2G_Ski_Lift
p2G_Sunset

**You will save your presentation as
2G_Packages_Firstname_Lastname**

Figure 2.45

(Project 2G–Packages continues on the next page)

Mastering PowerPoint

(Project 2G–Packages continued)

1. **Start** PowerPoint, and then from your student files, open **p2G_Packages**. **Save** your presentation as **2G_Packages_Firstname_Lastname**

2. Display **Slide 2**, and then change the bulleted list to **Numbering**. Insert a **Basic Shape Bevel** at **1 inch to the right of zero on the horizontal ruler** and at **0.5 inch below zero on the vertical ruler**. Size the bevel so that its **Height** is **1.3** inches and its **Width** is **3** inches. In the bevel, type **We'll customize your package; just call for reservations! Center** the text.

3. Select the shape so that its outer border is solid, and then duplicate the shape by using [Ctrl] + [D]. Drag the new shape down so that it almost touches the bottom of the slide. Replace the text with **Book two packages in one year; get a free weekend stay!**

4. Select both shapes, and then **Arrange** the shapes, using **Align Left** so that the left edge of the two shapes align. Apply a **Shape Style** found in the third row, **Light 1 Outline, Colored Fill – Accent 1** to both shapes.

5. Display **Slide 3**. In the placeholder on the left side of the slide, use the **Insert Picture from File** button in the placeholder to insert from your student files **p2G_Ski_Lift**. Change the **Picture Shape** under **Basic Shapes** to **Parallelogram**, and then apply the first **Reflection** effect—**Tight Reflection, touching.**

6. Display **Slide 4**, and then add a **New Slide** with the **Comparison** layout. Type and **Center** the title **Fifth Night Free Package** In the caption box on the left, type **Stay an extra day** and then in the caption box on the right, type **Enjoy the evening view**

(Project 2G–Packages continues on the next page)

Center both captions, and then in the content placeholder on the left, type the following bullet points:

Accommodations at the Summit Lodge

Book four nights, stay for free on the fifth

Complimentary breakfast every morning

7. Select the placeholder so that its outer edge displays as a solid line, and then change the **Line Spacing** to **1.5** and the **Font Size** to **20**. With the placeholder border displayed as a solid line, the change is applied to all of the text.

8. In the placeholder on the right side of the slide, use the **Insert Picture from File** button in the placeholder to insert from your student files **p2G_Sunset**. Apply the second **Glow Picture Effect** in the second row—**Accent color 2, 8 pt. glow**. **Save** the presentation.

9. Add a **New Slide** to the presentation with the **Content with Caption** layout. The slide title is **Fourth of July Celebration Package Center** the title and increase the **Font Size** to **24**. Remove the **Bold** formatting. In the text placeholder on the left of the slide, type **Stay Fourth of July weekend at the Summit Lodge and receive preferred seating at the evening fireworks show and complimentary tickets for four to our barbecue**

10. Change the **Font Size** of the text that you typed to **16**, and then change the **Line Spacing** to **2.5**. **Center** the text and apply **Italic**. In the placeholder on the right side of the slide, use the **Insert Picture from File** button to insert **p2G_Fireworks** from your student files.

11. Add a **New Slide** with the **Title and Content** layout. The slide title is **Summer Festivals** In the content placeholder, use the **SmartArt Graphic** button to insert a **List** graphic found in the fifth row—**Table List**. Apply the **3-D Powder SmartArt Style** to

Content-Based Assessments

(Project 2G–Packages continued)

the graphic. In the long rectangular box at the top of the SmartArt graphic, type **Stay For Any Weekend Festival** and then select the text and display the **WordArt Styles** gallery. In the first row of WordArt styles, apply **Fill – White, Outline – Accent 1** to the selection. In the three remaining boxes, type the following points, one in each box from left to right.

Free admission to festival

Complimentary lunch

Free parking or free trolley ride to event

12. Display **Slide 8**. Click the **Insert Picture from File** button in the placeholder to insert from your student files **p2G_Mountain**. Apply the second **Reflection** effect in the first row—**Half Reflection, touching**.

13. Display **Slide 2**, and then select the title. Change the **Font** to **Tahoma**. Use the **Format Painter** to apply the formatting to the titles on **Slides 3**, **4**, and **7**. (Hint: Double-click Format Painter so that you can apply the formatting multiple times).

14. In the **Transitions** gallery, under **Wipes**, apply the **Uncover Left-Up** transition, and then change the **Transition Speed** to **Medium** for all of the slides. View the **Slide Show** from the beginning.

15. Create a **Header and Footer** for the **Notes and Handouts**. Include only the **Date and time updated automatically**, the **Page number**, and a **Footer** with the file name **2G_Packages_Firstname_Lastname** using your own first and last name.

16. Check your *Chapter Assignment Sheet* or *Course Syllabus* or consult your instructor to determine if you are to submit your assignments on paper or electronically. To submit electronically, go to Step 18, and then follow the instructions provided by your instructor.

17. **Print Preview** your presentation and then print **Handouts, (4 slides per page)**.

18. **Save** your presentation, and then **Close** the file.

End **You have completed Project 2G**

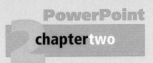

PowerPoint

chapter **two** ## Mastering PowerPoint

Project 2H—Family

In this project, you will apply the skills you practiced from the Objectives in Projects 2A and 2B.

Objectives: 2. *Insert and Format Pictures and Shapes;* **3.** *Apply Slide Transitions;* **4.** *Reorganize Presentation Text and Clear Formats;* **5.** *Create and Format a SmartArt Graphic.*

In the following Mastering PowerPoint project, you will create a presentation based on the activities that the Gillis family enjoyed while spending a day at Montagna del Pattino. Your completed presentation will look similar to Figure 2.46.

For Project 2H, you will need the following files:

New blank PowerPoint presentation
p2H_Baby
p2H_Group
p2H_Memories
p2H_Snowflake
p2H_Winner

You will save your presentation as 2H_Family_Firstname_Lastname

Figure 2.46

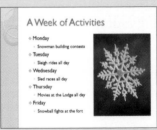

(Project 2H–Family continues on the next page)

Content-Based Assessments

Mastering PowerPoint

(Project 2H–Family continued)

1. **Start** PowerPoint, and then begin a new blank presentation. On the **Design tab**, display the **Themes** gallery, and then under **Built-In**, apply the **Solstice** theme. Change the **Theme Colors** to the fifth theme under **Built-In—Civic**. **Save** the file as **2H_Family_Firstname_Lastname**

2. The title of this presentation is **Family Friendly Activities** and the subtitle is **At Montagna del Pattino** From your student files, insert the **p2H_Group** picture. Adjust the picture **Height** to **4.5** and the **Width** to **3**. Drag the picture to the lower right corner of the slide. Change the picture shape to **Bevel**, and then apply a **Soft Edges Picture Effect** of **10 Point**.

3. Add a **New Slide** with the **Two Content** layout, and then in the title placeholder, type **A Week of Activities** In the content placeholder on the left, type the following bullet points, increasing and decreasing the list level as necessary:

   Monday

   Snowman building contests

   Tuesday

   Sleigh rides all day

   Wednesday

   Sled races

   Thursday

   Movies at the lodge

   Friday

   Snowball fights at the fort

4. Click the **Insert Picture from File** button in the placeholder on the right to insert from your student files **p2H_Snowflake**.

5. Add a **New Slide** with the **Picture with Caption** layout. In the title placeholder, type **Family Memories** and then apply **WordArt Style Gradient Fill – Black, Outline – White, Outer Shadow**. Increase the **Font Size** to **32** and **Center** the title. In the Picture placeholder, from your student files insert **p2H_Winner**. In the caption box below the picture, type **One of our sled race winners!** In the slide title, select the word *Family*, and then use **Format Painter** to apply the WordArt style to the caption. **Center** the caption and change the **Line Spacing** to **1.0**.

6. On the **Insert tab**, display the **Shapes** gallery. Under **Stars and Banners**, in the first row, click the second shape— **Explosion 2**. Draw a shape that extends from **zero on the horizontal** and **vertical rulers** to **4 1/2 to the right of zero on the horizontal ruler** and **3 below zero on the vertical ruler**. Type **First Place!** in the shape, and then change the **Font Size** to **28**. Display the **Shape Styles gallery**, and then in the fourth row apply **Subtle Effect – Accent 1**. Apply the **Bevel Shape Effect Soft Round**—the second effect in the second row.

7. Add a **New Slide** with the **Two Content** layout, and then in the title placeholder, type **A Great Place to Vacation!** In the content placeholder on the left, insert the **Vertical Process SmartArt** graphic. In the first box, type **Family!** In the second box, type **Snow!** In the last box, type **Fun!** Apply **SmartArt Style 3-D Polished** to the graphic.

8. In the placeholder on the right of the slide, from your student files, insert the picture **p2H_Memories**. Apply **Picture Style Rotated, White**, and then apply the **Glow Picture Effect—Accent color 1, 5 pt glow**.

(Project 2H–Family continues on the next page)

(Project 2H–Family continued)

9. Add a **New Slide** with the **Comparison** layout, and then in the title placeholder at the bottom of the slide, type **What Do Our Guests Say?** Click in the white placeholder at the top left of the slide, and then press ⇧Shift and click the white placeholder at the top right to select both placeholders. **Delete** both placeholders.

10. Click in the placeholder on the left, and then type **I had so much fun at Montagna del Pattino! You should bring your family for a day or a week of winter fun! They helped my parents plan our trip and they made sure that my sister and I had lots of fun in the snow.** Press Enter, and then type **Amy Gillis**

11. In the placeholder on the right, use the **Insert Picture from File** button to insert from your student files **p2H_Baby**. Change the shape of the picture to the **32-Point Star**, and then apply the **Soft Edges 50 Point Picture Effect** so that the baby almost appears to be crawling on the slide. Drag the picture to the right so that the points of the stars and its border box aligns with the right edge of the slide.

12. With the picture selected, press ⇧Shift, and then click the slide title to select both the picture and the title. On the **Drawing Tools Format tab**, in the **Arrange group**, click **Align**, and then click **Align Bottom** to align the bottom edges of the two objects. The baby displays slightly above the word *Say*.

13. Select the text in the bulleted list placeholder, and then on the **Home tab**, click the **Bullets** button to toggle the bullets off. **Center** all of the text in the placeholder.

Point to the placeholder's right-center sizing handle and drag to the right to **4.5 inches to the right of zero on the horizontal ruler** to resize the placeholder. Apply the **Shape Style** found in the fourth row—**Subtle Effect – Accent 3**, and then change the **Line Spacing** of the text to **2.0**.

14. Display **Slide 2**, and then click in the first bullet point—**Monday**. Change the Bullet style to **Star Bullets**. Use F4 or Format Painter to apply the same bullet style to each bullet point that includes a day of the week. In the fourth bullet point, **Copy** the words *all day* to the end of the sixth and eighth bullet points after the words *races*, and *lodge*.

15. Apply the **Box In** transition and change the **Transition Speed** to **Medium**. Click **Apply To All**, and then view the slide show from the beginning.

16. Create a **Header and Footer** for the **Notes and Handouts**. Include only the **Date and time updated automatically**, the **Page number**, and a **Footer** with the file name **2H_Family_Firstname_Lastname**

17. Check your *Chapter Assignment Sheet* or *Course Syllabus* or consult your instructor to determine if you are to submit your assignments on paper or electronically. To submit electronically, go to Step 19, and then follow the instructions provided by your instructor.

18. **Print Preview** your presentation, and then print **Handouts, (6 slides per page)**.

19. **Save** changes to your presentation, and then **Close** the file.

End **You have completed Project 2H**

Mastering PowerPoint

Project 2I — Summer

In this project, you will apply the skills you practiced from all the Objectives in Projects 2A and 2B.

Objectives: 1. *Format Slide Elements;* **2.** *Insert and Format Pictures and Shapes;* **3.** *Apply Slide Transitions;* **4.** *Reorganize Presentation Text and Clear Formats;* **5.** *Create and Format a SmartArt Graphic.*

In the following Mastering PowerPoint Assessment, you will edit a presentation that Kirsten McCarty, Director of Marketing, will be showing at a travel fair describing the summer activities at Montagna del Pattino. Your completed presentation will look similar to Figure 2.47.

For Project 2I, you will need the following files:

p2I_Art
p2I_Balloons
p2I_Fireworks
p2I_Summer

You will save your presentation as
2I_Summer_Firstname_Lastname

Figure 2.47

(Project 2I–Summer continues on the next page)

(Project 2I–Summer continued)

1. **Start** PowerPoint, and then from your student files open the file **p2I_Summer**. **Save** the presentation as **2I_Summer_Firstname_Lastname**

2. On **Slide 2**, apply a **WordArt Style—Gradient Fill – Accent 6, Inner Shadow** found in the fourth row—to the title, and then decrease the **Font Size** to **32**. Select the bulleted list placeholder so that its border displays as a solid line, and then display the **Bullets and Numbering** dialog box. Change the bullet style to the third style in the first row of the Bullets gallery—**Hollow Round Bullets**. Change the bullet **Color** to the first color under **Standard Colors—Dark Red**.

3. On **Slide 2**, display the **Shapes** gallery. Under **Basic Shapes**, insert the fifth shape in the second row—**Frame**. Position the pointer at **1.5 inches to the right of zero on the horizontal ruler** and at **1.5 inches above zero on the vertical ruler**. Draw the shape with a **Height** of **1.5** and a **Width** of **3.25**, using the **Format Tab** to adjust the size as necessary. In the frame, type **Reservations recommended at least two months in advance** Apply **Italic** and **Center** the text.

4. Duplicate the frame shape by using Ctrl + D, and then drag the duplicated shape down so that it is approximately 0.5 inch below the first shape. Align the left edges of the shapes, and then in the second shape, replace the text with **Check out our Stay and Play packages for special discounts** On the **Format tab**, click the **Shape Fill arrow**, and then under **Standard Colors**, click the first color—**Dark Red**. Use F4 to repeat the fill color formatting to the other frame shape.

5. Display **Slide 3**. In the placeholder on the right, use the **Insert Picture from File**

button to insert from your student files, **p2I_Art**. Change the **Picture Shape** to a **Rounded Rectangle**. Apply the fourth **Glow Effect** in the first row—**Accent color 4, 5 pt glow**.

6. Display **Slide 4**. Select the title, and then in the **Font group**, click the **Clear All Formatting** button to remove the WordArt formatting from the selection.

7. On **Slide 4**, right-click in the content placeholder text, and then point to **Convert to SmartArt**. Click **More SmartArt Graphics** to display the **Choose a SmartArt Graphics** dialog box. Click **Process**, and then in the first row, double-click the last graphic—**Alternating Flow** to convert the text to a diagram. Click in the **Mile 10** shape, and then in the **Create Graphic group**, click **Add Shape**. In the gray box, type **Finish** and then in the brown box, type **Summit Lodge**

8. Change the color of the SmartArt to the first **Accent 1** color—**Colored Outline - Accent 1**, and then apply **3-D Style Powder**.

9. Display **Slide 5**. Select the *Fireworks Display* text, and then apply the second **Word Art Style** in the first row. Change the **Text Fill** color to **Dark Red**. Use the **Format Painter** to apply the same formatting to the *Hot Air Balloon Race* text. In the placeholder on the left, use the **Insert Picture from File** button to insert the picture **p2I_Fireworks**. Apply the **Glow Picture Effect Accent color 2, 8 pt glow**.

10. In the placeholder on the right, use the **Insert Picture from File** button to insert the picture **p2I_Balloons**. Apply the **Soft Edges Picture Effect 5 Point**. Size the picture to a **Height** of 2.5 and a **Width** of

(Project 2I–Summer continues on the next page)

Content-Based Assessments

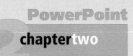
(Project 2I–Summer continued)

3.75 and then drag the picture up so that its top edge is positioned at **1 inch above zero on the vertical ruler**. It should *not* align with the fireworks picture.

11. Insert a 4-inch-wide **Text Box** positioned at **zero on the horizontal ruler** and at **2 inches below zero on the vertical ruler**. Type **Color lights up the sky in July and August. Join us for both events and enjoy a barbecue, carnival rides, and music.** Apply **WordArt Style Fill – None, Outline – Accent 2**, and then change the **Text Fill** to **Dark Red**. Apply **Italic**, and then change the **Font Size** to **16**. **Center** the text.

12. Use ⬆Shift to select the text box that you created in Step 11, the balloon picture, and the *Hot Air Balloon Race* text box. **Align Center** the three objects. (Hint: Use the Drawing Tools Format tab).

13. In the first row of the **Wipes** transitions, apply the **Wedge Transition** to all of the slides in the presentation, and then view the slide show.

14. Create a **Header and Footer** for the **Notes and Handouts**. Include only the **Date and time updated automatically**, the **Page number**, and a **Footer** with the file name **2I_Summer_Firstname_Lastname** using your own first and last name.

15. Check your *Chapter Assignment Sheet* or *Course Syllabus* or consult your instructor to determine if you are to submit your assignments on paper or electronically. To submit electronically, go to Step 17, and then follow the instructions provided by your instructor.

16. **Print Preview** your presentation, and then print **Handouts, (6 slides per page)**.

17. **Save** changes to your presentation, and then **Close** the presentation.

End **You have completed Project 2I** ————————————————

Content-Based Assessments

Business Running Case

Project 2J—Business Running Case

In this project, you will apply the skills you practiced in Projects 2A and 2B.

From My Computer, navigate to the student files that accompany this textbook. In the folder **03_business_running_case_pg37_86**, locate and open the folder for this chapter. Open and print the instructions for this project, which are provided to you in Adobe PDF format. Follow the instructions and use the skills you have gained thus far to assist Jennifer Nelson in meeting the challenges of owning and running her business.

 End **You have completed Project 2J** ——————————

Outcomes-Based Assessments

Rubric

The following outcomes-based assessments are *open-ended assessments*. That is, there is no specific correct result; your result will depend on your approach to the information provided. Make *Professional Quality* your goal. Use the following scoring rubric to guide you in *how* to approach the problem and then to evaluate *how well* your approach solves the problem.

The *criteria*—Software Mastery, Content, Format and Layout, and Process—represent the knowledge and skills you have gained that you can apply to solving the problem. The *levels of performance*—Professional Quality, Approaching Professional Quality, or Needs Quality Improvements—help you and your instructor evaluate your result.

	Your completed project is of Professional Quality if you:	Your completed project is Approaching Professional Quality if you:	Your completed project Needs Quality Improvements if you:
1-Software Mastery	Choose and apply the most appropriate skills, tools, and features and identify efficient methods to solve the problem.	Choose and apply some appropriate skills, tools, and features, but not in the most efficient manner.	Choose inappropriate skills, tools, or features, or are inefficient in solving the problem.
2-Content	Construct a solution that is clear and well organized, contains content that is accurate, appropriate to the audience and purpose, and is complete. Provide a solution that contains no errors of spelling, grammar, or style.	Construct a solution in which some components are unclear, poorly organized, inconsistent, or incomplete. Misjudge the needs of the audience. Have some errors in spelling, grammar, or style, but the errors do not detract from comprehension.	Construct a solution that is unclear, incomplete, or poorly organized, containing some inaccurate or inappropriate content; and contains many errors of spelling, grammar, or style. Do not solve the problem.
3-Format and Layout	Format and arrange all elements to communicate information and ideas, clarify function, illustrate relationships, and indicate relative importance.	Apply appropriate format and layout features to some elements, but not others. Overuse features, causing minor distraction.	Apply format and layout that does not communicate information or ideas clearly. Do not use format and layout features to clarify function, illustrate relationships, or indicate relative importance. Use available features excessively, causing distraction.
4-Process	Use an organized approach that integrates planning, development, self-assessment, revision, and reflection.	Demonstrate an organized approach in some areas, but not others; or, use an insufficient process of organization throughout.	Do not use an organized approach to solve the problem.

Outcomes-Based Assessments

Problem Solving

Project 2K—Adult Lessons

In this project, you will construct a solution by applying any combination of the skills you practiced from the Objectives in Projects 2A and 2B.

For Project 2K, you will need the following file:

New blank PowerPoint presentation

**You will save your presentation as
2K_Adult_Lessons_Firstname_Lastname**

Using the information provided, create a presentation that contains four to six slides that Dane Richardson, Director of Ski and Snowboard Instruction, can use to describe the adult ski and snowboard lessons offered at Montagna del Pattino. The presentation will be used as a part of a larger presentation on resort activities to be shown to an audience of varying skiing abilities at a regional ski and snowboard convention.

The resort offers Adult Group Lessons that are comprised of individuals with similar skill levels. Two-hour group lessons include equipment. Private lessons, which are one-on-one instruction geared toward an individual's skill level and preferences, are also available. The resort offers 8-week programs which are group lessons for those who prefer more in-depth, ongoing instruction. The resort also offers several specialty lessons. The Ladies Only group lessons are geared specifically toward women and participants are encouraged to bring a friend. The Backcountry Adventure is a chance for advanced skiers to explore lesser-known areas of the resort. Finally, the Racing Camps are for recreational skiers seeking to fine-tune their skills, and feature gate running and on-hill training.

Use the techniques that you learned in this chapter to insert and format graphics to visually enhance your presentation. The tone of the presentation should be positive and encouraging so that the audience—regardless of skill level—will be interested in visiting the resort and attending the Ski and Snowboard School. Add the file name to the Notes and Handouts footer and check the presentation for spelling errors. Save the presentation as **2K_Adult_Lessons_Firstname_Lastname** and submit it as directed.

Note: You can find many appropriate images available to Office users. To access these images, click the Insert tab, and then from the Illustrations group, click the Clip Art button. In the Clip Art task pane, type a key word—such as *ski*—in the *Search for* box. You can specify the image type (clip art or photographs) and where to search. The largest variety of photographs can be found by including Web Collections in the *Search in* box. You can also use images from earlier projects in this chapter, or images from your personal collection.

End **You have completed Project 2K**

Outcomes-Based Assessments

Problem Solving

Project 2L — Festivals

In this project, you will construct a solution by applying any combination of the skills you practiced from the Objectives in Projects 2A and 2B.

For Project 2L, you will need the following file:

New blank PowerPoint presentation

You will save your presentation as 2L_Festivals_Firstname_Lastname

In this project, you will create a presentation that Justin Mitrani, Hotel Manager, is creating as part of a collection of presentations, given to guests on CDs, that describes the seasonal festivals and events held at Montagna del Pattino. The events that are sponsored at the resort include a Celtic Festival, a Chili Cook-Off, and a Country Music Festival. The tone of the presentation should be fun and interesting so that guests will be encouraged to return to the resort during the events. Research these types of events on the Internet to develop content and use a SmartArt graphic to highlight the dates of the festivals. Include pictures and shapes that are relevant to the events and format the pictures, using the techniques that you learned in this chapter. (See the note at the end of Project 2K for hints about locating images.) Add the file name to the Notes and Handouts footer and check the presentation for spelling errors. Save the presentation as **2L_Festivals_Firstname_Lastname** and submit it as directed.

 You have completed Project 2L

Outcomes-Based Assessments

Problem Solving

Project 2M—Orientation

In this project, you will construct a solution by applying any combination of the skills you practiced from the Objectives in Projects 2A and 2B.

For Project 2M, you will need the following file:

New blank PowerPoint presentation

You will save your presentation as
2M_Orientation_Firstname_Lastname

In this exercise, you will create an orientation presentation consisting of four to six slides to be used by Justin Mitrani, Hotel Director for Montagna del Pattino. This presentation will be used to introduce new employees to the resort and to the importance of customer service. Begin the presentation with slides that include information about the resort. You can summarize from the following information, and you can expand upon this information by researching mountain ski resorts.

Montagna del Pattino was founded and built by the Blardone family in the 1950s. It has grown from one ski run and a small lodge to 50 trails, 6 lifts, a 300-room lodge, and a renowned ski and snowboard school. Luxurious condominiums on the property have ski in/ski out access. A resort store offers rental and sale of gear for enthusiasts who want the latest advances in ski and snowboard technology. A variety of quick service, casually elegant, and fine dining restaurants complete the scene for a perfect ski-enthusiast getaway.

Include at least two slides that describe why customer service and hospitality are important at the resort. Guests who return year after year are impressed by the friendly attitude and helpfulness of the staff and the cleanliness of the facilities. Stress the importance of greeting guests and making them feel at home, thus exemplifying the family-friendly atmosphere that is a hallmark of the resort. Use a process SmartArt graphic to illustrate how hospitality and customer service lead to satisfied guests.

The tone of this presentation is informative and should include examples of how customer service is provided on a daily basis. Keep this in mind when choosing a theme, diagrams, bullet styles, and pictures. (See the note at the end of Project 2K for hints about locating images.) Add the date and file name to the Notes and Handouts footer and check the presentation for spelling errors. Save the presentation as **2M_Orientation_Firstname_Lastname** and submit it as directed.

 End **You have completed Project 2M**

Outcomes-Based Assessments

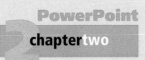

Problem Solving

Project 2N — Restaurants

In this project, you will construct a solution by applying any combination of the skills you practiced from the Objectives in Projects 2A and 2B.

For Project 2N, you will need the following file:

New blank PowerPoint presentation

You will save your presentation as
2N_Restaurants_Firstname_Lastname

In this exercise, you will create a presentation that contains information about the restaurants that are onsite at Montagna del Pattino resort. This presentation is being used by Justin Mitrani, Hotel Director, at a Chamber of Commerce meeting. Mr. Mitrani's purpose is to inform Chamber members of the restaurant and catering services available at the resort in an effort to expand catering, conference, and business meeting operations. Create a presentation about the restaurant services, using the following information.

The resort offers a variety of quick service, casually elegant, and fine dining restaurants. The Summit Clubhouse and the Montagna Vista Club are fine dining restaurants known for their superb buffets and desserts. The Mediterranean buffet includes Whole Chicken, slow-roasted and quartered, Rice Pilaf with Pine Nuts and Raisins, Classic Greek Salad with Vinaigrette, Hummus, and Baklava. The Italian buffet includes Lasagna, Italian Vegetable Sauté, Classic Caesar salad, Garlic Bread and Bread Sticks, and Cheesecake. Other buffets include the All American Barbecue, the Cajun Cookout, and the Heartland buffet. The Summit Clubhouse can accommodate large groups of up to 150 guests and the Montagna Vista Club is best suited for more intimate gatherings of no more than 65 guests. The restaurants offer full bar service, event-planning services, and coordination with hotel operations to accommodate conference guests who plan to stay overnight. The Summit Clubhouse includes three conference rooms off of the main banquet room that can be used for smaller group meetings. The resort recently hired a full-time conference and catering director who will act as a liaison with business representatives to coordinate event planning.

Using the preceding information, create a presentation with a minimum of six slides that describes the resort restaurants, menus, banquet and conference facilities, and services. Create a SmartArt graphic that demonstrates the catering and event-planning process. The process may include an initial meeting with the catering director, a meeting to choose

(Project 2N–Restaurants continues on the next page)

Problem Solving

(Project 2N–Restaurants continued)

the date and location, and other meetings to choose menus and finalize reservations. Illustrate your presentation with pictures that will entice the intended audience to use the Montagna del Pattino resort for their catering and business meeting needs. (See the note at the end of Project 2K for hints about locating images.) Add the date and file name to the Notes and Handouts footer and check the presentation for spelling errors. Save the presentation as **2N_Restaurants_Firstname_Lastname** and submit it as directed.

 End **You have completed Project 2N** ────────────

Outcomes-Based Assessments

Problem Solving

Project 2O — Triathlon

In this project, you will construct a solution by applying any combination of the skills you practiced from the Objectives in Projects 2A and 2B.

For Project 2O, you will need the following file:

New blank PowerPoint presentation

**You will save your presentation as
2O_Triathlon_Firstname_Lastname**

In this exercise, you will create a presentation to be shown by Montagna del Pattino's President, Albert Blardone, at a company meeting that details the Annual Triathlon sponsored by the resort. The presentation will explain the details of the triathlon including the events, the routes, major sponsors, prizes, and medical and security measures. The triathlon takes place in July and is attended by international competitors who excel in three sporting events—swimming, cycling, and running. The triathlon is open to men and women of all ages. Men and women compete concurrently but in separate categories. In addition to gender, the athletes are further categorized according to the following age brackets: 18 to 24; 25 to 35; 36 to 45; and over 45.

Conduct research on triathlon events and begin the presentation with at least two slides that describe traditional triathlon competitions. The next two slides should include the categories in which competitors are separated and a diagram that illustrates the race route. The 1600-meter swimming event takes place in Lake Hennessy, which adjoins Montagna del Pattino. The 50-mile cycling event begins at the lake and finishes at the Brownsville Town Square. The 26-mile marathon finishes at Montagna del Pattino Summit Lodge. Refer to Project 2I_Summer, Slide 4 to see an example of how this information can be included in a SmartArt graphic.

As you conduct your research, explore the types of sponsors involved in triathlon events and the prizes awarded to winners. Include this information on two slides and conclude the presentation with one slide that discusses the mobile medical facilities that will be available to competitors and bystanders as heat exhaustion can affect both athletes and fans. The event draws a large number of spectators, with rooms at the Summit Lodge typically reserved two months in advance. Use the techniques that you learned in this chapter to illustrate the presentation. (See the note at the end of Project 2K for hints about locating images.) Add the date and file name to the Notes and Handouts footer and check the presentation for spelling errors. Save the presentation as **2O_Triathlon_Firstname_Lastname** and submit it as directed.

End You have completed Project 2O

Outcomes-Based Assessments

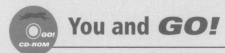

Project 2P — You and *GO!*

In this project, you will construct a solution by applying any combination of the skills you practiced from the Objectives in Projects 2A and 2B.

From My Computer, navigate to the student files that accompany this textbook. In the folder **04_you_and_go_pg87_102**, locate and open the folder for this chapter. Open and print the instructions for this project, which are provided to you in Adobe PDF format. Follow the instructions to create a presentation about a career in which you are interested.

 End You have completed Project 2P ——————————

GO! with Help

Project 2Q — *GO!* with Help

The PowerPoint Help system is extensive and can help you as you work. In this project, you will view information about creating a photo album in PowerPoint.

1 **Start** PowerPoint. On the right side of the Ribbon, click the **Microsoft Office PowerPoint Help** button to open the PowerPoint Help window. In the **Search** box, type **Create a Photo Album** and then press Enter.

2 In the displayed search results, click **Create a photo album**. Maximize the displayed window, and then read about photo albums and how you can create them in PowerPoint.

3 If you want, print a copy of the information by clicking the printer button at the top of Microsoft Office PowerPoint Help window.

4 Close the **Help** window, and then **Close** PowerPoint.

 End You have completed Project 2Q ——————————

Group Business Running Case

Project 2R—Group Business Running Case

In this project, you will apply the skills you practiced from the Objectives in Projects 2A and 2B.

Your instructor may assign this group case project to your class. If your instructor assigns this project, he or she will provide you with information and instructions to work as part of a group. The group will apply the skills gained thus far to help the Bell Orchid Hotel Group achieve its business goals.

End **You have completed Project 2R** —————————

3

chapter three

Enhancing a Presentation with Animation, Tables, and Charts

OBJECTIVES

At the end of this chapter you will be able to:

1. Customize Slide Backgrounds and Themes
2. Animate a Slide Show

OUTCOMES

Mastering these objectives will enable you to:

PROJECT 3A
Customize a Presentation

3. Create and Modify Tables
4. Create and Modify Charts

PROJECT 3B
Present Data with Tables and Charts

Select National Properties

Select National Properties is a diversified real estate company that develops, builds, manages, and acquires a wide variety of properties nationwide. Among the company's portfolio of properties are shopping malls, mixed-use town center developments, high-rise office buildings, office parks, industrial buildings and warehouses, multifamily housing developments, educational facilities, and hospitals. Residential developments are mainly located in and around the company's hometown, Chicago; commercial and public buildings in the portfolio are located nationwide. The company is well respected for its focus on quality and commitment to the environment and economic development of the areas where it operates.

Enhancing a Presentation with Animation, Tables, and Charts

Recall that the presentation theme applies a consistent look to a presentation. You can customize a presentation by modifying the theme and by applying animation to slide elements, and you can enhance your presentations by creating tables and charts that help your audience understand numeric data and trends just as pictures and diagrams help illustrate a concept. The data that you present should determine whether a table or a chart would most appropriately display your information. The charts most commonly used in PowerPoint presentations are bar, column, line, and pie. Styles applied to your tables and charts unify these slide elements by complementing your presentation theme.

Project 3A **New Homes**

In Activities 3.1 through 3.8, you will edit and format a presentation that Shaun Walker, President of Select National Properties, has created for a City Council meeting that describes a proposed residential development. Your completed presentation will look similar to Figure 3.1.

For Project 3A, you will need the following files:

p3A_Bedroom
p3A_Community
p3A_Family_Room
p3A_New_Homes

You will save your presentation as
3A_New_Homes_Firstname_Lastname

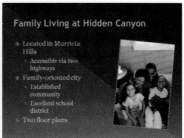

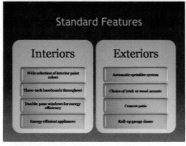

Figure 3.1
Project 3A—New Homes

Objective 1
Customize Slide Backgrounds and Themes

You have practiced customizing presentations by applying themes with unified design elements, backgrounds, and colors that provide a consistent look in your presentation. You can further customize a slide by changing the background color, applying a background style, or by inserting a picture on the slide background.

Activity 3.1 Applying a Background Style

Recall that the presentation theme is a coordinated, predefined set of colors, fonts, lines, and fill effects. In this activity, you will open a presentation in which the Verve theme is applied, and then you will change the theme colors for the entire presentation and the background style for the first slide.

> ## Note — Comparing Your Screen with the Figures in This Textbook
>
> Your screen will match the figures shown in this textbook if you set your screen resolution to 1024 x 768. At other resolutions, your screen will closely resemble, but not match, the figures shown. To view your screen's resolution, on the Windows desktop, right-click in a blank area, click Properties, and then click the Settings tab.

1 **Start** PowerPoint. From your student files, **Open** the file

p3A_New_Homes. From the **Office** menu [icon], click **Save As**, and then click the **Create New Folder** button [icon]. Navigate to the location where you are saving your solution files, create a folder with the name **PowerPoint Chapter 3** and then click **OK**. In the **File name** box, type **3A_New_Homes_Firstname_Lastname** and then click **Save** to save your file.

2 Click the **Design tab**, and then in the **Themes group**, click the **Colors** button. Click **Trek** to change the theme color for the entire presentation.

3 With **Slide 1** displayed, on the **Design tab**, in the **Background group**, click the **Background Styles** button to display the Background Styles gallery, as shown in Figure 3.2.

A *background style* is a slide background fill variation that combines theme colors in different intensities.

Figure 3.2

Background Styles gallery

4 Point to each of the background styles to use Live Preview to view the style on **Slide 1**. Then, in the first row, *right-click* **Style 2** to display the shortcut menu. Click **Apply to Selected Slides**.

The background style is applied to Slide 1.

5 **Save** your presentation.

More Knowledge

Applying Background Styles to All Slides in a Presentation

You do not need to display the shortcut menu to apply a background style to all of the slides in a presentation. Click the background style that you wish to apply and the style will be applied to all of the slides in the presentation.

Activity 3.2 Hiding Background Graphics

Slide themes and backgrounds often contain graphic elements that display on slides with various layouts. In the Verve theme applied to this presentation, the background includes a triangle and a line that intersect near the lower right corner of the slide. Sometimes the background graphics interfere with the slide content. When this happens, you can hide the background graphics.

1 Display **Slide 6** and notice that on this slide, you can clearly see the triangle and line on the slide background.

You cannot delete these objects because they are a part of the slide background.

2 Display **Slide 5**. On the **Design tab**, in the **Background group**, click to select the **Hide Background Graphics** check box, and then compare your slide with Figure 3.3.

The background objects no longer display behind the SmartArt diagram.

Hide Background Graphics
check box is checked

Figure 3.3

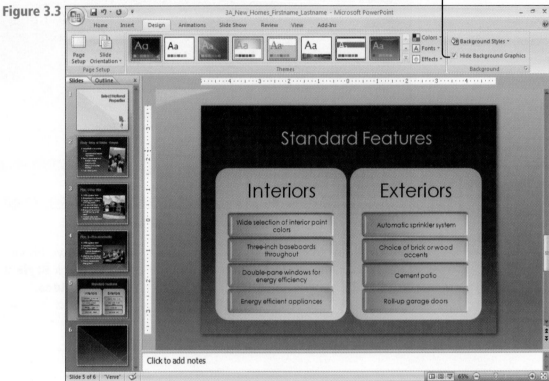

3 Display **Slide 1**. On the **Design tab**, in the **Background group**, select the **Hide Background Graphics** check box to toggle the graphics off.

4 Click the **Hide Background Graphics** check box again to toggle the graphics on.

5 **Save** the presentation.

Activity 3.3 Formatting a Slide Background with a Picture

You can insert a picture on a slide background so the image fills the entire slide.

1 Display **Slide 3**, and then click the **Home tab**. In the **Slides group**, click the **New Slide arrow**, and then click the **Title Only** layout.

2 Click the **Design tab**. In the **Background group**, click the **Hide Background Graphics** check box, and then click the **Background Styles** button. Below the displayed gallery, click **Format Background**.

The Format Background dialog box displays, providing options for customizing slide backgrounds.

3 If necessary, on the left side of the dialog box, click Fill. On the right side of the dialog box, under **Fill**, click the **Picture or texture fill** option button as shown in Figure 3.4, and then notice that on the slide background, a textured fill displays.

Your background may differ

Figure 3.4

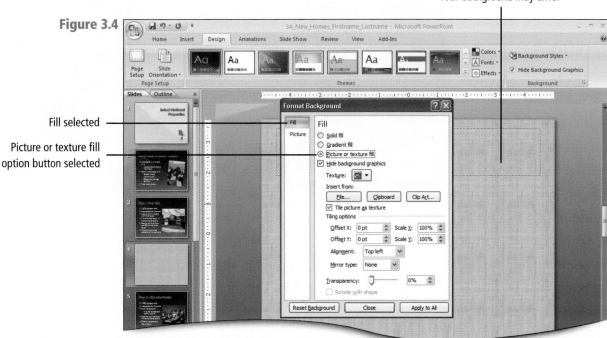

Fill selected

Picture or texture fill option button selected

4 Under **Insert from**, click the **File** button to display the **Insert Picture** dialog box. Navigate to the location where your student files are located, and then click **p3A_Bedroom**. Click **Insert**.

Notice that the picture displays on the background of Slide 4.

5 In the **Format Background** dialog box, under **Stretch options**, verify that the **Left**, **Right**, **Top**, and **Bottom Offsets** are set to **0%** and make changes as necessary. Compare your dialog box with Figure 3.5.

The Stretch options enable you to control the way in which the picture displays on the slide background by cropping portions of the picture and then stretching it to fit on the background. Setting the Offsets to 0% ensures that the slide background is formatted with the original picture in its entirety.

6 Click **Close** and notice that the picture has been applied to the slide background.

When a picture is applied to the slide background using the Format Background option, the picture is not treated as an object. Thus, you cannot move it or size it.

Picture displays on slide background

Figure 3.5

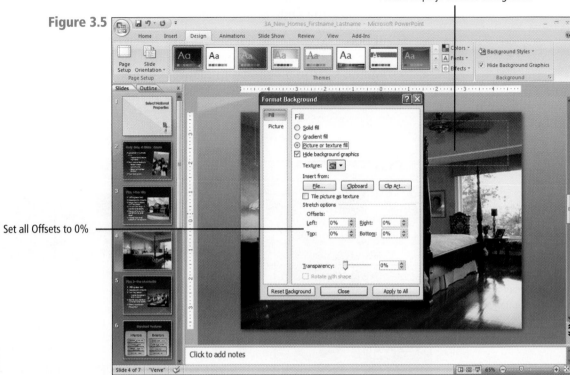

Set all Offsets to 0%

7 Click in the title placeholder, type **Master Bedroom** and then notice that the background picture does not provide sufficient contrast with the text to display the title effectively.

8 Point to the outer edge of the title placeholder so that the ⊕ pointer displays. Drag the title placeholder down and to the left so that its lower left corner aligns with the lower left corner of the slide. Release the mouse button, and then compare your slide with Figure 3.6.

The brown background of the floor provides good contrast for the title text.

Figure 3.6

Workshop

Overlaying Text on a Picture

When you insert a picture on a slide background, it is a good idea to choose a picture that has a solid area in which you can overlay a text box or title. For example, in the picture that you inserted on Slide 4, the lower left corner has a brown area that provides good contrast for light-colored text. When the picture that you choose does not contain a solid area, you can create one by filling the text box with color.

9 Display **Slide 5**, and then insert a **New Slide** with the **Title Only** layout.

10 On the **Design tab**, in the **Background group**, click the **Hide Background Graphics** check box, and then click the **Background Styles** button. Click **Format Background**. Under **Fill**, click the **Picture or texture fill** option button. Under **Insert from**, click **File**. Navigate to your student files, click **p3A_Family_Room**, and then click **Insert**. Under **Stretch options**, change as necessary the **Left**, **Right**, **Top**, and **Bottom Offsets** to **0%**. **Close** the **Format Background** dialog box to format the slide background with the picture.

11 In the title placeholder, type **Family Room** Select the text, and then on the Mini toolbar, click the **Font Color button arrow** to display the **Theme Colors gallery**. In the first row, click the first color, **Black**, **Background 1**. On the Mini toolbar, click the **Align Text Right** button.

12 Point to the outer edge of the placeholder to display the pointer, and then drag the placeholder up and to the right so that its upper right corner aligns with the upper right corner of the slide. Compare your slide with Figure 3.7.

Figure 3.7

13 Display **Slide 8**. Using the process that you practiced in **Step 10**, insert the picture **p3A_Community** on the background of **Slide 8**.

Notice that the background does not provide sufficient contrast for the slide title to be easily read. You can apply a Shape Style to the title placeholder so that the text is visible.

14 Click in the title placeholder, and then click the **Format tab**. In the **Shape Styles group**, click the **More** button. In the second row of the **Shape Styles gallery**, click the third style—**Colored Fill – Accent 2**.

15 Point to the outer edge of the placeholder to display the pointer, and then drag the placeholder down so that its bottom edge aligns with the bottom of the slide. Click outside of the placeholder, and then compare your slide with Figure 3.8.

Figure 3.8

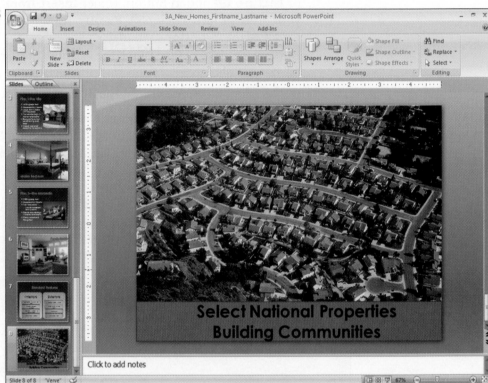

16 Save your presentation.

Activity 3.4 Applying a Background Fill Color and Resetting a Slide Background

1 Display **Slide 1**, and then click the **Design tab**. In the **Background group**, click the **Background Styles** button, and then click **Format Background**. In the **Format Background** dialog box, if necessary, click the Solid Fill option button, and then click the **Color** button. Under **Theme Colors**, in the last row, click the second color—**Black, Text 1, Lighter 5%**. Click **Close**.

The solid fill color is applied to the slide background.

2 On the **Design tab**, in the **Background group**, click the **Background Styles** button. Below the gallery, click **Reset Slide Background**.

After making many changes to a slide background, you may decide that the original theme formatting best displays the text and graphics on a slide. The Reset Slide Background feature restores the original theme formatting to a slide.

3 **Save** 🖫 the presentation.

Activity 3.5 Modifying Font Themes

Every presentation theme includes a ***font theme*** that determines the font applied to two types of slide text—headings and body. The ***headings font*** is applied to slide titles and the ***body font*** is applied to all other text. Sometimes the heading and body fonts are the same, but are different sizes. In other font themes, the heading and body fonts are different. When you apply a new font theme to the presentation, the text on every slide is updated with the new heading and body fonts.

1 If necessary, display **Slide 1**. Click anywhere in the title placeholder. Click the **Home tab**, and then in the **Font group**, click the **Font button arrow** Calibri (Headings) ▾. Notice that at the top of the Font list, under **Theme Fonts**, *Century Gothic (Headings)* and *Century Gothic (Body)* display as shown in Figure 3.9.

Figure 3.9

Theme fonts ——

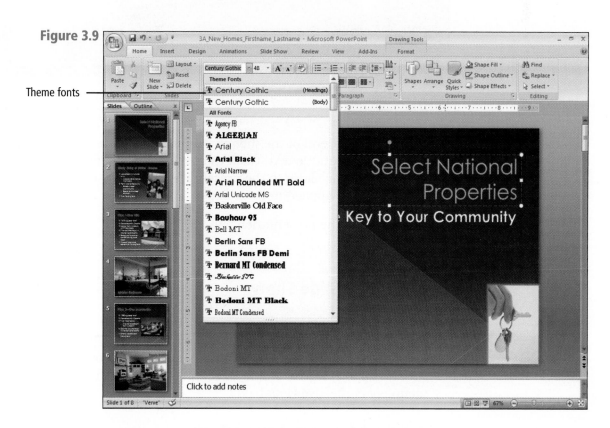

2 Click anywhere on the slide to close the Font list.

3 Click the **Design tab**, and then in the **Themes group**, click the **Fonts** button.

The list displays the name of each font theme and the pair of fonts in the theme. The first and larger font in each pair is the Headings font and the second and smaller font in each pair is the Body font.

4 Scroll the **Theme Fonts** list and notice that the last theme—*Verve*—is selected as shown in Figure 3.10.

Current font theme

Figure 3.10

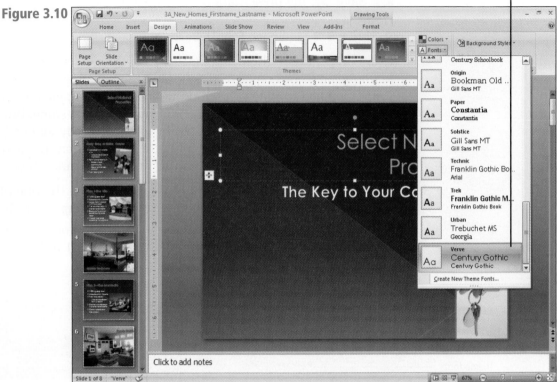

5 Point to several of the themes and watch as Live Preview changes the title and subtitle text. Click the **Urban** theme, and then scroll through the slides in the presentation, noticing that the font changes have been applied to every slide.

6 **Save** the presentation.

Objective 2
Animate a Slide Show

Animation effects are used to introduce individual slide elements so that the slide can progress one element at a time. When used correctly, animation effects focus the audience's attention, providing the speaker with an opportunity to emphasize important points using the slide element as an effective visual aid.

Activity 3.6 Applying Entrance Effects

Entrance effects are animations that bring a slide element onto the screen.

1 Display **Slide 1**. Click the **Animations tab**, and then in the

Transition to This Slide group, click the **More** button ▼. Under **Wipes**, click the transition that contains four arrows pointing inward toward a center box—**Box In**. Click the **Transition Speed arrow**, and then click **Medium**. Click the **Apply To All** button.

2 Display **Slide 2**, and then click the bulleted list placeholder. In the **Animations group**, click the **Custom Animation** button. At the top of the displayed **Custom Animation** task pane, click the **Add Effect** button, and then point to **Entrance**. Compare your screen with Figure 3.11.

A list of the most recently used animation effects displays. At the bottom of the list, the *More Effects* option displays.

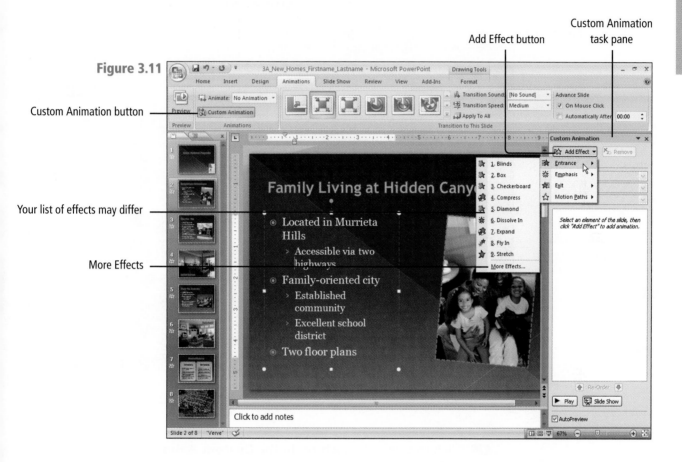

Figure 3.11

Custom Animation button

Add Effect button

Custom Animation task pane

Your list of effects may differ

More Effects

3 Click **More Effects** to display the **Add Entrance Effect** dialog box. Scroll through the list to view the *Basic*, *Subtle*, *Moderate*, and *Exciting* entrance effects.

4 At the bottom of the **Add Entrance Effect** dialog box, if necessary, click to select the **Preview Effect** check box. Click several of the effects in each of the four categories to view the animation.

5 Under **Basic**, click **Blinds**, and then click **OK**. Compare your screen with Figure 3.12.

Notice that the numbers *1, 2,* and *3* display to the left of the bulleted list placeholder, indicating the order in which the bullet points will display. For example, the first bullet point and its subordinate bullet are both numbered *1*. Thus, both will display at the same time.

In the task pane, the ***custom animation list*** indicates that an animation effect has been applied to the selected item. The custom animation list displays the animation sequences for a slide. The mouse image next to item 1 in the custom animation list indicates that the animation will display the bulleted list placeholder text when the left mouse button is clicked or when the Spacebar is pressed. Below item 1, a button with two downward-pointing arrows displays. This is the *Click to expand contents* button, which when clicked, displays the animation for bullet points 1, 2, and 3.

Figure 3.12

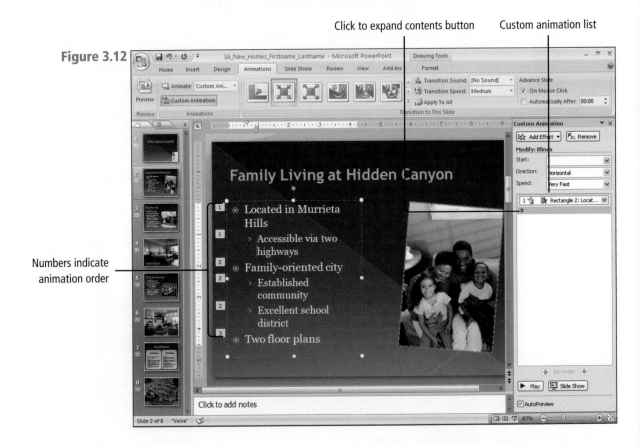

Click to expand contents button

Custom animation list

Numbers indicate animation order

6 Click to select the picture. In the **Custom Animation** task pane, click the **Add Effect** button, point to **Entrance**, and then click **More Effects**. In the displayed **Add Entrance Effect** dialog box, under **Basic**, click **Dissolve In**, and then click **OK**.

The task pane displays item number 4 in the custom animation list, and the number 4 also displays on the slide next to the picture. These numbers only display when the Custom Animation task pane is open.

7 At the bottom of the task pane, click the **Play** button.

For the active slide only, the slide transition and each animation display. Additionally, the task pane indicates the number of seconds that elapse with each animation. This is a good way to test the animations you have applied to a single slide, without switching to Slide Show view.

8 **Save** the presentation.

More Knowledge

Removing Animation Effects

You can remove animation that you have applied to a slide element by clicking the element in the Custom Animation task pane, and then clicking the Remove button. If you have applied an animation effect to a slide element, and then change your mind and decide to apply a different one, be sure to remove the animation that you do not wish to use. Otherwise, when you view your slide show, all of the animation effects will display one after another.

Activity 3.7 Setting Effect and Timing Options

After animation is applied, you can set *effect options*. Using effect options, you can change the direction of the effect and play a sound when an animation takes place. Effect options also enable you to control the levels of text that display. For example, you can animate text by first-level paragraphs, so that first-level bullet points and their subordinate text display all at once. Or, you can animate text by second-, third-, fourth-, or fifth-level paragraphs so that each bullet on the slide, regardless of level, displays individually. Finally, you can use the effect options to control how text displays when the next animation sequence occurs. For example, after you have discussed a bullet point, you can click the mouse button to display the next point and dim the previous point, thus keeping the audience focused on the new bullet point.

1 With **Slide 2** displayed, click in the bulleted list placeholder. If necessary, display the Custom Animation task pane by clicking the Custom Animation button, in the Animations group.

2 In the **custom animation list**, notice that item 1 is selected and a downward-pointing arrow displays to the right of the item. In the **custom animation list**, click the **item 1 arrow**, and then point to **Effect Options**, as shown in Figure 3.13.

Figure 3.13

Item 1 arrow

Effect Options

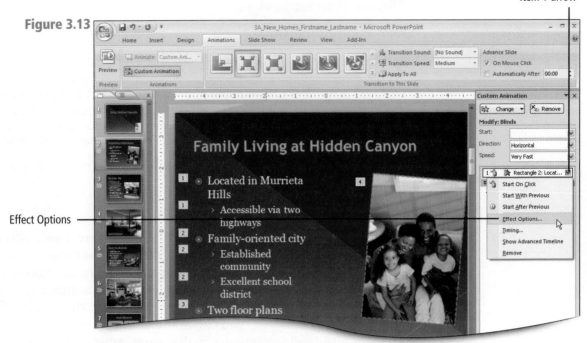

3 Click **Effect Options** to display the **Blinds** dialog box.

When you click the Effect Options command, the dialog box that displays is named according to the applied animation.

4 In the **Blinds dialog box**, if necessary, click the **Effect tab**. Under **Enhancements**, click the **After animation arrow**.

Use the After Animation options to choose how the text will display after it is animated and you click the mouse button. The default—*Don't Dim*—keeps the text onscreen without any changes. You can dim the text by choosing a color that blends with the slide background, or you can hide the text so that it does not display at all.

5 In the row of colors, click the **fifth color**, as shown in Figure 3.14, and then click **OK** to apply the effect option.

Figure 3.14

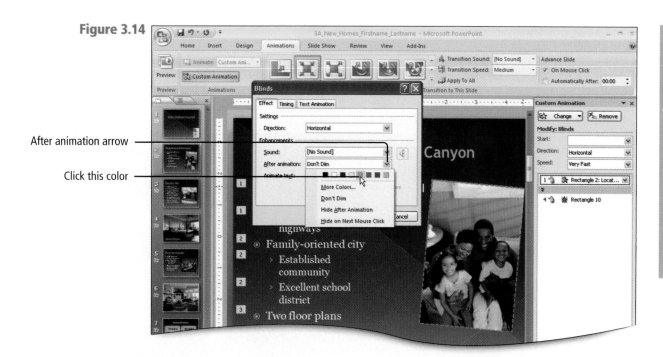

After animation arrow

Click this color

6 Click to select the picture. Near the top of the **Custom Animation** task pane, under **Modify: Dissolve In**, click the **Start arrow** to display three options—On Click, With Previous, and After Previous.

The *On Click* option begins the animation sequence for the selected slide element when the mouse button is clicked or the [Spacebar] is pressed. The *With Previous* option begins the animation sequence at the same time as the item preceding it in the custom animation list. The *After Previous* option begins the animation sequence for the selected slide element immediately after the completion of the previous animation or transition.

7 Click **After Previous**. In the **Custom Animation** task pane, under **Modify: Dissolve In**, click the **Speed arrow**, and then click **Fast**. Compare your task pane with Figure 3.15.

Figure 3.15

Change Start option

Change Speed

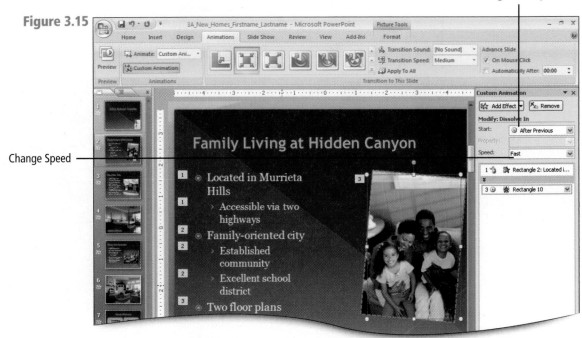

8 In the **Custom Animation** task pane, click **Play** to view the animation applied to the slide.

9 Display **Slide 4**, and then click in the title placeholder. In the **Custom Animation** task pane, click **Add Effect**, and then point to **Entrance**. Click **More Effects**. Under **Basic**, click **Fly In**, and then click **OK**.

10 In the **Custom Animation task pane**, click the **Start arrow**, and then click **After Previous** so that the title displays immediately after the slide transition. If necessary, click the **Direction arrow**, and then click **From Bottom**. In the **Custom Animation** task pane, click **Play** to view the animation applied to the slide.

11 Display **Slide 6**, and then click in the title placeholder. In the **Custom Animation** task pane, click **Add Effect**, and then point to **Entrance**.

Recall that the Animation Effects list displays the most recently applied animations.

12 In the **Animation Effects list**, click **Fly In**. Click the **Start arrow**, and then click **After Previous**. Click the **Direction arrow**, and then click **From Top**. In the **Custom Animation** task pane, click **Play** to view the animation applied to the slide.

13 **Close** ✕ the **Custom Animation** task pane, and then **Save** 🖫 the presentation.

Workshop

Applying Animation Effectively

It is not necessary to animate every item on every slide in your presentation. Too much animation can distract your audience by focusing their attention on what the presentation is going to do instead of the message that you are trying to convey. Remember, the purpose of animation is to draw attention to important text and graphics!

Activity 3.8 Applying Animation to a SmartArt Graphic

The most efficient method of animating a SmartArt graphic is to use one of the choices in the Animate list. Your animation choice can be modified using the Custom Animation task pane.

1 Display **Slide 7**, and then click anywhere in the *Interiors/Exteriors* SmartArt graphic to select it.

2 On the **Animations tab**, in the **Animations group**, click the **Animate arrow** to display the Animate list, as shown in Figure 3.16.

Animate arrow

Figure 3.16

Animate list

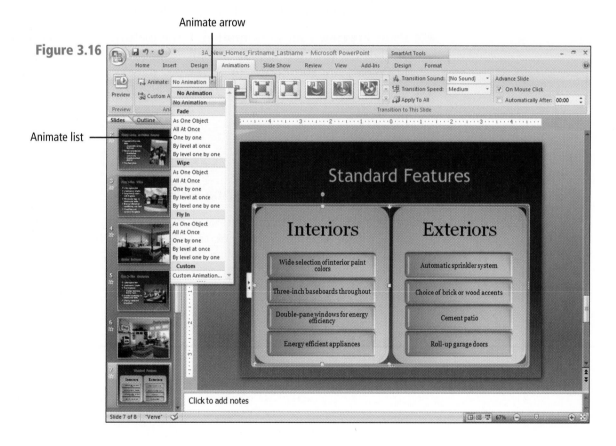

3 Point to several of the **Animate** options and notice as Live Preview displays the animation effects.

4 Under **Wipe**, click **By level at once**.

The *By level at once* option animates all shapes at the same level at the same time. In this case, the light-colored Interiors and Exteriors boxes will display at the same time, and then all of the gold boxes will display.

5 Click the **Slide Show tab**. In the **Start Slide Show group**, click **From Current Slide** to view the animation on Slide 7. Press [Spacebar] to advance through the SmartArt graphic animation effects. After the animations for Slide 7 are complete, press [Esc] to end the slide show and return to the presentation.

6 In the **Start Slide Show group**, click **From Beginning**, and then view your presentation, clicking the mouse button to advance through the slides. Notice the animation that is applied to each slide, and then when the black slide displays, click the mouse button one more time to display the presentation in Normal view.

7 Insert a **Header and Footer** for the **Notes and Handouts**. Include the **Date and time updated automatically**, the **Page number**, and a **Footer** with the file name 3A_New_Homes_Firstname_Lastname

8 Check your *Chapter Assignment Sheet* or *Course Syllabus* or consult your instructor to determine if you are to submit your assignments on paper or electronically. To submit electronically, go to Step 10, and then follow the instructions provided by your instructor.

9 **Print Preview** your presentation. If the pictures on the background of Slides 4, 6, and 8 do not display, Print Preview your presentation in Color. Print **Handouts, (4 slides per page)**.

10 **Save** the changes to your presentation, and then **Close** the presentation.

More Knowledge
Showing Selected Slides During a Slide Show

When you are delivering a presentation, you can right-click to display the shortcut menu, and then point to Go to Slide to view a list of the slides in the presentation. Then, click the slide that you want to display.

End You have completed Project 3A ————————————

Project 3B **Developments**

In Activities 3.9 through 3.14, you will add a table and two charts to a presentation that Shaun Walker, President of Select National Properties, is creating to apprise investors of the status of several new residential developments. Your completed presentation will look similar to Figure 3.17.

For Project 3B, you will need the following file:

p3B_Developments

You will save your presentation as
3B_Developments_Firstname_Lastname

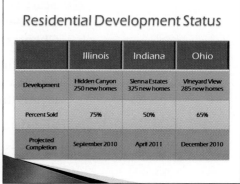

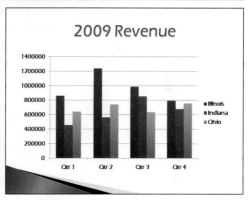

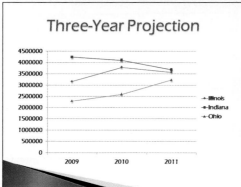

Figure 3.17
Project 3B—Developments

Objective 3
Create and Modify Tables

A *table* is a format for information that organizes and presents text and data in columns and rows. The intersection of a column and row is a *cell* and is the location in which you type text in a table.

Activity 3.9 Creating a Table

There are several ways to insert a table. You can create a table in Microsoft Office Word or Excel, and then paste and edit it in PowerPoint. You can also draw a table using the Draw Table pointer—a feature that is useful when the rows and columns contain cells of different sizes. You can insert a slide with a Content Layout and then click the Insert Table button, or you can click the Insert tab and then click Table. In this Activity, you will use a Content Layout to create a table.

1 **Start** PowerPoint, and then from your student files, open **p3B_Developments**. **Save** the presentation in your **PowerPoint Chapter 3** folder as **3B_Developments_Firstname_Lastname**

2 With **Slide 1** displayed, on the **Home tab**, in the **Slides group**, click the **New Slide** button to insert a slide with the **Title and Content** layout. In the title placeholder, type **Residential Development Status** and then **Center** the title.

3 In the content placeholder, click the **Insert Table** button to display the Insert Table dialog box, as shown in Figure 3.18.

In the Insert Table dialog box, you can enter the number of columns and rows that you want the table to contain.

Figure 3.18

Insert Table dialog box

Insert Table button

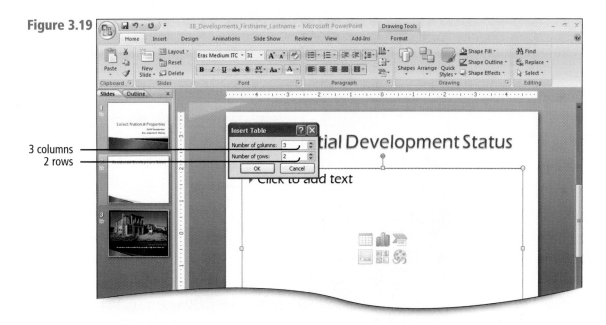

4 In the **Insert Table** dialog box, in the **Number of columns box** type **3** and then press Tab. In the **Number of rows** box type **2** and then compare your dialog box with Figure 3.19.

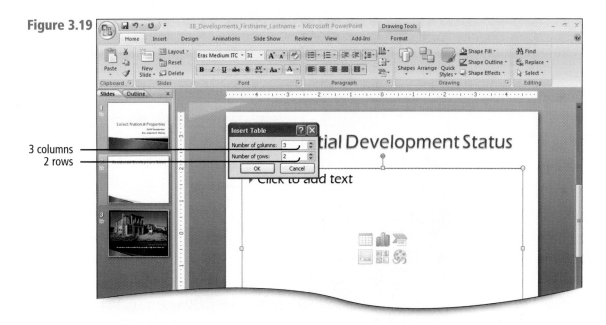

Figure 3.19

3 columns
2 rows

5 Click **OK** to create a table with three columns and two rows. Notice that the insertion point is blinking in the upper left cell of the table.

The table extends from the left side of the content placeholder to the right side and the three columns are equal in width. By default, a style is applied to the table.

6 With the insertion positioned in the first cell of the table, type **Illinois** and then press Tab.

Pressing Tab moves the insertion point to the next cell in the same row. If the insertion point is positioned in the last cell of a row, pressing Tab moves the insertion point to the first cell of the next row.

Alert!

Did you press Enter instead of Tab?

In a table, pressing Enter creates another line in the same cell, similar to the way you add a new bullet point in a content placeholder. If you press Enter by mistake, you can remove the extra line by pressing ←Bksp.

7 With the insertion point positioned in the second cell of the first row, type **Indiana** and then press Tab. Type **Ohio** and then press Tab to move the insertion point to the first cell in the second row, and then compare your table with Figure 3.20.

Figure 3.20

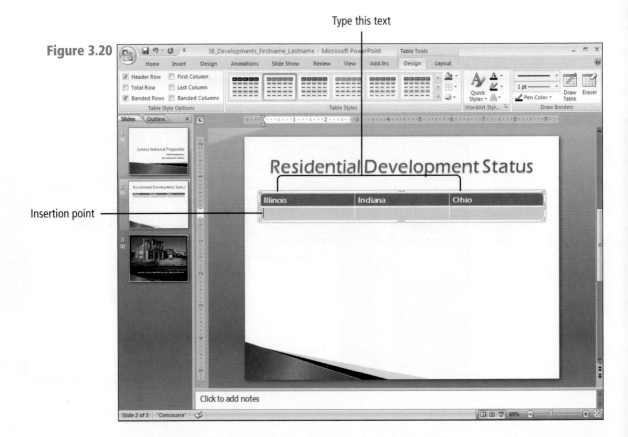

8 With the insertion positioned in the first cell of the second row, type **Hidden Canyon** and then press Enter to create a second line in the cell. Type **250 new homes** and then press Tab. Type **Sienna Estates** and then press Enter to create a second line in the cell. Type **325 new homes** and then press Tab. Type **Vineyard View** and then press Enter. Type **285 new homes** and then press Tab to insert a new blank row.

When the insertion point is positioned in the last cell of a table, pressing Tab inserts a new blank row at the bottom of the table.

9 In the first cell of the third row, type **September 2010** and then press Tab. Type **April 2011** and then press Tab Type **December 2010** and then compare your table with Figure 3.21.

Figure 3.21

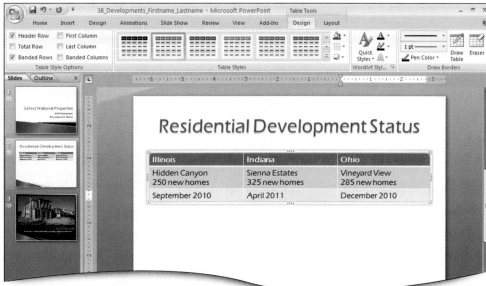

Alert!

Did you add an extra row to the table?

Recall that when the insertion point is positioned in the last cell of the table, pressing Tab inserts a new blank row. If you inadvertently inserted a blank row in the table, on the Quick Access Toolbar, click Undo.

10 **Save** 🖫 the presentation.

Activity 3.10 Modifying the Layout of a Table

You can modify the layout of a table by inserting or deleting rows and columns, changing the alignment of the text in a cell, adjusting the height and width of the entire table or selected rows and columns, and by merging multiple cells into one cell.

1 Click in any cell in the first column, and then click the **Layout tab**. In the **Rows & Columns group**, click the **Insert Left** button.

A new first column is inserted and the width of the columns is adjusted so that all four columns are the same width.

2 Click in the first cell in the *second row*, and then type **Development** Click in the first cell in the third row, type **Projected Completion** and then compare your table with Figure 3.22.

Figure 3.22

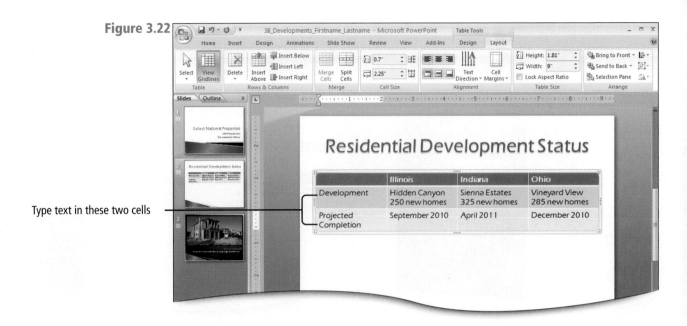

Type text in these two cells

3 With the insertion point positioned in the third row, on the **Layout tab**, in the **Rows & Columns group**, click the **Insert Above** button to insert a new third row. In the first cell type **Percent Sold** and then press Tab. Type the remaining three entries, pressing Tab to move from cell to cell: **75% 50%** and **65%**

More Knowledge

Deleting Rows and Columns

To delete a row or column from a table, click in the row or column that you want to delete. Click the Layout tab, and in the Rows & Columns group, click Delete. In the displayed list, click Delete Columns or Delete Rows.

4 At the center of the lower border surrounding the table, point to the four dots—the sizing handle—to display the ⬍ pointer, as shown in Figure 3.23.

When you drag the pointer down, an outline of the table displays, indicating the new size of the table.

Sizing handle

Figure 3.23

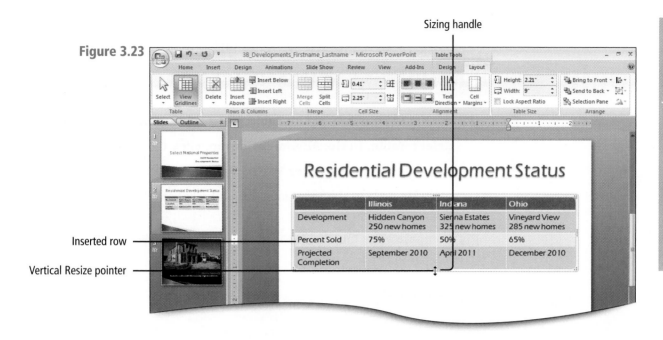

Inserted row

Vertical Resize pointer

---

5 Drag down until the lower left corner of the table outline touches the graphic in the lower left corner of the slide as shown in Figure 3.24, and then release the mouse button to size the table.

Figure 3.24

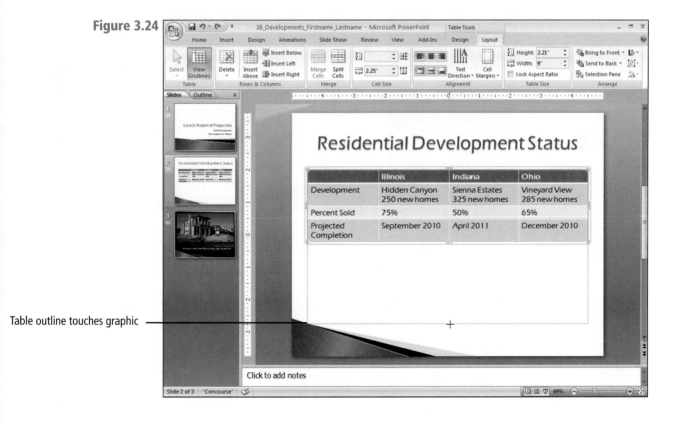

Table outline touches graphic

6 Click in the first cell of the table. On the **Layout tab**, in the **Cell Size group**, click the **Distribute Rows** ⊞ button.

The Distribute Rows option adjusts the height of the rows in the table so that they are equal.

7 On the **Layout tab**, in the **Table group**, click **Select**, and then click **Select Table**. In the **Alignment group**, click the **Center** button ▤, and then click the **Center Vertically** button ▤.

All of the text in the table is centered horizontally and vertically within the cells.

8 Compare your table with Figure 3.25, and then **Save** 🖫 your presentation.

Figure 3.25

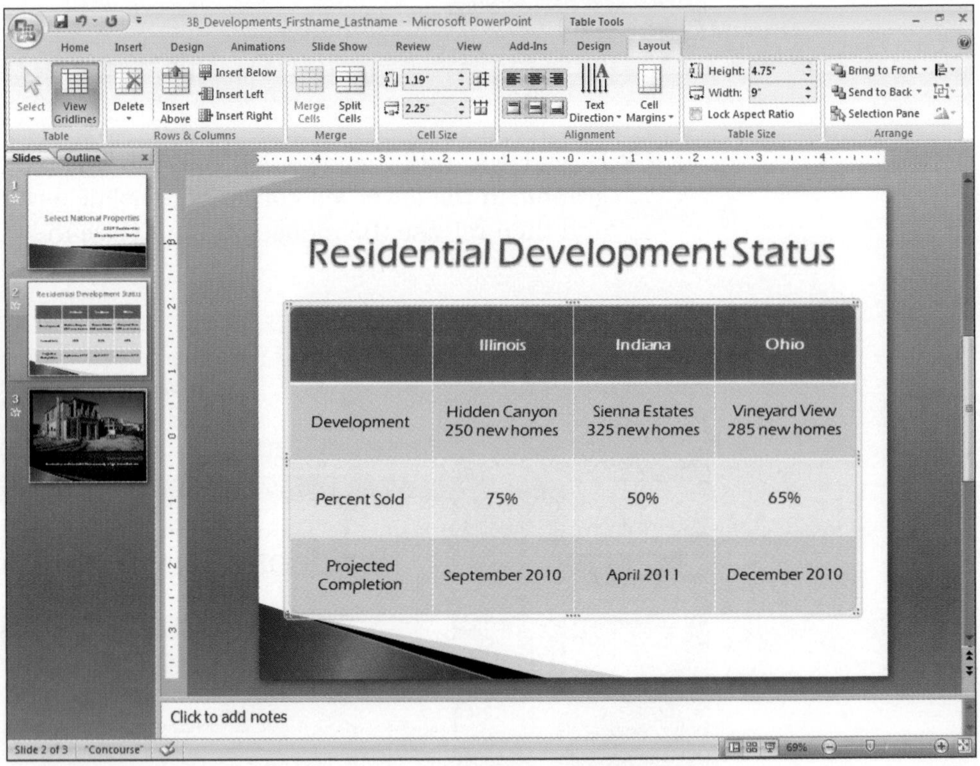

Activity 3.11 Modifying a Table Design

The most efficient way to modify the design of a table is to apply a *table style*. A table style formats the entire table so that it is consistent with the presentation theme. There are color categories within the table styles—Best Match for Document, Light, Medium, and Dark. The Best Match for Document styles provide the best choices for coordinating the table with the document theme.

1 Click in any cell in the table. Click the **Design tab**, and then in the **Table Styles group**, click the **More** button ▼. In the displayed **Table Styles gallery**, point to several of the styles to Live Preview the style.

2 Under **Best Match for Document**, click the second button—**Themed Style 1 – Accent 1**—to apply the style to the table.

3 On the **Design tab**, in the **Table Style Options group**, click to clear the **Banded Rows** check box. Notice that each row except the header row displays in the same color.

The check boxes in the Table Style Options group control where Table Style formatting is applied.

4 Click again to select the **Banded Rows** check box.

5 Move the pointer outside of the table so that is positioned to the left of the first row in the table to display the ➡ pointer, as shown in Figure 3.26.

Figure 3.26

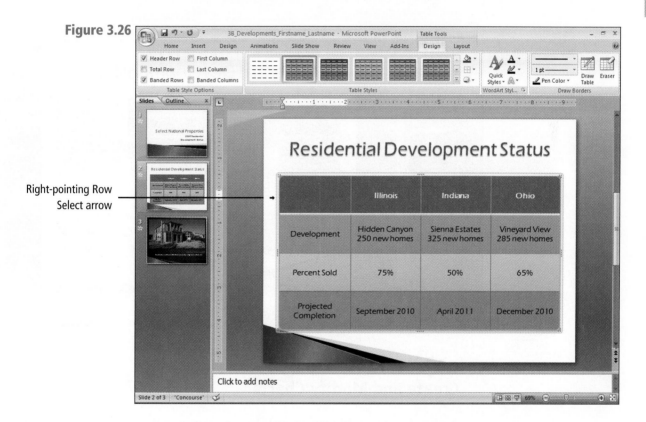

Right-pointing Row
Select arrow

6 With the ➡ pointer pointing to the first row in the table, click the mouse button to select the entire row so that you can apply formatting to the selection. Move the pointer into the selected row, and then right-click to display the Mini toolbar and shortcut menu. On the Mini toolbar, change the **Font Size** to **28**.

More Knowledge

Selecting Columns

To select an entire column, position the pointer above the column that you want to select to display the ⬇ pointer, and then click to select the column.

7 Verify that the first row is still selected. Click the **Design tab**, and then in the **Table Styles group**, click the **Effects** button. Point to **Cell Bevel**, and then under **Bevel**, click the first bevel— **Circle**.

The Bevel effect is applied to the first row in the table.

8 Click in a blank area of the slide, and then compare your slide with Figure 3.27. **Save** the presentation.

Figure 3.27

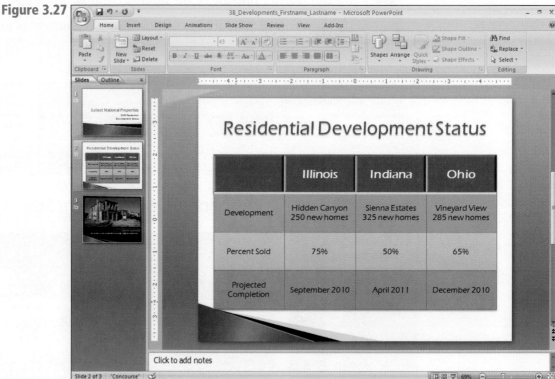

Objective 4
Create and Modify Charts

A **chart** is a graphic representation of numeric data and is often easier to understand than a table of numbers. Chart types frequently used in presentations include bar and column charts, pie charts, and line charts. When you create a chart in PowerPoint, the chart data is stored in an Excel worksheet that is incorporated in the PowerPoint file.

Activity 3.12 Creating a Column Chart and Applying a Chart Style

A **column chart** is useful for illustrating comparisons among related numbers. In this activity you will create a column chart that compares the quarterly 2009 revenue generated by the Residential Development Sector of Select National Properties.

1 Display **Slide 3**, and then add a **New Slide** with the **Title and Content** layout. In the title placeholder, type **2009 Revenue** and then **Center** the title.

2 In the content placeholder, click the **Insert Chart** button to display the **Insert Chart** dialog box. Drag the scroll box to view the types of charts that you can insert in your presentation, and then on the left side of the dialog box, if necessary, click Column.

3 Point to the first chart to display the ScreenTip *Clustered Column*, and then if necessary, click to select it. Compare your screen with Figure 3.28.

Figure 3.28

Clustered Column chart —

4 Click **OK**, and then compare your screen with Figure 3.29.

On the left side of your screen, the PowerPoint window displays a column chart. On the right side of your screen, a Microsoft Office Excel worksheet displays containing vertical columns and horizontal rows. Recall that the intersection of a column and a row forms a small rectangular box referred to as a cell. A cell is identified by the intersecting column letter and row number, which forms the **cell reference**.

The worksheet contains sample data in a data range outlined in blue, from which the chart in the PowerPoint window is generated. You can include additional data by dragging the lower right corner of the data range, and you can replace the sample data to update the chart. The column headings—*Series 1*, *Series 2*, and *Series 3* display in the chart **legend** and the row headings—*Category 1*, *Category 2*, *Category 3*, and *Category 4*—display as **category labels**. The legend identifies the patterns or colors that are assigned to the categories in the chart. The category labels display along the bottom of the chart to identify the categories of data.

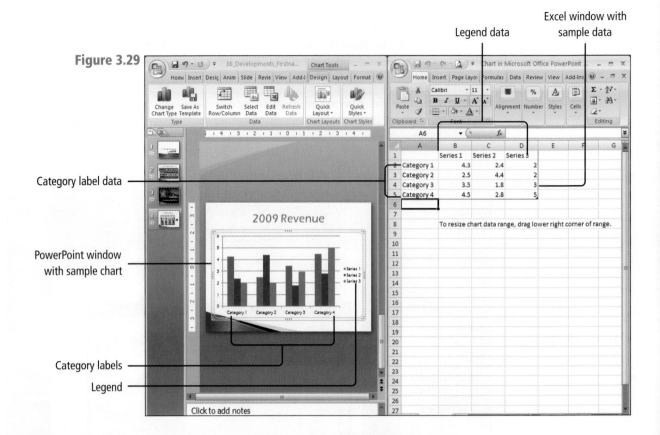

Figure 3.29

Excel window with sample data

Legend data

Category label data

PowerPoint window with sample chart

Category labels

Legend

5 In the Excel window, click in cell **B1**, which contains the text *Series 1*. Type **Illinois** and then press Tab to move to cell **C1**. Notice that the legend in the PowerPoint chart is updated to reflect the change in the Excel worksheet.

6 In cell **C1**, which contains the text *Series 2*, type **Indiana** and then press Tab to move to cell **D1**, which contains the text *Series 3*. Type **Ohio** and then press Tab. Notice that cell **A2**, which contains the text *Category 1*, is selected.

The blue box outlining the range of cells defines the area in which you are entering data. When you press tab in the rightmost cell, the first cell in the next row becomes the active cell. Compare your worksheet with Figure 3.30.

Type these column headings

Figure 3.30

Cell A2 selected

Legend updated to reflect Excel data

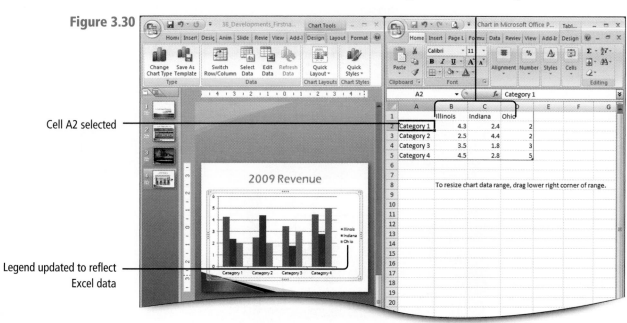

7 Beginning in cell **A2**, type the following data, pressing Tab to move from cell to cell.

	Illinois	Indiana	Ohio
Qtr 1	857300	453228	639852
Qtr 2	1235750	563214	741258
Qtr 3	987653	852147	632145
Qtr 4	789000	674982	

8 In cell **D5**, which contains the value 5, type 753951 and then press Enter so that cell D6 becomes the active cell.

Pressing Enter in the last cell of the blue outlined area maintains the existing data range. Pressing Tab expands the chart data range by including the next row.

9 Compare your worksheet and your chart with Figure 3.31. If you have made any typing errors, click in the cell that you want to change, and then retype the data.

Alert! **Did you press Tab after the last entry?**

If you pressed Tab after entering the data in cell D5, you expanded the chart range. In the Excel window, click Undo.

Each of the twelve cells containing the numeric data that you entered is a ***data point***—a value that originates in a worksheet cell. Each data point is represented in the chart by a ***data marker***—a column, bar, area, dot, pie slice, or other symbol in a chart that represents a single data point. Related data points form a ***data series***; for example, there is a data series for *Illinois*, *Indiana*, and *Ohio*. Each data series has a unique color or pattern represented in the chart legend.

Figure 3.31

Data markers (columns)
represent each data point

Verify that outlined area
does not include Row 6

Data entered in worksheet

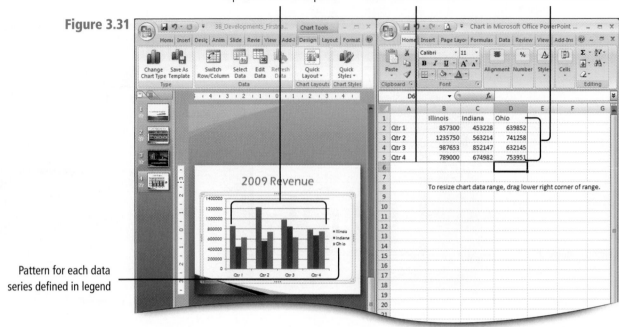

Pattern for each data
series defined in legend

10 In the **Excel window**, click the **Office** button , and then click **Close**.

You are not prompted to save the Excel worksheet because the work-sheet data is a part of the PowerPoint presentation. When you save the presentation, the Excel data is saved with it.

More Knowledge
Editing the Chart Data After Closing Excel

You can redisplay the Excel worksheet and make changes to the data after you have closed Excel. In PowerPoint, click the chart to select it, and then on the Design tab in the Data group, click Edit Data to redisplay the Excel worksheet.

11 If necessary, click on the chart so that it is selected. Click the **Design tab**, and then in the **Chart Styles group**,

click the **More** button ⬇.

The chart styles are numbered sequentially and ScreenTips display the style numbers.

12 In the displayed **Chart Styles gallery**, use the ScreenTips to locate **Style 20**. Click **Style 20** to apply the style to the chart.

13 **Save** 💾 the presentation.

Activity 3.13 Deleting Chart Data and Changing the Chart Type

To analyze and compare annual data over a three-year period, an additional chart must be inserted. Recall that there are a number of different types of charts that you can insert in a PowerPoint presentation. Once a chart has been created, you can easily change the chart type. In this Activity, you will create a column chart and then change it to a line chart.

1 With **Slide 4** displayed, add a **New Slide** with the **Title and Content** layout. In the title placeholder, type **Three-Year Projection** and then

Center ⬚ the title.

2 In the content placeholder, click the **Insert Chart** button ⬚. In the displayed **Insert Chart** dialog box, click the first **Column** chart—**Clustered Column**—and then click **OK**.

3 In the displayed Excel worksheet, click in cell **B1**, which contains the text *Series 1*. Type **Illinois** and then press Tab. Type **Indiana** and then press Tab. Type **Ohio** and then press Tab.

4 Beginning in cell **A2**, type the following data, pressing Tab to move from cell to cell. If you make any typing errors, click in the cell that you want to change, and then retype the data.

	Illinois	Indiana	Ohio
2009	3156951	4238714	2289746
2010	3786521	4095372	2589674
2011	3569782	3679850	3226915

5 In the Excel window, position the pointer over **row heading 5** so that the ➡ pointer displays as shown in Figure 3.32.

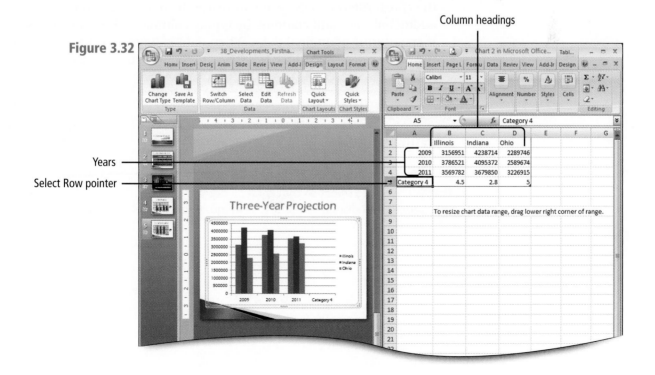

Figure 3.32

6 With the ➡ pointer displayed, click the right mouse button to select the row and display the shortcut menu as shown in Figure 3.33.

Figure 3.33

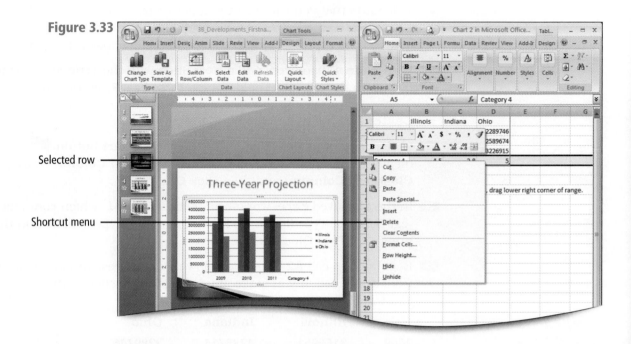

Selected row

Shortcut menu

7 From the shortcut menu, click **Delete** to delete the extra row from the worksheet.

The sample data in the worksheet contains four columns and four rows and the blue outline defining the chart data range is resized. You must delete columns and rows that you do not want to include in the chart. Alternatively, you can resize the data range. You can add additional rows and columns by typing column and row headings and then entering additional data. When data is typed in cells adjacent to the chart range, the range is resized to include the new data.

More Knowledge
Deleting Columns

To delete a worksheet column, position the pointer over the column letter that you want to select so that the ⬇ pointer displays. Right-click to select the column and display the shortcut menu. Click Delete.

■ **Close** X the Excel window.

■ If necessary, click the chart to select it, and then click the **Design tab**. In the **Type group**, click **Change Chart Type**. Under **Line**, click the fourth chart type—**Line with Markers**—and then click **OK**.

The column chart is converted to a *line chart*. A line chart is ideal for this data because line charts are used to show trends over time.

■ In the **Chart Styles group**, click the **More** button ⊡. In the displayed **Chart Styles gallery**, click **Style 26**, and then compare your slide with Figure 3.34.

Figure 3.34

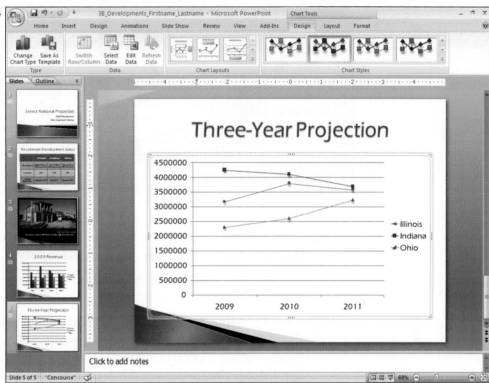

■ **Save** 🖫 the presentation.

Activity 3.14 Animating a Chart

■ Display **Slide 4**, and then click the column chart to select it.

■ Click the **Animations tab**, and then in the **Animations group**, click the **Animate arrow** to display the Animate list as shown in Figure 3.35.

Animate arrow

Figure 3.35

Animate list

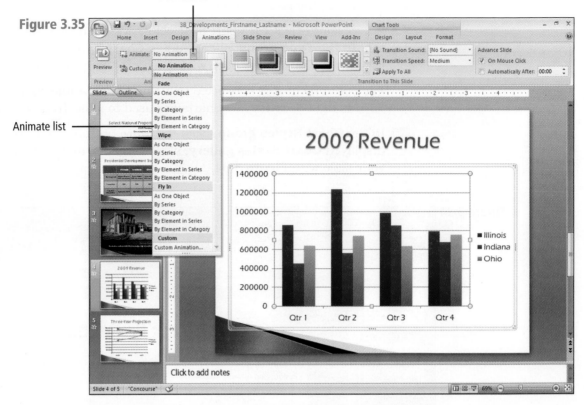

3 Point to several of the **Animate** options to Live Preview the animation effects. Then, under **Wipe**, click **By Category**.

In this chart, the *By Category* option animates the column data markers by Qtr.

4 Click the **Slide Show tab**. In the **Start Slide Show group**, click **From Current Slide** to view the animation on Slide 4. Press Spacebar to display the legend and labels. Press Spacebar again to display the Qtr 1 data. Continue to press Spacebar to advance through the remaining animation effects. After the animations for Slide 4 are complete, press Esc to end the slide show and return to the presentation.

5 Create a **Header and Footer** for the **Notes and Handouts**. Include the **Date and time updated automatically**, the **Page number**, and a **Footer** with the file name **3B_Developments_Firstname_Lastname**

6 Check your *Chapter Assignment Sheet* or *Course Syllabus* or consult your instructor to determine if you are to submit your assignments on paper or electronically. To submit electronically, go to Step 8, and then follow the instructions provided by your instructor.

7 **Print Preview** your presentation, and then print **Handouts, (6 slides per page)**.

8 **Save** the changes to your presentation, and then **Close** the presentation.

 You have completed Project 3B ⎯⎯⎯⎯⎯⎯

There's More You Can Do!

From My Computer, navigate to the student files that accompany this textbook. In the folder **02_theres_more_you_can_do_pg1_36**, locate and open the folder for this chapter. Open and print the instructions for this project, which are provided to you in Adobe PDF format.

Try IT!—Compress Pictures

In this Try IT! exercise, you will compress pictures in a presentation in order to reduce file size.

Content-Based Assessments

Summary

In this chapter, you formatted a presentation by applying background styles, inserting pictures on slide backgrounds, and by changing the theme fonts. You enhanced your presentation by applying animation effects and by changing effect and timing options. You practiced creating tables to present information in an organized manner and you used charts to visually represent data.

Key Terms

Content-Based Assessments

Matching

Match each term in the second column with its correct definition in the first column. Write the letter of the term on the blank line in front of the correct definition.

_____ **1.** A slide background fill variation that combines theme colors in different intensities.

_____ **2.** A theme that determines the font applied to two types of slide text—headings and body.

_____ **3.** The font applied to slide titles.

_____ **4.** The font applied to all slide text except titles.

_____ **5.** Effects used to introduce individual slide elements so that the slide can progress one element at a time.

_____ **6.** Animations that bring a slide element onto the screen.

_____ **7.** A list that indicates the animation effects applied to slide items.

_____ **8.** Animation options that include changing the direction of an effect and playing a sound when an animation takes place.

_____ **9.** A format for information that organizes and presents text and data in columns and rows.

_____ **10.** The intersection of a column and row.

_____ **11.** Formatting applied to an entire table so that it is consistent with the presentation theme.

_____ **12.** A graphic representation of numeric data.

_____ **13.** A type of chart used to compare data.

_____ **14.** A combination of the column letter and row number identifying a cell.

_____ **15.** A chart element that identifies the patterns or colors that are assigned to the categories in the chart.

A Animation effects

B Background style

C Body font

D Cell

E Cell reference

F Chart

G Column chart

H Custom animation list

I Effect options

J Entrance effects

K Font theme

L Headings font

M Legend

N Table

O Table style

Content-Based Assessments

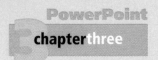

Fill in the Blank

Write the correct word in the space provided.

1. To help an audience understand numeric data and trends, insert a(n) _____ or a(n) _____ on a slide.

2. The charts most commonly used in PowerPoint presentations are _____, _____, _____, and _____.

3. When the background graphics interfere with slide content, you can _____ the background graphics.

4. When you insert a picture on a slide background, it is a good idea to choose a picture that has a(n) _____ area in which you can overlay a text box or title.

5. When you apply a new font theme to the presentation, the text on every slide is updated with the new _____ and _____ fonts.

6. Animation effects focus the audience's attention, providing the speaker with an opportunity to emphasize an important point using the slide element as an effective _____ _____.

7. The most efficient method of animating a SmartArt graphic is to use one of the choices in the _____ _____.

8. When you are delivering a presentation, you display the shortcut menu, and then point to _____ to view a list of the slides in the presentation.

9. You can modify the layout of a table by inserting or deleting _____ and _____.

10. The document matching styles provide the best choices for coordinating the table with the presentation _____.

11. When you create a chart in PowerPoint, the chart data is stored in a(n) _____ worksheet.

12. In a chart, categories of data are identified by _____ _____.

13. A chart value that originates in a worksheet cell is a(n) _____ _____.

14. A group of related data points is a(n) _____ _____.

15. A column, bar, area, dot, pie slice, or other symbol in a chart that represents a single data point is a(n) _____ _____.

Content-Based Assessments

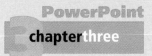
Project 3C — Seniors

In this project, you will apply the skills you practiced from the Objectives in Project 3A.

Objectives: 1. *Customize Slide Backgrounds and Themes;* **2.** *Animate a Slide Show.*

In the following Skills Review, you will edit a presentation created by Marla Rodriguez, the Marketing Director for Select National Properties, which describes a new real estate development in Illinois. Your completed presentation will look similar to the one shown in Figure 3.36.

For Project 3C, you will need the following files:

p3C_Seniors
p3C_Walkway

You will save your presentation as
3C_Seniors_Firstname_Lastname

Figure 3.36

(Project 3C–Seniors continues on the next page)

Content-Based Assessments

(Project 3C–Seniors continued)

1. **Start** PowerPoint. From your student files, **Open** the file **p3C_Seniors**. From the **Office** menu, click **Save As**, and then navigate to your **PowerPoint Chapter 3** folder. In the **File name** box, type **3C_Seniors_ Firstname_Lastname** and then click **Save** to save your presentation.

2. Click the **Design tab**, and then in the **Themes group**, click the **More** button to display the Themes gallery. Under **Built-In**, in the first row, click **Civic**. In the **Themes group**, click the **Colors** button, and then click **Office** to change the theme color for the entire presentation. In the **Background group**, click the **Background Styles** button to display the Background Styles gallery. In the second row, right-click **Style 7**. From the displayed shortcut menu, click **Apply to Selected Slides** to apply the style to **Slide 1**.

3. Display **Slide 2**. On the **Design tab**, in the **Background group**, click the **Background Styles** button to display the Background Styles gallery. In the last row, right-click **Style 11**, and then click **Apply to Selected Slides** to apply the style to **Slide 2**.

4. With **Slide 2** displayed, click the **Home tab**. In the **Slides group**, click the **New Slide arrow**, and then click the **Title Only** layout to create a new Slide 3. In the title placeholder, type **Take a Stroll Around the Lake** Click the **Design tab**, and then in the **Background group**, click to select the **Hide Background Graphics** check box so that the background graphics do not display.

5. In the **Background group**, click the **Background Styles** button, and then click **Format Background**. In the displayed **Format Background** dialog box, if necessary, on the left side of the dialog box,

click **Fill**. On the right side of the dialog box, under **Fill**, click the **Picture or texture fill** option button.

6. Under **Insert from**, click the **File** button. In the displayed **Insert Picture** dialog box, navigate to the location where your student files are located, and then click **p3C_Walkway**. Click **Insert**, and then under **Stretch options**, if necessary, change the **Left**, **Right**, **Top** and **Bottom Offsets** to 0% and then click **Close** to close the **Format Background** dialog box.

7. If necessary, click in the title placeholder. Click the **Format tab**, and then in the **Shape Styles group**, click the **Shape Fill** button. In the last row, click the fourth color—**Dark Blue, Text 2, Darker 50%** so that the text displays against the background.

8. Point to the outer edge of the placeholder to display the ⊕ pointer, and then drag the placeholder down so that its bottom edge aligns with the bottom of the slide. Point to the center, right sizing handle to display the ↔ pointer. Drag to the right so that the right side of the placeholder touches the right edge of the slide. Point to the center, left sizing handle to display the ↔ pointer. Drag to the left so that the left side of the placeholder touches the left edge of the slide.

9. Display **Slide 5**, and then select the subtitle text. On the **Home tab**, click the **Font Color button arrow**. Under **Theme Colors**, in the first row, click the seventh color—**Olive Green, Accent 3**. Click the **Design tab**. In the **Background group**, click the **Background Styles** button, and then click **Format Background**. In

(Project 3C–Seniors continues on the next page)

Content-Based Assessments

(Project 3C–Seniors continued)

the **Format Background** dialog box, if necessary, click the **Solid Fill** option button, and then click the **Color** button. Under **Theme Colors**, in the last row, click the fourth color—**Dark Blue, Text 2, Darker 50%**. Click **Close**.

10. Display **Slide 1**. On the **Design tab**, in the **Themes group**, click the **Fonts** button. Click the first font theme—**Office**, and then scroll through the slides in the presentation, noticing that the font changes have been applied to every slide.

11. Click the **Animations tab**, and then in the **Transition To This Slide group**, click the **More** button. Under **Wipes**, click **Box Out**. Click the **Transition Speed arrow**, and then click **Medium**. Click the **Apply To All** button.

12. Display **Slide 2**, and then click the bulleted list placeholder. In the **Animations group**, click the **Custom Animation** button. At the top of the displayed **Custom Animation** task pane, click the **Add Effect** button, and then point to **Entrance**. Click **More Effects** to display the **Add Entrance Effect** dialog box.

13. At the bottom of the **Add Entrance Effect** dialog box, if necessary, click to select the **Preview Effect** check box. Under **Basic**, click **Blinds**, and then click **OK**. In the **Custom Animation** list, click the **item 1 arrow**, and then click **Effect Options** to display the **Blinds** dialog box.

14. In the **Blinds dialog box**, if necessary, click the **Effect tab**. Under **Enhancements**, click the **After animation arrow**. In the row of colors, click the **fifth color**, and then click **OK** to apply the effect option.

15. Click to select the picture. In the **Custom Animation** task pane, click the **Add Effect** button, point to **Entrance**, and then click **More Effects**. In the displayed **Add Entrance Effect** dialog box, under **Basic**, click **Dissolve In**, and then click **OK**.

16. Near the top of the **Custom Animation** task pane, under **Modify: Dissolve In**, click the **Start arrow**, and then click **After Previous** to display the picture immediately after the last bulleted item displays. In the **Custom Animation task pane**, under **Modify: Dissolve In**, click the **Speed arrow**, and then click **Fast**.

17. Display **Slide 3**, and then click in the title placeholder. In the **Custom Animation** task pane, click **Add Effect**, and then point to **Entrance**. Click **More Effects**. Under **Basic**, click **Fly In**, and then click **OK**. In the **Custom Animation task pane**, click the **Start arrow**, and then click **After Previous** to display the title immediately after the slide transition. If necessary, click the **Direction arrow**, and then click **From Bottom**. **Close** the task pane.

18. Display **Slide 4**, and then select the **SmartArt graphic**. On the **Animations tab**, in the **Animations group**, click the **Animate arrow** to display the Animate list. Under **Wipe**, click **By level at once**.

19. Click the **Slide Show tab**. In the **Start Slide Show group**, click **From Beginning**, and then view your presentation, clicking the mouse button to advance through the slides. Notice the animation that is applied to each slide, and then when the black slide displays, click the mouse button one more time to display the presentation in Normal view.

20. Create a **Header and Footer** for the **Notes and Handouts**. Include only the **Date and time updated automatically**, the **Page**

(Project 3C–Seniors continues on the next page)

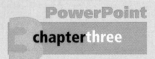

Skills Review

(Project 3C–Seniors continued)

number, and a **Footer** with the file name
3C_Seniors_Firstname_Lastname

21. Check your *Chapter Assignment Sheet* or
Course Syllabus or consult your instructor
to determine if you are to submit your
assignments on paper or electronically. To
submit electronically, go to Step 23, and

then follow the instructions provided by
your instructor.

22. **Print Preview** your presentation, and then
print **Handouts, (6 slides per page)**.

23. **Save** the changes to your presentation,
and then **Close** the presentation.

End You have completed Project 3C

Content-Based Assessments

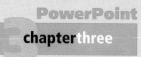
Skills Review

Project 3D — Commercial Developments

In this project, you will apply the skills you practiced from the Objectives in Project 3B.

Objectives: 3. *Create and Modify Tables;* **4.** *Create and Modify Charts.*

In the following Skills Review, you will add a table and two charts to a presentation that Shaun Walker, President of Select National Properties, is creating to apprise investors of the status of several new commercial developments. Your completed presentation will look similar to the one shown in Figure 3.37.

For Project 3D, you will need the following file:

p3D_Commercial_Developments

You will save your presentation as
3D_Commercial_Developments_Firstname_Lastname

Figure 3.37

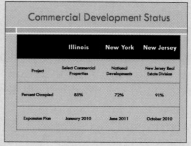

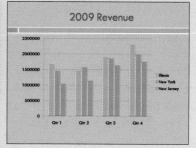

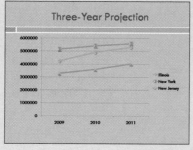

(Project 3D–Commercial Developments continues on the next page)

Skills Review

(Project 3D–Commercial Developments continued)

1. **Start** PowerPoint and from your student files, open **p3D_Commercial_ Developments**. **Save** the presentation in your **PowerPoint Chapter 3** folder as **3D_Commercial_Developments_ Firstname_Lastname**

2. With **Slide 1** displayed, on the **Home tab**, in the **Slides group**, click the **New Slide** button to insert a slide with the **Title and Content** layout. In the title placeholder, type **Commercial Development Status** and then **Center** the title.

3. In the content placeholder, click the **Insert Table** button. In the displayed **Insert Table** dialog box, in the **Number of columns box**, type **4** and then press Tab. In the **Number of rows** box, type **2**. Click **OK** to create a table with four columns and two rows.

4. Click in the second cell of the first row— the first cell will remain blank. Type **Illinois** and then press Tab. With the insertion point positioned in the third cell of the first row, type **New York** and then press Tab. Type **New Jersey** and then press Tab to move the insertion point to the first cell in the second row.

5. With the insertion point positioned in the first cell of the second row, type **Project** and then press Tab. Type **Select Commercial Properties** and then press Tab. Type **National Developments** and then press Tab. Type **New Jersey Real Estate Division** and then press Tab to insert a new blank row.

6. In the first cell of the third row, type **Expansion Plan** and then press Tab. Type **January 2010** and then press Tab Type **June 2011** and then press Tab. Type **October 2010**

7. With the insertion point positioned in the third row, click the **Layout tab**. In the **Rows & Columns group**, click the **Insert Above** button to insert a new third row. In the first cell of the newly inserted row, type **Percent Occupied** and then press Tab. Type the remaining three entries, pressing Tab to move from cell to cell: **85% 72%** and **91%**

8. If necessary, on the **View tab**, in the **Show/Hide group**, click to select the Ruler check box so that the Ruler displays. At the center of the lower border surrounding the table, point to the four dots—the sizing handle—to display the ↕ pointer. Drag down so that the bottom edge of the table is aligned at approximately **3 inches below zero on the vertical ruler**.

9. Click in the first cell of the table. On the **Layout tab**, in the **Cell Size group**, click the **Distribute Rows** button so that the four rows are equal in height. In the **Table group**, click **Select**, and then click **Select Table**. In the **Alignment group**, click the **Center** button, and then click the **Center Vertically** button.

10. Click the **Design tab**, and then in the **Table Styles group**, click the **More** button. Under **Light**, in the second row, click the first style—**Light Style 2**.

11. Move the pointer outside of the table so that is positioned to the left of the first row to display the → pointer. Click to select the entire row. Move the pointer into the selected row, and then right-click to display the Mini toolbar and shortcut menu. On the Mini toolbar, change the **Font Size** to **28**.

(Project 3D–Commercial Developments continues on the next page)

Content-Based Assessments

chapter three   Skills Review

(Project 3D–Commercial Developments continued)

12. With the first row still selected, click the **Design tab**. In the **Table Styles group**, click the **Effects** button. Point to **Cell Bevel**, and then under **Bevel**, click the first bevel—**Circle**.

13. Display **Slide 3**, and then insert a **New Slide** with the **Title and Content Layout**. In the title placeholder type **2009 Revenue** and then **Center** the title. In the content placeholder, click the **Insert Chart** button. In the displayed **Insert Chart** dialog box, point to the first chart to display the ScreenTip *Clustered Column*, and then if necessary, click to select it. Click **OK**.

14. In the **Excel** window, click in cell **B1**, which contains the word *Series 1*. Type **Illinois** and then press (Tab) to move to cell **C1** containing the word *Series 2*. Type **New York** and then press (Tab) to move to cell **D1**. Type **New Jersey**

15. Click in cell **A2**, and then type the data from the following table, pressing (Tab) to move from cell to cell. Be sure that you press (Enter) after the last entry—1753840—not (Tab).

	Illinois	New York	New Jersey
Qtr 1	1657305	1453230	1039855
Qtr 2	1434850	1563360	1141290
Qtr 3	1887640	1852175	1632785
Qtr 4	2286730	1974930	1753840

16. **Close** the Excel window. If necessary, click to select the chart. In the **Chart Tools**, click the **Design tab**, and then in the **Chart Styles group**, click the **More** button. In the displayed **Chart Styles gallery**, click **Style 26**. On the **Animations tab**, in the **Animations group**, click the **Animate**

arrow to display the Animate list. Under **Wipe**, click **As One Object**.

17. With **Slide 4** displayed, insert a **New Slide** with the **Title and Content Layout**. In the title placeholder type **Three-Year Projection** and then **Center** the title. In the content placeholder, click the **Insert Chart** button. In the displayed **Create Chart** dialog box, under **Line**, click **Line with Markers**, and then click **OK**.

18. In the displayed **Excel** worksheet, click in cell **B1**. Type **Illinois** and then press (Tab). Type **New York** and then press (Tab). Type **New Jersey** and then press (Tab).

19. Beginning in cell **A2**, enter the projected revenue for each state and each year as shown in the following table. If you make any typing errors, click in the cell that you want to change, and then retype the data.

	Illinois	New York	New Jersey
2009	4236950	5138726	3289728
2010	4896525	5395318	3589622
2011	5289862	5569857	4026935

20. Position the pointer over **row heading 5** to display the ➡ pointer. Click the right mouse button to select the row. From the displayed shortcut menu, click **Delete** to delete the extra row from the worksheet.

21. **Close** the Excel window. Click the **Design tab**. In the **Chart Styles group**, click the **More** button. In the displayed **Chart Styles gallery**, click **Style 26**.

22. Create a **Header and Footer** for the **Notes and Handouts**. Include only the **Date and**

(Project 3D–Commercial Developments continues on the next page)

Content-Based Assessments

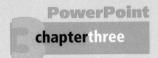
(Project 3D—Commercial Developments continued)

time updated automatically, the **Page number**, and a **Footer** with the file name 3D_Commercial_Developments_Firstname_ Lastname

23. Check your *Chapter Assignment Sheet* or *Course Syllabus* or consult your instructor to determine if you are to submit your assignments on paper or electronically. To

submit electronically, go to Step 25, and then follow the instructions provided by your instructor.

24. **Print Preview** your presentation, and then print **Handouts, (6 slides per page)**.

25. **Save** the changes to your presentation, and then **Close** the presentation.

 You have completed Project 3D

Content-Based Assessments

Mastering PowerPoint

Project 3E — Civic Center

In this project, you will apply the skills you practiced from the Objectives in Project 3A.

Objectives: 1. *Customize Slide Backgrounds and Themes;* **2.** *Animate a Slide Show.*

In the following Mastering PowerPoint project, you will edit a presentation that Shaun Walker, President of Select National Properties plans to show at a Farrington City Council meeting regarding the renovation of City Hall. Your completed presentation will look similar to Figure 3.38.

You will save your presentation as
3E_Civic_Center_Firstname_Lastname

Figure 3.38

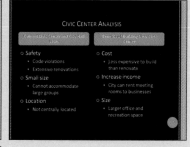

(Project 3E–Civic Center continues on the next page)

Content-Based Assessments

(Project 3E–Civic Center continued)

1. **Start** PowerPoint. From your student files, **Open** the file **p3E_Civic_Center**. **Save** the presentation in your **PowerPoint Chapter 3** folder as **3E_Civic_Center_ Firstname_ Lastname**

2. Apply the **Oriel Theme** to the presentation, and then change the presentation **Background** to the solid black **Style 4** for all of the slides in the presentation. Change the **Fonts** theme to the **Office** theme, which includes the *Cambria* and *Calibri* fonts. Display **Slide 3**, and then change the **Background** to **Style 12** using the **Apply to Selected Slides** option.

3. Display **Slide 4**, and then insert a **New Slide** with the **Title Only** layout. In the title placeholder, type **City of Farrington** and then **Center** the title. On the **Design tab**, in the **Background group**, click to select the **Hide Background Graphics** check box so that the background graphics do not display.

4. Change the **Background Style** by inserting a picture on the background using the **Format Background** dialog box. Under **Fill**, click the **Picture or texture fill** option button. From your student files, insert the file **p3E_City_Hall**, and then verify that the **Stretch options Offsets** are set to **0%**. **Close** the **Format Background** dialog box.

5. Select the title text, and then change the **Font Size** to **54**. Drag the title placeholder up and slightly to the right so that the top of the placeholder aligns with the top edge of the slide and the words *City of Farrington* are centered over *City Hall*.

6. Display **Slide 2**, and then click the bulleted list placeholder. Display the **Custom Animation** task pane, and then display the **Add Entrance Effect** dialog box.

Under **Subtle**, click **Expand**, and then click **OK** to apply the animation to the bulleted list.

7. In the **Custom Animation** list, click the **item 1 arrow**, and then click **Effect Options** to display the **Expand** dialog box. In the **Effect tab** of the **Expand dialog box**, under **Enhancements**, click the **After animation arrow**. In the row of colors, click the **third color**, and then click **OK** to apply the effect option.

8. Display **Slide 3**, and then select the **SmartArt graphic**. Display the **Animate** list, and then under **Fade**, click **As One Object**.

9. Display **Slide 5**, and then click in the title placeholder. In the **Custom Animation** task pane, click **Add Effect**, and then point to **Entrance**. Click **More Effects**. Under **Basic**, apply the **Fly In**, effect. In the **Custom Animation task pane**, click the **Start arrow**, and then click **After Previous** so that the title displays immediately after the slide transition. Click the **Direction arrow**, and then click **From Top**. **Close** the task pane.

10. Under **Wipes**, apply the **Split Horizontal In** transition to all the slides in the presentation. View the slide show from the beginning, clicking the mouse button to advance through the slides. Notice the animation that is applied to each slide, and then when the black slide displays, click the mouse button one more time to display the presentation in Normal view.

11. Create a **Header and Footer** for the **Notes and Handouts**. Include only the **Date and time updated automatically**, the **Page number**, and a **Footer** with the file name **3E_Civic_Center_ Firstname_Lastname**

(Project 3E–Civic Center continues on the next page)

Content-Based Assessments

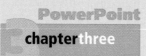
Mastering PowerPoint

(Project 3E–Civic Center continued)

12. Check your *Chapter Assignment Sheet* or *Course Syllabus* or consult your instructor to determine if you are to submit your assignments on paper or electronically. To submit electronically, go to Step 14, and then follow the instructions provided by your instructor.

13. **Print Preview** your presentation, and then print **Handouts, (6 slides per page)**.

14. **Save** the changes to your presentation, and then **Close** the presentation.

 End **You have completed Project 3E** _____

Content-Based Assessments

Mastering PowerPoint

Project 3F — Forest Glen

In this project, you will apply the skills you practiced from the Objectives in Project 3B.

Objectives: 3. *Create and Modify Tables;* **4.** *Create and Modify Charts.*

In the following Mastering PowerPoint project, you will edit a presentation that the Marketing Department will use to showcase the Forest Glen Lifestyle Center. Your completed presentation will look similar to Figure 3.39.

For Project 3F, you will need the following file:

p3F_Forest_Glen

You will save your presentation as
3F_Forest_Glen_Firstname_Lastname

Figure 3.39

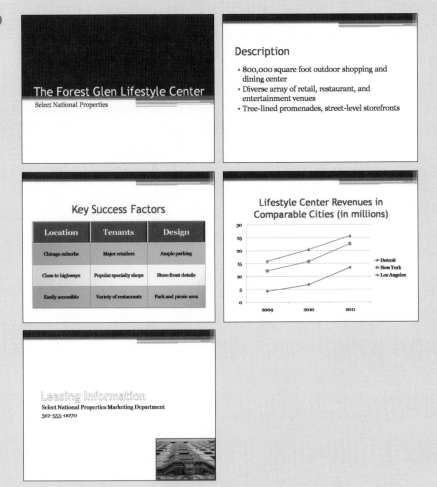

(Project 3F–Forest Glen continues on the next page)

(Project 3F–Forest Glen continued)

1. **Start** PowerPoint. From your student files, **Open** the file **p3F_Forest_Glen**. **Save** the file in your **PowerPoint Chapter 3** folder as 3F_Forest_Glen_Firstname_Lastname

2. Display **Slide 2**, and then insert a **New Slide** with the **Title and Content** layout. In the title placeholder, type **Key Success Factors** and then **Center** the title. In the content placeholder, insert a table with **3 columns** and **4 rows**. Type the following information in the table.

Location	Tenants	Design
Chicago suburbs	Major retailers	Ample parking
Close to highways	Popular specialty shops	Store front details
Easily accessible	Variety of restaurants	Park and picnic area

3. If necessary, display the Ruler. Size the table so that the bottom edge of the table is aligned at approximately **3 inches below zero on the vertical ruler**. On the **Layout tab**, in the **Cell Size group**, click the **Distribute Rows** button so that the four rows are equal in height. Select the table, and then **Center** the text horizontally and vertically in the cells.

4. Apply a **Best Match for Document** table style—**Themed Style 1 – Accent 2**, and in the **Table Style Options**, apply the **Header Row** and **Banded Row** options.

5. Select the first row of the table, change the **Font Size** to **28**, and then apply a **Cell Bevel** effect to the first row—**Circle**.

6. Insert a new slide with the **Title and Content Layout**. In the title placeholder, type **Lifestyle Center Revenues in Comparable Cities (in millions)** and then **Center** the title.

7. In the content placeholder, insert a **Clustered Column** chart, and then replace the data in the Excel window with the data below. Be sure to delete the extra row of data in **Row 5** in the Excel window.

	Detroit	New York	Los Angeles
2009	4.3	12.2	15.9
2010	6.9	15.8	20.4
2011	13.5	22.6	25.7

8. **Close** the Excel window. Select the chart, and then on the **Design tab**, in the **Type group**, click the **Change Chart Type** button. Under **Line**, click **Line with Markers**, and then apply chart **Style 26**.

9. Create a **Header and Footer** for the **Notes and Handouts**. Include only the **Date and time updated automatically**, the **Page number**, and a **Footer** with the file name 3F_Forest_Glen_Firstname_Lastname

10. Check your *Chapter Assignment Sheet* or *Course Syllabus* or consult your instructor to determine if you are to submit your assignments on paper or electronically. To submit electronically, go to Step 12, and then follow the instructions provided by your instructor.

11. **Print Preview** your presentation, and then print **Handouts, (6 slides per page)**.

12. **Save** the changes to your presentation, and then **Close** the presentation.

End **You have completed Project 3F**

Content-Based Assessments

Mastering PowerPoint

Project 3G—Restaurants

In this project, you will apply the skills you practiced from the Objectives in Projects 3A and 3B.

Objectives: 1. *Customize Slide Backgrounds and Themes;* **2.** *Animate a Slide Show;* **3.** *Create and Modify Tables;* **4.** *Create and Modify Charts.*

In the following Mastering PowerPoint project, you will edit a presentation that the president of Select National Properties will make to the National Restaurant Owners Association proposing new restaurant construction in the city of Monroe Heights. Your completed presentation will look similar to Figure 3.40.

For Project 3G, you will need the following files:

New blank PowerPoint presentation
p3G_Tables

You will save your presentation as
3G_Restaurants_Firstname_Lastname

Figure 3.40

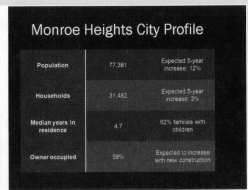

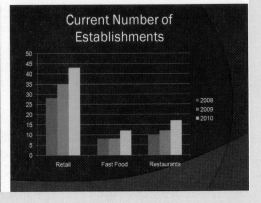

(Project 3G–Restaurants continues on the next page)

Content-Based Assessments

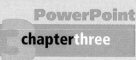
Mastering PowerPoint

(Project 3G–Restaurants continued)

1. **Start** PowerPoint and begin a new blank presentation. In the title placeholder, type **Presentation to the National Restaurant Owners Association** and then in the subtitle placeholder, type **Select National Properties**. **Save** the presentation in your **PowerPoint Chapter 3** folder as **3G_Restaurants_Firstname_Lastname**

2. Apply the **Technic** theme to the presentation, and then change the **Theme Colors** to **Solstice**. Hide the background graphics, and then display the **Format Background** dialog box. Use the **Picture or Texture fill option** to insert the **p3G_Tables** picture on the slide background. Verify that the **Stretch options Offsets** are set to **0%**.

3. Click in the title placeholder, and then on the **Format tab**, click the **Shape Fill** button, and then in the first row of colors, apply the **Brown, Background 2** fill to the title placeholder. In the **Size group**, change the **Height** to **1.5** and the **Width** to **10** and then **Center** the text. Move the title placeholder so that its lower edge aligns with the lower edge of the slide and the left and right edges of the slide and placeholder also align.

4. Click in the subtitle placeholder, and then change the **Shape Fill** color to **Black, Background 1**. Adjust the **Height** to **1.0** and the **Width** to **10** and then **Center** the text and change the **Font Size** to **28**. Drag the subtitle placeholder down so that its lower edge aligns with the top edge of the title placeholder and the left and right edges of the slide and placeholder also align.

5. Insert a **New Slide** with the **Title and Content** layout. Hide the background graphics on this slide.

6. In the title placeholder, type **Monroe Heights City Profile** and then **Center** the title. In the content placeholder, insert a table with **3 columns** and **4 rows**. Type the following table text.

Population	77,381	Expected 5-year increase: 12%
Households	31,482	Expected 5-year increase: 3%
Median years in residence	4.7	62% families with children
Owner occupied	59%	Expected to increase with new construction

7. If necessary, display the Ruler, and then adjust the size of the table so that its lower edge aligns at approximately **3 inches below zero on the vertical ruler**. Select the table, and then **Center** the text horizontally and vertically in the cells. Click **Distribute Rows** so that all of the rows are the same height.

8. Change the table **Design** by changing the **Table Style Options** so that only the **Banded Rows** and **First Column** check boxes are selected. In the **Tables Styles gallery**, under **Dark**, apply **Dark Style 1 – Accent 5**.

9. Add a slide with the **Two Content** layout. In the title placeholder, type **Increased Demand for New Restaurants in Monroe Heights** and then **Center** the title.

10. On **Slide 3**, hide the background graphics. In the placeholder on the left, insert a **SmartArt** graphic. In the **Choose a Smart Graphic** dialog box, click **Pyramid**, click the last pyramid graphic—**Segmented Pyramid**, and then click **OK**.

(Project 3G–Restaurants continues on the next page)

Mastering PowerPoint

(Project 3G–Restaurants continued)

11. In the top triangle shape, type **Large family base** and then click in the center triangle. Type **Clientele from nearby cities** and then click in the lower left triangle. Type **New theaters** and then click in the lower right triangle. Type **New retail outlets**

12. On the **SmartArt Tools**, click the **Design tab**, and then click **Change Colors**. Under **Colorful**, click the last color set—**Colorful Range – Accent Colors 5 to 6.** In the **SmartArt Styles group**, under **3-D**, apply the fourth effect—**Powder**.

13. In the placeholder on the right, type the following bullet points.

    Vibrant economic climate

    Growing population

    Community loyal to local merchants

    Close to major suburbs

    Small number of restaurants relative to population

14. Insert a **New Slide** with the **Title and Content** layout. In the title placeholder, type **Current Number of Establishments** and then **Center** the title.

15. In the content placeholder, insert a **Clustered Column** chart. In the **Excel** worksheet, type the following data, deleting extra columns and rows as necessary.

	2008	2009	2010
Retail	28	35	43
Fast Food	8	8	12
Restaurants	10	12	17

16. **Close** Excel, and then apply **Style 3** to the chart. Use the **Animate** list to apply the **Wipe By Category** animation.

17. Apply the **Wipe Down** transition, and then change the **Transition Speed** to **Medium**. Apply the transition setting to all of the slides in the presentation.

18. Display **Slide 3**, and then select the **SmartArt graphic**. Use the **Animate list** to apply the **Fade As One Object** animation. Click the bulleted list placeholder, and then use the **Custom Animation** task pane to apply the **Blinds Entrance Effect**. View the slide show from the beginning.

19. Create a **Header and Footer** for the **Notes and Handouts**. Include only the **Date and time updated automatically**, the **Page number**, and a **Footer** with the file name **3G_Restaurants_Firstname_Lastname**

20. Check your *Chapter Assignment Sheet* or *Course Syllabus* or consult your instructor to determine if you are to submit your assignments on paper or electronically. To submit electronically, go to Step 22, and then follow the instructions provided by your instructor.

21. **Print Preview** your presentation, and then print **Handouts, (4 slides per page).**

22. **Save** the changes to your presentation, and then **Close** the presentation.

 You have completed Project 3G

Content-Based Assessments

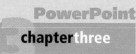

Mastering PowerPoint

Project 3H — Town Centers

In this project, you will apply the skills you practiced from the Objectives in Projects 3A and 3B.

Objectives: 1. *Customize Slide Backgrounds and Themes;* **2.** *Animate a Slide Show;* **4.** *Create and Modify Charts.*

In the following Mastering PowerPoint Assessment, you will edit a presentation that Randall Thomas, Select National Properties Chief Executive Officer, has created to explain the growth of mixed-use town centers in large cities. Your completed presentation will look similar to Figure 3.41.

For Project 3H, you will need the following files:

New blank PowerPoint presentation
p3H_Definition

You will save your presentation as
3H_Town_Centers_Firstname_Lastname

Figure 3.41

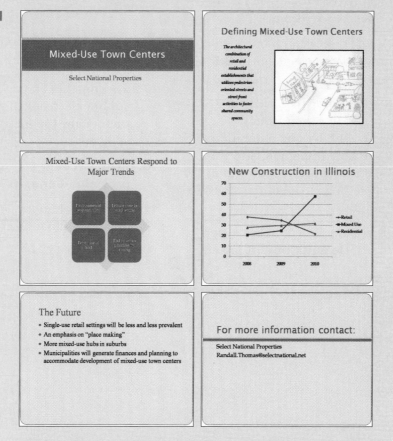

(Project 3H–Town Centers continues on the next page)

Content-Based Assessments

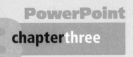

Mastering PowerPoint

(Project 3H–Town Centers continued)

1. **Start** PowerPoint and begin a new blank presentation. In the title placeholder, type **Mixed-Use Town Centers** In the subtitle placeholder, type **Select National Properties** and then **Save** the file in your **PowerPoint Chapter 3** folder as 3H_Town_Centers_Firstname_ Lastname

2. Apply the **Equity** theme to the presentation, and then apply **Background Style 2**. Apply the **Apex Fonts Theme** which consists of the *Lucida Sans* and *Book Antiqua* fonts.

3. From your student files, insert all of the slides from the **p3H_Definition** file. (**Hint**: click the **New Slide arrow**, and then click **Reuse Slides**). Display **Slide 2**, and then click in the text on the left side of the slide. Apply the **Compress Entrance Effect**. **Start** the effect **After Previous**, and change the **Speed** to **Medium**.

4. With **Slide 2** still displayed, move the picture so that its lower edge aligns at **2.5 inches below zero**.

5. Display **Slide 3**. Select the SmartArt graphic, and then use the **Animate** list to apply the **Wipe**, **One by one** animation. Apply the **Wipe Left** transition, and then set the **Transition Speed** to **Fast**. Apply the transition settings to all of the slides in the presentation.

6. With **Slide 3** still displayed, insert a **New Slide** with the **Title and Content** layout.

In the title placeholder, type **New Construction in Illinois** and then **Center** the title. In the content placeholder, insert a **Line with Markers** chart, and then enter the following data in the **Excel** worksheet:

	Retail	Mixed Use	Residential
2008	38	21	28
2009	35	25	30
2010	22	58	32

7. Delete the unused row, and then **Close** Excel. Apply **Chart Style 18**, and then view the slide show from the beginning of the presentation.

8. Create a **Header and Footer** for the **Notes and Handouts**. Include only the **Date and time updated automatically**, the **Page number**, and a **Footer** with the file name 3H_Town_Centers_Firstname_Lastname

9. Check your *Chapter Assignment Sheet* or *Course Syllabus* or consult your instructor to determine if you are to submit your assignments on paper or electronically. To submit electronically, go to Step 11, and then follow the instructions provided by your instructor.

10. **Print Preview** your presentation, and then print **Handouts, (6 slides per page)**.

11. **Save** the changes to your presentation, and then **Close** the presentation.

End You have completed Project 3H

Content-Based Assessments

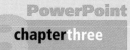
Mastering PowerPoint

Project 3I—Clients

In this project, you will apply the skills you practiced from all the Objectives in Projects 3A and 3B.

Objectives: 1. *Customize Slide Backgrounds and Themes;* **2.** *Animate a Slide Show;* **3.** *Create and Modify Tables;* **4.** *Create and Modify Charts.*

In the following Mastering PowerPoint Assessment, you will edit a presentation that Randall Thomas, Select National Properties Chief Executive Officer will present to a group of prospective clients. Your completed presentation will look similar to Figure 3.42.

For Project 3I, you will need the following files:

p3I_Clients
p3I_Building

You will save your presentation as
3I_Clients_Firstname_Lastname

Figure 3.42

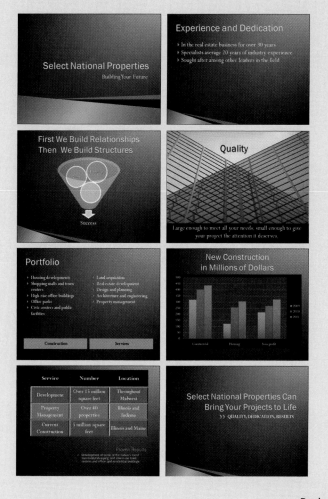

Content-Based Assessments

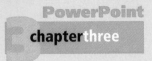
(Project 3I–Clients continued)

1. **Start** PowerPoint. From your student files, **Open** the file **p3I_Clients**. **Save** the file in your **PowerPoint Chapter 3** folder as **3I_Clients_Firstname_Lastname**

2. Apply **Background Style 8** to all of the slides in the presentation, and then change the **Fonts Theme** to **Equity**. Apply the **Split Vertical Out** transition to all of the slides in the presentation.

3. Display **Slide 3**, and then in the content placeholder, insert a **SmartArt** graphic. In the **Choose a SmartArt Graphic** dialog box, insert the **Process** type graphic—**Funnel**. On the **Design tab**, in the **Create Graphic group**, click the **Text Pane** button to display the text pane. Type the following text in each of the four bullet points:

   Integrity

   Trust

   Loyalty

   Success

4. **Close** the text pane. Apply the **Fade As one object** animation to the SmartArt graphic.

5. With **Slide 3** displayed, insert a **New Slide** with the **Title Slide** layout. In the title placeholder, type **Quality** and then in the subtitle placeholder, type **Large enough to meet all your needs; small enough to give your project the attention it deserves.** **Center** the title and subtitle text.

6. With **Slide 4** still displayed, hide the background graphics, and then on the **Background**, insert a picture from your student files—**p3I_Building**. Before closing the **Format Background** dialog box, verify that the **Stretch options Offsets** are set to **0%**.

7. Drag the title placeholder up so that the top edge of the placeholder aligns with the top edge of the slide and the word *Quality* is centered at the intersection of the two buildings. Select **Quality**, and then change the **Font Color** to **Black, Background 1**.

8. Select the subtitle placeholder, and then change the **Shape Fill** color to **Black, Background 1**. Size the placeholder so that it extends from the left edge to the right edge of the slide, and then drag the placeholder down so that its lower edge aligns with the lower edge of the slide.

9. Display **Slide 6**, and then in the content placeholder, insert a **Clustered Column** chart. In the **Excel** worksheet, enter the following data.

	2009	2010	2011
Commercial	318	402	435
Housing	122	257	305
Non-profit	216	268	322

10. Delete the unused row in the worksheet, and then **Close** Excel. Apply chart **Style 42**, and then from the **Animate** list, apply the **Fade By Category** animation.

(Project 3I–Clients continues on the next page)

Content-Based Assessments

Mastering PowerPoint

(Project 3I–Clients continued)

11. Display **Slide 7**, and then in the content placeholder, insert a **Table** with **3 columns** and **4 rows**. Type the following text in the table.

Service	Number	Location
Development	Over 15 million square feet	Throughout Midwest
Property Management	Over 40 properties	Illinois and Indiana
Current Construction	5 million square feet	Illinois and Maine

12. If necessary, display the Ruler. Size the table so that its lower edge aligns at approximately **1 inch below zero on the vertical ruler**. Distribute the rows, and then **Center** the text horizontally and vertically. In the **Tables Styles gallery**, apply **Dark Style 1 – Accent 1**. Select the entire table, and then change the **Font Size** to **28**. With the table still selected, apply the **Circle, Cell Bevel** effect.

13. Display **Slide 8**, and then select the title placeholder. Display the **Custom Animation** task pane, and then apply the **Blinds Entrance Effect**. **Start** the animation **After Previous**, and then change the **Speed** to **Fast**. Apply the same animation effect and settings to the subtitle, and then view the slide show from the beginning.

14. Create a **Header and Footer** for the **Notes and Handouts**. Include only the **Date and time updated automatically**, the **Page number,** and a **Footer** with the file name 3I_Clients_Firstname_Lastname

15. Check your *Chapter Assignment Sheet* or *Course Syllabus* or consult your instructor to determine if you are to submit your assignments on paper or electronically. To submit electronically, go to Step 17, and then follow the instructions provided by your instructor.

16. **Print Preview** your presentation, and then print **Handouts, (4 slides per page)**.

17. **Save** the changes to your presentation, and then **Close** the presentation.

End You have completed Project 3I

Content-Based Assessments

Business Running Case

Project 3J — Business Running Case

In this project, you will apply the skills you practiced in Projects 3A and 3B.

From My Computer, navigate to the student files that accompany this textbook. In the folder **03_business_running_case_pg37_86**, locate and open the folder for this chapter. Open and print the instructions for this project, which are provided to you in Adobe PDF format. Follow the instructions and use the skills you have gained thus far to assist Jennifer Nelson in meeting the challenges of owning and running her business.

 End **You have completed Project 3J** ——————————

Rubric

The following outcomes-based assessments are *open-ended assessments*. That is, there is no specific correct result; your result will depend on your approach to the information provided. Make *professional quality* your goal. Use the following scoring rubric to guide you in *how* to approach the problem and then to evaluate *how well* your approach solves the problem.

The *criteria*—Software Mastery, Content, Format and Layout, and Process— represent the knowledge and skills you have gained that you can apply to solving the problem. The *levels of performance*—Professional Quality, Approaching Professional Quality, or Needs Quality Improvements—help you and your instructor evaluate your result.

	Your completed project is of Professional Quality if you:	Your completed project is Approaching Professional Quality if you:	Your completed project Needs Quality Improvements if you:
1-Software Mastery	Choose and apply the most appropriate skills, tools, and features and identify efficient methods to solve the problem.	Choose and apply some appropriate skills, tools, and features, but not in the most efficient manner.	Choose inappropriate skills, tools, or features, or are inefficient in solving the problem.
2-Content	Construct a solution that is clear and well organized, contains content that is accurate, appropriate to the audience and purpose, and is complete. Provide a solution that contains no errors of spelling, grammar, or style.	Construct a solution in which some components are unclear, poorly organized, inconsistent, or incomplete. Misjudge the needs of the audience. Have some errors in spelling, grammar, or style, but the errors do not detract from comprehension.	Construct a solution that is unclear, incomplete, or poorly organized, containing some inaccurate or inappropriate content; and contains many errors of spelling, grammar, or style. Do not solve the problem.
3-Format and Layout	Format and arrange all elements to communicate information and ideas, clarify function, illustrate relationships, and indicate relative importance.	Apply appropriate format and layout features to some elements, but not others. Overuse features, causing minor distraction.	Apply format and layout that does not communicate information or ideas clearly. Do not use format and layout features to clarify function, illustrate relationships, or indicate relative importance. Use available features excessively, causing distraction.
4-Process	Use an organized approach that integrates planning, development, self-assessment, revision, and reflection.	Demonstrate an organized approach in some areas, but not others; or, use an insufficient process of organization throughout.	Do not use an organized approach to solve the problem.

Outcomes-Based Assessments

Problem Solving

Project 3K — Coral Ridge

In this project, you will construct a solution by applying any combination of the Objectives found in Projects 3A and 3B.

For Project 3K, you will need the following file:

New blank PowerPoint presentation

You will save your presentation as
3K_Coral_Ridge_Firstname_Lastname

Select National Properties has developed a new housing development in the suburbs of Chicago. Randall Thomas, CEO, will be making a presentation on the new community to prospective home buyers. The development—Coral Ridge—consists of 55 homes with two different floor plans. The first floor plan—The Oakmont—includes 1,700 square feet and has 3 bedrooms and 2 baths. There is a fireplace in the family room and the kitchen and bathrooms have tile countertops. The second floor plan—The Seneca—has 1,925 square feet with 4 bedrooms and 2 baths. There are fireplaces in the master bedroom and in the family room, and the bathrooms and kitchens have granite countertops. The community has an excellent school district and is accessible by major highways.

Create a presentation with six slides that describes the community and the development. Apply a design template of your choice, change the background style on at least one slide, and include a picture on the background of one slide. Using the information in the preceding paragraph, insert a slide with a table that compares the two floor plans. Apply slide transitions and animation. Add the file name to the Notes and Handouts footer and check the presentation for spelling errors. Save the presentation as **3K_Coral_Ridge_Firstname_Lastname** and submit it as directed.

Note: You can find many appropriate images available to Office users. To access these images, click the Insert tab, and then from the Illustrations group, click the Clip Art button. In the Clip Art task pane, type a key word—such as *construction*—in the *Search for* box. You can specify the image type (clip art or photographs) and where to search. The largest variety of photographs can be found by including Web Collections in the *Search in* box. You can also use images from earlier projects in this chapter, or images from your personal collection.

End You have completed Project 3K

Problem Solving

Project 3L — Land Development

In this project, you will construct a solution by applying any combination of the Objectives found in Projects 3A and 3B.

For Project 3L, you will need the following file:

New blank PowerPoint presentation

You will save your presentation as
3L_Land_Development_Firstname_Lastname

Select National Properties owns several land parcels in the growing community of Lake Monahan. The Chief Financial Officer, Morgan Bannon-Navarre, is creating a presentation for the members of the Lake Monahan Real Estate Association that describes the available parcels located in three areas of the city: North, South, and Central. Create a presentation with four to six slides describing the community and the parcels using the following information.

The City of Lake Monahan is a vacation destination for many out-of-state families. The lake provides opportunities for water sports, fishing, and boating. Select National Properties invested in the city by purchasing several land parcels approximately 15 years ago and is now ready to develop and sell the parcels.

In your presentation, insert one slide with a picture on the slide background that depicts the lake. (See the note at the end of project 3K for ideas on locating images). Insert a slide titled **Available Parcels** and use the data below to create a table describing the parcels.

	North	South	Central
Parcels	10	15	18
Size	.75 acres	1.2 acres	1.05 acres
Price	$45,000	$68,000	$52,000

Insert a slide with the title **Average Parcel Price** and then insert an appropriate chart using the following data.

	North	South	Central
2008	$22,300	$55,675	$41,375
2009	$32,500	$62,420	$45,850
2010	$45,000	$68,000	$52,000

Use formatting and animation techniques that you learned in this chapter to create a professional presentation. Add the file name to the Notes and Handouts footer and check for spelling errors. Save the presentation as **3L_Land_Development_Firstname_Lastname** and submit it as directed.

End **You have completed Project 3L**

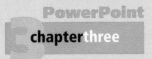

Problem Solving

Project 3M — Renovation

In this project, you will construct a solution by applying any combination of the Objectives found in Projects 3A and 3B.

> **For Project 3M, you will need the following files:**
>
> New blank PowerPoint presentation
> p3M_Scaffold
> p3M_Scaffold2

**You will save your presentation as
3M_Renovation_Firstname_Lastname**

Select National Properties' Vice President of Construction, Michael Wentworth, is presenting the status of The Lincoln Plaza—a large renovation project—to the project investors. Use the following information to create a presentation with at least four slides, including a table and a chart.

The Lincoln Plaza consists of three 10-story buildings on the perimeter of a large courtyard. The renovation is taking place in three overlapping phases: Exteriors which are 75 percent complete with an expected completion date of September 2009; Interior Infrastructure which is 55 percent complete with an expected completion date of June 2010; and Courtyard Enhancements which is 35 percent complete with an expected completion date of December 2010. The cost of each phase in millions is estimated as follows:

	Exterior	Interior	Courtyard
Labor	22.6	33.8	5.25
Materials	36.9	48.7	12.6

Apply an appropriate design and background style, and change the Fonts Theme. Format the background of one slide using one of the pictures provided with your student files—p3M_Scaffold or p3M_Scaffold2. Apply chart and table styles and slide transitions and animation. Add the file name to the Notes and Handouts footer and check for spelling errors. Save the presentation as **3M_Renovation_Firstname_Lastname** and submit it as directed.

 End **You have completed Project 3M** _____

Outcomes-Based Assessments

Problem Solving

Project 3N—High School

In this project, you will construct a solution by applying any combination of the Objectives found in Projects 3A and 3B.

For Project 3N, you will need the following file:

New blank PowerPoint presentation

You will save your presentation as
3N_High_School_Firstname_Lastname

Select National Properties has been chosen as one of three contractors bidding on the construction of a new high school in Monroe Heights. Company President Shaun Walker is making a presentation to the Monroe Heights School Board regarding the company's proposal. Create a presentation that includes one or two slides with information about the company, one slide with a table, one slide with a chart, and two slides that include slide backgrounds with pictures of school facilities. (See the note at the end of project 3K for ideas on locating images). Use the following information for your presentation.

Select National Properties is a diversified real estate company which develops, builds, manages, and acquires a wide variety of properties nationwide. Among the company's portfolio of properties are shopping malls, mixed-use town center developments, high-rise office buildings, office parks, industrial buildings and warehouses, multifamily housing developments, educational facilities, and hospitals. Residential developments are mainly located in and around the company's hometown, Chicago; commercial and public buildings in the portfolio are located nationwide. The company is well respected for its focus on quality and commitment to the environment and economic development of the areas where it operates. Use the information below to create a slide with a table using columns 1, 2, and 3 and a slide with a chart using columns 1 and 4.

	Description	Completion	Estimate
Buildings	45 classrooms	January 2010	$18.0 million
Network	Wireless access	July 2010	$0.5 million
Pool	Outdoor Olympic size with bleachers	December 2010	$1.5 million
Exteriors	Parking, landscape	July 2010	$5.0 million

Apply an appropriate design and background style and change the Fonts Theme. Apply chart and table styles and slide transitions and animation. Add the the file name to the Notes and Handouts footer and check for spelling errors. Save the presentation as **3N_High_School_Firstname_Lastname** and submit it as directed.

End **You have completed Project 3N**

Problem Solving

Project 30 — Recruiting

In this project, you will construct a solution by applying any combination of the Objectives found in Projects 3A and 3B.

For Project 30, you will need the following file:

New blank PowerPoint presentation

**You will save your presentation as
30_Recruiting_Firstname_Lastname**

To serve the growing national needs of the company, the Board of Directors for Select National Properties has decided to open an office in Austin, Texas. Nancy Chung, Human Resources Director, will be recruiting college graduates for professional opportunities in the new location. Use the following information to create a presentation that she can show at several colleges she is visiting.

Select National Properties is a diversified real estate company which develops, builds, manages, and acquires a wide variety of properties nationwide. The mission of Select National Properties is to be a leader in the real estate development business through a commitment to integrity, high ethical standards, and operational expertise. Among the company's portfolio of properties are shopping malls, mixed-use town center developments, high-rise office buildings, office parks, industrial buildings and warehouses, multifamily housing developments, educational facilities, and hospitals. Residential developments are mainly located in and around the company's hometown, Chicago; commercial and public buildings in the portfolio are located nationwide. The company is well respected for its focus on quality and commitment to the environment and economic development of the areas where it operates.

(Project 30–Recruiting continues on the next page)

Problem Solving

(Project 3O—Recruiting continued)

The following table includes information about the sales growth of Select National Properties in millions over the past 10 years.

Sector	2000	2005	2010
Residential	125	158	209
Commercial	167	219	282
Land	95	132	191

The following table summarizes the types of positions for which Nancy is recruiting.

Position	Description	Starting Salary
Civil Engineer	Applies knowledge of design, construction procedures, zoning and building codes, and building materials to render structural designs.	$45,000
Project Manager	Prepares and reviews facilities plans, construction contract bid documents, and specifications for projects. Monitors project progress and costs.	$53,000
Accountant	Performs professional accounting work, including auditing, analyzing, and verifying fiscal records and reports.	$38,000

Create a presentation that includes at least six slides, including background information on the company, and a table and a chart using the preceding information. Apply an appropriate design and background style and change the Fonts Theme. Apply chart and table styles, and slide transitions and animation. Add the file name to the Notes and Handouts footer and check for spelling errors. Save the presentation as **3O_Recruiting_Firstname_Lastname** and submit it as directed.

End **You have completed Project 3O** ————

Outcomes-Based Assessments

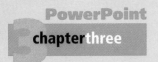
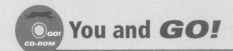 You and *GO!*

Project 3P — You and *GO!*

In this project, you will construct a solution by applying any combination of the skills you practiced from the Objectives in Projects 3A and 3B.

From My Computer, navigate to the student files that accompany this textbook. In the folder **04_you_and_go_pg87_102**, locate and open the folder for this chapter. Open and print the instructions for this project, which are provided to you in Adobe PDF format. Follow the instructions to create a presentation about the registration process at your school.

 You have completed Project 3P ————————

GO! with Help

Project 3Q — *GO!* with Help

There are a number of different types of charts that you can create in PowerPoint. Use Microsoft Office PowerPoint Help to learn about the different types of charts in PowerPoint.

1 **Start** PowerPoint. At the far right end of the Ribbon, click the **Microsoft Office PowerPoint Help** button.

2 In the **Type words to search for** box, type **Chart Types** and then press Enter.

3 Click the **Available chart types** link, and then read the information on each type of chart. When you are through, **Close** the Help window, and then **Close** PowerPoint.

 You have completed Project 3Q ————————

Group Business Running Case

Project 3R—Group Business Running Case

In this project, you will apply all the Objectives found in Projects 3A and 3B.

Your instructor may assign this group case project to your class. If your instructor assigns this project, he or she will provide you with information and instructions to work as part of a group. The group will apply the skills gained thus far to help the Bell Orchid Hotel Group achieve its business goals.

End **You have completed Project 3R** ─────────────

chapterfour

Enhance a Presentation with Advanced Table, Chart, and Animation Techniques

OBJECTIVES

At the end of this chapter you will be able to:

OUTCOMES

Mastering these objectives will enable you to:

1. Format Tables

2. Modify a Table Using the Draw Borders Feature

PROJECT 4A
Create and Format Tables

3. Create and Modify a Pie Chart

4. Apply Custom Animation Effects

PROJECT 4B
Present Information Using Charts and Advanced Animation Techniques

City of Lake Glendale

The City of Lake Glendale is a growing tourist destination located in Arizona. The year-round warm weather and the sun-drenched waters of the 23-mile long lake that the city borders make it a prime vacation setting for tourists who enjoy water activities. The city's growth and economic well being is closely tied to the burgeoning tourism industry. The City Council has responded to the city's growth by encouraging the development of new restaurants and hotels as well as retail establishments that cater to lakeside activities.

Enhance a Presentation with Advanced Table, Chart, and Animation Techniques

Tables and charts can be used to present information in an organized and effective manner. A well formatted table or chart enhances a presentation by providing your audience with a visual aid that quickly demonstrates important data. Your presentations can also be enhanced by applying animations, such as emphasis and exit effects, that draw attention to important slide elements. Animation options can be used to precisely control the timing of effects to achieve maximum impact.

Project 4A **Recreation**

In Activities 4.1 through 4.8 you will create a presentation that Marina Hernandez, Director of Parks and Recreation, is developing for a City Council meeting. The presentation will describe the children's recreation programs in the City of Lake Glendale. Your completed presentation will look similar to Figure 4.1.

For Project 4A, you will need the following files:

New blank PowerPoint presentation
p04A_Football
p04A_Soccer
p04A_Volleyball

**You will save your presentation as
4A_Recreation_Firstname_Lastname**

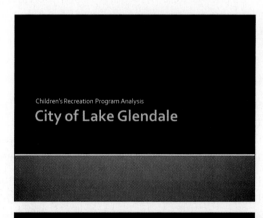

Figure 4.1
Project 4A—Recreation

Objective 1
Format Tables

Recall that a table is a format for information that organizes and presents text and data in columns and rows, and that the intersection of a column and row is a cell. A table can be quickly formatted by applying a Table Style. You can also format a table by merging and splitting table cells, adjusting row heights and column widths, and changing the text direction.

Activity 4.1 Creating a Table

> ## Note — Comparing Your Screen with the Figures in This Textbook
>
> Your screen will match the figures shown in this textbook if you set your screen resolution to 1024 x 768. At other resolutions, your screen will closely resemble, but not match, the figures shown. To view your screen's resolution, on the Windows desktop, right-click in a blank area, click Properties, and then click the Settings tab.

1 **Start** PowerPoint and begin a new blank presentation. From the **Office** menu [icon], click **Save As**. Navigate to the location where you are saving your files, create a folder with the name **PowerPoint Chapter 4** and then click **OK**. In the **File name** box, type **4A_Recreation_ Firstname_Lastname** and then click **Save** to save your presentation.

2 On the **Design** tab, in the **Themes** group, click the **More** button [icon], and then under **Built-In**, click the **Module theme**. In the title placeholder, type **City of Lake Glendale** and in the subtitle placeholder, type **Children's Recreation Program Analysis**

3 With **Slide 1** displayed, on the **Home tab**, in the **Slides group**, click the **New Slide** button to insert a slide with the **Title and Content** layout. In the title placeholder, type **Recreation Trends** and then **Center** [icon] the title. In the content placeholder, type each of the following four bullet points.

Preschool age children account for the largest number of enrollments

Organized sports are the most popular activities in the 11 to 18 age group

Mommy-and-Me classes fill more rapidly than other activities

Art and music classes continue to be popular across all age groups

4 With **Slide 2** displayed, on the **Home tab**, in the **Slides group**, click the **New Slide** button to insert a slide with the **Title and Content** layout. In the title placeholder, type **Highest Demand Activities** and then **Center** [icon] the title.

5 On the **Insert tab**, in the **Tables group**, click the **Table** button to display a grid with columns and rows, as shown in Figure 4.2.

You can drag to select the number of columns and rows that your table will contain.

Figure 4.2

Insert Table button

Table grid

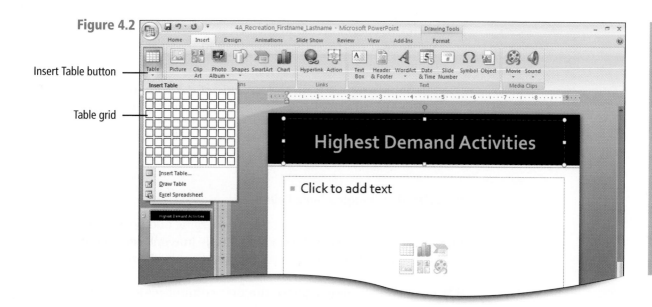

6 Move your pointer into the first box in the grid and notice that it is outlined, indicating that it is selected. A single cell displays in the slide. Drag to the right and down to select two columns and four rows as shown in Figure 4.3, noticing that a table displays on the slide.

Above the grid, the text *2x4 Table* displays, indicating the number of columns and rows that you have selected.

Indicates size of table   4 rows

Figure 4.3

2 columns

Table

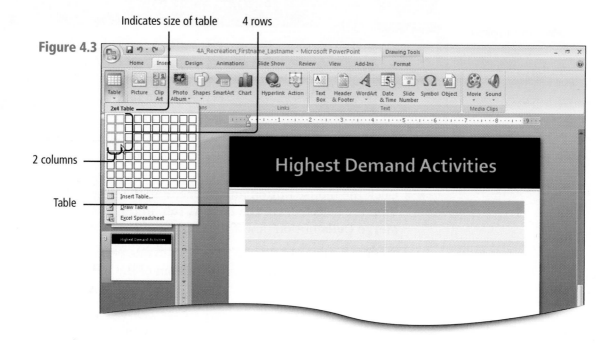

7 With two columns and four rows selected, click to create the table. Notice that the insertion point is blinking in the upper left cell of the table.

The table extends from the left side of the content placeholder to the right side, and the two columns are equal in width. By default, a Table Style is applied to the table.

8 **Save** 🖫 the presentation.

Activity 4.2 Merging Table Cells

You can modify the layout of a table by merging and splitting table cells. The **merge cells** feature combines selected cells into one cell. The **split cells** feature divides a selected cell into the number of cells that you specify.

1 Position the pointer above the first column to display the ⬇ pointer as shown in Figure 4.4.

Figure 4.4

Select Column pointer

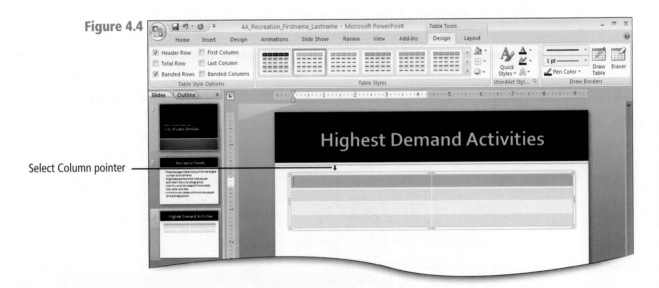

2 Click the mouse button and notice that all of the cells in the first column are selected. On the **Layout tab**, in the **Merge group**, click the **Merge Cells** button, and then compare your table with Figure 4.5.

The four selected cells are merged into one vertical cell that extends from the top of the table to the bottom of the table.

Merge Cells button

Figure 4.5

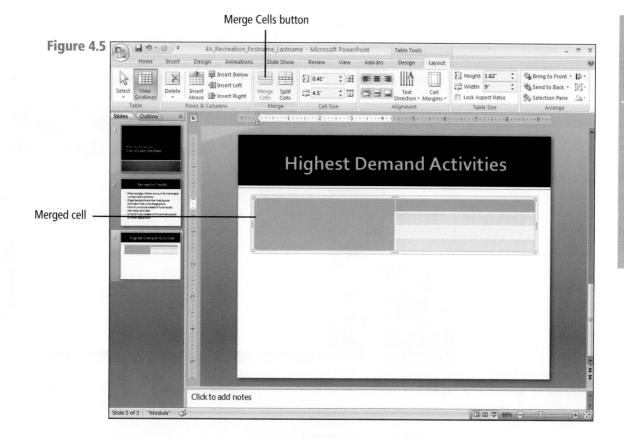

Merged cell

---

3 With the insertion point positioned in the merged cell, type **Participants Under 18 Years of Age** and then press [Tab]. Type the following text in the remaining four cells, pressing [Tab] to move from cell to cell.

Organized sports including football, soccer, and volleyball

Music lessons including guitar and voice training

Art lessons including animation and ceramics

Mommy-and-Me classes

4 Compare your slide with Figure 4.6, and then **Save** 🖫 your presentation.

Figure 4.6

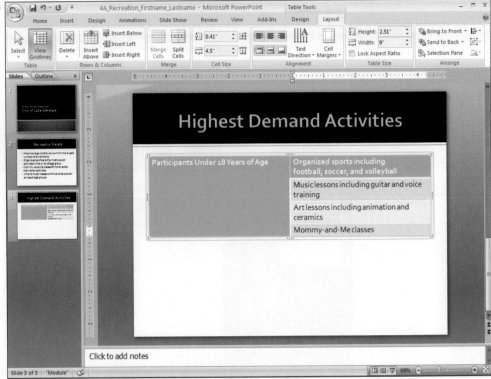

More Knowledge

Splitting Cells

To split a cell into multiple cells, click in the table cell that you want to split. On the Layout tab, in the Merge group, click the Split Cells button, and then enter the number of columns and rows into which you want to split the cell.

Activity 4.3 Adjusting Column Widths and Table Sizes

When a table is resized, the columns and rows are resized proportionately. You can adjust the width of individual columns if the information is best displayed in columns with varying widths.

1 Verify that the Rulers display. If they do not, click the View tab, and then in the Show/Hide group, click the Ruler check box.

2 Point to the border between the first and second column to display the ⊹ pointer, as shown in Figure 4.7.

Figure 4.7

Rulers displayed

Pointer positioned
between columns

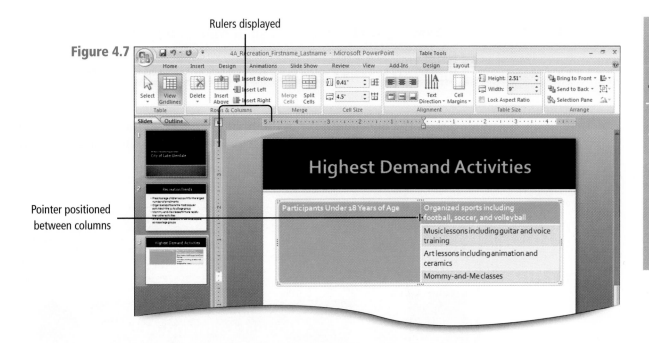

3 Drag to the left so that the dashed vertical line displays between
Under and *18* as shown in Figure 4.8.

The dashed vertical line indicates the size of the columns.

Figure 4.8

Drag pointer here

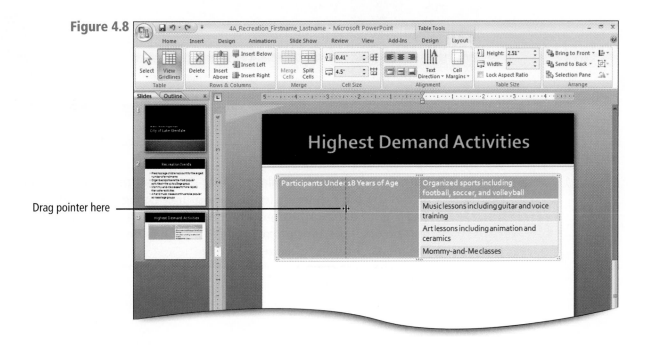

4 Release the mouse button to resize the columns.

The text in the first column wraps to three lines and the text in each
cell in the second column displays on one line.

5 At the bottom center of the border that surrounds the table, locate sizing handle, indicated by four dots. Point to the sizing handle to display the ⬍ pointer, as shown in Figure 4.9.

Figure 4.9

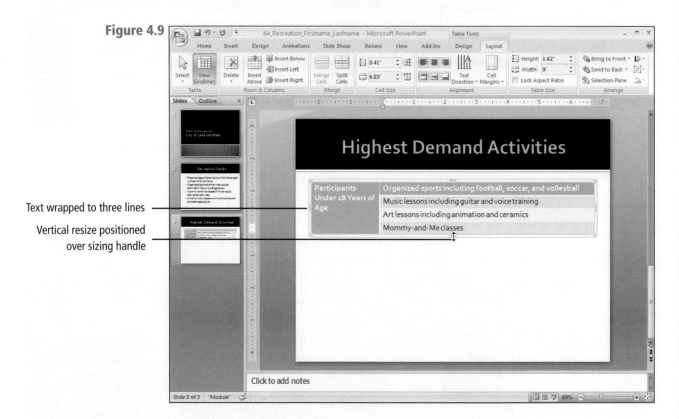

Text wrapped to three lines

Vertical resize positioned over sizing handle

6 With the ⬍ pointer displayed, drag down and notice that the new size of the table is indicated by an outline. Using the vertical ruler and Figure 4.10 as your guide, continue to drag down until the table outline displays at approximately **2.5 inches below zero**. Release the mouse button to resize the table.

Figure 4.10

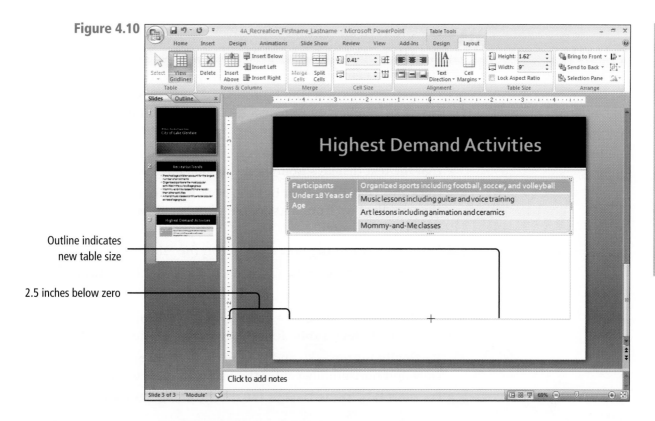

Outline indicates
new table size

2.5 inches below zero

7 **Save** 🖫 the presentation.

Activity 4.4 Changing Text Direction

When text is typed in a table, it displays horizontally from left to right.
You can change the text direction so that it displays vertically from top to
bottom or from bottom to top.

1 On **Slide 3**, click in the first column of the table. On the **Layout tab**,
in the **Alignment group**, click the **Text Direction** button to display
the gallery of text direction options as shown in Figure 4.11.

Text Direction options

Figure 4.11

2 Click **Rotate all text 90°**.

The text displays from top to bottom and is aligned at the right top edge of the column.

3 Click the **Text Direction** button again, and then click **Rotate all text 270°**. Notice that the text displays from bottom to top, and is aligned at the lower left edge of the column.

4 Click the **Text Direction** button again, and then click **Stacked**. Notice that the text displays from top to bottom, one character at a time.

5 Click the **Text Direction** button. click **Rotate all text 270°** so that the text displays from bottom to top and is aligned at the lower left edge of the column.

6 Select the text in the first column. On the Mini toolbar, click the **Font Size button arrow** 44 ▾, click **32**, and then **Center** ≡ the text.

7 On the **Layout tab**, in the **Table group**, click the **Select** button, and then click **Select Table**. In the **Alignment group**, click the **Center Vertically** button ▤, and then click the **Center** button ≣ to vertically and horizontally center the text within each cell.

8 On the **Table Tools Design tab**, in the **Table Styles group**, click the **More** button ▾. In the **Table Styles gallery**, under **Medium**, in the third row, click the second style—**Medium Style 3 – Accent 1**. In the **Table Style Options group**, *clear* the **Header Row** check box, and then select the **First Column** check box.

9 Compare your table with Figure 4.12, and then **Save** 🖫 the presentation.

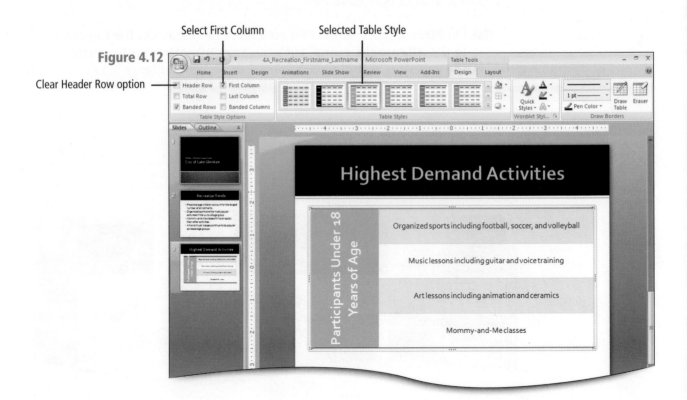

Figure 4.12

Select First Column

Selected Table Style

Clear Header Row option

Objective 2
Modify a Table Using the Draw Borders Features

The Draw Borders feature allows for exact placement of borders that are drawn in a table. Cells can be split and merged using the Draw Table and Eraser tools.

Activity 4.5 Inserting a Table on a Title Only Slide

When you insert a table on a slide with a content placeholder, the table extends from the left edge of the placeholder to the right edge of the placeholder. You can use a Title Only layout to insert a table that is not as wide as a content placeholder.

1 With **Slide 3** displayed, on the **Home tab**, in the **Slides group**, click the **New Slide button arrow** to display the **Layout gallery**. Click **Title Only**. In the title placeholder, type **Participation in Team Sports** and then **Center** 	the title.

Alert!

Did you insert a slide with the title and content layout?
If you clicked the New Slide button instead of the arrow, you inserted a slide with the Title and Content Layout. To change the layout, in the Slides group, click the Layout button, and then click Title Only.

---

2 On the **Insert tab**, in the **Tables group**, click the **Table** button to display the table grid. Drag to select **3 columns** and **3 rows**, as shown in Figure 4.13, and then click to create the table.

The Title Only layout does not include a content placeholder for the table. When a table is inserted on a slide that does not contain a content placeholder, the default width of the table is 6.67 inches and the table is positioned so that its upper edge aligns with the lower edge of the title placeholder.

Figure 4.13

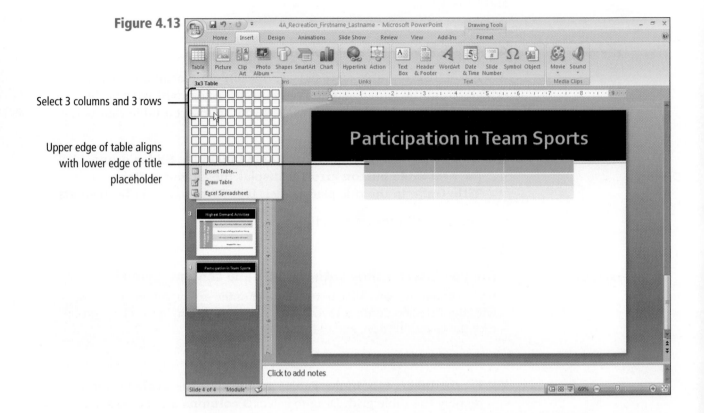

Select 3 columns and 3 rows

Upper edge of table aligns with lower edge of title placeholder

3 Point to the top border that surrounds the table to display the ⊕ pointer. Drag down approximately **0.5 inch** so that the top edge of the table aligns at **1.5 inches above zero**.

4 Point to the the sizing handle—the four dots at the bottom center of the table—to display the ↕ pointer. Drag down to **3 inches below zero** to resize the table, and then compare your table with the one in Figure 4.14.

Figure 4.14

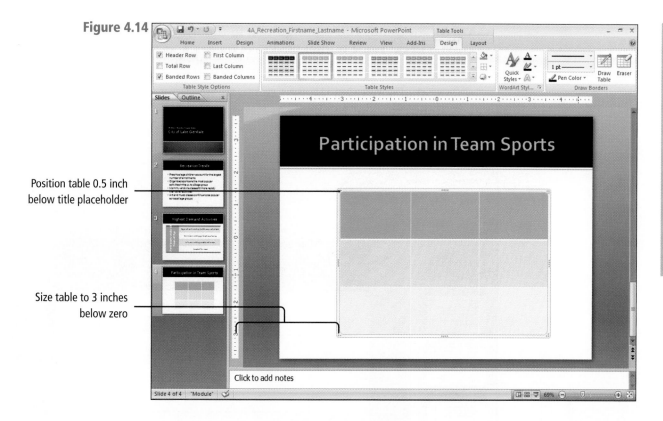

Position table 0.5 inch
below title placeholder

Size table to 3 inches
below zero

5 On the **Table Tools Design tab**, in the **Table Styles group**, click the **More** button ⏷. In the **Table Styles gallery**, under **Medium**, click the first style—**Medium Style 1**. In the **Table Style Options group**, clear the **Header Row** check box.

6 **Save** 💾 the presentation.

Activity 4.6 Applying Borders to a Table Using the Draw Table Feature

The Table Styles and Table Style Options apply borders and fill colors to a table, and the Merge options provide a method for combining and splitting cells. You can accomplish similar tasks by drawing the borders that you want to apply using the options in the Draw Borders group.

1 If necessary, click the table to select it. On the **Table Tools Design tab**, look at the **Draw Borders group** and notice the options that display. The table in Figure 4.15 describes each of the Draw Borders options.

Draw Borders options

Pen Style	Changes the style of the line used to draw borders
Pen Weight	Changes the thickness of the line used to draw borders
Pen Color	Changes the color of the line used to draw borders
Draw Table	Activates the Draw Table pointer used to draw the borders of a table
Eraser	Activates the Eraser pointer used to erase the borders of a table

Figure 4.15

2 On the **Table Tools Design tab**, in the **Draw Borders group**, click the **Draw Table** button, and then move the pointer into the table to display the ⟦🖉⟧ pointer. Position the pointer over the light gray border that separates the first cell in the first row from the second cell in the first row, as shown in Figure 4.16.

Figure 4.16

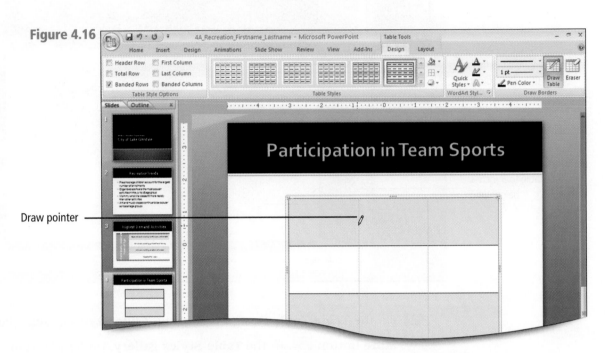

Draw pointer

3 Hold down the mouse button and drag down to the third row so that a dashed line covers the light gray line, as shown in Figure 4.17.

The light gray line that separates the first and second column provides a visual indication of the cell border, but when the table is viewed in the slide show, it will not display. The dashed line indicates where the solid black border will be drawn.

Figure 4.17

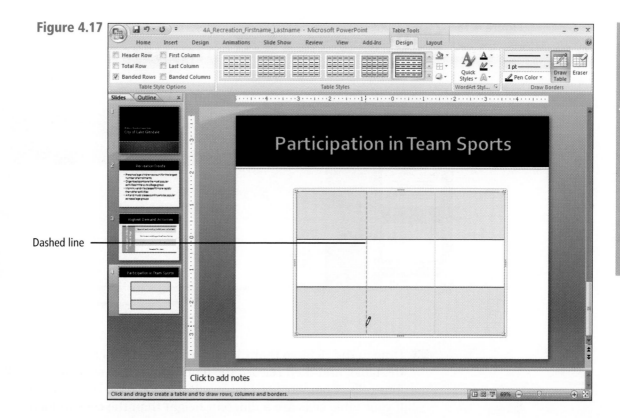

Dashed line

4 Release the mouse button to draw the solid, 1 pt, black border. Notice that the ⬚ pointer is still active.

Did you create a table border instead of a line?
When you released the mouse, did you create a table border instead of a line? If so, on the Quick Access Toolbar, click Undo. Then, repeat Steps 2, 3, and 4 and be sure to position the pointer directly over the border line to target the border.

5 Using the technique that you practiced in Steps 2, 3, and 4, apply a **solid, 1 pt, black border** to the light gray line separating the second and third columns so that all of the borders in the table display as solid black lines.

6 Position the ⬚ pointer at approximately the midpoint of the line that separates the first cell in the first row from the second cell in the first row as shown in Figure 4.18.

Figure 4.18

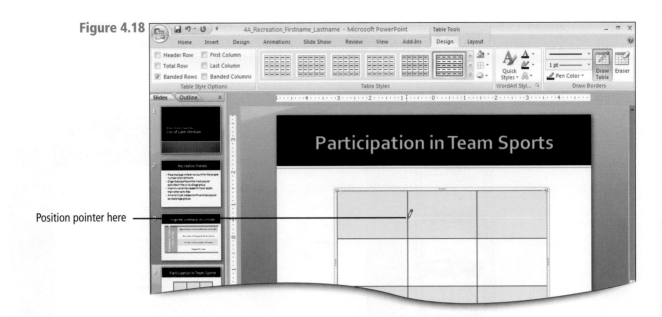

Position pointer here

7 Drag to the right so that the dashed line extends to the right edge of the table, and then release the mouse button to split the two cells into four cells. Compare your table with Figure 4.19. Do not be concerned if your table cells are a different height than the cells in Figure 4.19.

In addition to adding borders to *existing* cells, you can create *new* rows, columns, and cells using the Draw Borders feature.

Figure 4.19

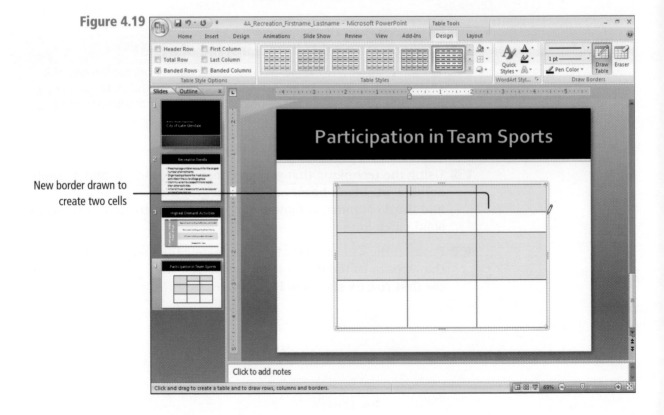

New border drawn to create two cells

Does the border extend across all three columns?

If you moved the mouse slightly to the left when drawing the line in Step 7, a cell was added in column one. On the Quick Access Toolbar, click the Undo button, and then repeat Steps 6 and 7.

8 Repeat Step 7 to draw two more lines in the second and third table rows, and then compare your table with Figure 4.20. Do not be concerned if your table's cells are a different height than those shown in Figure 4.20.

Draw these lines

Figure 4.20

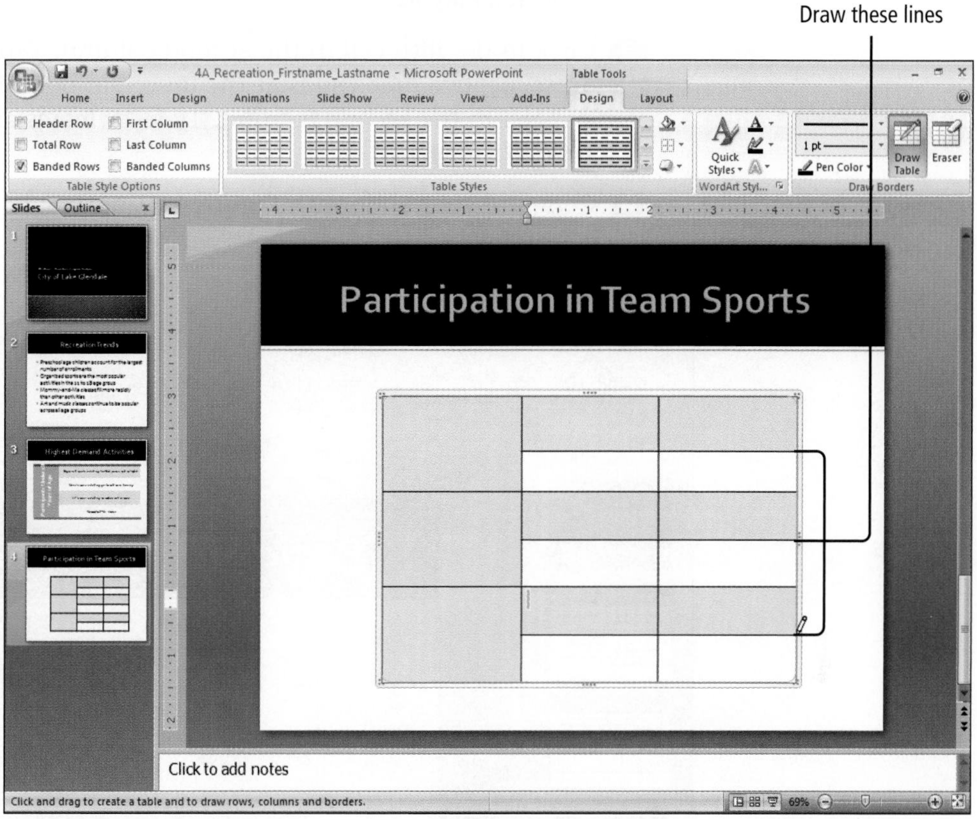

9 On the **Layout tab**, in the **Cell Size group**, click the **Distribute Rows** button so that all of the cells in the second and third columns are the same height.

10 Move the pointer back into the table and notice that the pointer is still active. Press [Esc] to display the pointer. **Save** the presentation.

More Knowledge

Activating the Draw Table Pointer

Changing the Pen Style, Pen Weight, and Pen Color options activates the Draw Table pointer.

Activity 4.7 Merging Cells Using the Eraser

Recall that the Merge Cells feature combines multiple cells into one cell. An alternative method of merging cells is the **Eraser**. You can use the Eraser to merge cells by deleting existing borders.

1 With **Slide 4** displayed, click in the first cell in the second column. Type **Soccer** and then press Tab two times so that the insertion point is positioned in the second cell in the second column. Type **22 Teams** and then press Tab. Type **250 Players**

2 Click in the third cell in the second column. Type **Football** and then press Tab two times so that the insertion point is positioned in the fourth cell in the second column. Type **4 Teams** and then press Tab. Type **160 Players**

3 Click in the fifth cell in the second column. Type **Volleyball** and then press Tab two times so that the insertion point is positioned in the last cell in the second column. Type **15 Teams** and then press Tab. Type **175 Players**

4 Compare your slide with Figure 4.21 and make any necessary corrections.

Figure 4.21

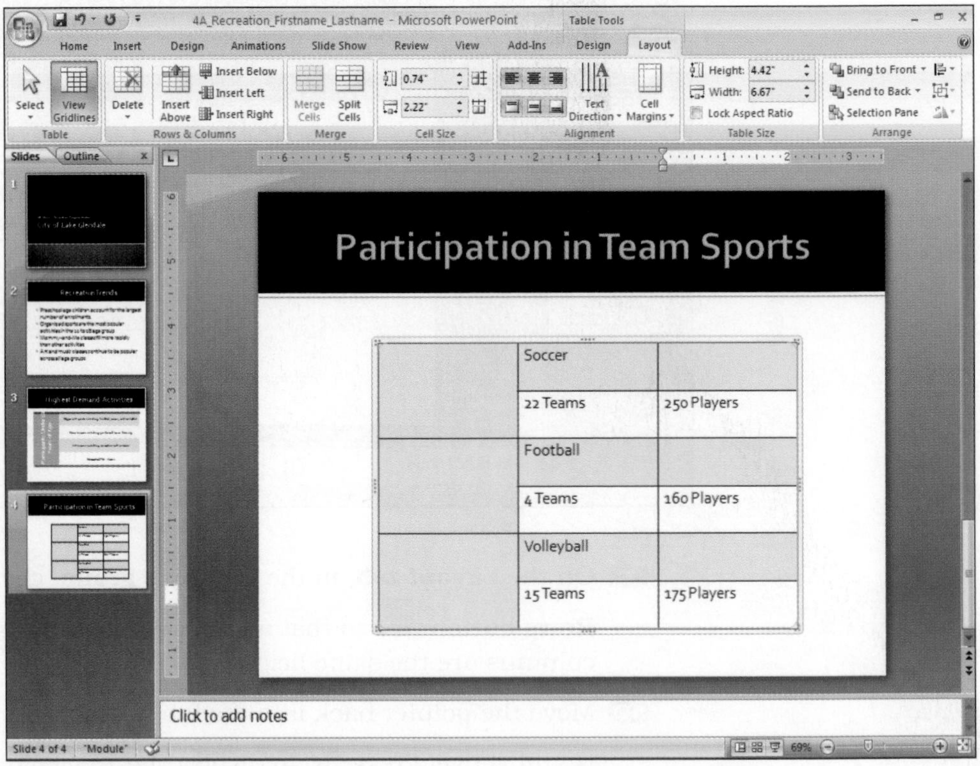

5 On the **Table Tools Design tab**, in the **Draw Borders** group, click the **Eraser** button. Position the [eraser] pointer over the border to the right of the word *Soccer* as shown in Figure 4.22.

Figure 4.22

Position Eraser pointer here ——————

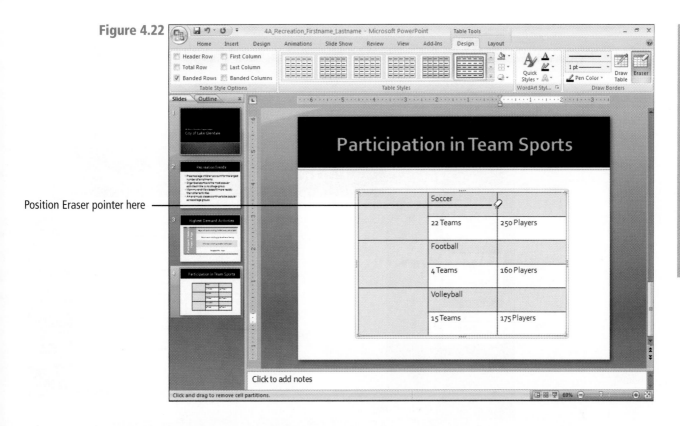

6 With the 🖉 pointer positioned over the border, click the left mouse button.

The border is erased and the two cells in columns two and three are merged. The 🖉 pointer remains active.

7 Using the technique that you just practiced, delete the borders to the right of the words *Football* and *Volleyball*, and then press Esc so that the Eraser is no longer active. Compare your table with the one in Figure 4.23.

Figure 4.23

These cells merged

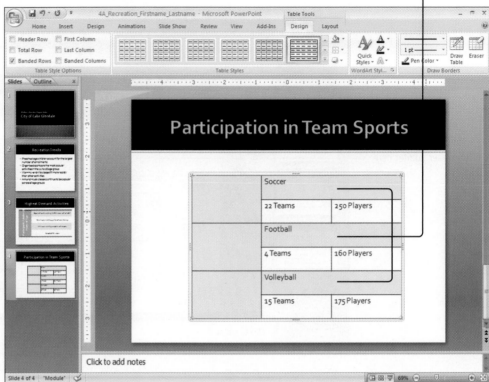

8 Drag to select all of the cells in **column 2** and **column 3**. Right-click over the selection, and then on the Mini toolbar, click the **Center** button ▤. Click the **Font Size button arrow** `44 ▾`, and then click **28**.

9 With **column 2** and **column 3** still selected, click the **Layout tab**. In the **Alignment group**, click the **Center Vertically** button ▤, and then **Save** 🖫 the presentation.

Activity 4.8 Filling a Cell with a Picture

Some Table Styles include shading in table cells. A table can also be formatted by filling a cell with a picture.

1 With **Slide 4** displayed, click in the first cell of the first row. On the **Table Tools Design tab**, in the **Table Styles group**, click the **Shading button arrow** 🎨 ▾, and then click **Picture**. Navigate to the location where your student data files are stored, and then click **p04A_Soccer**. Click **Insert**.

The cell is filled with the image of the soccer ball. You can still type in the cell if you choose to do so as the picture is part of the cell background.

Alert!

Is the cell filled with a color instead of a picture?

If you clicked the Shading *button* instead of the Shading *button arrow*, the cell was filled with the color displayed on the Shading button. On the Quick Access Toolbar, click the Undo button, and then repeat Step 1.

2 In the second and third cells of the first column, repeat Step 1, inserting **p04A_Football**, and **p04A_Volleyball**, and then compare your table with Figure 4.24.

Figure 4.24

Insert three pictures

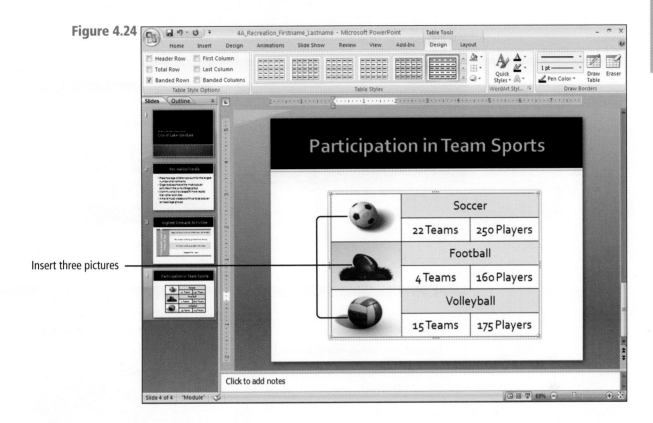

3 Insert a **Header and Footer** for the **Notes and Handouts**. Include the **Date and time updated automatically**, the **Page number**, and a **Footer** with the file name **4A_Recreation_Firstname_Lastname**

4 Check your *Chapter Assignment Sheet* or your *Course Syllabus* or consult your instructor to determine if you are to submit your assignments on paper or electronically. To submit electronically, go to Step 6, and then follow the instructions provided by your instructor.

5 **Print Preview** your presentation, and then print **Handouts (4 Slides Per Page)**.

6 **Save**  the changes to your presentation, and then close the presentation.

End You have completed Project 4A

Project 4B Analysis

In Activities 4.9 through 4.16, you will edit a presentation that Marina Hernandez, Director of Parks and Recreation, has created that presents an analysis of children's recreation programs in the City of Lake Glendale. Your completed presentation will look similar to Figure 4.25.

For Project 4B, you will need the following file:

p04B_Analysis

**You will save your presentation as
4B_Analysis_Firstname_Lastname**

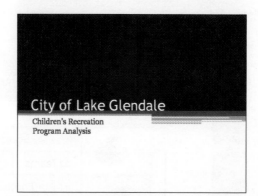

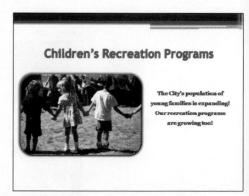

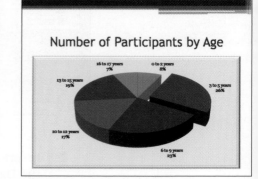

Figure 4.25
Project 4B—Analysis

Objective 3
Create and Modify a Pie Chart

Recall that a chart is a graphic representation of numeric data. A *pie chart* is used to illustrate percentages or proportions, and includes only one series of data.

Activity 4.9 Creating a Pie Chart and Widening an Excel Column

1 **Start** PowerPoint. From your student files, open the file **p04B_Analysis**. Display the **Office** menu , click **Save As**, and then navigate to your **PowerPoint Chapter 4** folder. In the **File name** box, type **4B_Analysis_ Firstname_Lastname** and then click **Save** to save your file.

2 Display **Slide 3**, and then add a **New Slide** with the **Title and Content** layout. In the title placeholder, type **Number of Participants by Age** and then **Center** the title.

3 In the content placeholder, click the **Insert Chart** button to display the **Insert Chart** dialog box. Click **Pie**, and then click the second pie chart—**Pie in 3-D**—as shown in Figure 4.26.

Figure 4.26

Pie in 3-D

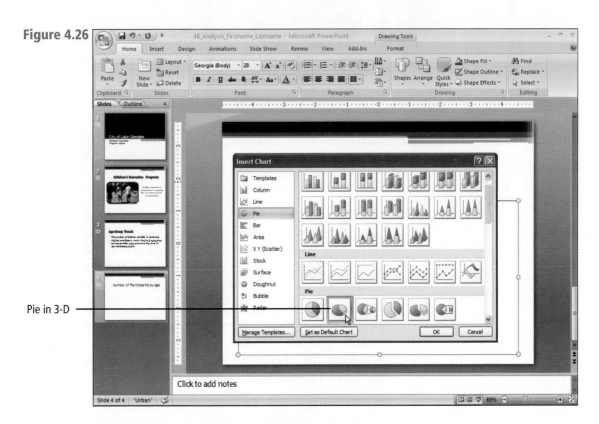

4 Click **OK**, and then compare your screen with Figure 4.27.

On the left side of your screen, the PowerPoint window displays a pie chart. On the right side of your screen, a Microsoft Office Excel worksheet displays. Recall that a pie chart includes only one series of data. Thus, the worksheet contains sample data for one data series.

Each of the cells containing the numeric data is a data point represented in the pie chart by a data marker. Recall that a data point is a value that originates in a worksheet cell, and that a data marker is a column, bar, area, dot, pie slice, or other symbol in a chart that represents a single data point. In this case, the data marker is a pie slice, each with a unique color.

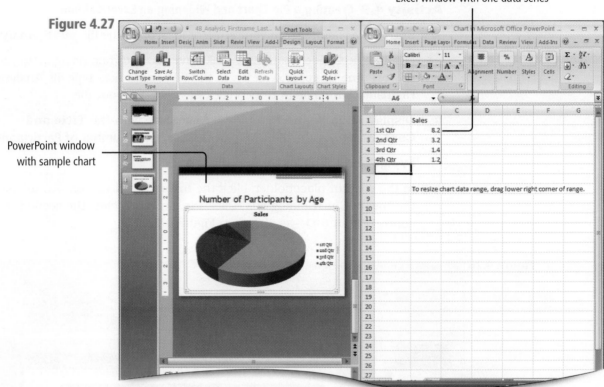

Figure 4.27

Excel window with one data series

PowerPoint window with sample chart

5. In the Excel window, click in cell **B1**, which contains the word *Sales*. Type **Number** and then press Tab to make cell **A2**, which contains the text *1st Qtr*, the active cell. Type **0 to 2 years** and then press Tab to move to cell **B2**. Notice that the legend in the PowerPoint chart is updated to reflect the change in the Excel worksheet.

6. In cell **B2**, type **240** and then press Tab to move to cell **A3**, which contains the text *2nd Qtr*. Type **3 to 5 years** and then press Tab to move to cell **B3**. Type **850** and then press Tab. In cell **A4**, type **6 to 9 years** and then press Tab. In cell **B4**, type **730** and then press Tab. In cell **A5**, type **10 to 12 years** and then press Tab. Type **550** and then press Tab.

Recall that the blue box outlining the chart data range defines the area in which you are entering data. When you press Tab in the last cell in the chart data range cell, the first cell in the next row becomes the active cell and the data range is expanded.

7. Compare your worksheet and your chart with Figure 4.28. If you have made any typing errors, click in the cell that you want to change, and then retype the data. Notice that in cell **A5**, two letters in the word *years* do not display.

If the text is too long for a cell and the cell to the right contains other data, only the text that will fit in the cell displays.

Data entered in worksheet

Figure 4.28

Part of word does not display

New row added to data range

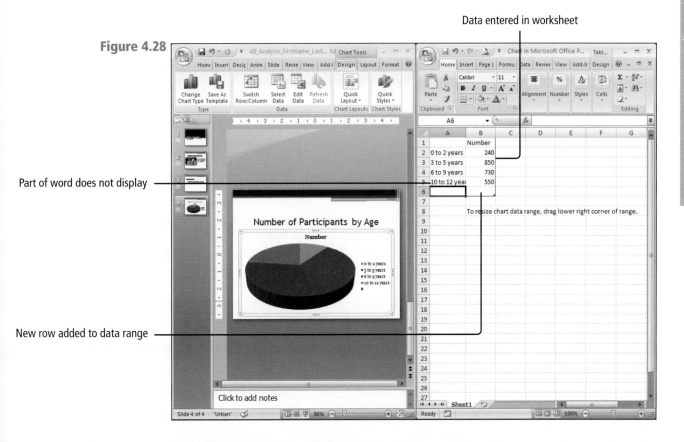

8 In the Excel window, in the **column heading area**, point to the vertical line between **column A** and **column B** to display the ⊞ pointer, as shown in Figure 4.29.

Position pointer between columns A and B

Figure 4.29

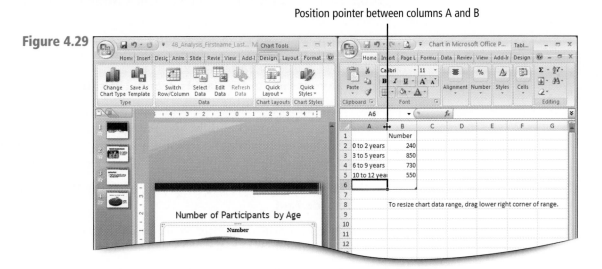

9 Double-click the mouse button to AutoFit the column width and display all of the text in cell **A5**.

AutoFit widens the column to accommodate the longest cell entry in the column. In this case, the column is widened so that all of the text in cell A5 displays.

10 In cell **A6**, type **13 to 15 years** and then press ⎄Tab. Type **620** and then press ⎄Tab. Type **16 to 17 years** and then press ⎄Tab. Type **240** and then press ⎄Enter.

11 **Close** ✕ the Excel window, and then Save 🖫 the presentation.

Activity 4.10 Modifying Chart Layout and Data Labels

Chart layout refers to the combination of chart elements that you want to display, including the title, legend, and data labels. In a pie chart, *data labels* are frequently used instead of a legend to identify the category name of each pie slice and to indicate the percentage of the total or a value that each slice represents.

1 With **Slide 4** displayed, if necessary, click the chart to select it. On the **Chart Tools Design tab**, in the **Chart Layouts group**, click the **More button** ⏷. From the displayed **Chart Layout gallery**, click **Layout 6**.

The applied chart layout includes a title, legend, and data labels with the percent that each slice represents of the total.

2 On the **Layout tab**, in the **Labels group**, click the **Legend** button.

The Legend gallery displays the legend placement options. You can turn the legend off, and you can move it so that it is positioned above, below, or to the side of the chart. The legend is often turned off in a pie chart because data labels are used to identify the pie slices.

3 Click **None** to turn off the legend. On the **Layout tab**, in the **Labels group**, click the **Chart Title** button. Click **None** to turn off the chart title.

The chart title is not necessary because the slide title identifies the chart.

4 On the **Layout tab**, in the **Labels group**, click the **Data Labels** button, and then click **Center**.

The pie chart is enlarged and the percentage data labels display close to the center of each slice. The Inside End option also enlarges the pie but displays the data labels near the inside edge of each slice.

5 On the **Layout tab**, in the **Labels group**, click the **Data Labels** button. Click **Outside End**.

The pie size is reduced slightly to accommodate the placement of the data labels outside of the pie.

6 On the **Layout tab**, in the **Labels group**, click the **Data Labels** button. Below the gallery, click **More Data Label Options**.

In the Format Data Labels dialog box, you can change the data labels that display by choosing the Series or Category name, the Value or Percentage, or the Leader Lines. When data labels are displayed outside of the pie, **leader lines** connect the pie slice to the data labels. In this dialog box, you can also change the position of the data labels.

7 Under **Label Contains**, select the **Category Name** check box, and then clear the **Show Leader Lines** check box. Under **Label Position**, click **Outside End**, and then compare your screen with Figure 4.30.

The Percentage check box is already selected because Layout 6, which was applied to the chart in Step 1, includes Percentage labels.

Figure 4.30

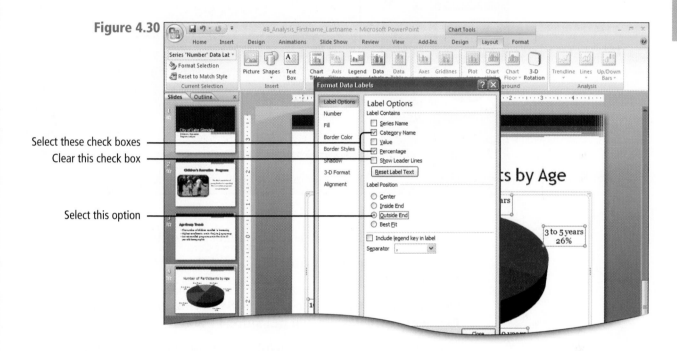

Select these check boxes
Clear this check box
Select this option

8 Click **Close** to apply the data label options. Notice that the slices are identified by data labels that display outside the pie, and that include the category name and the percentage that each slice represents.

9 Click anywhere outside of the pie so that it is not selected, and then **Save** 🖫 your presentation.

Activity 4.11 Selecting and Formatting Chart Elements

In addition to applying a chart layout and modifying the placement of chart elements, you can select and format individual chart elements, including the data labels, chart and plot areas, and the data markers.

1 With **Slide 4** displayed, click the pie so that it is selected, and then click any one of the data labels. Compare your slide with Figure 4.31.

All of the data labels are selected, indicating that formatting can be applied to all of the data labels at one time.

Figure 4.31

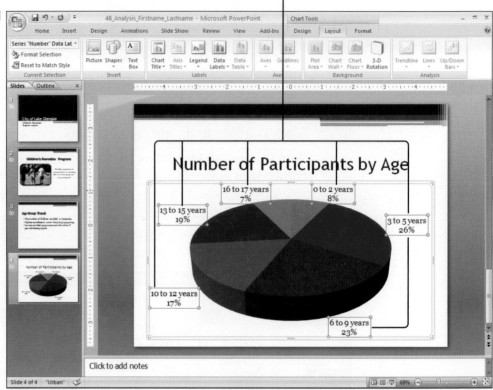

2. Right-click any of the selected data labels. On the Mini Toolbar, click

the **Font Size button arrow** , and then click **14** to resize all of the data labels.

3. On the **Layout tab**, in the **Current Selection group**, click the **Chart Elements arrow** as shown in Figure 4.32.

The Chart Elements arrow displays the list of elements in the selected chart. With the data labels selected in the chart, the *Series "Number" Data Labels* element is selected in the Chart Elements list.

Chart Elements arrow

Figure 4.32

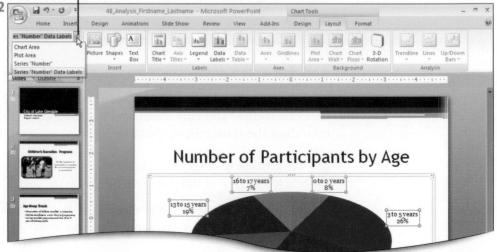

4 In the **Chart Elements list**, click **Chart Area**. In the **Current Selection group**, click **Format Selection** to display the Format Chart Area dialog box.

In this dialog box, you can format the ***Chart Area***—the area surrounding the chart enclosed by the blue outline. The dialog box title and the displayed options are context-sensitive and change depending upon the selection.

5 In the **Format Chart Area** dialog box, under **Fill**, click **Solid fill**.

Click the **Color** button ![color button], and then in the first column, click the third color—**White, Background 1, Darker 15%**.

6 On the left side of the **Format Chart Area dialog box**, click **3-D Format**. Under **Bevel**, click the **Top** button, and then under **Bevel**, in the last row, click **Divot**, as shown in Figure 4.33.

Top button

Figure 4.33

Click Divot

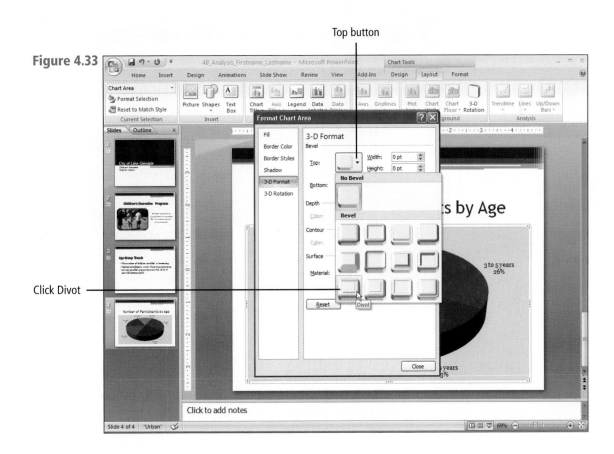

7 Click **Close** to apply the fill color and 3-D format to the chart area.

8 **Save** ![save icon] the presentation.

Activity 4.12 Exploding a Pie Slice

You can emphasize individual values or categories in a pie chart by exploding a selected pie slice. When you ***explode*** a pie slice, you emphasize the slice by pulling it out of the pie. In this Activity, you will emphasize the age group with the largest number of participants by exploding the *3 to 5 years* pie slice.

1 With **Slide 4** displayed, verify that the pie chart is selected, and then click anywhere on the pie so that each slice is surrounded by circles, indicating that all of the slices are selected.

2 Click the dark red **3-5 years pie slice** so that it is the only slice surrounded by circles, indicating that it is selected, as shown in Figure 4.34.

To select an individual pie slice, you must first select all of the slices.

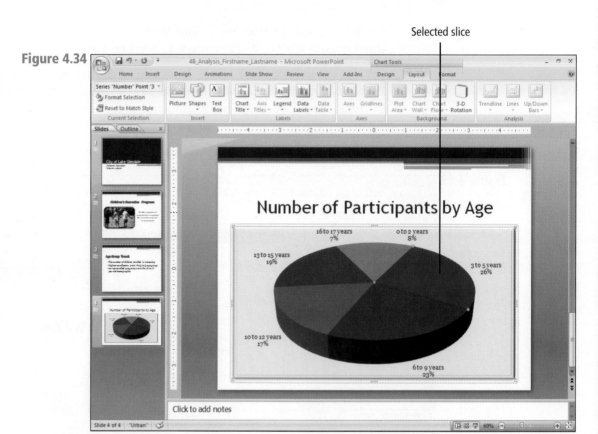

Selected slice

Figure 4.34

3 Point to the selected slice to display the pointer. Hold down the mouse button and drag to the right, noticing that as you do so, a dashed outline of the slice displays. Continue to drag to the right until the rounded edge of the dashed outline touches the *5* in *3-5 years*, as shown in Figure 4.35.

Drag to this location

Figure 4.35

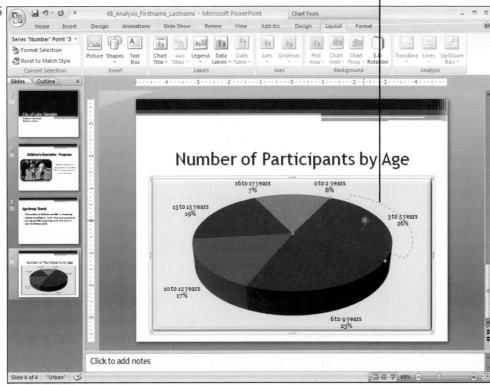

4 Release the mouse button to explode the pie slice, and then compare your slide with Figure 4.36. Notice that the pie size is adjusted so that the entire chart fits within the chart area.

Exploded pie slice

Figure 4.36

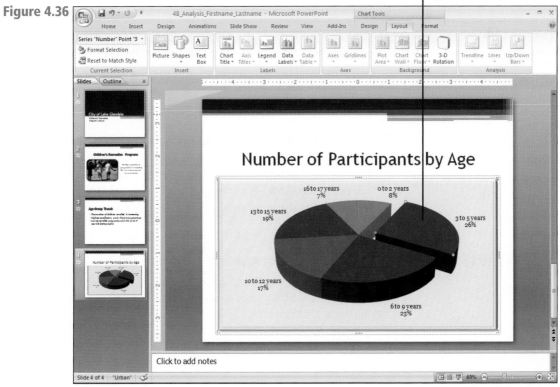

Is the entire pie exploded?

If all of the pie slices are exploded, then the *3 to 5 years* pie slice was not selected. On the Quick Access Toolbar, click Undo, and then repeat Steps 1-4, making sure that in Step 2, only the 3-5 years pie slice is selected.

5 **Save** 🖫 the presentation.

Objective 4
Applying Custom Animation Effects

Recall that animation effects are used to focus the audience's attention on individual slide elements. In addition to entrance effects, which introduce a slide element, you can apply emphasis and exit effects, and you can change the order and timing in which slide elements display.

Activity 4.13 Adding Entrance and Emphasis Effects

Recall that entrance effects are used to introduce slide elements. *Emphasis effects* draw attention to a slide element that is already displayed.

1 Display **Slide 2**, and then click the **picture** to select it.

2 On the **Animations tab**, in the **Animations group**, click the **Custom Animation** button. In the displayed **Custom Animation** task pane, click the **Add Effect** button, and then point to **Entrance**. Click **More Effects**, and then in the **Add Entrance Effect** dialog box, under **Basic**, click **Dissolve In**, and then click **OK**.

Recall that when a slide element is animated, a number displays to the left of the object indicating the order in which animation occurs and the animation effect is displayed in the Custom Animation task pane.

3 Click anywhere in the text *The City's population of young families is expanding!* and notice that the text *Our recreation programs are growing too!* is not enclosed within the placeholder.

Animation can be precisely controlled when text is contained within separate text boxes that can be animated individually.

4 In the **Custom Animation** task pane, click the **Add Effect** button, and then point to **Entrance**. In the displayed list, click **Fly In**. In the **Custom Animation** task pane, under **Modify: Fly In**, click the **Direction arrow**, and then click **From Right** to change the direction from which the text moves onto the slide.

Is the Fly In effect missing from the list?

If the Fly In effect is missing from the list, in the Custom Animation task pane, click Add Effect, and then point to Entrance. Click More Effects, and then in the Add Entrance Effect dialog box, under Basic, click Fly In, and then click OK.

5 Click the **picture**. In the **Custom Animation** task pane, click the **Add Effect** button, and then point to **Emphasis**. Click **More Effects**, and then scroll the **Emphasis** effects list to display the **Exciting** category. Under **Exciting**, click **Blink**, and then click **OK**.

When you run the slide show, the Blink effect will emphasize the picture after the first textbox displays.

6 Compare your screen with Figure 4.37 and notice that three items display in the custom animation list.

The picture displays twice in the list because both entrance and emphasis effects have been applied. The yellow star next to the picture in item 3 indicates that the applied animation is an emphasis effect.

Picture displays twice

Figure 4.37

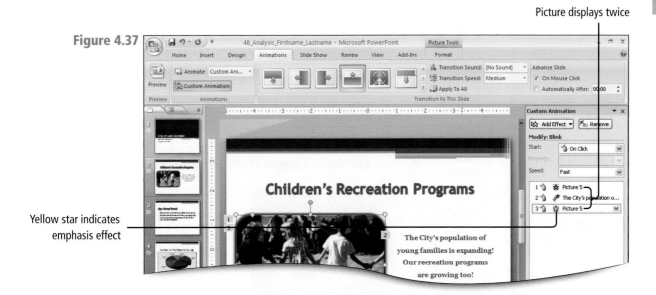

Yellow star indicates emphasis effect

7 Click anywhere in the text *Our recreation programs are growing too!* In the **Custom Animation** task pane, click the **Add Effect** button, and then point to **Entrance**. In the displayed list, click **Fly In**. In the **Custom Animation** task pane, under **Modify: Fly In**, click the **Direction arrow**, and then click **From Right** to change the direction from which the text moves onto the slide.

8 At the bottom of the **Custom Animation** task pane, click the **Play** button to display the animation applied to the slide elements.

9 **Save** the presentation.

Activity 4.14 Adding Exit Effects

Exit effects are animations that move a slide element off the screen and are commonly used when the presenter wants another slide element to take its place. In this activity, you will add an exit effect to the first text box on Slide 2 so that during the slide show, the text box exits the slide before the second text box displays.

1 On **Slide 2**, click the first text box—*The City's population of young families is expanding!* In the **Custom Animation** task pane, click the

Add Effect button, and then point to **Exit**. Click **More Effects**, and then under **Basic**, click **Fly Out**. Click **OK**.

▣ Compare your slide with Figure 4.38 and notice that in the custom animation list, item 5 displays three red stars, indicating that an exit effect has been applied.

The list contains entrance effects that are indicated by green stars, an emphasis effect indicated by a yellow star, and an exit effect indicated by red stars. The shape and number of stars that display provides a visual indication of the type of animation applied. For example, items 1 and 3 display a single star, indicating that the object stays in place when animated. Items 2, 4, and 5 show multiple stars indicating movement.

Figure 4.38

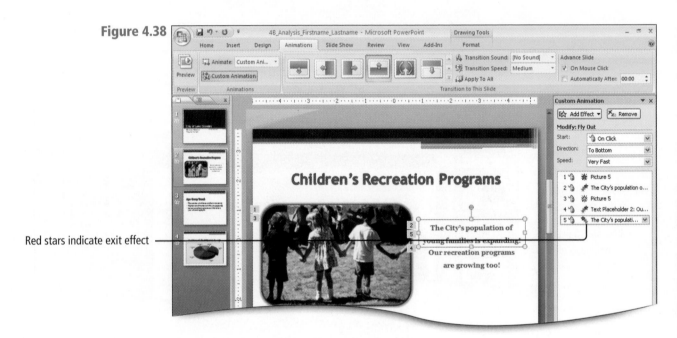

Red stars indicate exit effect

▣ In the **Custom Animation** task pane, click the **Play** button to view the animation.

The picture displays followed by the first text box. The picture is then animated with the emphasis effect, and then the second text box displays. Lastly, the first text box moves off the screen. To correctly animate this slide, the first text box should move off the screen prior to the display of the second text box. In the next Activity, you will change animation order.

▣ **Save** 🖫 the presentation.

Activity 4.15 Changing Animation Order and Setting Animation Timing

Slide elements display during a slide show in the order in which animation is applied. In the Custom Animation task pane, you can change the order in which slide elements are animated, and you can control the timing of when an animated object displays.

1 In the **Custom Animation** task pane, in the **custom animation list**, click **item 5**.

2 Below the **custom animation list**, click the **Re-Order up arrow** two times to move the **item 5** exit effect up to the **item 3** position in the list. Compare your screen with Figure 4.39.

Figure 4.39

Exit effect moved to item 3 position

Click Re-Order Up arrow two times

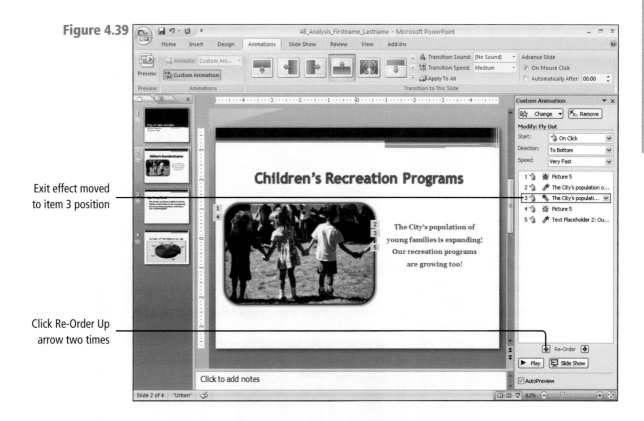

3 In the task pane, click the **Slide Show** button and then click the mouse button to view the animation sequence. Notice that the animations display in the following order: the picture dissolves, the first text box displays, the first text box moves off the screen, the picture blinks, the second text box displays. When **Slide 3** displays, press [Esc] to end the slide show.

Although you can click the left mouse button to advance through the slide transitions and animations, recall that you can advance the animations either at the same time as the previous animation, or immediately following the previous animation without clicking the mouse button.

4 Display **Slide 2**. In the **custom animation list**, click **item 1** to select it. Under **Modify: Dissolve In**, click the **Start arrow**, and then click **After Previous**.

Recall that the After Previous option begins the animation sequence for the selected slide element immediately after the completion of the previous animation or transition. In this instance, the previous animation is the slide transition. Thus, the slide will transition onto the screen and the picture will immediately display with the Dissolve In Entrance effect. Notice that the items are renumbered, beginning with zero. The picture is treated as zero because it displays immediately upon completion of the slide transition.

5 In the **custom animation list**, click **item 3**—the Emphasis effect for the picture—so that it is selected. Under **Modify: Blink**, click the **Start arrow**, click **With Previous**, and then compare your screen with Figure 4.40.

The With Previous option begins the animation sequence at the same time as the item preceding it in the custom animation list. Thus, the text box exit effect and the picture Emphasis effect will occur at the same time. The picture Emphasis effect is no longer numbered as it is treated as part of the item 2 animation sequence.

With Previous selected

Figure 4.40

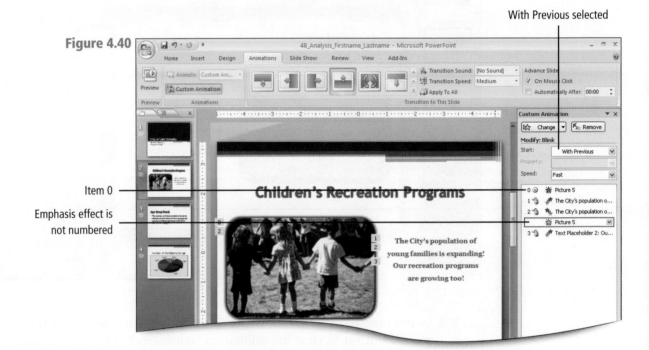

Item 0

Emphasis effect is not numbered

6 In the **custom animation list**, click **item 3**—the Entrance effect for the second text box. In the **Custom Animation** task pane, under **Modify: Fly In**, click the **Start arrow**, and then click **With Previous**.

The text box is part of the item 2 animation sequence. Thus, the first text box Exit effect, the picture Emphasis effect, and the second text box Entrance effect will occur simultaneously.

7 At the bottom of the task pane, click the **Slide Show** button. After the picture displays, click the mouse button to display the first text box. Click the mouse button again to move the text box off the screen, emphasize the picture with the blink animation, and move the second text box onto the screen.

8 Press [Esc] after the second text box displays to end the slide show, and then **Save** 💾 the presentation.

Activity 4.16 Changing and Removing Animation Effects

After animation is applied, you can change the effect or remove it. Using the Change command in the Custom Animation task pane ensures that you are changing the effect, not adding a new effect. If you add an effect that you do not need, you can use the Remove command in the Custom Animation task pane to delete the animation from the slide.

1 Display **Slide 1**, and then click the title placeholder. At the top of the **Custom Animation** task pane, click the **Remove** button.

The item is removed from the custom animation list and the number 1 is removed from the slide. Thus, the Entrance effect is removed from the title.

2 Display **Slide 3**. In the **custom animation list**, click **item 1**.

When you click an item in the custom animation list, the Add Effect button changes to the Change button, as shown in Figure 4.41.

Change button

Figure 4.41

Selected item

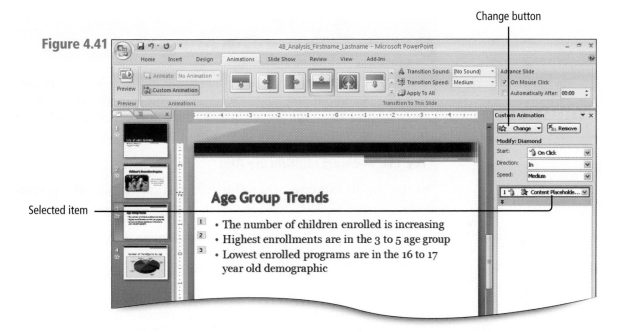

Age Group Trends

- The number of children enrolled is increasing
- Highest enrollments are in the 3 to 5 age group
- Lowest enrolled programs are in the 16 to 17 year old demographic

Alert!

Is the Change button activated?
To activate the Change button, you must click the item in the custom animation list. If instead you select the item on the slide, the Change button is not activated and you will add a new effect rather than change an existing effect.

3 In the **Custom Animation** task pane, click the **Change** button, point to **Entrance**, and then click **More Effects**. Under **Basic**, click **Peek In**, and then click **OK**.

4 On the **Slide Show tab**, in the **Start Slide Show group**, click **From Beginning**, and then click or press Spacebar to advance the presentation.

5 Create a **Header and Footer** for the **Notes and Handouts**. Include the **Date and time updated automatically,** the **Page number**, and a **Footer** with the file name **4B_Analysis_Firstname_Lastname**

6 Check your *Chapter Assignment Sheet* or your *Course Syllabus* or consult your instructor to determine if you are to submit your assignments on paper or electronically. To submit electronically, go to step 8, and then follow the instructions provided by your instructor.

7 **Print Preview** your presentation, and then print **Handouts (4 Slides Per Page)**.

8 **Save** the changes to your presentation, and then close the presentation.

End **You have completed Project 4B** ——————————

There's More You Can Do!

From My Computer, navigate to the student files that accompany this textbook. In the folder **02_theres_more_you_can_do**, locate and open the folder for this chapter. Open and print the instructions for this project, which are provided to you in Adobe PDF format.

Try IT! 1—Insert Multimedia Files

In this Try It! exercise, you will insert multimedia files in a presentation.

Content-Based Assessments

Summary

In this chapter, you enhanced your presentation by applying animation effects and by changing effect and timing options. You practiced advanced table formatting techniques to present information and you created a pie chart to visually represent data.

Key Terms

Content-Based Assessments

Matching

Match each term in the second column with its correct definition in the first column. Write the letter of the term on the blank line in front of the correct definition.

_____ **1.** A feature that combines selected cells into one cell.

_____ **2.** A feature that divides a selected cell into the number of cells that you specify.

_____ **3.** A feature that merges cells by deleting existing borders.

_____ **4.** A type of chart that is used to illustrate percentages or proportions.

_____ **5.** A feature that widens the column to accommodate the longest cell entry in the column.

_____ **6.** The combination of displayed chart elements, including the title, legend, and data labels.

_____ **7.** Labels that identify pie slices and that indicate the percentage of the total or a value that each slice represents.

_____ **8.** Lines that connect a pie slice to its corresponding data label.

_____ **9.** The area surrounding a chart.

_____ **10.** An animation effect that draws attention to a slide element that is currently displayed.

_____ **11.** Animations that move a slide element off the screen.

_____ **12.** The task pane in which you can change the order of animated slide elements.

_____ **13.** In the Custom Animation Task Pane, the button that deletes a selected animation from the animation sequence.

_____ **14.** An animation option that begins the animation sequence immediately after the previously animated item.

_____ **15.** An animation option that begins the animation sequence at the same time as the item preceding it in the Custom Animation list.

A AutoFit

B Chart Area

C Chart layout

D Custom animation

E Data labels

F Emphasis effect

G Eraser

H Exit effects

I Leader lines

J Merge cells

K Pie chart

L Remove

M Split cells

N Start After Previous

O Start With Previous

Content-Based Assessments

Fill in the Blank

Write the correct word in the space provided.

1. A _____ is a format for information that organizes and presents text and data in columns and rows.

2. The intersection of a column and row is a _____.

3. A table can be quickly formatted by applying a _____ _____.

4. You can modify the layout of a table by merging and _____ table cells.

5. When a table is created, the columns are _____ in width.

6. You can _____ the direction in which text displays so that it displays vertically from top to bottom or from bottom to top.

7. The _____ _____ feature allows for exact placement of borders that are drawn in a table.

8. A _____ is a graphic representation of numeric data.

9. A pie chart is used to illustrate percentages or proportions, and includes only _____ series of data.

10. When a pie chart is created, each of the cells in the Excel worksheet containing the numeric data is a _____ _____.

11. When a pie chart is created, the Excel worksheet contains sample data for one _____ _____.

12. You can emphasize individual values or categories in a pie chart by _____ a selected pie slice.

13. In the custom animation list, a _____ star indicates an Entrance effect.

14. In the custom animation list, a _____ star indicates an Emphasis effect.

15. In the custom animation list, a _____ star indicates an Exit effect.

Content-Based Assessments

Skills Review

Project 4C—Adults

In this project, you will apply the skills you practiced from the Objectives in Project 4A.

Objectives: 1. *Format Tables;* **2.** *Modify a Table Using the Draw Borders Feature.*

In the following Skills Review, you will you will create a presentation that Marina Hernandez, Director of Parks and Recreation, is developing for a City Council meeting that describes the adult recreation programs in the City of Lake Glendale. Your completed presentation will look similar to the one shown in Figure 4.42.

For Project 4C, you will need the following files:

New blank PowerPoint presentation
p04C_Dance
p04C_Weights
p04C_Sports

You will save your presentation as 4C_Adults_Firstname_Lastname

Figure 4.42

(Project 4C–Adults continues on the next page)

Content-Based Assessments

(Project 4C–Adults continued)

1. **Start** PowerPoint and begin a new blank presentation. On the **Office** menu, click **Save As**, and then navigate to your **PowerPoint Chapter 4** folder. In the **File name** box, type **4C_Adults_Firstname_Lastname** and then click **Save** to save your file.

2. On the **Design** tab, in the **Themes** group, click the **Median theme**. In the **Themes group**, click the **Colors** button, and then click **Civic** to change the theme color. In the title placeholder, type **City of Lake Glendale** and in the subtitle placeholder type **Recreation Analysis, Adult Programs**

3. Verify that the Rulers display. If they do not, click the View tab, and then in the Show/Hide group, select the Ruler check box. With **Slide 1** displayed, on the **Home tab**, in the **Slides group**, click the **New Slide** button to insert a slide with the **Title and Content** layout. In the title placeholder, type **Adult Recreation Trends** and then **Center** the title. In the content placeholder, type each of the following three bullet points.

   Team soccer and volleyball are the fastest growing activities
   Additional business and computer classes should be offered
   Fitness classes continue to be the most popular activities

4. With **Slide 2** displayed, on the **Home tab**, in the **Slides group**, click the **New Slide** button to insert a slide with the **Title and Content** layout. In the title placeholder, type **Highest Demand Activities** and then **Center** the title.

5. On the **Insert tab**, in the **Tables group**, click the **Table** button. Move your pointer into the first box in the grid, and then drag to the right and down to select **2 columns** and **3 rows**. Click to create the table.

(Project 4C–Adults continues on the next page)

6. Position the pointer above the first column to display the ⬇ pointer, and then select all of the cells in the first column. On the **Layout tab**, in the **Merge group**, click the **Merge Cells** button so that the three cells are merged into one.

7. With the insertion point positioned in the merged cell, type **Participants Over 18 Years of Age** and then press ⟨Tab⟩. Type the following text in the remaining three cells, pressing ⟨Tab⟩ to move from cell to cell.

   Organized sports including softball, soccer, and volleyball
   Fitness classes
   Business and computer classes

8. Point to the border between the first and second column to display the ⧫ pointer. Drag to the left until the dashed vertical line displays to the right of the word *Over*. Release the mouse button to resize the columns.

9. At the bottom center of the border that surrounds the table, point to the sizing handle—the four dots—to display the ↕ pointer. Using the vertical ruler as your guide, drag down so that the lower edge of the table extends to approximately **2.5 inches below zero**. Release the mouse button to resize the table.

10. Click in the first column of the table. On the **Layout tab**, in the **Alignment group**, click the **Text Direction** button. Click **Rotate all text 270°**.

11. Select the text in the first column, and then change the **Font Size** to **40. Center** the text. On the **Layout tab**, in the **Table group**, click the **Select** button, and then click **Select Table**. In the **Alignment group**, click the **Center Vertically** button.

(Project 4C–Adults continued)

12. On the **Table Tools Design tab**, in the **Table Styles group**, click the **More** button to display the **Table Styles gallery**. Under **Medium**, in the third row, click the second style—**Medium Style 3 – Accent 1**. In the **Table Style Options group**, *clear* the **Header Row** check box, and then select the **First Column** check box. **Save** your presentation.

13. With **Slide 3** displayed, on the **Home tab**, in the **Slides group**, click the **New Slide button arrow**, and then insert a slide with the **Title Only** layout. In the title placeholder, type **Participation in Team Sports** and then **Center** the title.

14. On the **Insert tab**, in the **Tables group**, click the **Table** button to display the table grid, and then drag to select **3 columns** and **3 rows**. Point to the top border that surrounds the table to display the ⬚ pointer. Drag down approximately 0.5 inch so that the top edge of the table aligns at **1.5 inches above zero**. Point to the four dots at the bottom center of the table—the sizing handle—to display the ⬍ pointer. Drag down to **3 inches below zero** to resize the table.

15. On the **Table Tools Design tab**, in the **Table Styles group**, click the **More** button to display the **Table Styles gallery**. Under **Medium**, click the first style—**Medium Style 1**. In the **Table Style Options group**, *clear* the **Header Row** check box.

16. On the **Table Tools Design tab**, in the **Draw Borders group**, click the **Draw Table** button, and then move the pointer into the table to display the ✎ pointer. Position the pointer over the light gray border that separates the first cell in the first row from the second cell in the first row. Hold down the mouse button and drag down to the third row so that a dashed line covers the light gray line. Release the mouse button to draw the solid, 1 pt, black border.

17. Using the technique that you practiced in Step 16, apply a solid black border to the light gray line separating the second and third columns.

18. Position the ✎ pointer at approximately the midpoint of the line that separates the first cell in the first row from the second cell in the first row. Drag to the right so that the dashed line extends to the right edge of the table, and then release the mouse button to split the two cells into four cells. Repeat this technique to draw two more lines in the second and third table rows. Press [Esc] so that the Draw Table pointer is no longer active. If you inadvertently draw a line that extends into the first column, click the **Undo** button and try again.

19. On the **Layout tab**, in the **Cell Size group**, click the **Distribute Rows** button so that all of the cells in the second and third columns are the same height.

20. With **Slide 4** displayed, click in the first cell in the second column. Type **Dance** and then press [Tab] two times so that the insertion point is positioned in the second cell in the second column. Type **5 Classes** and then press [Tab]. Type **125 Members**

21. Click in the third cell in the second column. Type **Weight Training** and then press [Tab] two times so that the insertion point is positioned in the fourth cell in the second column. Type **8 Classes** and then press [Tab]. Type **80 Members**

22. Click in the fifth cell in the second column. Type **Team Sports** and then press [Tab] two

(Project 4C–Adults continues on the next page)

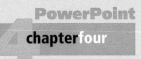
(Project 4C–Adults continued)

times so that the insertion point is positioned in the last cell in the second column. Type **28 Teams** and then press Tab. Type **225 Players**

23. On the **Table Tools Design tab**, in the **Draw Borders** group, click the **Eraser** button.

    Position the pointer over the border to the right of the word *Dance*, and then click to delete the line. Using the technique that you just practiced, delete the borders to the right of the words *Weight Training* and *Team Sports*. Press Esc so that the Eraser is no longer active.

24. Drag to select all of the cells in **Columns 2** and **3**. **Center** the text and then change the **Font Size** to **24**. With **Columns 2** and **3** still selected, click the **Layout tab**. In the **Alignment group**, click the **Center Vertically** button.

25. In the table, click in the first cell of the first row. On the **Table Tools Design tab**, in the **Table Styles group**, click the **Shading button arrow**, and then click

Picture. Navigate to the location where your student data files are stored, click **p04C_Dance**, and then click **Insert**. In the second and third cells of the first column, repeat this technique inserting **p04C_Weights**, and **p04C_Sports**.

26. Create a **Header and Footer** for the **Notes and Handouts**. Include the **Date and time updated automatically**, the **Page number**, and a **Footer** with the file name **4C_Adults_Firstname_Lastname**

27. Check your *Chapter Assignment Sheet* or your *Course Syllabus* or consult your instructor to determine if you are to submit your assignments on paper or electronically. To submit electronically, go to step 29, and then follow the instructions provided by your instructor.

28. **Print Preview** your presentation, and then print **Handouts (4 Slides Per Page)**.

29. **Save** the changes to your presentation, and then close the presentation.

End **You have completed Project 4C** ——————————

Content-Based Assessments

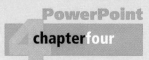
Skills Review

Project 4D — Adult Analysis

In this project, you will apply the skills you practiced from the Objectives in Project 4B.

Objectives: 3. *Create and Modify a Pie Chart;* **4.** *Apply Custom Animation Effects.*

In the following Skills Review, you will edit a presentation that Marina Hernandez, Director of Parks and Recreation, has created for a City Council meeting that presents an analysis of adult recreation programs in the City of Lake Glendale. Your completed presentation will look similar to the one shown in Figure 4.43.

For Project 4D, you will need the following file:

p04D_Adult_Analysis

You will save your presentation as
4D_Adult_Analysis_Firstname_Lastname

Figure 4.43

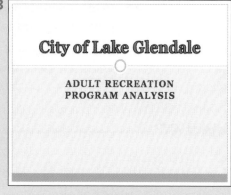

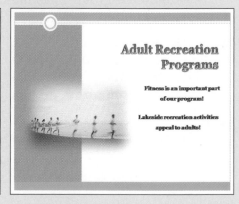

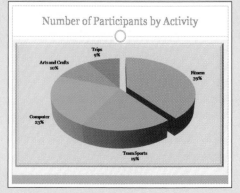

(Project 4D–Adult Analysis continues on the next page)

Content-Based Assessments

(Project 4D–Adult Analysis continued)

1. **Start** PowerPoint and from your student files, open **p04D_Adult_Analysis**. Save the file in your **PowerPoint Chapter 4** folder as 4D_Adult_Analysis_Firstname_Lastname

2. Display **Slide 3** and then add a **New Slide** with the **Title and Content Layout**. In the title placeholder type **Number of Participants by Activity**

3. In the content placeholder, click the **Insert Chart** button. Click **Pie**, click the second pie chart—**Pie in 3-D**—and then click **OK**. In the Excel window, click in cell **B1**. Type **Number** and then press Tab. Type the remaining data from the following table, pressing Enter after the last entry.

Fitness	480
Team Sports	225
Computer	280
Arts and Crafts	125
Trips	110

4. In the Excel window, in the column heading area, point to the vertical line between **column A** and **column B** to display the ⊹ pointer. Double-click the mouse button to AutoFit the column width and display all of the text in cell A5. Close the Excel window.

5. On the **Chart Tools Design tab**, in the **Chart Layouts group**, click the **More** button. From the displayed **Chart Layout gallery**, click **Layout 6**.

6. On the **Layout tab**, in the **Labels group**, click the **Legend** button. Click **None** to turn off the legend. In the **Labels group**, click the **Chart Title** button. Click **None** to turn off the chart title. In the **Labels group**, click the **Data Labels** button, and then click **More Data Label Options**. Under **Label Contains**, select the **Category Name** check box, and then *clear*

the **Show Leader Lines** check box. Under **Label Position**, click **Outside End**. Click **Close** to apply the data label options.

7. On the **Layout tab**, in the **Current Selection group**, click the **Chart Elements arrow**. In the displayed **Chart Elements list**, click **Chart Area**. In the **Current Selection group**, click the **Format Selection** button. In the **Format Chart Area** dialog box, under **Fill**, click **Solid fill**. Click the **Color** button, and then in the seventh column, click the fourth color—**Gold, Accent 3, Lighter 40%**.

8. On the left side of the **Format Chart Area** dialog box, click **3-D Format**. Under **Bevel**, click the **Top** button, and then under **Bevel**, in the last row, click **Divot**. Click **Close** to apply the fill color and 3-D format to the chart area.

9. With **Slide 4** displayed, click any one of the data labels so that all are selected. Right-click any of the selected data labels, and then change the **Font Size** to **14**.

10. Click anywhere on the pie so that each slice is surrounded by circles, indicating that all of the slices are selected. Click the **Fitness** pie slice so that it is the only slice that is selected. Point to the selected slice to display the ⬚ pointer. Hold down the mouse button and drag to the right, until the rounded edge of the dashed outline touches the percent sign—%. Release the mouse button to explode the pie slice. **Save** your presentation.

11. Display **Slide 2**, and then click the picture to select it. On the **Animations tab**, in the **Animations group**, click the **Custom Animation** button. In the displayed **Custom Animation** task pane, click the **Add Effect** button, and then point to **Entrance**. In the displayed list, click **Dissolve In**.

(Project 4D–Adult Analysis continues on the next page)

(Project 4D–Adult Analysis continued)

12. Click anywhere in the text *Fitness is an important part of our program!* In the **Custom Animation** task pane, click the **Add Effect** button, and then point to **Entrance**. In the displayed list, click **Fly In**. In the **Custom Animation** task pane, under **Modify: Fly In**, click the **Direction arrow**, and then click **From Right** to change the direction from which the text moves onto the slide.

13. Click the picture. In the **Custom Animation** task pane, click the **Add Effect** button, and then point to **Emphasis**. Click **More Effects**, and then scroll the **Emphasis** effects list to display the **Exciting** category. Under **Exciting**, click **Blink**, and then click **OK**.

14. Click anywhere in the text *Lakeside recreation activities appeal to adults!* In the **Custom Animation** task pane, click the **Add Effect** button, and then point to **Entrance**. In the displayed list, click **Fly In**. In the **Custom Animation** task pane, under **Modify: Fly In**, click the **Direction arrow**, and then click **From Right** to change the direction from which the text moves onto the slide.

15. Click the first text box—*Fitness is an important part of our program!* In the **Custom Animation** task pane, click the **Add Effect** button, and then point to **Exit**. Click **More Effects**, and then under **Basic**, click **Fly Out**. Click **OK**.

16. In the **custom animation list**, click **item 5**. Below the **custom animation list**, click the **Re-Order up arrow** two times to move the item 5 Exit effect up to the item 3 position in the list.

17. In the **custom animation list**, click **item 1** to select it. **Under Modify: Dissolve In**, click the **Start arrow**, and then click **After**

Previous. In the **custom animation list**, click **item 3**—the Emphasis effect for the picture. Under **Modify: Blink**, click the **Start arrow**, and then click **With Previous**.

18. In the **custom animation list**, click **item 3**—the Entrance effect for the second text box. In the **Custom Animation** task pane, under **Modify: Fly In**, click the **Start arrow**. Click **With Previous**. **Save** your presentation.

19. Display **Slide 1**, and then click the title placeholder. In the **Custom Animation** task pane, click the **Remove** button.

20. Display **Slide 3**. In the **custom animation list**, click **item 1**.

21. In the **Custom Animation** task pane, click the **Change** button, point to **Entrance**, and then click **More Effects**. Under **Basic**, click **Peek In**, and then click **OK**. On the **Slide Show tab**, in the **Start Slide Show group**, click **From Beginning**, and then click or press Spacebar to advance the presentation.

22. Create a **Header and Footer** for the **Notes and Handouts**. Include the **Date and time updated automatically**, the **Page number**, and a **Footer** with the file name **4D_Adult_Analysis_Firstname_Lastname**

23. Check your *Chapter Assignment Sheet* or your *Course Syllabus* or consult your instructor to determine if you are to submit your assignments on paper or electronically. To submit electronically, go to Step 25, and then follow the instructions provided by your instructor.

24. **Print Preview** your presentation, and then print **Handouts (4 Slides Per Page)**.

25. **Save** the changes to your presentation, and then close the presentation.

End You have completed Project 4D

Content-Based Assessments

Mastering PowerPoint

Project 4E — Traffic

In this project, you will apply the skills you practiced from the Objectives in Project 4A.

Objectives: 1. *Format Tables;* **2.** *Modify a Table Using the Draw Borders Feature.*

In the following Mastering PowerPoint project, you will edit a presentation that Jason Chou, Chairman of the Lake Glendale Traffic Commission, is preparing for an upcoming Traffic Commission meeting. Your completed presentation will look similar to Figure 4.44.

For Project 4E, you will need the following files:

p04E_Bus
p04E_Cars
p04E_Signal
p04E_Traffic

You will save your presentation as 4E_Traffic_Firstname_Lastname

Figure 4.44

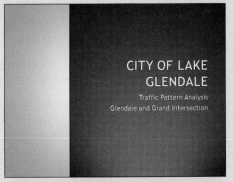
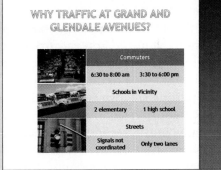
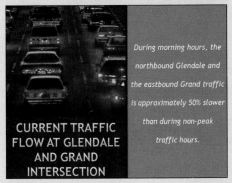
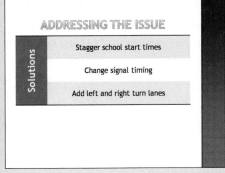

(Project 4E–Traffic continues on the next page)

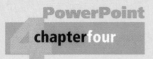

(Project 4E–Traffic continued)

1. **Start** PowerPoint and from your student files, open **p04E_Traffic**. **Save** the file in your **PowerPoint Chapter 4** folder as 4E_Traffic_Firstname_Lastname

2. If necessary, display the rulers and **Slide 1**. Insert a **New Slide** with the **Title Only** layout. In the title placeholder, type **Why Traffic at Grand and Glendale Avenues?** and then **Center** the title.

3. Insert a **Table** with **3 columns** and **3 rows**. Move the table so that the top edge of the table aligns at **1.5 inches above zero**. Resize the table so that its lower edge aligns at **3 inches below zero**.

4. On the **Table Tools Design tab**, in the **Draw Borders group**, click the **Pen Color** button, and then click the first color— **White, Background 1**—to change the border color to white and to activate the Draw Table pointer.

5. Position the pointer at approximately the midpoint of the line that separates the first cell in the first row from the second cell in the first row, and then draw a line that extends to the right edge of the table, splitting the two cells into four cells. Repeat this technique to draw two more lines in the second and third table rows. Notice that the first column contains three cells and the second and third columns each contain six cells.

6. Distribute the rows so that all of the cells in the second and third columns are the same height, and then press [Esc] so that the Draw Table pointer is no longer active. Click in the first cell in the second column. Type the following table text in **columns 2** and **3**, leaving cells blank as indicated.

Commuters	
6:30 to 8:00 am	3:30 to 6:00 pm
Schools in Vicinity	
2 elementary	1 high school
Streets	
Signals not coordinated	Only two lanes

7. Activate the **Eraser** pointer, and then delete the borders to the right of the words *Commuters*, *Schools in Vicinity*, and *Streets*. **Center** all of the table text horizontally and vertically within the cells.

8. In the first column, modify the **Shading** in each cell by inserting the following pictures: **p04E_Cars**, **p04E_Bus**, and **p04E_Signal**.

9. Display **Slide 3**, and then insert a **New Slide** with the **Title and Content** layout. In the title placeholder, type **Addressing the Issue** and then **Center** the text. Insert a **Table** with **2 columns** and **3 rows**. **Merge** the cells in the first column.

10. In the merged cell, type **Solutions** and then press [Tab]. Type the following text in the remaining three cells:

    Stagger school start times
    Change signal timing
    Add left and right turn lanes

11. Select the text in **column 2**, and then change the **Font Size** to **24**.

12. Size the first column so that it is slightly wider than the text *Solutions*. Using the bottom center sizing handle, size the table so that its lower edge of the table extends to approximately **1 inch below zero**. Select the text in the first column, and then change the **Text Direction** to **Rotate all text 270°** and the **Font Size** to **32**.

(Project 4E–Traffic continues on the next page)

Content-Based Assessments

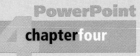
(Project 4E–Traffic continued)

13. Apply **Table Style Medium Style 3 – Accent 1**, and then *clear* the **Header Row** check box and select the **First Column** check box. Select the entire table, and then **Center** the text horizontally and vertically within the cells.

14. Create a **Header and Footer** for the **Notes and Handouts**. Include the **Date and time updated automatically**, the **Page number**, and a **Footer** with the file name **4E_Traffic_ Firstname_Lastname**

15. Check your *Chapter Assignment Sheet* or your *Course Syllabus* or consult your instructor to determine if you are to submit your assignments on paper or electronically. To submit electronically, go to Step 17, and then follow the instructions provided by your instructor.

16. **Print Preview** your presentation, and then print **Handouts (4 Slides Per Page)**.

17. **Save** the changes to your presentation, and then close the presentation.

End **You have completed Project 4E** ——————————

Content-Based Assessments

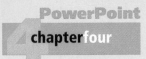
Mastering PowerPoint

Project 4F—Water

In this project, you will apply the skills you practiced from the Objectives in Project 4B.

Objectives: 3. *Create and Modify a Pie Chart;* **4.** *Apply Custom Animation Effects.*

In the following Mastering PowerPoint project, you will create a presentation that the Lake Glendale Water Department Chief, Mark Aldrian, will use to present information to the Commissioners of the Department of Water. Your completed presentation will look similar to Figure 4.45.

> **For Project 4F, you will need the following files:**
>
> New blank PowerPoint presentation
> p04F_Reservoir

**You will save your presentation as
4F_Water_Firstname_Lastname**

Figure 4.45

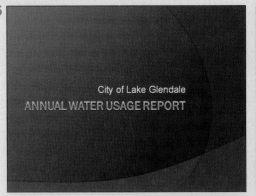

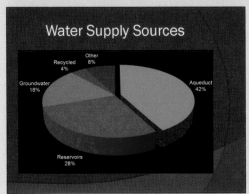

(Project 4F–Water continues on the next page)

Content-Based Assessments

(Project 4F–Water continued)

1. **Start** PowerPoint and begin a new blank presentation. Apply the **Technic** theme, and then change the **Colors Theme** to **Concourse**. In the title placeholder, type Annual Water Usage Report and then change the **Font Size** to **36**. In the subtitle placeholder, type City of Lake Glendale and then change the **Font Size** to **28**. **Save** the file in your **PowerPoint Chapter 4** folder as 4F_Water_Firstname_Lastname

2. Insert a **New Slide** with the **Title and Content** layout. In the title placeholder type Water Department Information and then **Center** the title. In the content placeholder, type the following bullet points.

120,000 acre-feet of water delivered annually

66,000 residents served

Funded by sales of water services

Over 1,200 miles of pipe

Approximately 4,300 fire hydrants

3. Insert a **New Slide** with the **Title and Content Layout**. In the title placeholder, type Water Supply Sources and then **Center** the title. In the content placeholder, insert a **Pie in 3-D** chart.

4. In the Excel window, in cell **B1**, type Percent and then press Tab. Type the remaining data from the following table:

Aqueduct	42%
Reservoirs	28%
Groundwater	18%
Recycled	4%
Other	8%

5. In the Excel window, **AutoFit column A**, and then **Close** the Excel window. Apply chart **Layout 6**, and then turn off the **Legend** and the **Chart Title**. Display the **Category Name** and **Percentage Data Labels** displayed on the **Outside End** of

the chart. Do not show leader lines. Change the **Font Size** for the **Data Labels** to **16**, and then explode the largest slice of the pie.

6. On the **Layout tab**, in the **Current Selection group**, click the **Chart Elements arrow**, click **Chart Area**. Display the **Format Chart Area** dialog box, and then apply a **Solid Fill—Black, Background 1**, and a **3-D Format—Top Bevel, Circle**.

7. Insert a **New Slide** with the **Picture with Caption** layout. In the title placeholder, type Lake Glendale Water Department and then change the **Font Size** to **28**. In the subtitle placeholder, type Quenching the City's Thirst and then change the **Font Size** to **28**.

8. In the picture placeholder, from your student files, insert **p04F_Reservoir**. Apply the **Dissolve In Entrance effect** to the picture, and change the **Start** setting to **After Previous**.

9. Select the text **Lake Glendale Water Department** text box, and then apply the **Fly In Entrance effect**. Change the **Direction** to **From Right** and change the **Start** setting to **After Previous**.

10. Select the picture, and then apply the **Blink Emphasis effect**. Select the **Quenching the City's Thirst** text box, and then apply the **Fly In Entrance effect**. Change the **Direction** to **From Right**, and then change the **Start** setting to **With Previous**.

11. Select the text **Lake Glendale Water Department** text box, and then apply the **Fly Out Exit effect**. Change the **Start** setting to **With Previous**.

12. Apply the **Wipe Down** transition to all of the slides in the presentation, and then view the Slide Show from the beginning.

(Project 4F–Water continues on the next page)

Content-Based Assessments

Mastering PowerPoint

(Project 4F—Water continued)

13. Create a **Header and Footer** for the **Notes and Handouts**. Include the **Date and time updated automatically**, the **Page number**, and a **Footer** with the file name **4F_Water_Firstname_Lastname**

14. Check your *Chapter Assignment Sheet* or your *Course Syllabus* or consult your instructor to determine if you are to submit your assignments on paper or electronically.

To submit electronically, go to step 16, and then follow the instructions provided by your instructor.

15. **Print Preview** your presentation, and then print **Handouts (4 Slides Per Page)**.

16. **Save** the changes to your presentation, and then close the presentation.

End You have completed Project 4F ―――――――――――――――

Mastering PowerPoint

Project 4G—Employees

In this project, you will apply the skills you practiced from the Objectives in Projects 4A and 4B.

Objectives: 1. *Format Tables;* **3.** *Create and Modify a Pie Chart.*

In the following Mastering PowerPoint project, you will edit a presentation that Lake Glendale Human Resources Director Kaitlyn Hughes has created to summarize a portion of the city's annual human resources survey. Your completed presentation will look similar to Figure 4.46.

For Project 4G, you will need the following file:

p04G_Employees

You will save your presentation as
4G_Employees_Firstname_Lastname

Figure 4.46

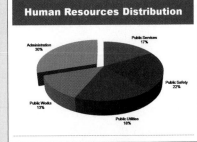
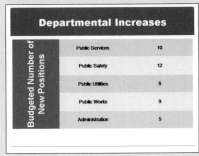

(Project 4G–Employees continues on the next page)

(Project 4G–Employees continued)

1. **Start** PowerPoint. From your student files, Open the file **p04G_Employees**. Save the file in your **PowerPoint Chapter 4** folder as 4G_Employees_Firstname_Lastname

2. Display **Slide 3**, and then add a **New Slide** with the **Title and Content** layout. The slide title is **Human Resources Distribution**

3. In the content placeholder, insert a **Pie in 3-D** chart. In the Excel window, in cell **B1**, type **Number** and then type the remaining data shown in the following table. **AutoFit column A** so that all of the text displays.

	Number
Public Services	35
Public Safety	45
Public Utilities	38
Public Works	28
Administration	62

4. Close the Excel window and, if necessary, select the chart. Modify the chart **Layout** so that the **Legend** and **Chart Title** do not display. Change the **Data Labels** options so that the **Category Name** and **Percentage** display on the **Outside End** of the chart. Select the **Data Labels** and change the **Font Size** to **14**, and then explode the largest pie slice.

5. Insert a **New Slide** with the **Title and Content** layout. In the title placeholder, type **Departmental Increases** and then insert a **Table** with **3 columns** and **5 rows**.

6. **Merge** the cells in the first column, type **Budgeted Number of New Positions** and then type the following text in the remaining cells.

Public Services	10
Public Safety	12
Public Utilities	8
Public Works	9
Administration	5

7. Size the first column so that the text *Budgeted Number* displays on the first line and the remaining text wraps to the second line. Select **columns 2** and **3**, and then **Distribute** them so that they are the same width. Size the table so that its lower edge extends to approximately **2.5 inches below zero**.

8. In the first column, change the **Text Direction** to **Rotate all text 270°**, and then change the **Font Size** to **32**.

9. Select all of the table text, and then **Center** the text horizontally and vertically within the cells. Change the **Table Style** to **Medium Style 2 – Accent 6**, and then change the **Table Style Options** by clearing the **Header Row** check box, and by selecting the **First Column** check box.

10. Apply the **Wipe Down** transition and change the **Transition Speed** to **Medium**. Apply the transition setting to all of the slides in the presentation. View the slide show from the beginning.

11. Create a **Header and Footer** for the **Notes and Handouts**. Include the **Date and time updated automatically**, the **Page number**, and a **Footer** with the file name **4G_Employees_Firstname_Lastname**

12. Check your *Chapter Assignment Sheet* or your *Course Syllabus* or consult your instructor to determine if you are to submit your assignments on paper or electronically. To submit electronically, go to step 14, and then follow the instructions provided by your instructor.

13. **Print Preview** your presentation, and then print **Handouts (6 Slides Per Page)**.

14. **Save** the changes to your presentation, and then close the presentation.

End **You have completed Project 4G**

Content-Based Assessments

Mastering PowerPoint

Project 4H — Visitors

In this project, you will apply the skills you practiced from the Objectives in Projects 4A and 4B.

Objectives: 1. *Format Tables;* **2.** *Modify a Table Using the Draw Borders Feature;* **4.** *Apply Custom Animation Effects.*

In the following Mastering PowerPoint Assessment, you will edit a presentation that Jennifer Moore, Director of Tourism for the City of Lake Glendale, has created for a vacation expo. Your completed presentation will look similar to Figure 4.47.

For Project 4H, you will need the following files:

p04H_Visitors
p04H_Lake
p04H_Plaza
p04H_Golf

**You will save your presentation as
4H_Visitors_Firstname_Lastname**

Figure 4.47

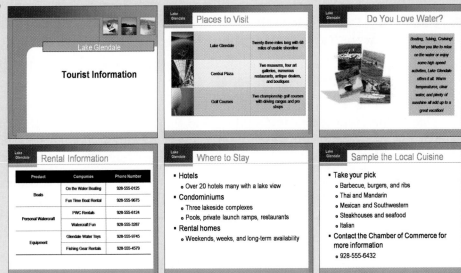

(Project 4H–Visitors continues on the next page)

Content-Based Assessments

(Project 4H–Visitors continued)

1. **Start** PowerPoint. From your student files, open the file **p04H_Visitors**. **Save** the file in your **PowerPoint Chapter 4** folder as **4H_Visitors_Firstname_Lastname**

2. With **Slide 1** displayed, add a **New Slide** with the **Title and Content** layout. In the title place-holder, type **Places to Visit** and then insert a **Table** with **3 columns** and **3 rows**.

3. Leave the first column blank, and then in the second and third columns, type the following text.

Lake Glendale	Twenty-three miles long with 68 miles of usable shoreline	
Central Plaza	Two museums, four art galleries, numerous restaurants, antique dealers, and boutiques	
Golf Courses	Two championship golf courses with driving ranges and pro shops	

4. Adjust the width of the first column so that it is approximately one-half of its original size, and then **Distribute columns 2** and **3** so that they are the same width. Size the table so that its lower edge extends to approximately **2.5 inches below zero**, and then **Center** the text in **columns 2** and **3** horizontally and vertically in the cells. **Distribute** the table rows.

5. Change the **Table Style** to the **Best Match for Document Themed Style 1 – Accent 1**, and then modify the **Table Style Options** by *clearing* the **Header Row** check box.

6. In the first cell of each row, modify the **Shading** by inserting the following pictures: **p04H_Lake, p04H_Plaza**, and **p04H_Golf**.

7. Display **Slide 3** and then add a **New Slide** with the **Title and Content** layout. In the title placeholder, type **Rental Information** and then insert a **Table** with **3 columns** and **4 rows**. Change the **Table Style** to **Medium Style 3**, and then modify the **Table Style Options** so that only the **Header Row** is selected. *Clear* all other **Table Style Options** check boxes.

8. Size the table so that its lower edge extends to approximately **2.5 inches below zero**, and then type the following text in the table, leaving the remaining cells blank.

Product	Companies	Phone Number
Boats		
Personal Watercraft		
Equipment		

9. Activate the ✐ pointer, and then drag the pointer over each of the gray lines in the table to format the borders as solid black lines.

10. In the second table row—below the header row—use the ✐ pointer to draw a line that splits the two cells in the second and third columns into four cells. Do not be concerned if the cells are not the same height.

(Project 4H– Visitors continues on the next page)

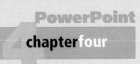

Mastering PowerPoint

(Project 4H–Visitors continued)

11. Repeat the technique that you practiced in Step 10 in the third and fourth table rows. Press [Esc] to turn off the Draw Table pointer. In the **Layout tab**, in the **Cell Size group**, click the **Distribute Rows** button.

12. Type the remaining text as shown in the following table, and then **Center** all of the table text horizontally and vertically in the cells.

Product	Companies	Phone Number
Boats	On the Water Boating	928-555-0125
	Fun Time Boat Rental	928-555-9675
Personal Watercraft	PWC Rentals	928-555-6124
	Watercraft Fun	928-555-3287
Equipment	Glendale Water Toys	928-555-9745
	Fishing Gear Rentals	928-555-4579

13. Display **Slide 1**, and then apply the **Uncover Left** transition at **Medium** speed to all of the slides in the presentation. Select the slide title—**Tourist Information**—and then display the **Custom Animation** task pane. Apply the **Box Entrance effect**, and then change the **Start** setting to **With Previous** so that the title displays after the slide transition.

14. Select the picture of the person on the jet ski—the left picture. Apply the **Blink Emphasis effect**. Select the picture of the person jumping on a wakeboard—the right picture—and then apply the **Blink Emphasis effect**. Select the picture of the lake, and then apply the **Blink Emphasis effect**. Hold down [Ctrl], and then in the **custom animation list**, click the three items with the yellow star so that all three are selected. Click the **Start arrow**, and then click **After Previous** to apply the same start setting to each selected item.

15. Select the slide subtitle—**Lake Glendale**—and then apply the **Box Entrance Effect**. Change the **Start** setting to **With Previous**.

16. In the **Custom Animation** task pane, click the **Lake Glendale item** so that it is selected, and then use the **Re-Order Up arrow** to move the item so that it is first in the custom animation list.

17. In the **Custom Animation** task pane, click the **Rectangle 4 item** so that it is selected, and then use the **Re-Order Down arrow** to move the item so that it is last in the custom animation list.

18. Display **Slide 3**, and then select the group of pictures. Apply the **Grow/Shrink Emphasis Effect**, and then change the **Start** setting to **After Previous**. Display **Slide 7**, and then in the **custom animation list**, select **item 2**. **Change** the **Entrance effect** to **Diamond**, and then change the **Speed** to **Fast** and the **Start** setting to **With Previous**.

19. On **Slide 7**, select the **Lake Glendale** text box below the picture, and then apply the **Fly Out Exit effect**. Select the **Visit Us Soon!** text box, and then apply the **Dissolve In Entrance effect**. Change the **Start** setting to **With Previous** so that it displays as the Lake Glendale text box exits the screen. View the slide show from the beginning.

20. Create a **Header and Footer** for the **Notes and Handouts**. Include the **Date and time updated automatically**, the **Page number**, and a **Footer** with the file name 4H_Visitors_Firstname_Lastname

(Project 4H– Visitors continues on the next page)

PowerPoint
chapter four   Mastering PowerPoint

(Project 4H–Visitors continued)

21. Check your *Chapter Assignment Sheet* or your *Course Syllabus* or consult your instructor to determine if you are to submit your assignments on paper or electronically. To submit electronically, go to step 23, and then follow the instructions provided by your instructor.

22. **Print Preview** your presentation, and then print **Handouts (4 Slides Per Page)**.

23. **Save** the changes to your presentation, and then close the presentation.

End **You have completed Project 4H** ——————————————————————————

Content-Based Assessments

Mastering PowerPoint

Project 4I — Finances

In this project, you will apply the skills you practiced from all the Objectives in Projects 4A and 4B.

Objectives: 1. *Format Tables;* **2.** *Modify a Table Using the Draw Borders Feature;* **3.** *Create and Modify a Pie Chart;* **4.** *Apply Custom Animation Effects.*

In the following Mastering PowerPoint Assessment, you will create a presentation that Gary Miller, Controller for the City of Lake Glendale, will present to the City Council that details the City's year-to-date financial reports. Your completed presentation will look similar to Figure 4.48.

For Project 4I, you will need the following files:

p04I_Administration
p04I_Services
p04I_Works
p04I_Safety
p04I_Utilities
p04I_Logo

You will save your presentation as
4I_Finances_Firstname_Lastname

Figure 4.48

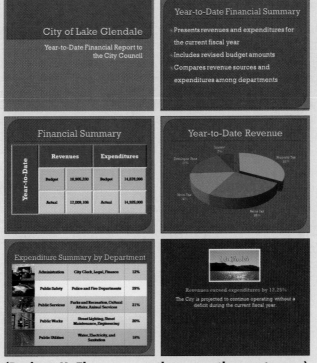

(Project 4I–Finances continues on the next page)

Mastering PowerPoint

(Project 4I–Finances continued)

1. **Start** PowerPoint and begin a new blank presentation. Apply the **Foundry** theme, and then change the **Theme Colors** to **Concourse**. For the presentation title, type **City of Lake Glendale** and for the subtitle, type **Year-to-Date Financial Report to the City Council Save** the file in your **PowerPoint Chapter 4** folder as **4I_Finances_Firstname_Lastname**

2. Insert a **New Slide** with the **Title and Content** layout. In the title placeholder, type **Year-to-Date Financial Summary** and then in the content placeholder, type the following bullet points.

   Presents revenues and expenditures for the current fiscal year

   Includes revised budget amounts

   Compares revenue sources and expenditures among departments

3. Select the text in the content placeholder, and then change the **Line Spacing** to **1.5**. Insert a **New Slide** with the **Title and Content** layout. In the title placeholder, type **Financial Summary** and then **Center** the title. In the content placeholder, insert a **Table** with **5 columns** and **3 rows**, and then adjust the table size so that its lower edge extends to **2.5 inches below zero**. Change the **Table Style** to **Medium Style 2 – Accent 4**.

4. **Merge** the three cells in the first column. Type **Year-to-Date** and then change the **Text Direction** to **Rotate all text 270°**. Change the **Font Size** to **32**, and then in the remaining cells, type the following information, leaving cells blank as indicated.

Revenues		Expenditures	
Budget	16,905,230	Budget	14,876,098
Actual	17,009,108	Actual	14,925,008

5. Use the **Eraser** to remove the border between the **Revenues** cell and the blank cell, and then use the **Eraser** again to remove the border between the **Expenditures** cell and the blank cell. Change the **Font Size** of **Revenues** and **Expenditures** to **28**. Select the entire table, and then **Center** the text horizontally and vertically within the cells. With the entire table still selected, modify the **Table Style Effects** by applying the first **Cell Bevel—Circle**.

6. Insert a **New Slide** with the **Title and Content** layout. Type and **Center** the slide title **Year-to-Date Revenue** and then in the content placeholder, insert a **Pie in 3-D** chart. In the Excel window, in cell **B1**, type **Income in Millions** and then beginning in cell **A2**, type the remaining data from the following table.

Property Tax	5.6
Sales Tax	4.3
Hotel Tax	2.7
Developer Fees	3.2
Interest	1.2

7. **AutoFit column A**, and then close the Excel window. Modify the chart layout by turning off the **Legend** and the **Chart Title**. Display the **Category Name** and **Percentage Data Labels** on the **Outside End** of the pie. Explode the largest pie slice, and then change the **Font Size** for all of the data labels to **16**.

(Project 4I– Finances continues on the next page)

(Project 4I–Finances continued)

8. Insert a **New Slide** with the **Title and Content** layout. Type and **Center** the slide title **Expenditure Summary by Department** and then change the **Font Size** to **36** so that the entire title fits on one line. Insert a **Table with 3 columns** and **5 rows**, and then size the table so that its lower edge extends to **3 inches below zero**. Change the **Table Style** to the **Best Match for Document Themed Style 1 – Accent 1**, and then *clear* the **Header Row** check box.

9. Point to the border separating the second and third columns to display the pointer. Using the horizontal ruler as your guide, drag to the right so that the dashed vertical line is positioned at approximately **3 inches after zero** and the last column is approximately 1 inch wide.

10. Select **columns 1** and **2**, and then use the **Distribute Columns** feature so that the two columns are equal in width. On the **Design tab**, in the **Draw Borders group**, change the **Pen Color** to the fifth color in the first row—**Turquoise, Accent 1**. Create a new first column by drawing a border that extends from the top of the table to the bottom of the table, positioned at **3 inches before zero** on the horizontal ruler. (Hint: Position the pointer slightly below the top border of the table.)

11. In the first column, modify the **Shading** by inserting the following pictures in each cell: **p04I_Administration**, **p04I_Safety**, **p04I_Services**, **p04I_Works**, and **p04I_Utilities**. In the remaining columns, type the following text.

Administration	City Clerk, Legal, Finance	12%
Public Safety	Police and Fire Departments	29%
Public Services	Parks and Recreation, Cultural Affairs, Animal Services	21%
Public Works	Street Lighting, Street Maintenance, Engineering	20%
Public Utilities	Water, Electricity, and Sanitation	18%

12. Select the table, and then **Center** the text horizontally and vertically within the cells.

13. Insert a **New Slide** with the **Section Header** layout. In the title placeholder, type **Revenues exceed expenditures by 12.25%**. Change the **Font Size** to **24**, and then **Center** the text. In the subtitle placeholder type **The City is projected to continue operating without a deficit during the current fiscal year**. Change the **Font Size** to **24**, and then **Center** the text.

14. From your student files, **Insert** the **Picture p04I_Logo**, and then drag the picture up so that it is positioned above the first text box. Display the **Custom Animation** task pane, and then apply the **Dissolve In Entrance effect** to the picture. Change the **Start** timing to **With Previous**.

15. Select the title placeholder—**Revenues exceed expenditures by 12.25%**. Apply the **Peek In Entrance effect**, change the **Start** timing to **After Previous**, and then change the **Speed** to **Fast**. Select the subtitle placeholder—**The City is projected to continue operating without a deficit during the current fiscal year**. Apply the **Peek In Entrance effect**, and then change the **Direction** to **From Top**.

(Project 4I– Finances continues on the next page)

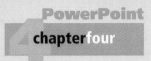

chapterfour   Mastering PowerPoint

(Project 4I–Finances continued)

16. Select the picture and apply the **Transparency Emphasis effect**. Change the **Start** timing to **With Previous**. Apply the **Box In Transition** at **Medium Speed** to all slides in the presentation, and then view the slide show from the beginning.

17. Create a **Header and Footer** for the **Notes and Handouts**. Include the **Date and time updated automatically**, the **Page number**, and a **Footer** with the file name 4I_Finances_Firstname_Lastname

18. Check your *Chapter Assignment Sheet* or your *Course Syllabus* or consult your instructor to determine if you are to submit your assignments on paper or electronically. To submit electronically, go to step 20, and then follow the instructions provided by your instructor.

19. Print Preview your presentation, and then print **Handouts (6 Slides Per Page)**.

20. Save the changes to your presentation, and then close the presentation.

End **You have completed Project 4I**

Content-Based Assessments

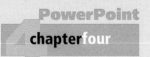

Project 4J—Business Running Case

In this project, you will apply the skills you practiced from the Objectives in Projects 4A and 4B.

From My Computer, navigate to the student files that accompany this textbook. In the folder **03_business_running_case**, locate and open the folder for this chapter. Open and print the instructions for this project, which are provided to you in Adobe PDF format. Follow the instructions and use the skills you have gained thus far to assist Jennifer Nelson in meeting the challenges of owning and running her business.

End **You have completed Project 4J** ————————————

Rubric

The following outcomes-based assessments are *open-ended assessments*. That is, there is no specific correct result; your result will depend on your approach to the information provided. Make *professional quality* your goal. Use the following scoring rubric to guide you in *how* to approach the problem and then to evaluate *how well* your approach solves the problem.

The *criteria*—Software Mastery, Content, Format and Layout, and Process—represent the knowledge and skills you have gained that you can apply to solving the problem. The *levels of performance*—Professional Quality, Approaching Professional Quality, or Needs Quality Improvement—help you and your instructor evaluate your result.

	Your completed project is of Professional Quality if you:	Your completed project is Approaching Professional Quality if you:	Your completed project Needs Quality Improvements if you:
1-Software Mastery	Choose and apply the most appropriate skills, tools, and features and identify efficient methods to solve the problem.	Choose and apply some appropriate skills, tools, and features, but not in the most efficient manner.	Choose inappropriate skills, tools, or features, or are inefficient in solving the problem.
2-Content	Construct a solution that is clear and well organized, contains content that is accurate, appropriate to the audience and purpose, and is complete. Provide a solution that contains no errors of spelling, grammar, or style.	Construct a solution in which some components are unclear, poorly organized, inconsistent, or incomplete. Misjudge the needs of the audience. Have some errors in spelling, grammar, or style, but the errors do not detract from comprehension.	Construct a solution that is unclear, incomplete, or poorly organized, containing some inaccurate or inappropriate content; and contains many errors of spelling, grammar, or style. Do not solve the problem.
3-Format and Layout	Format and arrange all elements to communicate information and ideas, clarify function, illustrate relationships, and indicate relative importance.	Apply appropriate format and layout features to some elements, but not others. Overuse features, causing minor distraction.	Apply format and layout that does not communicate information or ideas clearly. Do not use format and layout features to clarify function, illustrate relationships, or indicate relative importance. Use available features excessively, causing distraction.
4-Process	Use an organized approach that integrates planning, development, self-assessment, revision, and reflection.	Demonstrate an organized approach in some areas, but not others; or, use an insufficient process of organization throughout.	Do not use an organized approach to solve the problem.

Outcomes-Based Assessments

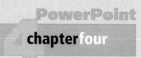

Problem Solving

Project 4K — City Profile

In this project, you will construct a solution by applying any combination of the Objectives found in Projects 4A and 4B.

For Project 4K, you will need the following file:

New blank PowerPoint presentation

You will save your presentation as
4K_City_Profile_Firstname_Lastname

The City of Lake Glendale is participating in a Housing Development Fair sponsored by the state of Arizona. Sienna Davidson, Director of Economic Development for the City of Lake Glendale, is preparing a city profile that she will use as part of her presentation at the fair. The fair is attended by people from many Southwestern states who are interested in learning more about home ownership opportunities in Arizona.

The City of Lake Glendale is home to approximately 65,890 residents with another 5,200 residents who own vacation property and who live in the city during peak summer vacation months. Children attend school at one of the eight elementary schools—8,800 students; two junior high schools—2,450 students; and three high schools—6,730 students. Adults enjoy access to community college courses and can earn a bachelors degree through the college's partnerships with local universities. The city enjoys a large tax base as boating and water loving visitors bring approximately $20 million dollars to the city on an annual basis. The 23-mile long Lake Glendale is home to a number of boat, jet ski, and fishing competitions and attracts visitors and residents to its calm blue waters. Vacation rental properties are tremendously popular. The number of properties listed with local rental property management companies are: Condominiums, 285; Studio apartments, 82; Houses, 165; Town Homes, 98. During summer months, property management companies routinely sell out of their weekend inventory. The newly built Glendale City Hospital provides emergency and urgent care as well as state-of-the-art operating rooms. Other attractions include two museums, a playhouse, and numerous antique stores and restaurants.

Create a presentation that describes the City of Lake Glendale using the information in the preceding paragraph. Apply a design template of your choice and include at least six slides. Organize the information in your presentation using at least one table, and create a Pie in 3-D chart using the vacation rental property information. Format the table and chart using the skills that you practiced in this chapter, including merging

(Project 4K–City Profile continues on the next page)

Problem Solving

(Project 4K—City Profile continued)

cells, drawing borders, rotating text, and exploding pie slices. Apply slide transitions and animation and insert pictures as necessary. Add the file name and page number to the Notes and Handouts footer and check the presentation for spelling errors. Save the presentation as **4K_City_Profile_Firstname_Lastname** and submit it as directed.

Note: You can find many appropriate images available to Microsoft Office users. To access these images, click the Insert tab, and then from the Illustrations group, click the Clip Art button. In the Clip Art task pane, type a key word—such as *lake*—in the *Search for* box. You can specify the image type (clip art or photographs) and where to search. The largest variety of photographs can be found by including Web Collections in the *Search in* box. You can also use images from earlier projects in this chapter, or images from your personal collection.

 You have completed Project 4K ——————————

Outcomes-Based Assessments

Problem Solving

Project 4L—Mall Construction

In this project, you will construct a solution by applying any combination of the Objectives found in Projects 4A and 4B.

For Project 4L, you will need the following file:

New blank PowerPoint presentation

You will save your presentation as
4L_Mall_Construction_Firstname_Lastname

The City Council of Lake Glendale is exploring the possibility of purchasing a large land parcel adjacent to the city limits for development of a new shopping mall. The City Controller, Gary Miller, is working with the Planning and Engineering departments to develop a presentation for the City Council regarding the purchase. Gary is responsible for developing the slides that include the cost estimates. Create a presentation titled **Glendale Shopping Mall** and then apply a theme of your choice. In the second slide, describe the parcel using the following information. The parcel is 20 acres and is located adjacent to the city, making utility construction feasible. There are two freeway off ramps that provide easy access and the land is flat and will require minimal grading. Storm drains and other utilities are nearby making construction in the area less expensive.

Insert a slide titled **Cost Summary** and use the data below to create a Pie in 3-D chart. Display category names and percentages, and format the chart using the skills that you practiced in this chapter.

	Cost
Land purchase	3,750,000
Land development	2,550,000
Utilities	5,450,000
Construction	8,235,000

Insert a slide with the title **Land and Utilities Cost Itemization** and then create a table using the following data. Format the table by merging cells, rotating text, applying table styles and adjusting column width.

(Project 4L–Mall Construction continues on the next page)

Outcomes-Based Assessments

Problem Solving

(Project 4L—Mall Construction continued)

Summary	Land Development Costs	
	Survey	850,000
	Soil Tests	765,000
	Grading	935,000
	Utilities Cost	
	Sewer	2,885,000
	Water	1,400,500
	Power and Telephone	1,164,500

Use animation techniques that you learned in this chapter to create a professional presentation. Add the file name and page number to the Notes and Handouts footer and check for spelling errors. Save the presentation as **4L_Mall_Construction_Firstname_Lastname** and submit it as directed.

End **You have completed Project 4L** ——————————

Outcomes-Based Assessments

Problem Solving

Project 4M—Rebate

In this project, you will construct a solution by applying any combination of the Objectives found in Projects 4A and 4B.

> **For Project 4M, you will need the following files:**
>
> New blank PowerPoint presentation
> p04M_Refrigerator
> p04M_Window
> p04M_Pool

You will save your presentation as
4M_Rebate_Firstname_Lastname

The City of Lake Glendale is participating in a rebate program that provides residents with the opportunity to turn in an older window or appliance and purchase a newer window or appliance that conserves energy. Twice a year, the city sponsors a Business Expo and the Engineering department is developing a presentation for residents who attend the Expo to learn about the Consumer Rebate Program. Create a presentation titled **Consumer Rebate Program** and subtitled **Improving Energy Efficiency** and then apply a design theme of your choice. Insert two slides that describe the program based on the following information.

The Consumer Rebate Program promotes energy- and water-efficient products and is designed to encourage Lake Glendale residents to install qualifying products in their homes. The products that qualify for the program are refrigerators, pool equipment, and windows. To qualify for the program, residents must fill out an application after purchasing and installing a product. Before making a purchase, residents must confirm that the product they are purchasing is eligible. If residents install the product themselves, a paid receipt for each item is necessary. If a contractor is hired, a copy of the signed and dated contract must be provided. Residents should submit the proof of purchase and installment along with the application and wait four to six weeks to receive the rebate.

Insert a slide with the Title and Content layout. In the title placeholder, type **Rebate Information** and then insert a table with 3 columns and 4 rows, and then apply a table style. Leave the first column blank, and then type the following information in the second and third columns.

(Project 4M–Rebate continues on the next page)

PowerPoint
chapterfour

Problem Solving

(Project 4M—Rebate continued)

Product	Rebate
Refrigerators	$85 each
Pool Pump	$75 each
Dual Pane Windows	$15 each

In the first column, insert the following pictures beginning in the second row: **p04M_Refrigerator**, **p04M_Pool**, and **p04M_Window**. Merge the first and second cells in the first row, and then change font sizes and alignment using the skills that you practiced in this chapter so that the table is appropriately formatted. Apply slide transitions and animation. Add the file name and page number to the Notes and Handouts footer and check for spelling errors. Save the presentation as **4M_Rebate_Firstname_Lastname** and submit it as directed.

End **You have completed Project 4M**———————————

Problem Solving

Project 4N — Power Usage

In this project, you will construct a solution by applying any combination of the Objectives found in Projects 4A and 4B.

For Project 4N, you will need the following file:

p04N_Power_Usage

You will save your presentation as
4N_Power_Usage_Firstname_Lastname

The Lake Glendale Power Department Chief Engineer, Sara Woodley, has been asked to present information on the Power Department to the Board of Commissioners. From your student files, open **p04N_Power_Usage**. Insert a new third slide titled **Lake Glendale Power Supply** and insert a table with 3 columns and 4 rows. Merge the first column and type **Sources** in the merged cell. Type the following information in the remaining cells, and then format the table using the skills that you practiced in this chapter.

Coal	32%
Natural Gas	28%
Hydroelectric	31%
Renewables	9%

Insert a fourth slide titled **Annual Electricity Usage** and insert a Pie in 3-D chart. Use the following data to create the chart.

	Megawatt Hours
Residential	705500
Commercial	1322600
Industrial	587900

Display category and percentage data labels and explode the largest slice of the pie. Apply slide transitions to all of the slides in the presentation. On Slide 5, apply Entrance effects to the picture and two text boxes. Apply an Emphasis effect to the picture and an Exit effect to the first text box. Change the animation order and timing so that the elements display in the following order with the following settings:

- Picture, Entrance effect, With Previous

- First text box, Entrance effect, After Previous

- Picture, Emphasis effect, On Click

(Project 4N–Power Usage continues on the next page)

Problem Solving

(Project 4N—Power Usage continued)

- First text box, Exit effect, With Previous
- Second text box, Entrance effect, With Previous

Add the file name and page number to the Notes and Handouts footer and check for spelling errors. Save the presentation as **4N_Power_Usage_Firstname_Lastname** and submit it as directed.

 You have completed Project 4N ————————

Outcomes-Based Assessments

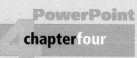
Problem Solving

Project 4O — Retirement

In this project, you will construct a solution by applying any combination of the Objectives found in Projects 4A and 4B.

For Project 4O, you will need the following file:

New blank PowerPoint presentation

You will save your presentation as
4O_Retirement_Firstname_Lastname

The City of Lake Glendale Human Resources Director is presenting information to city employees during the Employee Benefit Fair on the status of the City's Deferred Compensation Plan. The presentation will include information on the investments that the city offers for employees. The city has hired an independent brokerage firm to handle deferred compensation transactions, and employees may choose from a number of different mutual funds that vary in risk from moderate to aggressive. Statements are sent to employees on a quarterly basis but employees may change their investments options at anytime via the Plan Web site. Employees are eligible to invest in the Deferred Compensation Plan after their probation period has ended. Create a presentation that includes two slides describing the new Deferred Compensation Plan based on the information in the previous paragraph. Apply a theme to the presentation and then insert a slide that includes a table with 3 columns and 6 rows with the following information.

Capital Funds	Aggressive Portfolio	
	Can withstand market fluctuations	At least 10 years from retirement
	Moderate Portfolio	
	Willing to balance risk and growth over time	Five to ten years to retirement
	Conservative Portfolio	
	High priority on principal security	Approaching retirement

Merge the cells in the first column and then change the text direction and format of *Capital Funds*. Merge cells in columns 2 and 3 in rows 1, 3, and 5 so that the *Aggressive Portfolio*, *Moderate Portfolio*, and *Conservative Portfolio* text is centered over the cells in the rows below each merged cell. Use the skills that you practiced in this chapter to format the table appropriately, including applying table styles and drawing table borders.

(Project 4O–Retirement continues on the next page)

Problem Solving

(Project 4O—Retirement continued)

In addition to the Deferred Compensation Plan, the City Retirement Plan is a mandatory benefit in which employees contribute a percentage of their paycheck and the city matches the contribution. Insert a slide with a 3-D Pie chart that illustrates the percentage of each type of fund in which the city invests Retirement Plan contributions based on the data in the following table.

	Percent
Large Capital Funds	38%
International Funds	19%
Bonds	22%
Small Capital Funds	12%
Stable Value	9%

Display category and percentage data labels and explode the largest slice of the pie. Apply slide transitions and animation to the presentation. Add the file name to the Notes and Handouts footer and check for spelling errors. Save the presentation as **4O_Retirement_Firstname_Lastname** and submit it as directed.

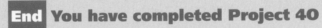

End **You have completed Project 4O**

Outcomes-Based Assessments

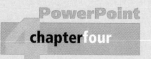
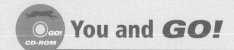

Project 4P — You and *GO!*

In this project, you will construct a solution by applying any combination of the Objectives found in Projects 4A and 4B.

From My Computer, navigate to the student files that accompany this textbook. In the folder **04_you_and_go**, locate and open the folder for this chapter. Open and print the instructions for this project, which are provided to you in Adobe PDF format. Follow the instructions to create a presentation describing the recreation programs in the city in which you live.

End **You have completed Project 4P** _____

GO! with Help

Project 4Q — *GO!* with Help

If you have created a chart in Microsoft Excel, you do not need to recreate it in PowerPoint. Instead, you can copy the chart from Excel to a PowerPoint slide. Use Microsoft PowerPoint Help to learn how to copy an Excel chart.

1 **Start** PowerPoint. At the far right end of the Ribbon, click the **Microsoft Office PowerPoint Help** button.

2 In the **Type words to search for** box, type **insert an Excel chart** and then press Enter.

3 Click the **Copy Excel data or charts to PowerPoint** link. Under **What do you want to do?** click **Copy a chart to a PowerPoint presentation**, and then read the steps and tips for copying an Excel chart. When you are through, close the Help window, and then **Exit** PowerPoint.

End **You have completed Project 4Q** _____

5 chapterfive

Delivering Custom Presentations

OBJECTIVES
At the end of this chapter you will be able to:

OUTCOMES
Mastering these objectives will enable you to:

1. Use Graphic Elements to Enhance a Slide
2. Work with Grouped Objects

PROJECT 5A
Enhance a Presentation Using Advanced Graphic Techniques

3. Insert Hyperlinks and Action Buttons
4. Create and Deliver Custom Shows

PROJECT 5B
Customize a Presentation for Your Audience

Sierra Vista Community College

Sierra Vista Community College is a large community college in California with a diverse student population. The college offers three associates degrees in 15 academic areas, and offers certificate programs, adult education, and continuing education on campus as well as online. The college serves the student body and surrounding community through partnerships with local businesses and nonprofit organizations, and makes positive contributions to the community by offering relevant curricula and high-quality learning experiences.

Delivering Custom Presentations

When you are preparing a PowerPoint presentation, it is a good idea to consider the types of questions that your audience may ask. If you can anticipate some of these inquiries, you can prepare slides that contain information relevant to the questions. These slides may contain information, graphics, or links to websites that will provide further insight into the topic.

Project 5A **Certificates**

In Activities 5.1 through 5.7, you will create a presentation that Nancy Kim, faculty member in the Computer Technology department, is developing to inform students of the certificate programs available in the Computer Technology department. Your completed presentation will look similar to Figure 5.1.

**You will save your presentation as
5A_Certificates_Firstname_Lastname**

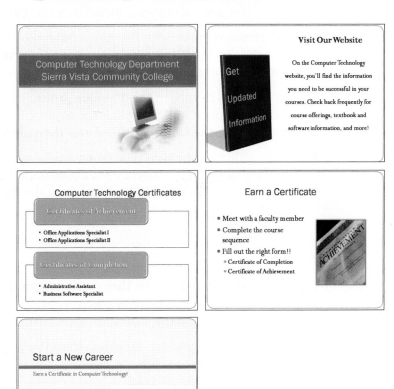

Figure 5.1
Project 5A—Certificates

Objective 1
Use Graphic Elements to Enhance a Slide

The pictures that you insert in a presentation should illustrate important information while enhancing the overall appearance of the slide. Grouping, recoloring, and rotating pictures are PowerPoint graphic techniques that will help you to ensure that your pictures provide maximum impact while still coordinating with your presentation design.

Activity 5.1 Inserting and Recoloring a Picture

You may find a picture that perfectly illustrates an important point on a slide, but clashes with your slide design. You can use PowerPoint to recolor your pictures so that the pictures coordinate with your design and color themes.

1 **Start** PowerPoint and begin a new blank presentation. From the **Office** menu , click **Save As**, and then navigate to the location where you are saving your files. Click the **Create New Folder** button , create a folder with the name **PowerPoint Chapter 5** and then click **OK**. In the **File name** box, type **5A_Certificates_Firstname_Lastname** and then click **Save** to save your file.

2 On the **Design** tab, in the **Themes** group, click the **More** button , and then under **Built-In**, click the **Equity** theme. In the **Themes group**, click the **Colors** button, and then click **Origin**.

3 In the title placeholder, type **Computer Technology Department** and then press Enter. Type **Sierra Vista Community College** and then select the title text. On the Mini toolbar, click the **Font Color button arrow** , and then in the first row, click the eighth color—**Light Yellow, Accent 4**.

4 Select and Delete the subtitle placeholder.

5 On the **Insert tab**, in the **Illustrations group**, click the **Picture** button. Navigate to the location where your student files are stored, click **p05A_Keyboard**, and then click **Insert**. Point to the picture to display the pointer, and then drag the picture to the right so that its right edge aligns with the right edge of the slide. Part of the title will be covered.

The colors of the picture are very bright and clash with the presentation design.

6 On the **Format tab**, in the **Adjust group**, click the **Recolor** button to display the **Recolor gallery**, as shown in Figure 5.2.

Using the Recolor gallery, you can change the overall color of a picture. For example, you can change a color picture to a gray tone or to another selected color tone so that it coordinates with the presentation theme colors.

Figure 5.2

Recolor button —

Recolor gallery —

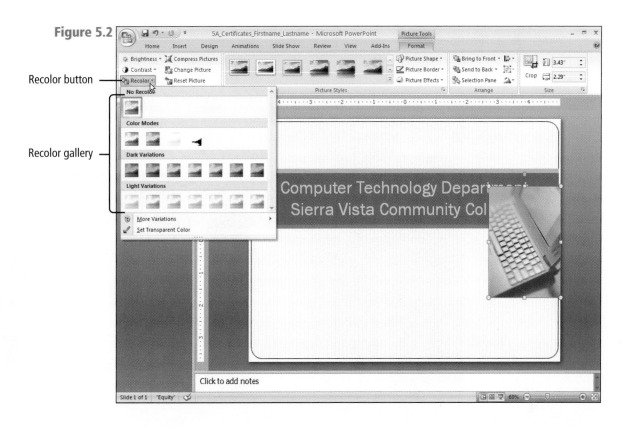

7 Point to several of the **Color Modes** and **Dark** and **Light Variations** to view the effect that the color will have on the picture. Then, under **Dark Variations**, click the first color—**Text color 2 Dark**.

The entire picture is reformatted in a gray tone.

8 From your student files, **Insert** the picture **p05A_Computer**. Drag down and to the right so that the lower right corner of the picture aligns with the lower right corner of the slide. The computer picture will overlap the keyboard picture. On the **Format tab**, in the **Size group**, click in the **Height box** [image]. Type **3.5** and then press Enter to change the size of the picture.

Do not be concerned if when you resize the picture, it no longer aligns with the lower right corner of the slide. You do not need to move the picture.

9 On the **Format tab**, in the **Adjust group**, click the **Recolor** button to display the **Recolor gallery**. Under **Light Variations**, click the first button—**Background color 2 Light**, and then compare your slide with Figure 5.3.

Figure 5.3

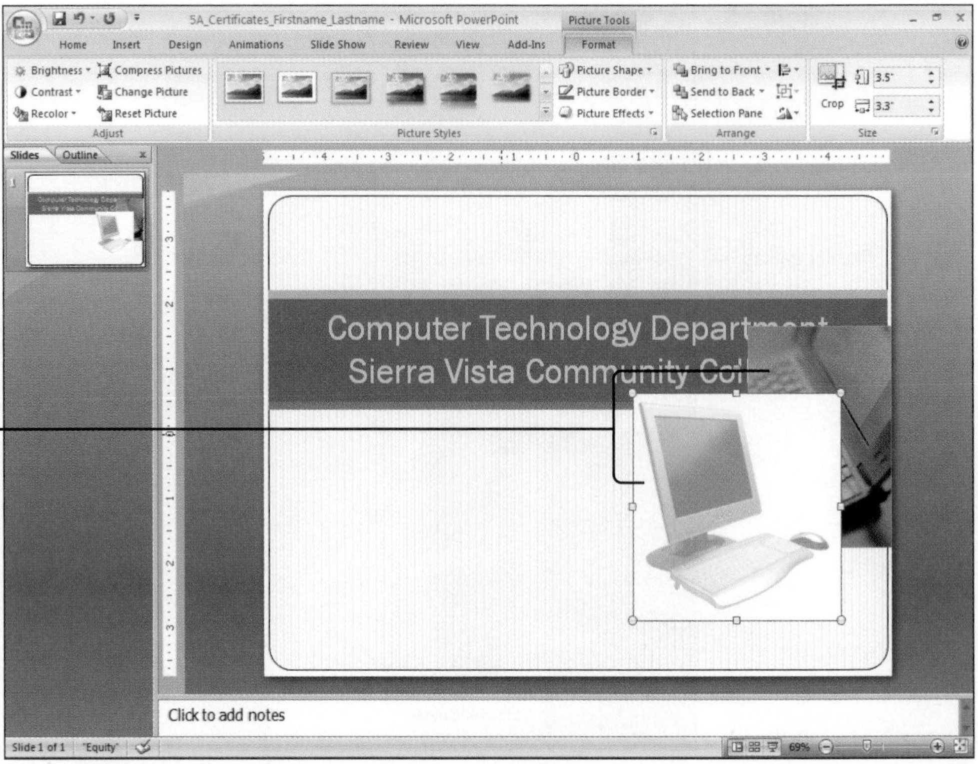

Recolored pictures

10 From your student files, **Insert** the picture **p05A_Mouse**. On the **Format tab**, in the **Adjust group**, click the **Recolor** button to display the **Recolor gallery**. Under **Dark Variations**, click the first button— **Text color 2 Dark.**

11 **Save** 🖫 the presentation.

More Knowledge
Additional Recolor Options

Below the Recolor gallery is the More Variations command. When you point to *More Variations*, the theme colors display. You can choose to apply any color to the picture, and you can display additional colors by clicking the More Colors option.

Activity 5.2 Rotating a Picture

Pictures and other objects can be rotated using the Rotate and Flip commands or by using the rotation handle.

1 If necessary, select the picture of the computer mouse. On the

Format tab, in the **Arrange group**, click the **Rotate** button 🔄▾. Point to **Rotate Right 90°** and notice the rotation applied to the picture, as shown in Figure 5.4.

Figure 5.4

Rotate button —

Picture rotated 90° —

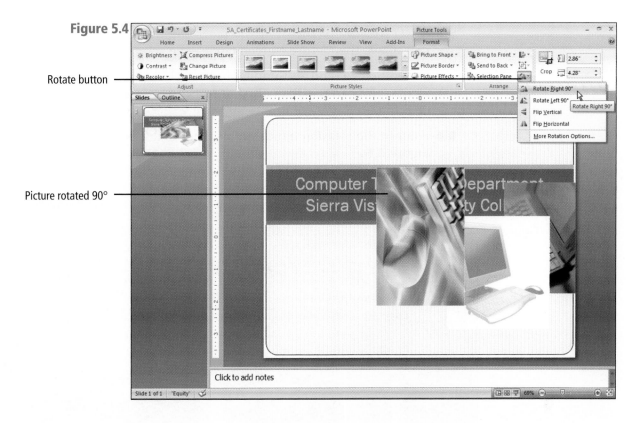

2 Point to each of the rotation options to view the effect that each has on the picture. Notice that the Flip Horizontal and Flip Vertical commands flip the picture 180°.

3 Click **Flip Horizontal** to create a mirror image of the picture by flipping it 180°, as shown in Figure 5.5.

Figure 5.5

Picture flipped horizontally —

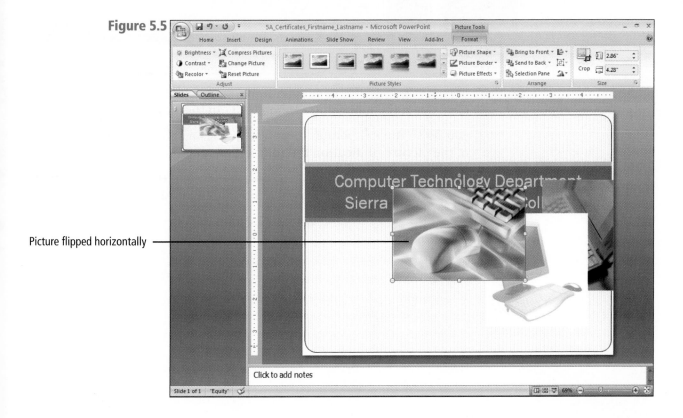

4 Select the first picture that you inserted—the keyboard—and notice that above the picture a green circle—the rotation handle—displays.

In addition to rotating and flipping objects in 90° and 180° increments, you can use the ***rotation handle*** to rotate an object in any direction in any increment.

5 Point to the rotation handle to display the ⟳ pointer as shown in Figure 5.6.

Figure 5.6

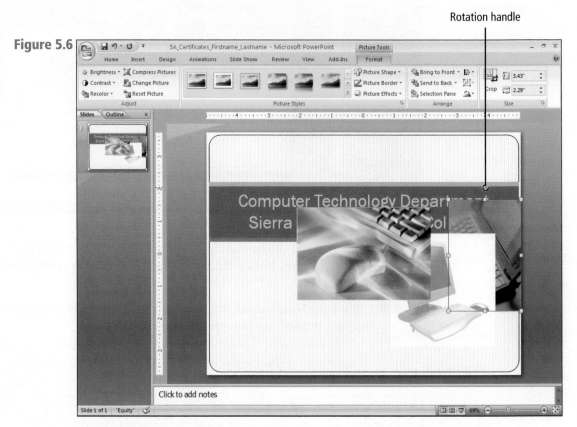

6 Hold down the mouse button and drag to the right, noticing that as you do so the ⟳ pointer displays, as does a semi-transparent image of the picture, indicating the rotation position.

7 Rotate the picture until the upper left corner of the semi-transparent image aligns with the green rotation handle as shown in Figure 5.7.

Semi-transparent image
aligns with green rotation handle

Figure 5.7

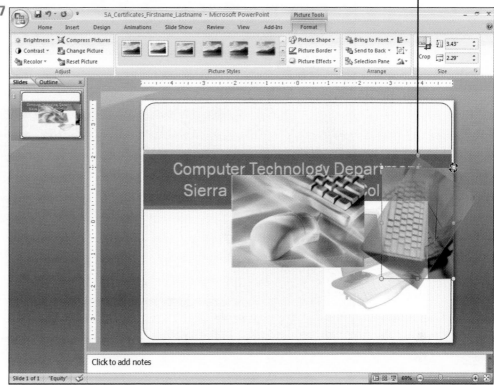

8 Release the mouse button to rotate the picture, and then compare your slide with Figure 5.8.

Do not be concerned that a portion of the rotated picture is outside of the slide as you will adjust the picture in a later activity.

Figure 5.8

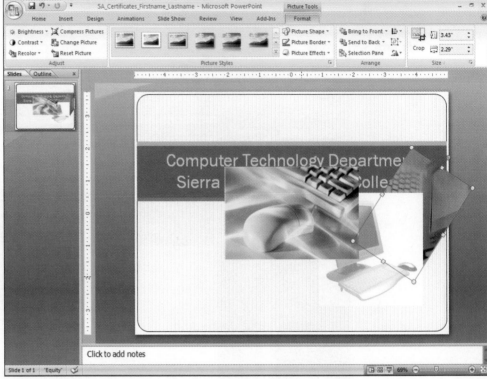

9 **Save** 💾 your presentation.

More Knowledge

Rotating an Object in 15° Increments

Hold down [⇧ Shift] while rotating an object to constrain the rotation to 15° increments.

Activity 5.3 Cropping a Picture

Cropping or trimming a picture emphasizes part of the picture by removing unwanted vertical or horizontal edges.

1 Select the picture of the computer mouse. On the **Format tab**, in the **Size group**, click the **Crop** button and then notice that the picture is surrounded by cropping handles, as shown in Figure 5.9.

You can crop a picture using any of the cropping handles. The left and right handles remove unwanted portions of the picture from the left or right sides of the picture. The top and bottom cropping handles remove unwanted portions of the picture from the top or bottom of the picture. The corner handles remove unwanted portions of the picture from the top or bottom *and* the sides.

Figure 5.9

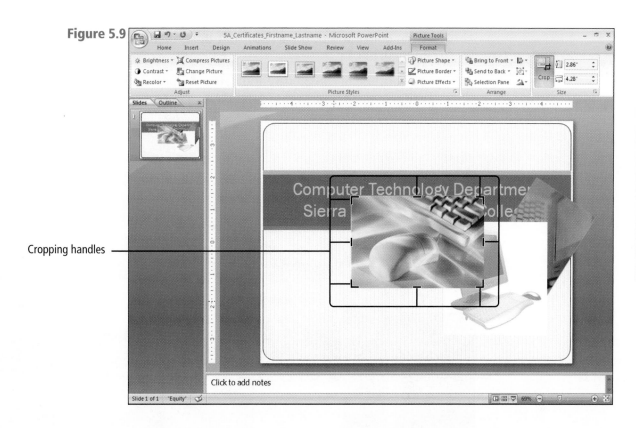

Cropping handles ——

2 Position the pointer over the top-right corner cropping handle and notice that the pointer displays in the same shape as the cropping handle, as shown in Figure 5.10.

Position pointer here

Figure 5.10

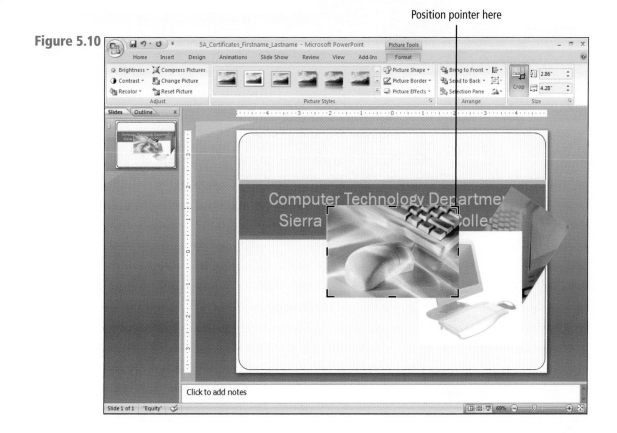

3 Drag down and to the left so that the crop outline displays as shown in Figure 5.11.

The outline of the picture indicates the portion of the picture that will *remain*. The portion of the picture outside of the outline will be cropped.

Crop picture as shown

Figure 5.11

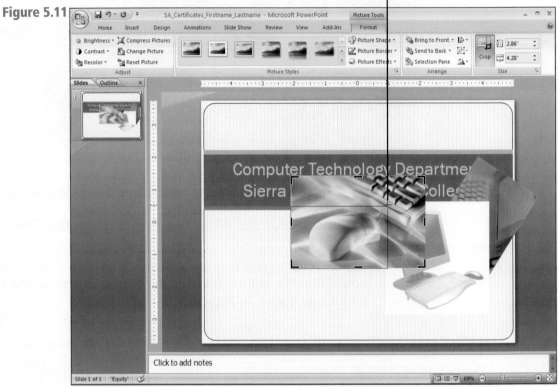

4 Release the mouse button to crop the picture.

The crop feature eliminated the keyboard from the picture, thus emphasizing the mouse.

5 On the **Format tab**, in the **Size group**, click the **Crop** button to turn off the Crop feature. Alternatively, press Esc to turn off the Crop feature.

6 **Save** 🖫 your presentation.

More Knowledge

Zooming in on a Slide

The Zoom Slider—located in the lower right corner of the PowerPoint window to the right of the View buttons—can be used to increase and decrease the size of the slide in the Slide pane. You may find that as you crop, size, and position graphics, you may need a larger view of the slide. Drag the Zoom slider as necessary to adjust the size of the slide in the Slide pane.

Activity 5.4 Changing Object Order

When objects are inserted on a slide, they often overlap. For example, on the first slide of the **5A_Certificates** presentation, the three pictures overlap each other in a stack. The first picture inserted—the keyboard—is at the bottom of the stack. The second picture inserted—the computer—is in the middle of the stack. The last picture inserted—the mouse—is at the top of the stack. You can change the order of the pictures by moving them backwards and forwards in the stack. The Table in Figure 5.12 describes the object order options.

Object Order Options

Option	Description
Bring to Front	Places the selected object in front of all other overlapping objects
Bring Forward	Moves the selected object one object closer to the top of the stack
Send to Back	Places the selected object behind all other overlapping objects
Send Backward	Moves the selected object one object closer to the bottom of the stack

Figure 5.12

1 Select the picture of the mouse. On the **Format tab**, in the **Picture Styles group**, click the **Picture Effects** button. Point to **Soft Edges**, and then click **25 Point**.

2 Select the picture of the computer. On the **Format tab**, in the **Picture Styles group**, click the **Picture Effects** button. Point to **Soft Edges**, and then click **25 Point**.

3 Select the picture of the keyboard. On the **Format tab**, in the **Picture Styles group**, click the **Picture Effects** button. Point to **Soft Edges**, and then click **50 Point**.

The computer picture overlaps the keyboard, thus hiding part of the keyboard picture. You can change the object order so that the keyboard displays on top of the computer.

4 With the keyboard selected, on the **Format tab**, in the **Arrange group**, click the **Bring To Front** button.

The keyboard moves to the front of the stack and is visible above the computer.

5 Point to the keyboard to display the 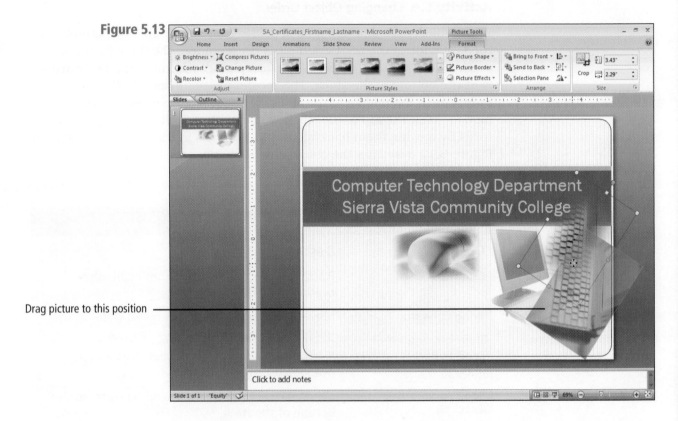 pointer, and then drag down so that the lower corner sizing handle touches the lower edge of the slide, as shown in Figure 5.13.

With the keyboard at the front of the stack of pictures, it obscures part of the computer picture.

Figure 5.13

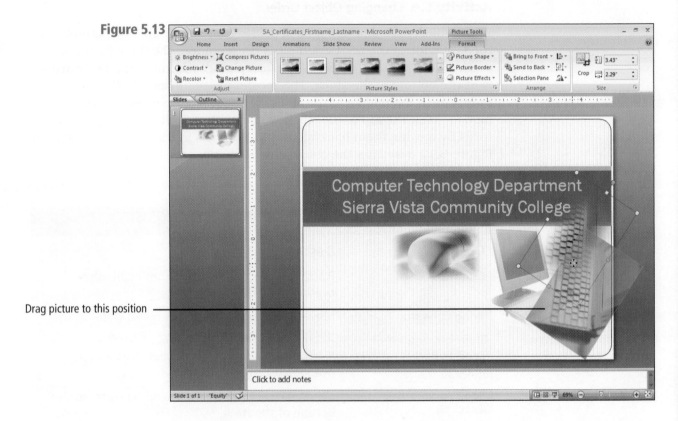

Drag picture to this position ———

6 To complete the collection of pictures, select the mouse picture, and then drag down and to the right so that the mouse overlaps the computer picture, as shown in Figure 5.14.

Figure 5.14

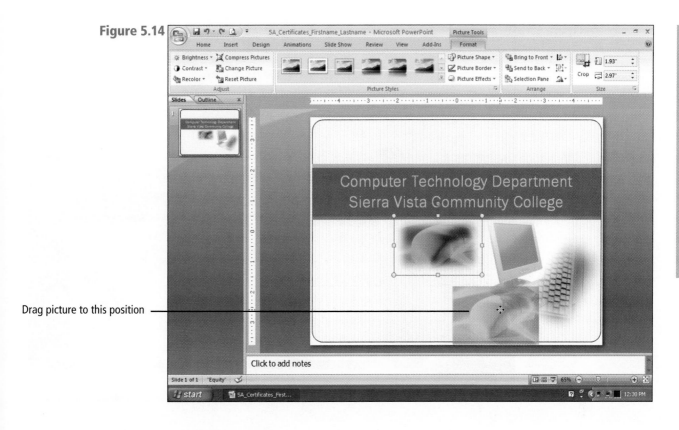

Drag picture to this position ——————

7 Save 💾 the presentation.

Objective 2
Work with Grouped Objects

When objects are inserted on a slide, animation and formatting are applied individually to each object. Some slides may contain a group of objects that should be treated as one unit, rather than as several individual elements. For example, Slide 1 in your **5A_Certificates_Firstname_Lastname** presentation contains three pictures. Each of these pictures is currently formatted separately. If the three objects are converted to a *group*—treated as one object—they can be sized, moved, and formatted all at one time.

Activity 5.5 Grouping Objects

To group objects on a slide, you must first select each object that you want to include in the group. In this Activity, you will group the three pictures on Slide 1.

1 With **Slide 1** displayed, hold down ⬆Shift, and then click each of the three pictures so that all three are selected as shown in Figure 5.15.

Sizing handles surround each individual picture, indicating that all three are selected.

Figure 5.15

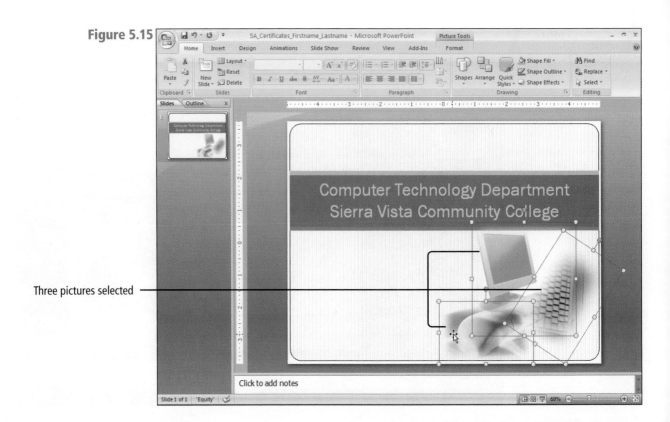

Three pictures selected

> **2** On the **Format tab**, in the **Arrange group**, click the **Group** button
> ![icon], and then click **Group**. Notice that sizing handles enclose the
> entire group of pictures, as shown in Figure 5.16, indicating that the
> three pictures can now be formatted and edited as one single object.

Figure 5.16

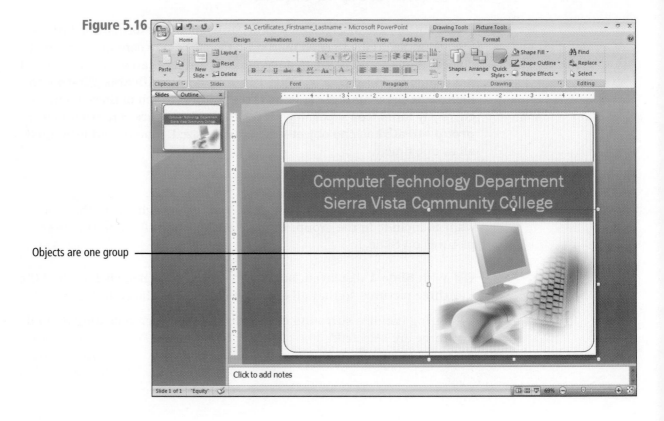

Objects are one group

3 **Save** the presentation.

<table>
<tr><td>**Another Way**</td><td>**To select multiple objects**

To select multiple objects, on the Home tab, in the Editing group, click the Select button, and then click Selection Pane. Hold down Ctrl, and then in the Selection pane, click each object that you want to select.</td></tr>
</table>

Activity 5.6 Moving, Sizing, and Formatting Grouped Objects

A grouped object can be moved or formatted as one unit, or individual objects within the group can be moved and formatted.

1 If necessary, select the group of images. On the **Picture Tools Format tab**, in the **Adjust group**, click the **Recolor** button. Under **Light Variations**, click the second variation—**Accent color 1 Light**.

The entire group is recolored.

2 On the **Format tab**, in the **Size group**, click in the **Height box** 2", type **3.5** and then click in the **Width box** 2.67". Type **4** and then press Enter to resize the entire group.

3 The arrow keys on your keyboard can be used to *nudge*—move objects in small increments. Press → six times to nudge the grouped object to the right.

4 Press ↓ six times to nudge the grouped object down. Click anywhere on the slide so that the group is not selected, and then compare your slide with Figure 5.17.

Figure 5.17

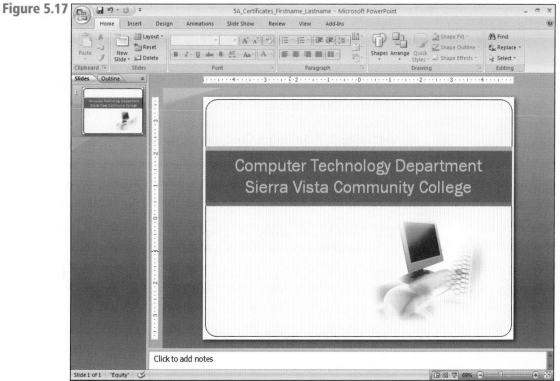

5 Select the group. Click the keyboard and notice that the group is surrounded by a dashed border and the keyboard is surrounded by a solid border, as shown in Figure 5.18.

Formatting will only be applied to the object with the solid border—the keyboard. The keyboard is very light and would be best displayed with a darker color variation.

Figure 5.18

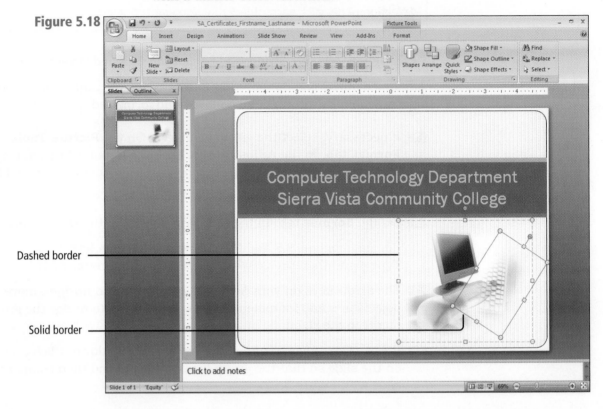

Dashed border

Solid border

6 On the **Format tab**, in the **Adjust group**, click the **Recolor** button. Under **Dark Variations**, click the second variation—**Accent color 1 Dark**.

7 Formatting for the group is complete. Click anywhere on the slide so that the group is not selected, and then **Save** 🖫 your presentation.

Activity 5.7 Saving a Group as a Picture

A group can be saved as a picture so that you can insert it on another slide or in another presentation. Although you can copy and paste a group, saving it as a picture facilitates easy sharing among presentations.

1 Point to the grouped object, and then click the right mouse button to select the group and display the shortcut menu.

2 Point to **Save as Picture**, as shown in Figure 5.19, and then click.

Figure 5.19

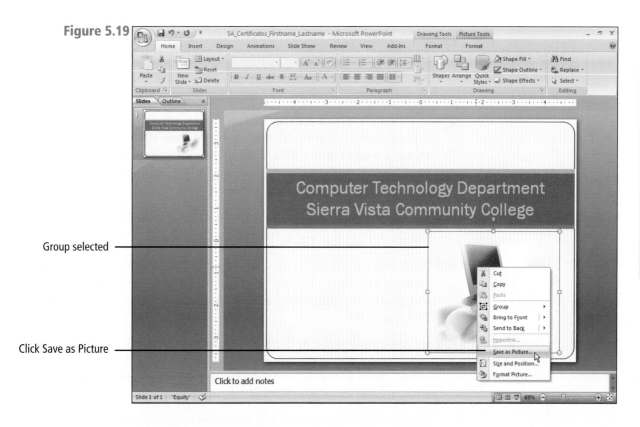

Group selected

Click Save as Picture

3 In the **Save As Picture** dialog box, navigate to your **PowerPoint Chapter 5** folder. Click the **Save as type arrow** to display picture file types from which you can choose to save your picture, as shown in Figure 5.20.

Figure 5.20

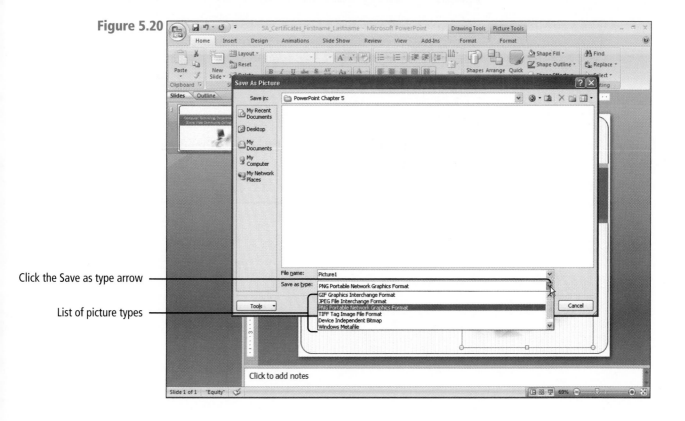

Click the Save as type arrow

List of picture types

4 Click **JPEG File Interchange Format**. In the **File name** box, type **5A_Picture_Firstname_Lastname** and then click **Save** to save your file.

Saving the file as a JPEG image results in a good quality compressed picture with a smaller file size than other picture file types.

5 On the **Home tab**, in the **Slides group**, click the **New Slide arrow**, and then click **Reuse Slides**. In the **Reuse Slides** task pane, click **Open a PowerPoint File**, and then navigate to the location where your student files are stored. Click **p05A_Slides**, and then click **Open**.

6 In the **Reuse Slides** task pane, right click **Slide 1**, and then click **Insert All Slides**. **Close** ⊠ the **Reuse Slides** task pane.

7 Display **Slide 4**, and then insert a **New Slide** with the **Section Header** layout. In the title placeholder, type **Start a New Career** and in the subtitle placeholder type **Earn a Certificate in Computer Technology!**

8 On the **Insert tab**, in the **Illustrations group**, click the **Picture** button. Navigate to your **PowerPoint Chapter 5** folder, and then click the picture that you just created—**5A_Picture_Firstname_Lastname**. Click **Insert** to insert the picture.

The file that you inserted is no longer a group—the individual elements cannot be edited or formatted—but all picture styles and formatting options can be applied to the picture.

Note — Background of Groups Saved as Pictures

When a group is saved as a picture, the background of the saved picture is white. In this presentation, the slide background is very light so the saved picture blends into the slide background. When a saved picture is inserted on a slide with a colored background, the picture's white background displays more prominently.

---

9 Drag the picture down so that it is positioned as shown in Figure 5.21.

Figure 5.21

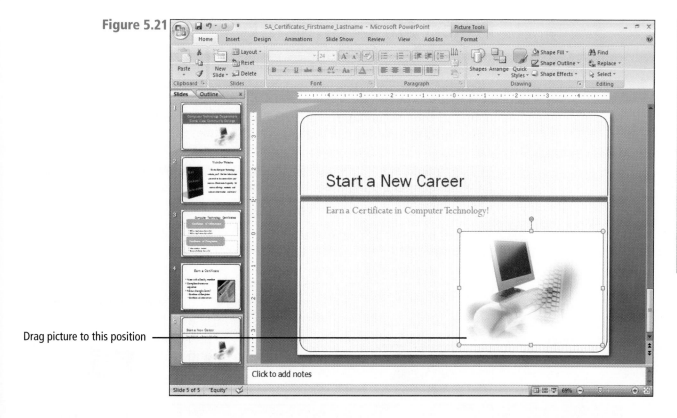

Drag picture to this position

10 Create a **Header and Footer** for the **Notes and Handouts**. Include the **Date and time updated automatically**, the **Page number,** and a **Footer** with the file name **5A_Certificates_Firstname_Lastname**

11 Check your *Chapter Assignment Sheet* or your *Course Syllabus* or consult your instructor to determine if you are to submit your assignments on paper or electronically. To submit electronically, go to Step 13, and then follow the instructions provided by your instructor.

12 **Print Preview** your presentation, and then print **Handouts (6 Slides Per Page).**

13 **Save** ![save icon] the changes to your presentation, and then close the presentation.

End **You have completed Project 5A** ————————————

Project 5B **Community**

In Activities 5.8 through 5.14, you will edit a presentation that Brock Klein, Director of the Sierra Vista Learning Community Project, has created to show to faculty and administrators who are interested in participating in the college Learning Community project. Your completed presentation will look similar to Figure 5.22.

For Project 5B, you will need the following file:

p05B_Community

You will save your presentation as
5B_Community_Firstname_Lastname

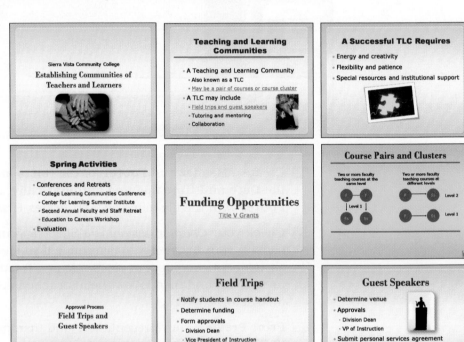

Figure 5.22
Project 5B—Community

Objective 3
Insert Hyperlinks and Action Buttons

A **hyperlink** is a button, text, or image that when selected, activates another information resource. Hyperlinks in a presentation give the speaker easy access to related information contained on another slide in the current presentation, in another presentation, in a file created in another application, or to a Web page.

Activity 5.8 Inserting a Hyperlink to a Web Page

Information on the World Wide Web is viewed with a **browser**, software that lets you view and navigate on the Web. A hyperlink can be created that launches your Web browser and connects to a Web page.

1 **Start** PowerPoint. From your student files, open the file **p05B_ Community**. From the **Office** menu [icon], click **Save As**, and then navigate to your **PowerPoint Chapter 5** folder. In the **File name** box, type **5B_Community_Firstname_Lastname** and then click **Save** to save your file.

2 Display **Slide 5**, and then select the text **Title V Grants**. On the **Insert tab**, in the **Links group**, click the **Hyperlink** button.

In the Insert Hyperlink dialog box, you can enter a Web address to display a Web page during the presentation.

3 Under **Link to**, if necessary, click **Existing File or Web Page**. In the **Address box**, type **www.ed.gov/programs/idueshsi** as shown in Figure 5.23.

This is the **URL**—Uniform Resource Locator or Web address—for the Department of Education Title V Grants Program—a resource for Learning Community Funding.

Figure 5.23

Type URL here

4 In the upper right corner of the **Insert Hyperlink** dialog box, click the **ScreenTip** button.

In the Set Hyperlink ScreenTip dialog box, in the ScreenTip text box, you can type the text that you want to display when you point to the hyperlink during the slide show.

5 Type **Department of Education** and then click **OK**. In the **Insert Hyperlink** dialog box, click **OK**, and then click anywhere on the slide to cancel the selection.

Notice that the hyperlink text is underlined and is a different color from the rest of the slide text. During the slide show, you can click the hyperlink and your Internet connection will launch and display the Web site.

6 To test your hyperlink, on the **Slide Show tab**, in the **Start Slide Show group**, click the **From Current Slide** button. Point to the hyperlink—**Title V Grants**—to display the 🖑 pointer and the *Department of Education* ScreenTip, as shown in Figure 5.24.

Figure 5.24

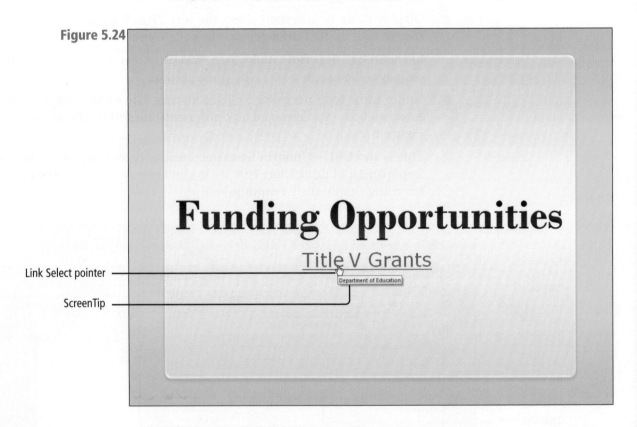

Link Select pointer

ScreenTip

Funding Opportunities
<u>Title V Grants</u>
Department of Education

7 Click the hyperlink to launch your browser and the Web page.

8 After you have viewed the Web page, close your browser to return to the slide presentation. Press [Esc] to end the presentation.

9 **Save** 🖫 the presentation.

Activity 5.9 Inserting a Hyperlink to Another Slide

Recall that when you are preparing a PowerPoint presentation, it is a good idea to consider the types of questions that your audience may ask so that you can prepare additional slides that contain information relevant to the questions. Use a hyperlink to display a slide that contains additional information about the topic.

1 Display **Slide 2**, and then select the third bullet point—*May be a pair of courses or course cluster.*

2 On the **Insert tab**, in the **Links group**, click the **Hyperlink** button.

In addition to creating a hyperlink to a Web site, you can use this dialog box to create a hyperlink to another slide within the presentation. In this case, another slide in the presentation illustrates the concept of a pair of courses. A hyperlink can be used to display the slide that illustrates the concept. The slide show can then be returned to the current slide so that the presenter may continue the presentation.

3 Under **Link to**, click **Place in This document**.

When Place in This Document is selected, you can choose to link to the first or last slides, the next or previous slides, or you can choose a specific slide in the presentation.

4 In the **Select a place in this document** area, under **Slide Titles**, click **6. Course Pairs and Clusters**, as shown in Figure 5.25.

Figure 5.25

Click Place in This Document

Select Slide 6

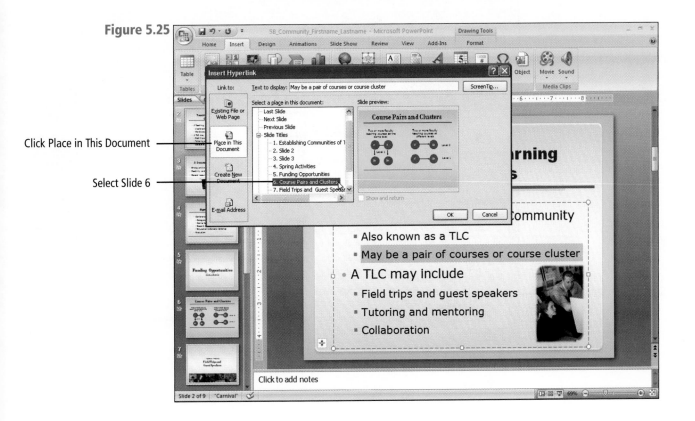

5 Click **OK** to create the hyperlink as indicated by the underlined text.

During the slide show, when the hyperlink is clicked, Slide 6 will display. In the next activity, you will create a link from Slide 6 back to Slide 2.

6 **Save** 🖫 your presentation.

Activity 5.10 Creating an Action Button to Link to Another Slide

An ***action button*** is a type of hyperlink created using an AutoShape. During a presentation, you can click an action button to execute the action that has been assigned to the button. For example, you can create an action button that opens another PowerPoint presentation or that displays another slide. In this activity you will create an action button on Slide 6 that returns the presentation to Slide 2.

1 Display **Slide 6**. If necessary, display the rulers.

Recall that in the previous Activity, you created a hyperlink to Slide 6. After Slide 6 displays during the slide show, the presentation must return to Slide 2 so that the slide show can continue.

2 On the **Insert tab**, in the **Illustrations group**, click the **Shapes** button. Under **Action Buttons**, point to the seventh button—**Action Button: Return**—as shown in Figure 5.26.

Figure 5.26

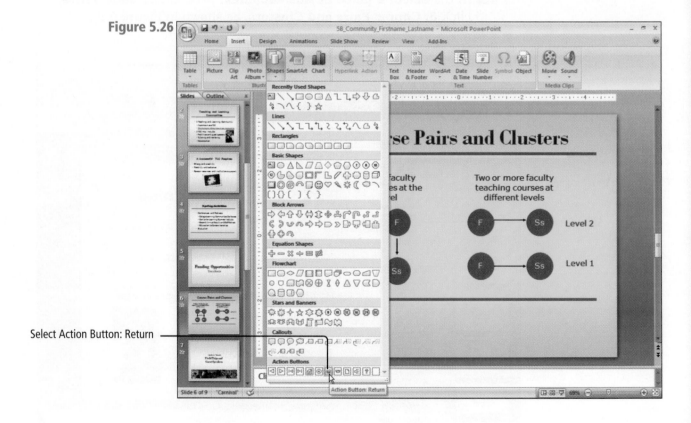

Select Action Button: Return

3 Click the **Return** action button. Position the displayed ⊞ pointer at **3.5 inches after zero on the horizontal ruler** and at **2.5 inches below zero on the vertical ruler**, and then click the mouse button.

An approximately 1-inch square action button is inserted on the slide and the Action Settings dialog box displays, in which you can indicate the action that takes place when the action button is clicked during a slide presentation.

4 In the **Action Settings** dialog box, under **Action on click**, notice that the **Hyperlink to** box displays *Last Slide Viewed*, as shown in Figure 5.27.

When you create an action button using the *Action Button: Return*, by default, the setting returns the presentation to the previous slide that was viewed. Other settings include Next Slide, Previous Slide, First Slide, and Last Slide. In this case, the last slide viewed is Slide 2. During the presentation, the action button—when clicked—will return the presentation to Slide 2.

Figure 5.27

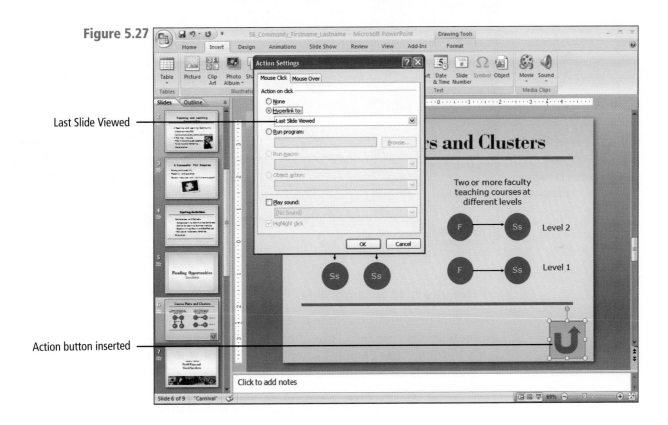

Last Slide Viewed

Action button inserted

5 In the **Action Settings** dialog box, click **OK**.

6 If necessary, select the action button. On the **Format tab**, in the **Size group**, click in the **Height box** [⊞ 2″ ⇕]. Type **0.5** and then click in the **Width box** [⊞ 2.67″ ⇕]. Type **0.5** and then press [Enter] to resize the action button.

7 With the action button still selected, in the **Shape Styles group**, click the **Shape Effects** button, and then point to **Bevel**. Under **Bevel**, click the first type—**Circle**.

8 Point to the action button to display the ⬚ pointer and then drag the action button down and to the right so that its lower right corner aligns with the lower right corner of the slide.

9 Click anywhere on the slide so that nothing is selected, and then compare your slide with Figure 5.28. **Save** 🖫 your presentation.

Figure 5.28

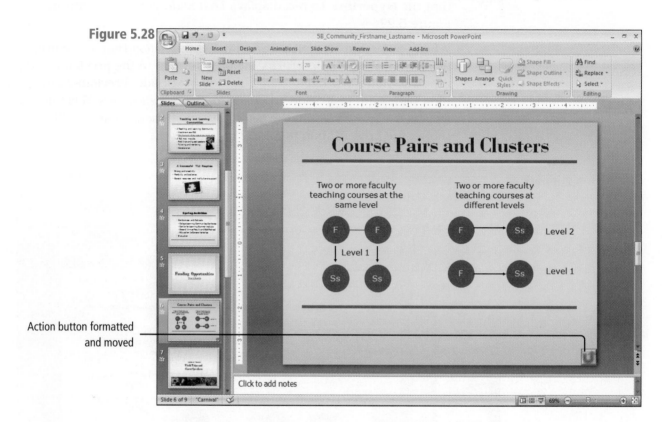

Action button formatted and moved

Activity 5.11 Hiding a Slide

In this presentation, Slide 6 should not display unless the action button on Slide 2 is clicked. Thus, Slide 6 must be formatted as a hidden slide. A *hidden slide* displays when the action button or hyperlink to which it is linked is clicked during an onscreen presentation. Hidden slides are useful because they enable you to create a slide that you can display only if necessary. For example, questions may arise during the presentation or clarification may be needed on a certain point. If the speaker can anticipate some of these questions, a hidden slide can be prepared, and then displayed only when necessary. In this Activity, you will hide Slide 6, and then test your hyperlink and action button.

1 If necessary, display **Slide 6**. On the **Slide Show tab**, in the **Set Up group**, click the **Hide Slide** button. Notice that in the Slides/Outline pane, the number 6 displays with a diagonal line through it and the slide thumbnail is transparent, indicating that the slide is hidden. Compare your screen with Figure 5.29.

Figure 5.29

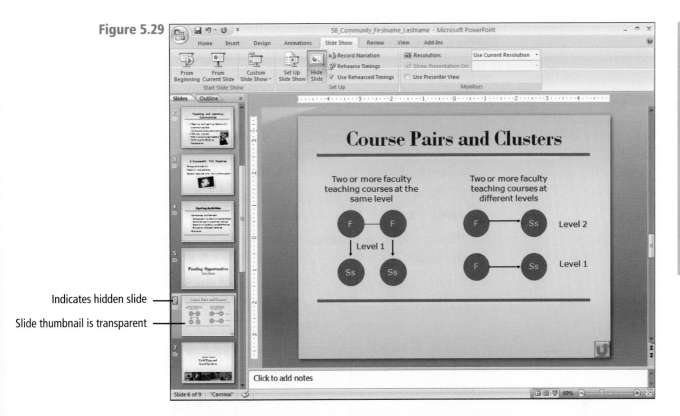

Indicates hidden slide —

Slide thumbnail is transparent —

2 Display **Slide 2**, and then on the **Slide Show tab**, in the **Start Slide Show group**, click the **From Current Slide** button. Click one time to display the first bullet point and its subordinate bullet points. Point to the hyperlink—*May be a pair of courses or course cluster*—to display the 🖑 pointer, and then click to display **Slide 6**.

3 View **Slide 6**. Point to the action button in the lower right corner of the slide to display the 🖑 pointer, and then click the action button.

The presentation returns to Slide 2, at the exact point you left the slide.

4 Continue to view the remainder of the slide show, and on **Slide 5**, click the hyperlink to launch your browser and open the Web page. Close the browser window to return to **Slide 5**. Continue to click the mouse button until the next slide displays.

Notice that Slide 6 does *not* display because it is hidden, and instead Slide 7—*Field Trips and Guest Speakers*—displays after Slide 5.

5 Press [Esc] to end the slide show, and then **Save** 🖫 the presentation.

Objective 4
Create and Deliver Custom Shows

When you deliver a presentation to more than one audience at different times, you may want to create a ***custom show***—a presentation within a presentation in which you group several slides to be shown to a particular audience. For example, in this presentation, the first six slides are relevant for every audience to whom it is shown. The last three slides are only relevant to faculty. Thus, a custom show can be created so that when faculty view the presentation, the speaker can show the last three slides and then return to the main presentation.

Activity 5.12 Creating a Custom Show

In this Activity, you will create a custom show using Slides 7, 8, and 9.

1 On the **Slide Show tab**, in the **Start Slide Show group**, click the **Custom Slide Show** button, and then click **Custom Shows**. In the **Custom Shows** dialog box, click the **New** button.

2 In the displayed **Define Custom Show** dialog box, in the **Slide show name** box, type **Trips and Speakers**

3 Under **Slides in presentation**, click **7. Field Trips and Guest Speakers**. Hold down ⇧Shift, and then click **9. Guest Speakers**.

Slides 7, 8, and 9 are selected as shown in Figure 5.30.

Type custom show name

Figure 5.30

Three slides selected

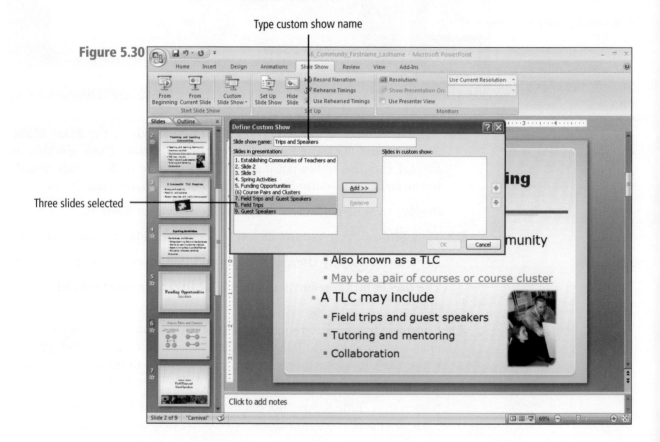

4 Click **Add**, and then compare your screen with Figure 5.31.

The three selected slides will be added to the custom show that you are creating—Trips and Speakers.

Figure 5.31

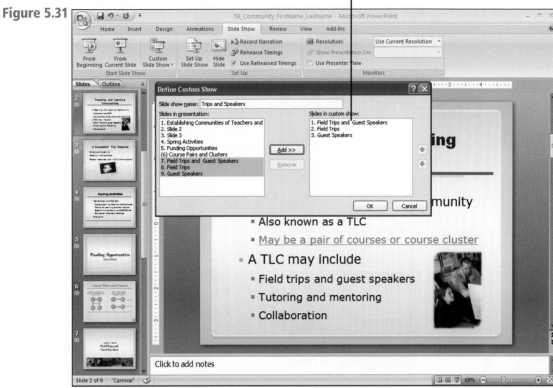

◪ Click **OK** to display the **Custom Shows** dialog box and notice that the Trips and Speakers custom show displays in the *Custom shows* list.

◪ Click **Close**, and then **Save** ▣ the presentation.

Activity 5.13 Creating a Hyperlink to a Custom Show

You can create a hyperlink to a custom show from any slide within the presentation.

▨ Display **Slide 2**. Select the text in the fifth bullet point—*Field trips and guest speakers*.

▨ On the **Insert tab**, in the **Links group**, click the **Action** button. On the **Mouse Click tab**, click the **Hyperlink to** option button, and then click the **Hyperlink to arrow** as shown in Figure 5.32.

Figure 5.32

Select Hyperlink to
option button

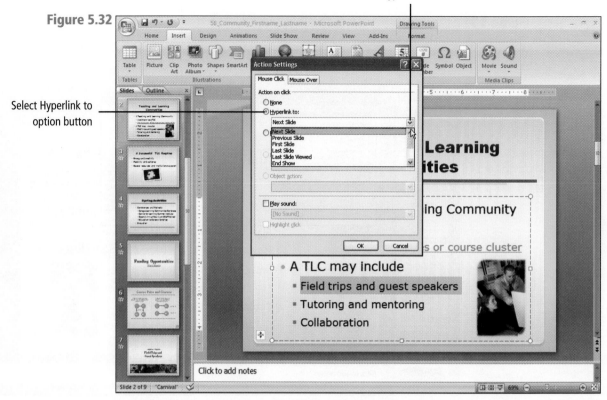

3 Scroll the **Hyperlink to** list, and then click **Custom Show**. In the **Link To Custom Show** dialog box, click **Trips and Speakers**. At the bottom of the **Link To Custom Show** dialog box, select the **Show and return** check box, as shown in Figure 5.33.

When the Show and return check box is selected, the slide show will return to Slide 2 after the three slides in the custom show have been viewed.

Figure 5.33

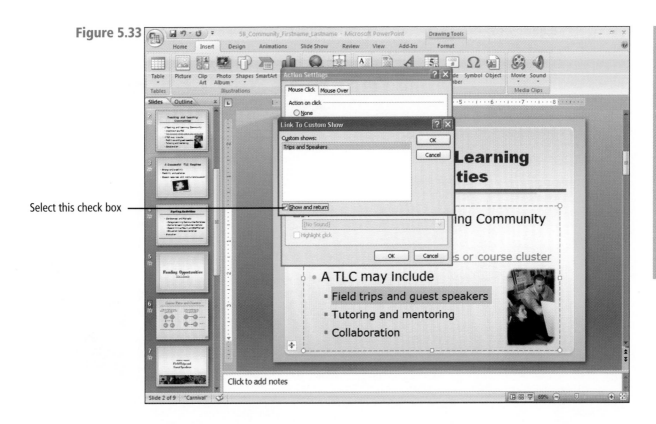

Select this check box

4 Click **OK**, and then in the **Action Settings** dialog box, click **OK**.

The underlined, colored text indicates that the text is a hyperlink.

5 In the **Slides/Outline pane**, scroll so that you can view **Slides 7, 8, and 9**. Click **Slide 7**. Hold down ⇧Shift, and then click **Slide 9** so that Slides 7, 8, and 9 are selected. On the **Slide Show tab**, in the **Set Up group**, click **Hide Slide** to hide the three selected slides.

Hiding the three slides in the custom show prevents the slides from being viewed unless the hyperlink on Slide 2 is clicked.

6 **Save** 🖫 the presentation.

Activity 5.14 Using On-Screen Navigation Tools

During a slide show, *navigation tools* display in the lower left corner of the slide. You can use navigation tools to display the presentation slides in any order while the slide show is running.

1 On the **Slide Show tab**, in the **Start Slide Show group**, click the **From Beginning** button. Click the mouse button to display **Slide 2**.

2 Point to the lower left corner of the slide and notice that a left-pointing arrow displays, as shown in Figure 5.34.

The left-pointing arrow is a navigation tool that when clicked, displays the previous slide.

Teaching and Learning Communities

Navigation tool

3 Move the pointer slightly to the right and notice that a pen displays.

The pen can be used to **annotate** a presentation by writing notes on the slide while the slide show is running.

4 Move the pointer to the right and notice that a slide button displays.

5 Click the **slide button** to display the shortcut menu. Point to **Go to Slide** and notice that the slide numbers and titles display as shown in Figure 5.35.

You can navigate to any slide in the presentation using the Go to Slide option. Thus, if an audience member has a question that is relevant to another slide, you can easily display the slide without exiting the presentation.

Figure 5.35

Slide numbers and titles

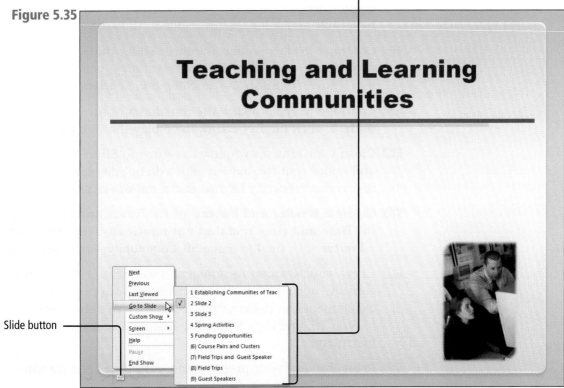

Slide button

6 Click **4 Spring Activities** to display the fourth slide.

7 With **Slide 4** displayed, on your keyboard, press B.

The B key is a toggle key that displays a black screen. During a slide show, it may be desirable to pause a presentation so that a discussion can be held without the distraction of the presentation visuals. Rather than turning off the projection system or ending the slide show, you can display the slide as a black screen, and then redisplay the same slide when you are ready to resume the presentation.

8 On your keyboard, press B to redisplay **Slide 4**, and then press Esc to end the show.

Note — Displaying a White Screen

Press the W key to display a white screen instead of a black screen.

9 Read Steps 10 through 14 to review the animation and hyperlink sequence that you will follow during this slide show. Then complete Steps 10 through 14.

10 View the slide show from the beginning, and on **Slide 2**, click the first hyperlink to display **Slide 6**.

11 On **Slide 6,** click the **action button** to redisplay **Slide 2**. Click to display the second set of bullet points, and then click the second hyperlink to display the first slide in the custom show.

12 Continue to click so that the three slides in the custom show display. Notice that when the custom show is complete, the presentation returns to **Slide 2**—*Teaching and Learning Communities*.

13 Continue to click to view the remainder of the presentation and on **Slide 5**, click the **hyperlink** to display the Web page.

14 **Close** your browser window to return to **Slide 5**. Click one last time and notice that the hidden slides do not display, and the presentation ends. Press any key to return to PowerPoint.

15 Create a **Header and Footer** for the **Notes and Handouts**. Include the **Date and time updated automatically**, the **Page number**, and a **Footer** with the file name **5B_Community_Firstname_Lastname**

16 Check your *Chapter Assignment Sheet* or your *Course Syllabus* or consult your instructor to determine if you are to submit your assignments on paper or electronically. To submit electronically, go to Step 18, and then follow the instructions provided by your instructor.

17 **Print Preview** your presentation, and then click **Handouts (3 Slides Per Page)**.

18 **Save** 🖫 the changes to your presentation, and then close the presentation.

End **You have completed Project 5B** ———————————

🔘 There's More You Can Do!

From My Computer, navigate to the student files that accompany this textbook. In the folder **02_theres_more_you_can_do** locate and open the folder for this chapter. Open and print the instructions for this project, which are provided to you in Adobe PDF format.

Try It! 1—Annotate a Presentation

In this Try It! exercise, you will use the pen to annotate a slide during a slide show.

Content-Based Assessments

Summary

In this chapter, you formatted pictures by cropping, recoloring, and rotating them. You practiced grouping pictures, and then saved your grouped object as a picture so that it could be inserted in another location. You customized a presentation by creating hyperlinks and action buttons to Web pages, other slides, and custom shows, and you practiced using onscreen navigation tools during a slide show.

Key Terms

Action button 340	**Custom show** 343	**Navigation tools** 347
Annotate 348	**Group** 329	**Nudge** 331
Browser 337	**Hidden slide** 342	**Rotation handle** 322
Cropping 324	**Hyperlink** 337	**URL** 337

Matching

Match each term in the second column with its correct definition in the first column. Write the letter of the term on the blank line in front of the correct definition.

_____ **1.** A feature used to rotate an object in any direction in any increment.

_____ **2.** The action of trimming a picture to remove unwanted vertical or horizontal edges.

_____ **3.** Several objects treated as one unit.

_____ **4.** The action of moving objects in small increments using the directional arrow keys.

_____ **5.** A button, text, or image that when selected, activates another information resource.

_____ **6.** Software that enables you to view and navigate on the Web.

_____ **7.** The acronym for Uniform Resource Locator.

_____ **8.** A slide that displays only when the action button to which it is linked is clicked during an onscreen presentation.

_____ **9.** A type of hyperlink created using an AutoShape.

_____ **10.** A presentation within a presentation in which you group several slides to be shown to a particular audience.

_____ **11.** To write notes on the slide while the slide show is running.

_____ **12.** Buttons used during a slide show to display slides in any order.

_____ **13.** A command that, during the slide show, enables you to navigate to any slide in the presentation.

_____ **14.** During a slide show, the B key is used to pause the presentation and display this type of screen.

_____ **15.** During a slide show, the W key is used to pause the presentation and display this type of screen.

A Action button

B Annotate

C Black

D Browser

E Cropping

F Custom show

G Go to Slide

H Group

I Hidden slide

J Hyperlink

K Navigation tools

L Nudge

M Rotation handle

N URL

O White

Content-Based Assessments

Fill in the Blank

Write the correct word in the space provided.

1. When preparing a PowerPoint presentation, it is a good idea to consider the types of _____ that your audience may ask.

2. Using the _____ gallery, you can change the overall color of a picture.

3. Pictures and other objects can be rotated using the Rotate and Flip commands or by using the _____ _____.

4. The Flip Horizontal and Flip Vertical commands flip the picture _____°.

5. The rotation handle is a _____ colored circle.

6. When a picture is cropped, the _____ handles remove unwanted portions of the picture from the top or bottom *and* the sides.

7. When a picture is cropped, the outline of the picture indicates the portion of the picture that will _____.

8. When a picture is cropped, the portion of the picture_____ of the outline will be cropped.

9. You can change the order of the pictures by moving them backwards and forwards in the _____.

10. To place the selected object in front of all other overlapping objects, click _____ _____ _____.

11. To place the selected object behind all other overlapping objects, click _____ _____ _____.

12. To move the selected object one object closer to the front of the stack, click _____ _____.

13. To move the selected object one object closer to the bottom of the stack, click _____ _____.

14. A _____ can be created that launches your Web browser and connects to a Web page.

15. When you create an action button using *Action Button: Return*, the presentation returns to the _____ slide that was viewed.

Content-Based Assessments

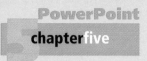

Skills Review

Project 5C — Visual Arts

In this project, you will apply the skills you practiced from the Objectives in Project 5A.

Objectives: 1. *Use Graphic Elements to Enhance a Slide;* **2.** *Work with Grouped Objects.*

In the following Skills Review, you will create the first few slides of a presentation that Judy Benson, faculty member in the Visual Arts department, will show at a student information meeting. Your completed presentation will look similar to the one shown in Figure 5.36.

For Project 5C, you will need the following files:

New blank PowerPoint presentation
p05C_Brushes
p05C_Film
p05C_Reel
p05C_Program

You will save your presentation as
5C_Visual_Arts_Firstname_Lastname

Figure 5.36

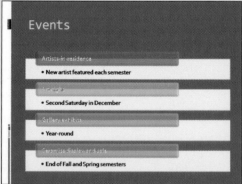
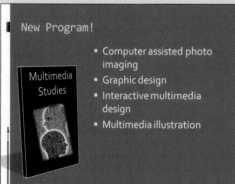

(Project 5C–Visual Arts continues on the next page)

Content-Based Assessments

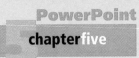
(Project 5C–Visual Arts continued)

1. **Start** PowerPoint and begin a new blank presentation. On the **Design tab**, in the **Themes group**, click the **More** button, and then under **Built-In**, click the **Metro** theme. In the **Background group**, click the **Background Styles** button, and then in the third row, click the third style—**Style 11**. From the **Office** menu, click **Save As**, and then navigate to your **PowerPoint Chapter 5** folder. In the **File name** box, type 5C_Visual_Arts_Firstname_Lastname and then click **Save** to save your file.

2. In the title placeholder, type **Visual Arts Department** and then in the subtitle place-holder type **Sierra Vista Community College**

3. On the **Insert tab**, in the **Illustrations group**, click the **Picture** button. Navigate to the location where your student files are stored, click **p05C_Reel**, and then click **Insert**. Hold down `⇧ Shift`, and then drag the picture up so that its top edge touches the top edge of the slide. Recall that press-ing `⇧ Shift` while dragging enables you to drag an object in a straight line.

4. From your student files, insert the picture **p05C_Brushes**. Drag the picture up and to the right so that its upper right corner aligns with the upper right corner of the slide.

5. From your student files, insert the **p05C_Film** picture. On the **Format tab**, in the **Adjust group**, click the **Recolor** but-ton to display the Recolor gallery. Under **Dark Variations**, click the third button— **Accent color 2 Dark**. On the **Format tab**, in the **Arrange group**, click the **Rotate** button, and then click **Flip Horizontal** to create a mirror image of the picture by flipping it 180°.

6. Select the picture of the reel, and then drag it down and to the right so that it is positioned below the brushes and to the right of the film pictures. Point to the green rotation handle to display the ⟳ pointer. Hold down the mouse button and drag counterclockwise to the left so that the upper right corner of the semi-transparent image aligns above the green rotation handle. A portion of the picture will be hidden behind the brushes picture.

7. Select the picture of the brushes. On the **Format tab**, in the **Size group**, click the **Crop** button. Position the pointer over the center, right cropping handle and then drag to the left so that the crop outline displays at approximately **4 inches to the right of zero on the horizontal ruler**. On the **Format tab**, in the **Size group**, click the **Crop** button to turn off the Crop feature.

8. If necessary, select the picture of the brushes. On the **Format tab**, in the **Picture Styles group**, click the **Picture Effects** button. Point to **Soft Edges**, and then click **50 Point**. Apply the same **Soft Edges Picture Effect** to the pictures of the reel and the film.

9. Select the picture of the film, and then drag to the right so that its left edge aligns at approximately **0 inches on the hori-zontal ruler**. The film picture overlaps the reel. Select the brushes and drag down so that the top edge of the brushes picture aligns at approximately **2 inches above zero on the vertical ruler**. Select the reel, and then on the **Format tab**, in the **Arrange group**, click the **Bring To Front** button. Compare your slide to Figure 5.36 at the beginning of this Skills Review and make adjustments to the placement of your pictures as necessary.

10. Hold down `⇧ Shift`, select the film and the brushes, and if necessary the reel, so that

(Project 5C–Visual Arts continues on the next page)

(Project 5C–Visual Arts continued)

all three pictures are selected. On the **Format tab**, in the **Arrange group**, click the **Group** button, and then click **Group**. On the **Format tab**, in the **Size group**, click in the **Height box**. Type **4** and then click in the **Width box**. Type **4.5** and then press **Enter** to resize the entire group.

11. Point to the grouped object, and then right-click to select the group and display the shortcut menu. Click **Save as Picture**. In the displayed **Save As Picture** dialog box, navigate to your **PowerPoint Chapter 5** folder. Click the **Save as type arrow** to display the picture file types from which you can choose to save your picture. Click **JPEG File Interchange Format**. In the **File name** box, type **5C_Art_Firstname_Lastname** and then click **Save** to save your file.

12. On the **Home tab**, in the **Slides group**, click the **New Slide arrow**, and then click **Reuse Slides**. In the **Reuse Slides** task pane, click **Open a PowerPoint File**, and then navigate to the location where your student files are stored. Click **p05C_Program**, and then click **Open**. In the **Reuse Slides** task pane, right-click **Slide 1**, and then click **Insert All Slides**. **Close** the **Reuse Slides** task pane.

13. Display **Slide 3**, and then insert a **New Slide** with the **Section Header** layout. In the title placeholder type **For More Information** and in the subtitle placeholder type **Contact the Visual Arts Department at 617-555-0987**

14. On the **Insert tab**, in the **Illustrations group**, click the **Picture** button. Navigate to your **PowerPoint Chapter 5** folder, and then click the picture that you just created—**5C_Art_Firstname_Lastname**. Click **Insert** to insert the picture. Drag the picture down and to the right so that its top edge aligns at **1 inch above zero on the vertical ruler** and its left edge aligns at **1 inch to the left of zero on the horizontal ruler**.

15. With the picture selected, on the **Format tab**, in the **Picture Styles group**, click the **Picture Effects** button. Point to **Soft Edges**, and then click **50 Point**.

16. Create a **Header and Footer** for the **Notes and Handouts**. Include the **Date and time updated automatically**, the **Page number,** and a **Footer** with the file name **5C_Visual_Arts_Firstname_Lastname**

17. Check your *Chapter Assignment Sheet* or your *Course Syllabus* or consult your instructor to determine if you are to submit your assignments on paper or electronically. To submit electronically, go to Step 19, and then follow the instructions provided by your instructor.

18. **Print Preview** your presentation, and then print **Handouts (4 Slides Per Page)**.

19. **Save** the changes to your presentation, and then close the presentation.

End **You have completed Project 5C**

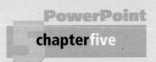

Skills Review

Project 5D — Curriculum

In this project, you will apply the skills you practiced from the Objectives in Project 5B.

Objectives: 3. *Insert Hyperlinks and Action Buttons;* **4.** *Create and Deliver Custom Shows.*

In the following Skills Review, you will edit a presentation that Jennifer Davies, Chairperson of the Curriculum and Instruction committee at Sierra Vista Community College, has created to describe the types of classes offered at the college. Your completed presentation will look similar to the one shown in Figure 5.37.

For Project 5D, you will need the following file:

p05D_Curriculum

**You will save your presentation as
5D_Curriculum_Firstname_Lastname**

Figure 5.37

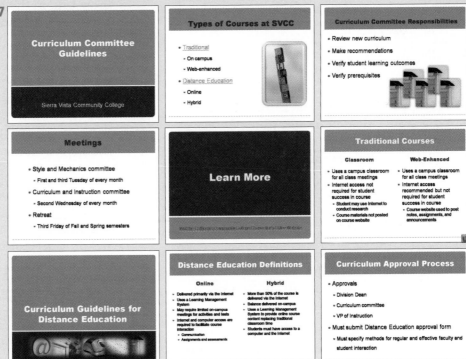

(Project 5D–Curriculum continues on the next page)

Content-Based Assessments

(Project 5D–Curriculum continued)

1. **Start** PowerPoint. From your student files, open the file **p05D_Curriculum**. Display the **Save As** dialog box, and then navigate to your **PowerPoint Chapter 5** folder. In the **File name** box, type 5D_Curriculum_ Firstname_Lastname and then click **Save** to save your file.

2. Display **Slide 5**, and then select the subtitle text—*Visit the California Community College Chancellor's Office Website*. On the **Insert tab**, in the **Links group**, click the **Hyperlink** button. Under **Link to**, if necessary, click **Existing File or Web Page**. In the address box type **www.cccco.edu/**

3. In the upper right corner of the **Insert Hyperlink** dialog box, click the **ScreenTip** button. In the **Set Hyperlink ScreenTip** dialog box, in the **ScreenTip text** box, type **Chancellor's Office** and then click **OK**. In the **Insert Hyperlink** dialog box, click **OK**.

4. Display **Slide 2**, and then select the first bullet point—*Traditional*. On the **Insert tab**, in the **Links group**, click the **Hyperlink** button. Under **Link to**, click **Place in This document**. In the **Select a place in this document** area, under **Slide Titles**, click **6. Traditional Courses**. Click **OK** to create the hyperlink as indicated by the underlined text.

5. Display **Slide 6**. If necessary, display the rulers. On the **Insert tab**, in the **Illustrations group**, click the **Shapes** button. Under **Action Buttons**, click the seventh button—**Action Button: Return**.

   Position the displayed ⊞ pointer at **3.5 inches after zero on the horizontal ruler** and at **2.5 inches below zero on the vertical ruler**, and then click the mouse button.

6. In the **Action Settings** dialog box, under **Action on click**, notice that the

   Hyperlink to box displays *Last Slide Viewed*. In the **Action Settings** dialog box, click **OK**. With the Return shape still selected, on the **Format tab**, in the **Shape Styles group**, click the **Shape Effects** button, and then point to **Bevel**. Under **Bevel**, click the first type—**Circle**.

7. If necessary, select the action button. On the **Format tab**, in the **Size group**, click in the **Height** box. Type **0.5** and then click in the **Width** box. Type **0.5** and then press Enter to resize the action button. Point to the action button to display the ✛ pointer and then drag the action button down and to the right so that its lower right corner aligns with the lower right corner of the slide.

8. If necessary, display **Slide 6**. On the **Slide Show tab**, in the **Set Up group**, click the **Hide Slide** button.

9. On the **Slide Show tab**, in the **Start Slide Show group**, click the **Custom Slide Show** button, and then click **Custom Shows**. In the **Custom Shows** dialog box, click the **New** button. In the displayed **Define Custom Show** dialog box, in the **Slide show name** box, type Distance Education

10. Under **Slides in presentation**, click **7. Curriculum Guidelines for Distance Education**. Hold down △ Shift, and then click **9. Curriculum Approval Process** to select **Slides 7, 8,** and **9**. Click **Add**, and then click **OK**. In the **Custom Shows** dialog box, click **Close**.

11. Display **Slide 2**. Select the fourth bullet point—*Distance Education*. On the **Insert tab**, in the **Links group**, click the **Action** button. On the **Mouse Click tab**, click the **Hyperlink to** option button, and then

(Project 5D–Curriculum continues on the next page)

(Project 5D–Curriculum continued)

click the **Hyperlink to arrow**. Scroll the **Hyperlink to** list, and then click **Custom Show**. In the **Link To Custom Show** dialog box, click **Distance Education**. At the bottom of the **Link To Custom Show** dialog box, select the **Show and return** check box. Click **OK**, and then in the **Action Settings** dialog box, click **OK** to create the hyperlink to the custom show.

12. In the **Slides/Outline pane**, scroll so that you can view **Slides 7**, **8**, and **9**. Click **Slide 7**. Hold down ⟨⇧ Shift⟩, and then click **Slide 9** so that Slides 7, 8, and 9 are selected. On the **Slide Show tab**, in the **Set Up group**, click **Hide Slide** to hide the three selected slides.

13. Read Steps 14 and 15 to review the animation and hyperlink sequence that you will follow during this slide show.

14. View the slide show from the beginning, and when the first hyperlink on **Slide 2** displays, click the hyperlink to display **Slide 6**. On **Slide 6**, click the **action button** to redisplay **Slide 2**. Click to display the second set of bullet points, and then click the second hyperlink to display the first slide in the custom show.

15. Continue to click so that the three slides in the custom show display. Notice that

when the custom show is complete, the presentation returns to **Slide 2**—*Types of Courses at SVCC*. Continue to click to view the remainder of the presentation and on **Slide 5**, click the **hyperlink** to display the Web page. **Close** your browser window to return to **Slide 5**. Click one last time and notice that the hidden slides do not display, and the presentation ends. Press any key to return to PowerPoint.

16. Create a **Header and Footer** for the **Notes and Handouts**. Include the **Date and time updated automatically**, the **Page number**, and a **Footer** with the file name **5D_Curriculum_Firstname_Lastname**

17. Check your *Chapter Assignment Sheet* or your *Course Syllabus* or consult your instructor to determine if you are to submit your assignments on paper or electronically. To submit electronically, go to Step 19, and then follow the instructions provided by your instructor.

18. **Print Preview** your presentation, and then print **Handouts (3 Slides Per Page)**.

19. **Save** the changes to your presentation, and then close the presentation.

 End You have completed Project 5D ──────────

Content-Based Assessments

Mastering PowerPoint

Project 5E — Alumni

In this project, you will apply the skills you practiced from the Objectives in Project 5A.

Objectives: 1. *Use Graphic Elements to Enhance a Slide;* **2.** *Work with Grouped Objects.*

In the following Mastering PowerPoint project, you will create the first few slides of a presentation that Kevin Perez, President of the Sierra Vista Community College Alumni Association, will show at a college informa- tion meeting. Your completed presentation will look similar to the one shown in Figure 5.38.

For Project 5E, you will need the following files:

New blank PowerPoint presentation
p05E_Graduate
p05E_Diploma
p05E_Information

You will save your presentation as
5E_Alumni_Firstname_Lastname

Figure 5.38

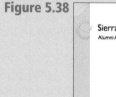

(Project 5E–Alumni continues on the next page)

Content-Based Assessments

chapterfive Mastering PowerPoint

(Project 5E–Alumni continued)

1. **Start** PowerPoint and begin a new blank presentation. Apply the **Solstice** theme. **Save** the file in your **PowerPoint Chapter 5** folder as **5E_Alumni_Firstname_Lastname**

2. In the title placeholder, type **Sierra Vista Community College** and then in the subtitle placeholder type **Alumni Association**

3. From your student files, **Insert** the picture **p05E_Graduate**, and then drag the picture down and to the right so that its lower right corner aligns with the lower right corner of the slide. **Crop** the picture using the top center cropping handle so that the gift does not display. (Hint: When you finish cropping the picture, its Height will be approximately 2.75 inches). Format the picture by applying a **Soft Edges 25 Point** picture effect.

4. From your student files, **Insert** the picture **p05E_Diploma**, and then **Rotate** the picture by applying the **Flip Horizontal** command. Drag the picture down and to the right so that its right edge aligns at **3.5 inches after zero on the horizontal ruler** and its bottom edge aligns at **3 inches after zero on the vertical ruler**. Apply a **Soft Edges 25 Point** picture effect, and then in the **Arrange group**, click **Send to Back** so that the diploma picture is behind the graduation cap picture.

5. Select and **Group** the two pictures and then **Recolor** the group with the **Light Variation—Accent color 5 Light**.

6. Save the group as a picture in your **PowerPoint Chapter 5** folder. Change the

file type to **JPEG File Interchange Format** and change the file name to **5E_Graduation_Firstname_Lastname**

7. Use the **Reuse Slides** command to insert all of the slides in the **p05E_Information** presentation. Display **Slide 4**, and then insert a **New Slide** with the **Picture with Caption** layout. In the title placeholder, type **Join the Alumni Association!** and in the caption placeholder below the picture placeholder, type **This is your chance to give back!** Change the title and caption **Font Size** to **24**.

8. In the picture placeholder, insert the picture that you saved in your **PowerPoint Chapter 5** folder—**5E_Graduation_Firstname_Lastname**. Display the **Picture Effects Bevel gallery**, and then apply the last **Bevel—Art Deco**.

9. Create a **Header and Footer** for the **Notes and Handouts**. Include the **Date and time updated automatically**, the **Page number**, and a **Footer** with the file name **5E_Alumni_Firstname_Lastname**

10. Check your *Chapter Assignment Sheet* or your *Course Syllabus* or consult your instructor to determine if you are to submit your assignments on paper or electronically. To submit electronically, go to Step 12, and then follow the instructions provided by your instructor.

11. **Print Preview** your presentation, and then print **Handouts (6 Slides Per Page)**.

12. **Save** the changes to your presentation, and then close the presentation.

End **You have completed Project 5E**

PowerPoint

chapterfive

Mastering PowerPoint

Project 5F—Student Services

In this project, you will apply the skills you practiced from the Objectives in Project 5B.

Objectives: 3. *Insert Hyperlinks and Action Buttons* **4.** *Create and Deliver Custom Shows.*

In the following Mastering PowerPoint project, you will edit a presentation that James Nishime, Dean of Student Services, has created to apprise students and faculty of the programs offered by Student Services. Your completed presentation will look similar to the one shown in Figure 5.39.

For Project 5F, you will need the following files:

p05F_Student_Services

You will save your presentation as 5F_Student_Services_Firstname_Lastname

Figure 5.39

(Project 5F–Student Services continues on the next page)

Content-Based Assessments

(Project 5F–Student Services continued)

1. **Start** PowerPoint. From your student files, **Open** the file **p05F_Student Services**. **Save** the file in your **PowerPoint Chapter 5** folder as 5F_Student_Services_Firstname_Lastname

2. Display **Slide 2**, and then select the first bullet point—*U.S. Department of Education.* **Insert** a **Hyperlink** to the **Web Page www.ed.gov** and then change the **ScreenTip** to **Department of Education**

3. Display **Slide 3**, and then select the first bullet point—*Individualized tutoring.* **Insert** a **Hyperlink** to **Slide 6. Tutoring Program**. On **Slide 6**, insert an **Action Button—Action Button: Return** positioned at **3.5 inches after zero on the horizontal ruler**, and at **2.5 inches below zero on the vertical ruler** so that the action button, when clicked returns to the *Last Slide Viewed.*

4. If necessary, select the action button and apply a **Bevel Shape Effect —Circle**. Size the action button so that its **Height** and **Width** are both **0.5** and then move the action button to the lower right corner of the slide. **Hide Slide 6**.

5. Create a **Custom Show** with the name **Faculty Involvement** that includes **Slides 7, 8**, and **9**. Display **Slide 3**, and then select

the last bullet point—*Faculty involvement.* Insert a link to the **Custom Show— Faculty Involvement**. Select the **Show and return** check box so that the presentation returns to **Slide 3** after the custom show is viewed. **Hide Slides 7, 8**, and **9**.

6. View the Slide Show from the beginning and click each hyperlink and action button to view the hidden slides and Web page.

7. Create a **Header and Footer** for the **Notes and Handouts**. Include the **Date and time updated automatically**, the **Page number**, and a **Footer** with the file name 5F_Student_Services_Firstname_Lastname

8. Check your *Chapter Assignment Sheet* or your *Course Syllabus* or consult your instructor to determine if you are to submit your assignments on paper or electronically. To submit electronically, go to Step 10, and then follow the instructions provided by your instructor.

9. **Print Preview** your presentation, and then print **Handouts (3 Slides Per Page)**.

10. **Save** the changes to your presentation, and then close the presentation.

End You have completed Project 5F ————————————————

Content-Based Assessments

Mastering PowerPoint

Project 5G — Online

In this project, you will apply the skills you practiced from the Objectives in Projects 5A and 5B.

Objectives: 1. *Use Graphic Elements to Enhance a Slide;* **3.** *Insert Hyperlinks and Action Buttons* **4.** *Create and Deliver Custom Shows.*

In the following Mastering PowerPoint project, you will edit a presentation that Robert Miller, Dean of Information Technology at Sierra Vista Community College, has created to inform students of the online programs offered at the college. Your completed presentation will look similar to the one shown in Figure 5.40.

For Project 5G, you will need the following files:

p05G_Online
p05G_Key

**You will save your presentation as
5G_Online_Firstname_Lastname**

Figure 5.40

(Project 5G–Online continues on the next page)

Content-Based Assessments

(Project 5G–Online continued)

1. **Start** PowerPoint. From your student files, open the file **p05G_Online**. **Save** the file in your **PowerPoint Chapter 5** folder as 5G_Online_Firstname_Lastname

2. Display **Slide 7**. In the content placeholder on the right, use the **Insert Picture From File** button to insert **p05G_Key** from your student files. **Recolor** the picture using **Accent color 6 Light**. Apply two **Picture Effects**: Glow—**Accent color 6, 18 pt glow**, and **Shadow—Inside Center**.

3. Display **Slide 8**, and then select the first bullet point—*FAFSA information*. Insert a **Hyperlink** to the Web Page **www.fafsa.ed.gov** and then change the **ScreenTip** to **Financial Aid**

4. Display **Slide 2**, and then select the second bullet point—*On the Web*. Insert a **Hyperlink** to **Slide 6. How Do I Access SVCCOnline?**

5. On **Slide 6**, insert an **Action Button—Action Button: Return** positioned at **3.5 inches after zero on the horizontal ruler** and at **2.5 inches below zero on the vertical ruler** so that the action button, when clicked, returns to the *Last Slide Viewed*. Apply a **Bevel Shape Effect—Circle**—to the action button. Size the action button so that its **Height** and **Width** are both **1 inch** and then move the action button to the lower right corner of the slide. **Hide Slide 6**.

6. Create a **Custom Show** with the name **Financial Aid** that includes **Slides 7** and **8**. Display **Slide 3**, and then select the last

bullet point—*Access financial aid information*. Insert an **Action** link to the **Custom Show—Financial Aid**. Select the **Show and return** check box so that the presentation returns to **Slide 3** after the custom show is viewed. **Hide** the slides in the custom show so that they only display if the custom show is viewed during the slide show.

7. Apply the **Box In Transition** at **Medium Speed** to all of the slides in the presentation. On **Slides 2**, **3**, and **4** apply the **Custom Animation Entrance effect—Blinds**—to each of the content placeholders. View the Slide Show from the beginning and click each hyperlink and action button to view the hidden slides and Web page.

8. Create a **Header and Footer** for the **Notes and Handouts**. Include the **Date and time updated automatically**, the **Page number**, and a **Footer** with the file name 5G_Online_Firstname_Lastname

9. Check your *Chapter Assignment Sheet* or your *Course Syllabus* or consult your instructor to determine if you are to submit your assignments on paper or electronically. To submit electronically, go to Step 11, and then follow the instructions provided by your instructor.

10. **Print Preview** your presentation, and then print **Handouts (4 Slides Per Page)**.

11. **Save** the changes to your presentation, and then close the presentation.

End **You have completed Project 5G**

Content-Based Assessments

Mastering PowerPoint

Project 5H—Natural Science

In this project, you will apply the skills you practiced from the Objectives in Projects 5A and 5B.

Objectives: 1. *Use Graphic Elements to Enhance a Slide;* **2.** *Work with Grouped Objects.*

In the following Mastering PowerPoint project, you will create the first few slides of a presentation that Dave Douglass, Dean of the Natural Science Division, will show at a college and career day at a local high school. Your completed presentation will look similar to the one shown in Figure 5.41.

For Project 5H, you will need the following files:

New blank PowerPoint presentation
p05H_Microscope
p05H_Dish
p05H_Experiment
p05H_Science

You will save your presentation as
5H_Natural_Science_Firstname_Lastname

Figure 5.41

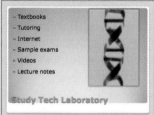

(Project 5H–Natural Science continues on the next page)

Content-Based Assessments

Mastering PowerPoint

(Project 5H–Natural Science continued)

1. Start PowerPoint and begin a new blank presentation. Apply the **Aspect** theme, and then change the **Layout** to **Section Header**. **Save** the file in your **PowerPoint Chapter 5** folder as 5H_Natural_Science_Firstname_Lastname

2. In the title placeholder, type **Natural Science Division** and then in the text placeholder type **Sierra Vista Community College**

3. From your student files, **Insert** the picture **p05H_Experiment**, and then drag the picture to the right so that its right edge aligns with the right edge of the slide. **Crop** the picture using the left center cropping handle so that the bottle on the left side of the picture does not display. Format the picture by applying a **Soft Edges 50 Point** picture effect.

4. From your student files, **Insert** the picture **p05H_Microscope**, and then **Rotate** the picture by applying the **Flip Horizontal** command. Drag the picture up so that its top edge aligns with the top of the grey rounded rectangle, and then drag the picture to the right so that its right edge aligns at **3.5 inches after zero on the horizontal ruler**. Apply a **Soft Edges 50 Point** picture effect, and then **Recolor** the picture using the **Grayscale Color Mode**. Click **Send to Back** so that the microscope is behind the bottles.

5. From your student files, insert the picture **p05H_Dish**, and then size the picture so that its **Height** and **Width** are **2.5** inches. Drag the picture so that its lower edge aligns just above the title text and so that its right edge aligns at **3 inches after zero on the horizontal ruler**. Format the picture by applying a **Soft Edges 25 Point** picture effect, and then use the **Send to**

Back command to move the picture of the dishes behind the microscope and the beakers.

6. Select and **Group** the three pictures and then save the group as a picture in your **PowerPoint Chapter 5** folder. Change the file type to **JPEG File Interchange Format** and change the file name to 5H_Science_Logo_Firstname_Lastname

7. Use the **Reuse Slides** command to insert all of the slides in the **p05H_Science** presentation. Display **Slide 4**, and then insert a **New Slide** with the **Picture with Caption** layout. In the title placeholder type **Natural Science Division** and in the caption placeholder to the right of the picture placeholder type **Visit the Natural Science Division and learn more about the courses, faculty, and resources available at Sierra Vista Community College.** Change the caption **Font Size** to **18**, change the **Line Spacing** to **1.5**, **Center** the text, and then apply **Italic**.

8. In the picture placeholder, insert the picture that you saved in your **PowerPoint Chapter 5** folder—**5H_Science_Logo_Firstname_Lastname**. Apply the **Glow Picture Effect—Accent color 1, 18 pt glow**.

9. Create a **Header and Footer** for the **Notes and Handouts**. Include the **Date and time updated automatically**, the **Page number,** and a **Footer** with the file name 5H_Natural_Science_Firstname_Lastname

10. Check your *Chapter Assignment Sheet* or your *Course Syllabus* or consult your instructor to determine if you are to submit your assignments on paper or electronically. To submit electronically, go to

(Project 5H–Natural Science continues on the next page)

Content-Based Assessments

(Project 5H–Natural Science continued)

Step 12, and then follow the instructions provided by your instructor.

11. Print Preview your presentation, and then print **Handouts (6 Slides Per Page)**.

12. Save the changes to your presentation, and then close the presentation.

 End **You have completed Project 5H** ⎯⎯⎯⎯⎯⎯⎯⎯⎯⎯⎯⎯⎯⎯

Content-Based Assessments

Mastering PowerPoint

Project 5I — Activities

In this project, you will apply the skills you practiced from the Objectives in Projects 5A and 5B.

Objectives: 1. *Use Graphic Elements to Enhance a Slide;* **2.** *Work with Grouped Objects;* **3.** *Insert Hyperlinks and Action Buttons* **4.** *Create and Deliver Custom Shows.*

In the following Mastering PowerPoint project, you will create the first few slides of a presentation that Kevin Perez, President of the Sierra Vista Community College Alumni Association, will show at a college information meeting. Your completed presentation will look similar to the one shown in Figure 5.42.

For Project 5I, you will need the following files:

p05I_Activities
p05I_Beaker
p05I_Earth
p05I_Scope

You will save your presentation as
5I_Activities_Firstname_Lastname

Figure 5.42

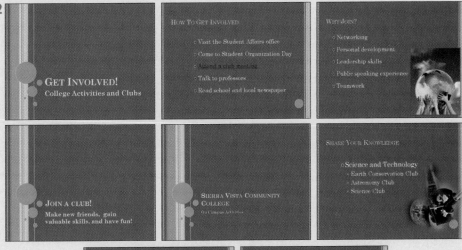

(Project 5I–Activities continues on the next page)

(Project 5I–Activities continued)

1. **Start** PowerPoint. From your student files, **Open** the file **p05I_Activities**. **Save** the file in your **PowerPoint Chapter 5** folder as 5I_Activities_Firstname_Lastname

2. Display **Slide 6**. From your student files, **Insert** the picture **p05I_Scope**. Drag the picture down and to the right so that its lower edge aligns at **3.5 inches below zero on the vertical ruler** and its right edge aligns at **4 inches after zero on the horizontal ruler**.

3. **Rotate** the picture to the right so that the upper left corner of the semitransparent image aligns with the green rotation handle. The rightmost sizing handle will touch the right edge of the slide and the lowest corner of the picture will extend just below the bottom edge of the slide. **Recolor** the picture using the **Grayscale Color Mode**, and then format the picture by applying a **Soft Edges 50 Point** picture effect.

4. From your student files, **Insert** the picture **p05I_Beaker**, and then **Crop** the picture from the right so that only the beaker displays. **Recolor** the picture using **Accent color 1 Dark**, and then apply the **Flip Horizontal** command. Apply a **Soft Edges 50 Point** picture effect, and then hold down ⇧Shift and drag the picture to the right so that its left edge aligns at approximately **1 inch after zero on the horizontal ruler**.

5. From your student files, insert the picture **p05I_Earth**, and then drag the picture down and to the right so that its right edge aligns at approximately **3 inches after zero on the horizontal ruler** and its bottom edge aligns at approximately **3 inches after zero on the vertical ruler**. **Recolor** the picture using **Accent color 2 Dark**, and then apply a **Soft Edges 50 Point**

picture effect. Use the **Send to Back** command to move the picture of the earth to the bottom of the stack of pictures.

6. Select and **Group** the three pictures and then use the → and ↓ keys as necessary to nudge the group so that its lower right corner aligns with the lower right corner of the slide.

7. Display **Slide 8**, and then select the first bullet point—*Phi Theta Kappa*. Insert a **Hyperlink** to the **Web Page** www.ptk.org and change the **ScreenTip** to **Phi Theta Kappa**

8. Create a **Custom Show** with the name **Clubs** that includes **Slides 5**, **6**, **7**, and **8**. Display **Slide 2**, and then select the third bullet point—*Attend a club meeting*. Insert an **Action** link to the **Custom Show—Clubs**. Select the **Show and return** check box so that the presentation returns to **Slide 2** after the custom show is viewed. **Hide** the slides in the custom show so that they only display if the custom show is viewed during the slide show.

9. Apply the **Wipe Down Transition** at **Medium Speed** to all of the slides in the presentation. On **Slides 2** and **3** apply the **Custom Animation Entrance effect—Peek In**—to each of the content placeholders. View the Slide Show from the beginning and click each hyperlink to view the hidden slides and Web page.

10. Create a **Header and Footer** for the **Notes and Handouts**. Include the **Date and time updated automatically**, the **Page number**, and a **Footer** with the file name 5I_Activities_Firstname_Lastname

11. Check your *Chapter Assignment Sheet* or your *Course Syllabus* or consult your instructor to determine if you are to

(Project 5I–Activities continues on the next page)

Content-Based Assessments

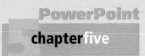
(Project 5I–Activities continued)

submit your assignments on paper or electronically. To submit electronically, go to Step 13, and then follow the instructions provided by your instructor.

12. **Print Preview** your presentation, and then print **Handouts (4 Slides Per Page)**.

13. **Save** the changes to your presentation, and then close the presentation.

 You have completed Project 5I

Content-Based Assessments

Project 5J—Business_Running_Case

In this project, you will apply the skills you practiced from all the Objectives in Projects 5A and 5B.

From My Computer, navigate to the student files that accompany this textbook. In the folder **03_business_running_case**, locate and open the folder for this chapter. Open and print the instructions for this project, which are provided to you in Adobe PDF format. Follow the instructions and use the skills you have gained thus far to assist Jennifer Nelson in meeting the challenges of owning and running her business.

Rubric

The following outcomes-based assessments are *open-ended assessments*. That is, there is no specific correct result; your result will depend on your approach to the information provided. Make *professional quality* your goal. Use the following scoring rubric to guide you in *how* to approach the problem and then to evaluate *how well* your approach solves the problem.

The *criteria*—Software Mastery, Content, Format and Layout, and Process—represent the knowledge and skills you have gained that you can apply to solving the problem. The *levels of performance*—Professional Quality, Approaching Professional Quality, or Needs Quality Improvement—help you and your instructor evaluate your result.

	Your completed project is of Professional Quality if you:	Your completed project is Approaching Professional Quality if you:	Your completed project Needs Quality Improvements if you:
1-Software Mastery	Choose and apply the most appropriate skills, tools, and features and identify efficient methods to solve the problem.	Choose and apply some appropriate skills, tools, and features, but not in the most efficient manner.	Choose inappropriate skills, tools, or features, or are inefficient in solving the problem.
2-Content	Construct a solution that is clear and well organized, contains content that is accurate, appropriate to the audience and purpose, and is complete. Provide a solution that contains no errors of spelling, grammar, or style.	Construct a solution in which some components are unclear, poorly organized, inconsistent, or incomplete. Misjudge the needs of the audience. Have some errors in spelling, grammar, or style, but the errors do not detract from comprehension.	Construct a solution that is unclear, incomplete, or poorly organized, containing some inaccurate or inappropriate content; and contains many errors of spelling, grammar, or style. Do not solve the problem.
3-Format and Layout	Format and arrange all elements to communicate information and ideas, clarify function, illustrate relationships, and indicate relative importance.	Apply appropriate format and layout features to some elements, but not others. Overuse features, causing minor distraction.	Apply format and layout that does not communicate information or ideas clearly. Do not use format and layout features to clarify function, illustrate relationships, or indicate relative importance. Use available features excessively, causing distraction.
4-Process	Use an organized approach that integrates planning, development, self-assessment, revision, and reflection.	Demonstrate an organized approach in some areas, but not others; or, use an insufficient process of organization throughout.	Do not use an organized approach to solve the problem.

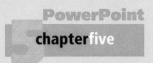

Problem Solving

Project 5K—Overview

In this project, you will construct a solution by applying any combination of the Objectives found in Projects 5A and 5B.

For Project 5K, you will need the following file:

New blank PowerPoint presentation

You will save your presentation as
5K_Overview_Firstname_Lastname

Sierra Vista Community College is hosting a Welcome Day for students the Friday before the Fall semester begins. Deena Yates, Vice President of Student Services, will be making a presentation on Welcome Day that provides students with an overview of the college. Create the first three slides of a presentation that describes Sierra Vista Community College using the information in the following paragraph. Apply a design template of your choice.

Sierra Vista Community College is a large community college in California with a diverse student population. The college offers three associates degrees in 15 academic areas and offers certificate programs, adult education, and continuing education on campus and online. The college serves the student body and surrounding community through partnerships with local businesses and nonprofit organizations, and makes positive contributions to the community by offering relevant curricula and high-quality learning experiences.

Create a fourth presentation slide based on the following information. On this slide, insert a hyperlink to the Accrediting Commission for Community and Junior Colleges at www.accjc.org.

Sierra Vista Community College is accredited by the Accrediting Commission for Community and Junior Colleges. Additionally, the college is noted for its high transfer rate to four-year universities and outstanding completion rates for students who earn A.A. degrees and certificates.

Insert a fifth slide using the Section Header layout that ends the presentation by encouraging students to attend SVCC. Then, create two additional hidden slides for a custom show entitled Certificate Programs. On these two slides, include information from the following paragraph.

SVCC offers certificate programs in Business, Computer Information Technology, Child Development, Fashion, Fire Technology, Machine Shop

(Project 5K–Overview continues on the next page)

Problem Solving

(Project 5K–Overview continued)

Technology, Nursing, Photography, and Radiological Technology. The programs are designed in conjunction with industry experts and local advisory committee input. Some programs prepare students for outside certification that meets industry standards, while others prepare students for a specific occupation. Programs are reviewed yearly to ensure quality and workforce standards.

On the fourth slide, create a link to the custom show. Apply slide transitions and animation and insert pictures as necessary. Add the file name and page number to the Notes and Handouts footer and check the presentation for spelling errors. Save the presentation as **5K_Overview_Firstname_Lastname** and submit it as directed.

 End **You have completed Project 5K** ————————————

Outcomes-Based Assessments

Problem Solving

Project 5L — Music

In this project, you will construct a solution by applying any combination of the Objectives found in Projects 5A and 5B.

For Project 5L, you will need the following file:

New blank PowerPoint presentation

**You will save your presentation as
5L_Music_Firstname_Lastname**

The Dean of the Music Division, David Robinson, will be making a presentation to a local foundation considering a donation to the division. Create four slides for this presentation that describe the music program based on the information in the following paragraph.

Sierra Vista Community College offers more than 75 courses in Music, ranging from basic instrumental skills to jazz band arrangement and composing. The curriculum covers traditional and contemporary courses, and is offered by a diverse faculty experienced in all aspects of the music field. To develop an appreciation of music, classes are taught in literature, vocal, instrumental, and electronic techniques. The curriculum is reviewed yearly and new courses are added and existing courses changed to reflect the needs of today's competitive music industry. A number of instrumental and choral groups are composed of dedicated faculty and students who participate in ensembles that provide a variety of performance experiences for the benefit of the students, the college, and the community.

Apply a design theme of your choice and insert two or three pictures on the first slide. Recolor, crop, and format the pictures as necessary so that the pictures can be grouped and saved as a picture. Insert the saved picture on the last slide of the presentation. Use animation techniques to create a professional presentation. Add the file name and page number to the Notes and Handouts footer and check for spelling errors. Save the presentation as **5L_Music_Firstname_Lastname** and submit it as directed.

Note: You can find many appropriate images available to Microsoft Office users. To access these images, click the Insert tab, and then from the Illustrations group, click the Clip Art button. In the Clip Art task pane, type a key word—such as *music*—in the *Search for* box. You can specify the image type (clip art or photographs) and where to search. The largest variety of photographs can be found by including Web Collections in the *Search in* box. You can also use images from earlier projects in this chapter, or images from your personal collection.

End You have completed Project 5L

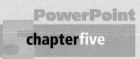

Problem Solving

Project 5M — Clubs

In this project, you will construct a solution by applying any combination of the Objectives found in Projects 5A and 5B.

> **For Project 5M, you will need the following file:**
>
> p05M_Clubs

**You will save your presentation as
5M_Clubs_Firstname_Lastname**

The President of the Associated Student Body will be making a presentation at a membership event for students interested in joining or starting a club on campus. From your student files, open the presentation **p05M_Clubs**. Hide Slides 7 and 8, and then create a custom show named **Funding** using Slides 7 and 8. On Slide 3, create a link to the custom show and be sure that after the custom show is viewed, the presentation returns to Slide 3. On Slide 1, insert two or three pictures. (See the note at the end of Project 5L for hints about locating images.) Recolor, crop, and format the pictures as necessary so that the pictures can be grouped and saved as a picture. Insert the saved picture on Slide 6. Apply slide transitions and animation. Add the file name and page number to the Notes and Handouts footer and check for spelling errors. Save the presentation as **5M_Clubs_Firstname_Lastname** and submit it as directed.

End You have completed Project 5M ———————

Outcomes-Based Assessments

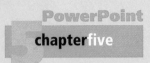

Problem Solving

Project 5N—Library

In this project, you will construct a solution by applying any combination of the Objectives found in Projects 5A and 5B.

For Project 5N, you will need the following file:

New blank PowerPoint presentation

You will save your presentation as
5N_Library_Firstname_Lastname

The Director of Library Services for Sierra Vista Community College would like to develop a presentation that librarians can use in their Library 101—Introduction to Library Services course. The presentation will inform students of some of the services that are available at the SVCC library. Using a design template of your choice, create a presentation with four slides from the information in the following paragraph.

The Sierra Vista Community College library is a multi-million dollar structure with a staff of ten librarians and six classified staff. The library's holdings exceed 135,000 volumes in the general book collection, over 250 periodical subscriptions, approximately 1,500 titles in electronic databases, 1,250 paperbacks, and approximately 2,500 items in media collections including CDs, and video and audio cassettes. The library's instructional program includes classes, workshops, and tutorials that are attended by approximately 2,500 students each year. The library's Web site offers students and faculty access to the majority of its resources, and the library's periodical and reference databases are accessible from off-campus.

Create two additional slides that describe the library's borrowing policy based on the following information. Add the two slides to a custom show named **Borrowing Terms** and then create a link to the show from one of the first four slides that you created.

To borrow resources from the Sierra Vista Community College library, a student or employee I.D. card is required; however, adult residents of the Sierra Vista Community College District and SVCC Alumni may also borrow materials. Most borrowed items can be renewed three times either online or in person at the Circulation Desk. Items that are currently checked out can be placed on hold using online library services. When

(Project 5N–Library continues on the next page)

PowerPoint
chapterfive

Problem Solving

(Project 5N–Library continued)

the item is available, the library will send an email to the specified email address. The item is held at the Circulation Desk for five days.

Add the file name and page number to the Notes and Handouts footer and check for spelling errors. Save the presentation as **5N_Library_Firstname_Lastname** and submit it as directed.

End **You have completed Project 5N** ———————————————

Outcomes-Based Assessments

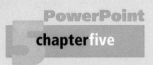
Problem Solving

Project 50—Athletics

In this project, you will construct a solution by applying any combination of the Objectives found in Projects 5A and 5B.

For Project 50, you will need the following file:

New blank PowerPoint presentation

You will save your presentation as
50_Athletics_Firstname_Lastname

The Athletics Division at Sierra Vista Community College is sponsoring a student information night in an effort to encourage promising athletes to attend SVCC and participate in the sports program. Create a presentation that introduces prospective athletes to the program using a design template of your choice. On the title slide, insert three pictures and use the skills that you practiced in this chapter to recolor, change the order, crop, and group the pictures so that they can be saved as one picture. Create the content for the next two or three slides based on the information in the following paragraphs, and then insert the picture that you saved from the first slide on the last slide of the presentation.

The Sierra Vista Community College Physical Education Division sponsors the following intercollegiate teams that play in the West Coast Conference.

Fall	**Spring**
Men/Women Cross Country	Men/Baseball
Men/Women Soccer	Women/Softball
Women/Water Polo	Men/Women Track and Field
Women/Volleyball	Men/Women Swimming and Diving
Men/Football	Women/Badminton
Men/Women Basketball	

The college Athletics program is housed in the athletic complex that includes a state-of-the-art gymnasium, stadium, and aquatics center. The gymnasium includes basketball courts, men's and women's locker rooms, three workout and fitness rooms, classrooms, faculty offices, and a counseling center dedicated to student athletes. The Physical Education division prides itself not only for its dedication to athletics but also on its commitment to help student athletes succeed in their college academic programs. Student athletes have access to two academic counselors who work only with athletes, a tutoring center, and a computer classroom equipped with ten computer stations.

(Project 50–Athletics continues on the next page)

Outcomes-Based Assessments

Problem Solving

(Project 5O–Athletics continued)

Add the file name to the Notes and Handouts footer and check for spelling errors. Save the presentation as **5O_Athletics_Firstname_ Lastname** and then submit it as directed.

 End **You have completed Project 5O** ——————————

Outcomes-Based Assessments

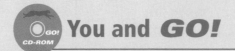 You and *GO!*

Project 5P—You and *GO!*

In this project, you will construct a solution by applying any combination of the skills you practiced from the Objectives in Projects 5A and 5B.

From My Computer, navigate to the student files that accompany this textbook. In the folder **04_you_and_go**, locate and open the folder for this chapter. Open and print the instructions for this project, which are provided to you in Adobe PDF format. Follow the instructions to create a presentation describing a major course of study in which you are interested.

GO! with Help

Project 5Q—*GO!* with Help

The color of a picture can be altered using the Transparency, Brightness, and Contrast commands. Use Microsoft PowerPoint Help to learn how to change the color of a picture using these tools.

1 **Start** PowerPoint. At the far right end of the Ribbon, click the **Microsoft Office PowerPoint Help** button.

2 In the **Type words to search for** box, type **change picture brightness** and then press [Enter].

3 Click the **Change the brightness, contrast, or transparency of a picture** link, and then read the information and steps for each option. When you are through, **Close** the Help window, and then close PowerPoint.

End **You have completed Project 5Q** ————————————

chapter**six**

Create Templates, Photo Albums, and Web Pages

OBJECTIVES

At the end of this chapter you will be able to:

1. Create a Template by Modifying Slide Masters
2. Edit a Presentation

3. Create a Photo Album
4. Share Files with Other Users

OUTCOMES

Mastering these objectives will enable you to:

PROJECT 6A
Customize a Presentation by Modifying the Master Slides

PROJECT 6B
Create a Photo Album Presentation for Web Page Viewing

Adventure Valley Resort

Adventure Valley Resort is a family-oriented resort complex that includes a theme park with rides and arcade games and a water park with numerous rides, slides, a wave pool, and a lazy river. The resort complex is anchored by two hotels and a shopping and restaurant area. Whether guests spend a day or a week, resort management is committed to providing a safe, clean, and exciting environment where families can relax and enjoy the amenities, the rides, and the resort entertainment.

Create Templates, Photo Albums, and Web Pages

Collaboration is a critical skill in today's business world, and developing the skills to use PowerPoint collaboratively can improve presentation design and content. Presentations can be edited and formatted by multiple users with the insertion of comments and by collaborating on design elements that reflect a company's style. Additionally, presentations can be shared among users and between applications by importing and exporting files from and to Microsoft Word. Completed presentations can be shared with many viewers by saving files for viewing on the Web.

Project 6A **Vacation**

In Activities 6.1 through 6.8, you will create a presentation that Mark Lewis, Adventure Valley Resort Director, is developing for a tourism exhibit. Your completed presentation will look similar to Figure 6.1.

For Project 6A, you will need the following files:

New blank PowerPoint presentation
p06A_Vacation
p06A_Logo

**You will save your presentation as
6A_Vacation_Firstname_Lastname**

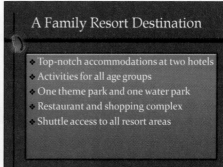

Figure 6.1
Project 6A—Vacation

Objective 1
Create a Template by Modifying Slide Masters

Microsoft Office PowerPoint 2007 includes a number of professionally designed themes that you can apply to your presentations. You can customize a theme by modifying the slide master. The **slide master** is a slide that holds the information about formatting and text that displays on every slide in your presentation, including placeholder positions, background design, theme formatting, bullets, and font styles. After you have designed and customized the slide master, you can save it as a template that can be applied to any presentation that you create.

Activity 6.1 Displaying and Editing Slide Masters

In PowerPoint 2007, each theme includes a slide master that when modified, the changes are applied to every slide in the presentation. Additionally, within each theme, each slide layout includes a slide master that when modified affects only those slides to which the layout has been applied.

Note — Comparing Your Screen with the Figures in This Textbook

Your screen will match the figures shown in this textbook if you set your screen resolution to 1024 x 768. At other resolutions, your screen will closely resemble, but not match, the figures shown. To view your screen's resolution, on the Windows desktop, right-click in a blank area, click Properties, and then click the Settings tab.

1 **Start** PowerPoint and begin a new blank presentation. Recall that by default, the theme applied to a new blank presentation is the Office theme.

2 On the **View tab**, in the **Presentation Views group**, click the **Slide Master** button. Alternatively, press ⬆Shift, and then in the lower right corner of your screen, click the Normal button 🔲 .

The left side of your window displays the slide masters for each layout in the Office theme and the Slide pane displays the slide master for the Title Slide layout.

3 Point to the first slide master and notice the ScreenTip *Office Theme Slide Master: used by slide(s) 1*. Also notice that the remaining slide masters are smaller, indented, and connected to the topmost master in a hierarchical structure. Compare your screen with Figure 6.2.

The first slide master controls the theme and overall design of the presentation. Changes made to this slide master affect all master layouts, whereas changes made to the other master layouts affect only the slide layout on which the change was made.

Figure 6.2

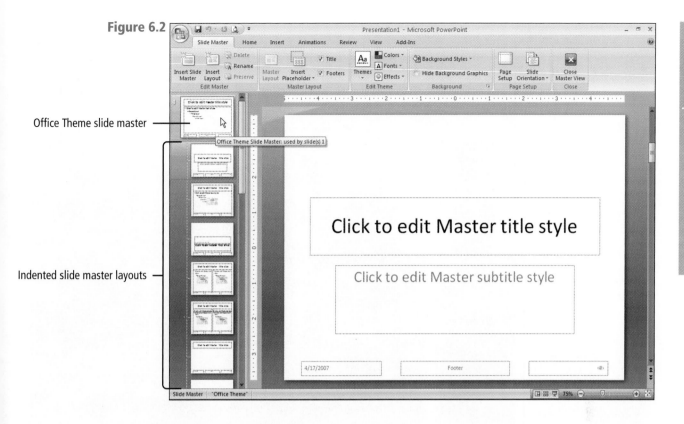

Office Theme slide master ⎯

Indented slide master layouts ⎯

4 Click the first slide master—**Office Theme Slide Master: used by slide(s) 1** so that it displays in the slide pane. On the **Slide Master tab**, in the **Background group**, click the **Background Styles** button, and then click **Style 3**.

The blue background is applied to each slide master layout.

5 Select the title placeholder text, and then on the **Home tab**, in the **Font group**, click the **Font button arrow** Calibri (Headings) ▾ . Click **Book Antiqua**.

The Book Antiqua font is applied to the theme slide master and thus is also applied to the title placeholders on all of the slide master layouts.

6 Click in the content placeholder, and then click the dashed edge of the content placeholder so that it displays as a solid line. Recall that when the border surrounding a placeholder is solid, all of the text within the placeholder is selected. On the **Home tab**, in the **Font group**, click the **Font button arrow** Calibri (Headings) ▾ , and then click **Constantia**.

The text in the content placeholders on every slide layout is changed to Constantia.

7 Compare your screen with Figure 6.3, and then leave the presentation open for the next activity.

Figure 6.3

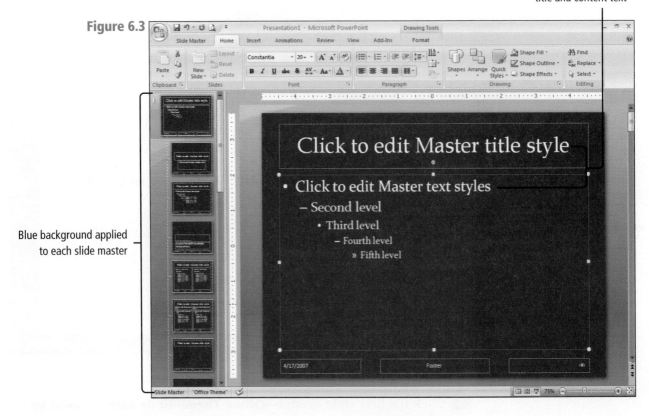

Font changes made to
title and content text

Blue background applied
to each slide master

Activity 6.2 Saving a Presentation as a Template

When the slide master is modified, the changes apply only to the presentation which you are editing or formatting. Save the presentation as a template if you would like to apply the slide master changes to other presentations. For example, you can create a presentation that includes company logos, text, and colors that many people within an organization can apply to their presentations. By saving the presentation as a template, the formatting can be applied to any presentation in the same manner in which a theme is applied.

1 From the **Office** menu [icon], click **Save As**. At the bottom of the **Save As** dialog box, click the **Save as type arrow**, and then click **PowerPoint Template**. Notice that the **Save in** box displays the *Templates* folder name. Compare your screen with Figure 6.4.

Figure 6.4

Save as type arrow

Templates folder displays

Change type to
PowerPoint Template

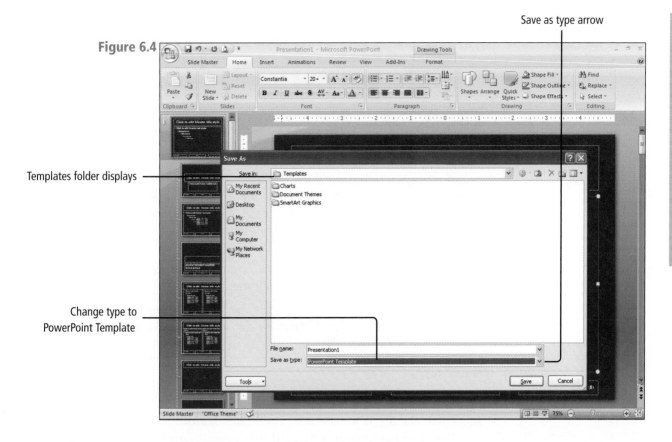

2 Navigate to the location where you are saving your solution files, and then click the **Create New Folder** button ![icon]. Create a folder with the name **PowerPoint Chapter 6** and then click **OK**. In the **File name** box, type **6A_Template_Firstname_Lastname** and then click **Save**.

The file is saved as a PowerPoint template with a file extension of .potx.

Workshop

Working with Slide Masters

When you are formatting a presentation and want to change a format that will affect every slide, modify the slide master. For example, if the theme that you apply includes a title placeholder in which the titles are left-aligned and your presentation would best display with centered titles, change the alignment on the slide master so that you do not have to change every slide. It is not necessary to save the modified slide master as a template unless you are planning to use the same formatting on multiple presentations.

Activity 6.3 Formatting a Slide Master with a Gradient Fill

The background on individual slide master layouts can be modified to override the formatting on the theme slide master. In this Activity, you will apply a gradient fill to the Title Slide layout master.

1 Click the second slide master—**Title Slide Layout: used by slide(s) 1**. On the **Slide Master tab**, in the **Background group**, click the **Background Styles** button, and then click **Format Background**.

2 Under **Fill**, click **Gradient fill**, and notice the change in the background fill. Recall that a gradient fill is a color combination in which one color fades into another. The gradient fill options are described in the table in Figure 6.5.

Gradient Fill Options

Option	Description
Preset colors	Built-in gradient fill color options.
Type	There are five types of gradient fills—linear, radial, rectangular, path, and shade from title. The types determine the angle and directions from which the gradient fill is applied.
Direction and Angle	Determine the progression of colors from one area of the slide to another.
Gradient stops	Determines the color, position, and transparency values of the gradient fill. Each color used in the gradient fill must be included as a gradient stop.

Figure 6.5

3 Click the **Type arrow**, and then click **Radial** to view the change in the slide background. Repeat this process and click each **Type** option to view how the different types affect the background. After you have viewed each Type option, click the **Type arrow**, and then click **Linear**. Click the **Direction arrow**, and then click the second option—**Linear Down**.

4 Under **Gradient Stops**, click the **Stop 1 arrow** to display the three gradient stops as shown in Figure 6.6.

The list of gradient stops—Stop 1, Stop 2, and Stop 3, indicate that there are three colors in the gradient fill.

Figure 6.6

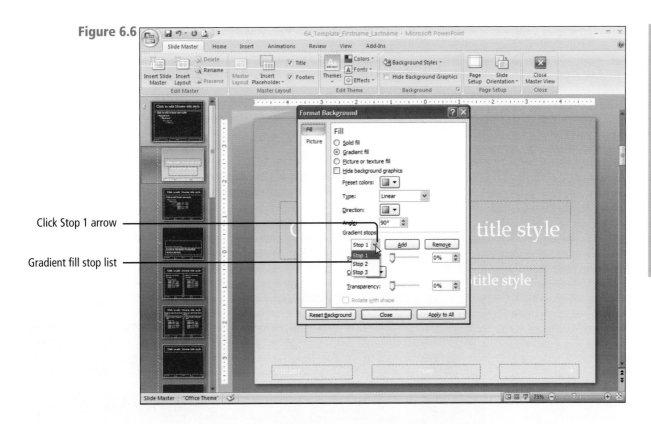

Click Stop 1 arrow

Gradient fill stop list

5 Click **Stop 3**, and then click **Remove** to remove Stop 3 from the gradient fill and to display the settings for **Stop 2**.

6 With **Stop 2** displayed, click the **Color button arrow** to display the **Theme Colors gallery**. Under **Theme Colors**, in the third column, click the last color—**Dark Blue, Background 2, Darker 50%.**

7 Click the **Stop 2 arrow**, and then click **Stop 1**. Click the **Color button arrow** Under **Theme Colors**, click the first color— **Black, Background 1,** and then click **Close** to apply the gradient fill to the title slide master.

8 **Save** the presentation template.

More Knowledge

Changing the Stop Position and Transparency Values

You can use the slider tools in the Format Background dialog box to change the Stop position and Transparency values of the selected Stop color. The Stop position determines the location on the slide where the color begins to fade into the next color. The Transparency value determines the opaqueness of the selected Stop color.

Activity 6.4 Formatting Slide Masters by Adding Pictures and Shapes

1 If necessary, select the second slide master—**Title Slide Layout: used by slide(s) 1**.

2 On the **Insert tab**, in the **Illustrations group**, click the **Shapes button**, and then under **Rectangles**, click the first shape—**Rectangle**. Position the ⊞ pointer in the upper left corner of the slide, and then drag to the right and down to draw a rectangle that extends to **3 inches before zero on the horizontal ruler** and to the bottom of the slide. Compare your slide with Figure 6.7.

Figure 6.7

Draw this rectangle ———

3 On the **Format tab**, in the **Shape Styles group**, click the **More** button ⊞. In the displayed **Shapes Styles gallery**, in the last row, click the second style—**Intense Effect-Accent 1**. In the **Size group**, click in the **Width** box ⊞ 2.67" ⬍, type **1.75** and then press Enter to resize the rectangle.

4 On the **Insert tab**, in the **Illustrations group**, click **Picture**. Navigate to the location where your student files are stored, and then click **p06A_Logo**. Click **Insert**. On the **Format tab**, in the **Size group**, click in the **Height** box ⊞ 2" ⬍, type **2** and then press Enter to resize the picture. Drag the picture up and to the left so that its upper left corner aligns with the upper left corner of the slide, and then compare your slide with Figure 6.8.

Figure 6.8

Size picture

Position picture

5 With the picture selected, hold down Ctrl and press D.

Recall that Ctrl+D creates a duplicate of the selected object.

6 Drag the new picture down and to the left so that its top edge aligns at **1 inch above zero on the vertical ruler** and its left edge aligns with the left edge of the slide.

7 Hold down Ctrl and press D to create another picture. Drag the new picture down so that its lower left corner aligns with the lower left corner of the slide.

8 Hold down Shift and click the top two pictures so that all three pictures are selected. On the **Format tab**, in the **Picture Styles group**, click the **Picture Effects** button, and then point to **Soft Edges**. Click **25 Point**.

9 Click on a blank area of the slide so that nothing is selected, and then compare your slide with Figure 6.9. Make adjustments as necessary.

Figure 6.9

Formatted pictures

10 **Save** ![save icon] the presentation template.

11 Display the third slide master—**Title and Content Layout: used by no slides**. On the **Insert tab**, in the **Illustrations group**, click **Shapes**. Under **Rectangles**, click the second shape—**Rounded Rectangle**. Position the pointer on the left edge of the slide at **2 inches above zero**, and then drag up and to the right so that the top edge of the rectangle touches the bottom of the title placeholder and extends to the right edge of the slide as shown in Figure 6.10.

The rectangle is positioned between the title and content placeholders.

Figure 6.10

Draw rectangle

12 On the **Format tab**, in the **Shape Styles group**, click the **More** button 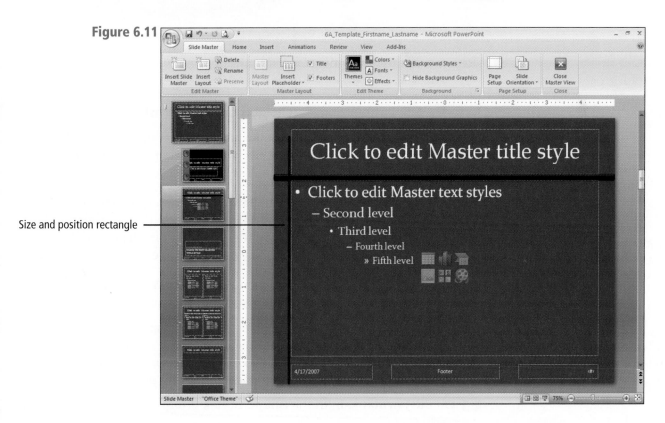, and then in the first column of the **Shapes Styles gallery**, click the last style—**Intense Effect-Dark 1**.

13 With the rectangle selected, hold down Ctrl and press D to create another rectangle. On the **Format tab**, in the **Size group**, click in the **Height** box. Type **.05** and then click in the **Width** box. Type **7** and then press Enter to size the rectangle.

14 On the **Format tab**, in the **Arrange group**, click the **Rotate** button, and then click **Rotate Right 90°** so that the two rectangles are intersecting. Drag the rectangle down and to the left so that it aligns with the left edge of the title and content placeholders and its lower edge aligns with the lower edge of the slide. Click in a blank area of the slide, and then compare your screen with Figure 6.11.

Figure 6.11

Size and position rectangle

15 On the **Insert tab**, in the **Illustrations group**, click **Picture**, and then navigate to the location where your student files are stored. Click **p06A_Logo**, and then click **Insert**. On the **Format tab**, in the **Size group**, click in the **Height** box. Type **1.4** and then press Enter to size the picture.

16 On the **Format tab**, in the **Picture Styles group**, click the **Picture Effects** button. Point to **Soft Edges**, and then click **25 Point**. Drag the picture so that it is positioned over the intersection of the two black rectangles as shown in Figure 6.12.

Figure 6.12

Move picture to this position

17 **Save** 🖫 the presentation template.

Activity 6.5 Customizing Placeholders on a Slide Master

In addition to modifying slide master backgrounds and adding objects to a slide master, you can change the size, position, and format of placeholders.

1 With the **Title and Content Layout** slide master displayed, click in the content placeholder. Notice that the picture that you inserted in the previous activity is covering the first bullet in the content placeholder. On the **Format tab**, in the **Size group**, click in the **Height** box 🔲 2" ⬍. Type **4.5** and then click in the **Width** box 🔲 2.67" ⬍. Type **8.5** and then press Enter to resize the placeholder.

2 Point to the outer edge of the placeholder to display the 🔆 pointer, and then drag the placeholder down and to the right so that its top edge aligns at **1.5 inches above zero on the vertical ruler** and its right edge aligns with the right edge of the title placeholder.

3 On the **Format tab**, in the **Shape Styles group**, click the **More** button ⬇. In the displayed **Shapes Styles gallery**, in the last row, click the second style—**Intense Effect-Accent 1**.

The size, position, and style of the content placeholder make it display prominently on the slide. In order to coordinate the placeholder with the other slide elements, small amounts of black can be added to the design.

4 With the content placeholder selected, on the **Format tab**, in the **Shape Styles group**, click the **Shape Effects** button. Point to **Glow**, and then below the **Glow Variations gallery**, click **More Glow Colors**. Click the first color—**Black, Background 1** to add a slight black glow effect to the outside of the placeholder. Click in a blank area of the slide, and then compare your screen with Figure 6.13.

Figure 6.13

Content placeholder aligns with title placeholder

Placeholder formatted with Shape Style and Black Glow effect

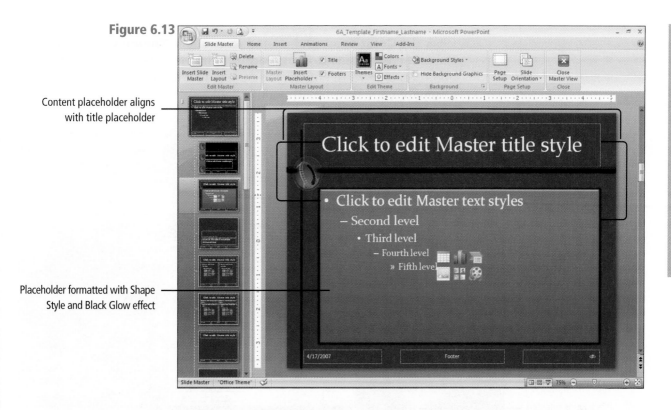

5. Recall that in addition to containing information about the slide background and the graphics contained in a presentation, the slide master also includes font and bullet information. Click anywhere in the first line of the content placeholder—**Click to edit Master text styles**.

6. On the **Home tab**, in the **Paragraph group**, click the **Bullets button arrow** to display the **Bullets gallery**.

Alert!

Did the bullet disappear?

If you clicked the Bullets *button* instead of the Bullets button *arrow*, then the bullet symbol was removed from the line. On the Quick Access Toolbar, click Undo to redisplay the bullet, and then repeat Step 6.

7. Below the **Bullets gallery**, click **Bullets and Numbering**. In the displayed **Bullets and Numbering** dialog box, in the second row, click **Star Bullets**.

Alert!

Are the Star Bullets missing from the dialog box?

If the Star Bullets do not display, click the second bullet that displays in the second row, and then at the bottom of the Bullets and Numbering dialog box, click the Reset button so that the default bullet styles display.

8 Click the **Color arrow** 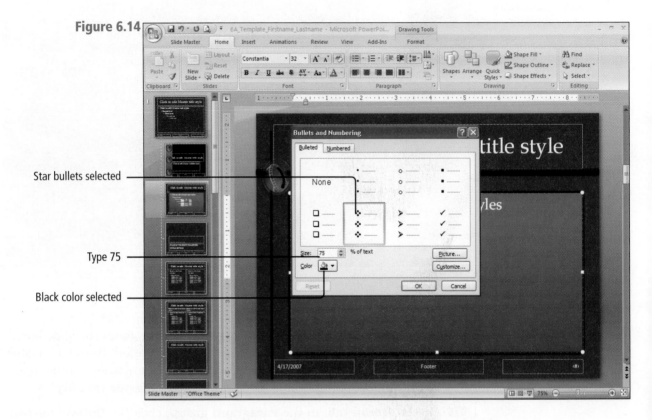, and then under **Theme Colors**, click the first color—**Black, Background 1**. In the **Size** box, select *100* and then type **75** to change the bullets to 75% of the size of the text. Compare your screen with Figure 6.14.

Figure 6.14

Star bullets selected

Type 75

Black color selected

9 Click **OK** to apply the bullet formatting.

10 Formatting for the template is complete. **Save** 🖫 and close ✕ the presentation template.

More Knowledge

Inserting Placeholders on a Slide Master

You can insert a new placeholder anywhere on a slide master. On the Slide Master tab, in the Master Layout group, click the Insert Placeholder button, and then select the type of placeholder that you want to insert. Use the ➕ pointer to draw the placeholder.

Activity 6.6 Applying a Template to a Presentation

In this activity, you will apply the template that you created to an existing presentation.

1 If necessary **Start** PowerPoint. From your student files, open the file

p06A_Vacation. From the **Office** menu 🗔, click **Save As**, and then navigate to your **PowerPoint Chapter 6** folder. In the **File name**

box, type **6A_Vacation_Firstname_Lastname** and then click **Save** to save your file.

2 On the **Design tab**, in the **Themes group**, click the **More** button, ▼ and then below the **Themes gallery**, click **Browse for Themes**. Navigate to your **PowerPoint Chapter 6** folder, and then click your template file **6A_Template_Firstname_Lastname**. Click **Apply**. Notice that the entire presentation is formatted with the template that you created. Compare your screen with Figure 6.15.

In the status bar, your template name displays.

Slides formatted with Title layout from template

Figure 6.15

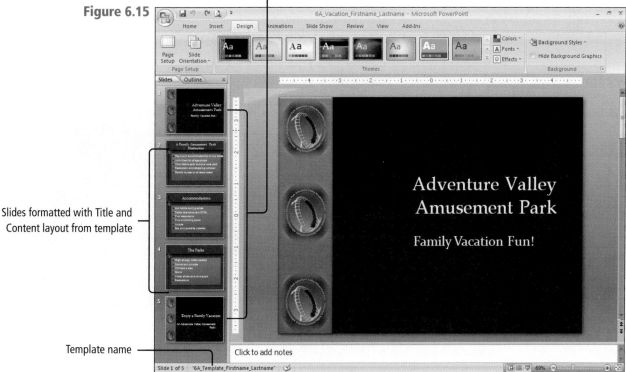

Slides formatted with Title and Content layout from template

Template name

3 **Save** 🖫 the presentation.

Objective 2
Edit a Presentation

Presentations are frequently reviewed by several people so that input on design and content is accomplished collaboratively. You can use the Review tab to insert, edit and delete comments about the presentation.

Activity 6.7 Inserting Comments

While you are reviewing a presentation, you may add **comments** that function as electronic sticky notes within your presentation and contain reviewer questions or thoughts.

1 Display **Slide 1**. On the **Review tab**, in the **Comments group**, click **New Comment**.

A comment opens displaying the user information in the PowerPoint Options dialog box and the current date. An insertion point is blinking in the comment indicating that you can type. In the upper left corner of the slide, a User name comment button displays the initials of the person whose name is entered in the user information in the PowerPoint Options dialog box. This information is followed by the number of the comment. Comments are numbered sequentially in the order in which they are entered.

2 Type **This presentation includes information about the entire resort. Please replace all instances of Park with Resort.** Compare your screen with Figure 6.16.

Figure 6.16

User name comment button

Comment

3 Click anywhere on the slide to close the comment so that it no longer displays.

4 In the upper left corner of the slide, click the **User name comment button** to open the comment.

When the comment is open, you can view it but you cannot change it. To change the comment you must use the Edit Comment command.

Alert!

Is your user name comment button missing from the slide?
If the user name comment button does not display, on the Review tab, in the Comments group, click the Show Markup button to display the comment button.

5 On the **Review tab**, in the **Comments group**, click **Edit Comment** to expand the comment box for editing. Alternatively, double click the User name comment button.

6 Click in front of the word *Park*, type **Amusement** and then press Spacebar. Click anywhere on the slide to close the comment.

7 **Save** 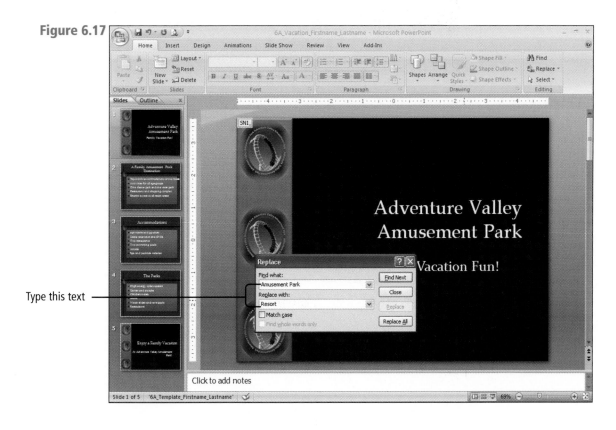 the presentation.

More Knowledge

Deleting a Comment

To delete a comment, right-click on the comment to display the shortcut menu, and then click Delete Comment. Alternatively, on the Review tab, in the Comments group, click the Delete button.

Activity 6.8 Finding and Replacing Text

The Replace command enables you to quickly locate all occurrences of specified text and replace it with alternative text. In this Activity, you will replace all occurrences of *Amusement Park* with *Resort*.

1 Display **Slide 1**. On the **Home tab**, in the **Editing group**, click the **Replace** button. In the **Replace** dialog box, click in the **Find what** box. Type **Amusement Park** and then in the **Replace with** box, type **Resort** and compare your screen with Figure 6.17.

Figure 6.17

Type this text

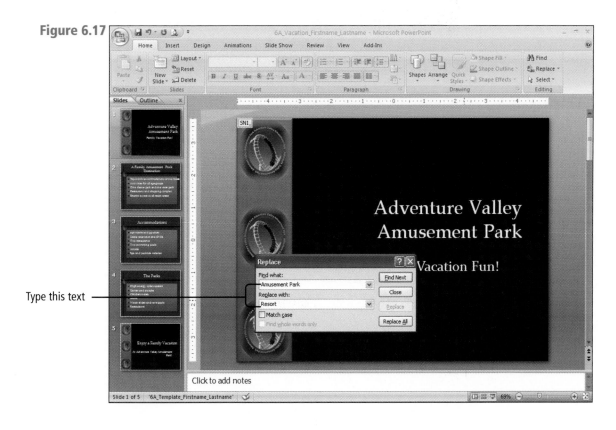

2 In the **Find and Replace** dialog box, click the **Replace All** button.

A message box displays indicating the number of replacements that were made.

3 Click **OK** to close the message box, and then in the **Replace** dialog box, click the **Close** button.

4 Create a header and footer for the **Notes and Handouts**. Include the **Date and time updated automatically**, the **Page number**, and a **Footer** with the file name **6A_Vacation_Firstname_Lastname**

5 Check your *Chapter Assignment Sheet* or your *Course Syllabus* or consult your instructor to determine if you are to submit your assignments on paper or electronically. To submit electronically, go to Step 8, and then follow the instructions provided by your instructor.

6 **Print Preview** your presentation, and in the **Page Setup group**, click the **Print What arrow**. Click **Handouts (6 Slides Per Page)**, and then in the **Preview group**, click **Next Page** to display the text of the comment inserted on Slide 1.

7 Print **Handouts (6 Slides Per Page)**.

8 **Save** 🖫 the changes to your presentation, and then close the presentation.

End **You have completed Project 6A** ——————————

Project 6B **Album**

In Activities 6.9 through 6.13, you will create and edit a photo album that Adventure Valley Resort will post on their Web page to showcase poolside activities available for resort guests. Your completed presentation will look similar to Figure 6.18. You will save your presentation as 6B_Album_Firstname_Lastname.

For Project 6B, you will need the following files:

New blank PowerPoint presentation
p06B_Outline
p06B_Pool1
p06B_Pool2
p06B_Pool3
p06B_Pool4
p06B_Pool5
p06B_Pool6
p06B_Pool7

You will save your presentation, your Web page, and your document as
6B_Album_Firstname_Lastname,
6B_Web_Album_Firstname_Lastname, and
6B_Handouts_Firstname_Lastname

Figure 6.18
Project 6B—Album

Objective 3
Create a Photo Album

You can use Microsoft Office PowerPoint 2007 to create a *photo album*—a presentation composed of pictures. The pictures can be added all at once to your presentation photo album using a digital camera, a scanner, files saved on a disk, or a Web camera. You can format the photo album by adding captions, templates, text boxes, and frames.

Activity 6.9 Inserting a Photo Album

1 **Start** PowerPoint and begin a new blank presentation. On the **Insert tab**, in the **Illustrations group**, click the **Photo Album** button. Alternatively, click the Photo Album button arrow, and then click New Photo Album.

In the displayed Photo Album dialog box, you can view a list of the pictures you have added, preview a picture, set picture options, move and format the pictures that you add, and choose a layout for your photo album.

2 Under **Insert picture from**, click **File/Disk** to open the **Insert New Pictures** dialog box.

In the Insert New Pictures dialog box, you can choose the pictures that you want to add to the photo album. You can add all of the pictures at one time, or you can add a few, and then add more later.

3 Navigate to your student files, and then click **p06B_Pool1**. Hold down ⧉Shift, and then click **p06B_Pool7** so that seven pictures are selected, as shown in Figure 6.19.

Recall that pressing ⧉Shift while selecting enables you to select continuous items in a list.

Figure 6.19

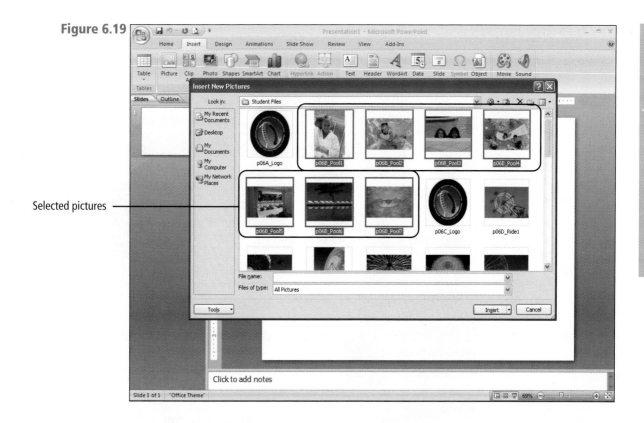

Selected pictures —

4 Click **Insert**, and notice that the **Photo Album** dialog box displays
and the file names are listed under *Pictures in album*, as shown in
Figure 6.20.

A preview of one of the pictures displays in the Preview box and
below the Preview box, flip, contrast, and brightness buttons display
so that you can adjust the pictures, if necessary. Your pictures may
display in a different order than those in Figure 6.20.

Preview

Figure 6.20

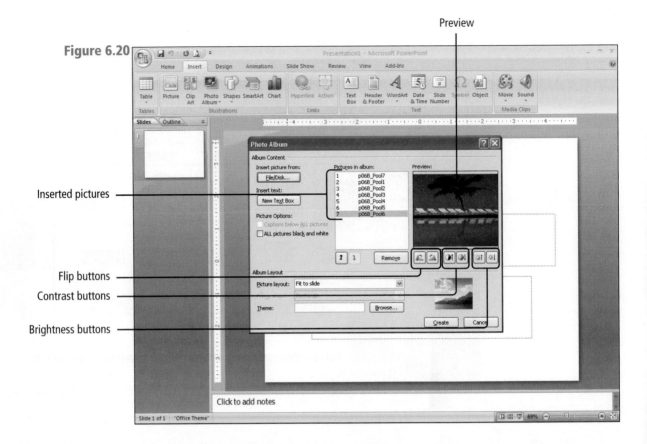

Inserted pictures

Flip buttons
Contrast buttons

Brightness buttons

5 Under **Pictures in album**, click each picture to preview it. Then, click **p06B_Pool7**. Below the **Picture in album list**, click the **Remove** button to delete the picture from the list.

6 Click **p06B_Pool1**—the picture of the woman on the lounge chair—so that it is selected. Below the **Pictures in album box**, locate the up and down arrows as shown in Figure 6.21.

Using the up and down arrows, you can rearrange the pictures in the album.

Figure 6.21

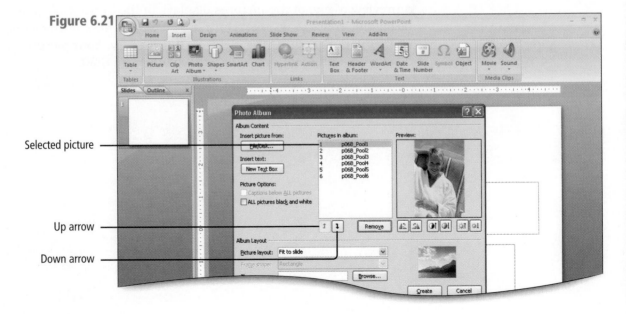

Selected picture

Up arrow
Down arrow

7 With **p06B_Pool1** selected, click the down arrow until **p06B_Pool1** is the fifth picture in the list. Under **Pictures in album**, click **p06B_ Pool6**—the picture of the palm tree and lounge chairs. Click the up arrow until **p06B_Pool6** is the first picture in the list. Compare your screen with Figure 6.22, and use the up and down arrows as necessary so that your pictures are in the same order as those in the figure.

Figure 6.22

Rearranged list ⎯⎯⎯⎯⎯⎯

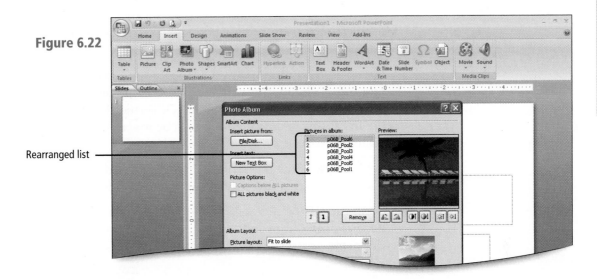

8 Under **Album Layout**, click the **Picture layout arrow**, and then click **1 picture**. Click the **Frame shape arrow**, and then click **Rounded Rectangle**. Click the **Browse button**, and then in the **Choose Theme** dialog box, click **Concourse**, and then click **Select**. Compare your screen with Figure 6.23.

Figure 6.23

Album layout options ⎯⎯⎯⎯

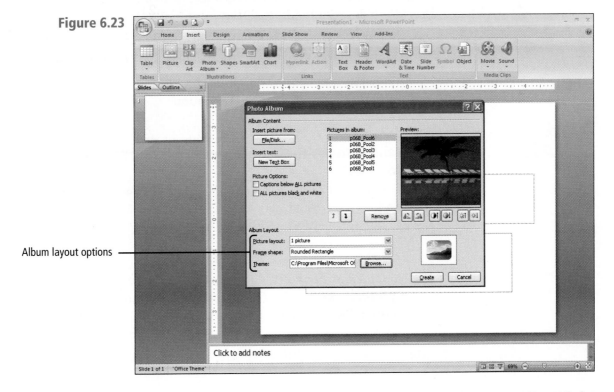

Note Adding Captions to Photo Albums

You can select the *Captions below ALL pictures* check box to add a caption below every picture in your presentation. By default, the caption includes the file name of the picture. You can type a new caption under the picture, but you cannot delete a caption or move it as these actions result in deleting and moving the associated picture.

9 In the **Photo Album** dialog box, click **Create** to insert the photo album.

A new presentation with the Concourse theme opens, and the layout and frame shape that you selected are applied to the photo album slides. Additionally, a title slide is inserted that includes the title Photo Album. A subtitle may also be inserted depending upon your system settings.

10 Replace the title text—*Photo Album*—with **Adventure Valley Resort** and then replace the subtitle text with **Water Activities**

11 From the **Office** menu 📳, click **Save As**, and then navigate to your **PowerPoint Chapter 6** folder. In the **File name** box, type **6B_Album_ Firstname_Lastname** and then click **Save** to save your file.

Activity 6.10 Modifying a Photo Album

After a photo album is created, you can change the layout and frame shape, and you can add new pictures and text. When you modify the photo album, your changes affect the entire album, so it is best not to format your slides until you are finished inserting pictures and laying out your Photo Album. Changes that you make to slide backgrounds, textboxes, and animation schemes will be lost if you make the changes prior to updating the photo album.

1 On the **Insert tab**, in the **Illustrations group**, click the **Photo Album button arrow**, and then click **Edit Photo Album**.

The displayed Edit Photo Album dialog box includes the pictures and settings for the current photo album.

Alert!

Are the pictures that you inserted missing from the dialog box?

If the dialog box does not contain the pictures or settings from the photo album that you created, click Cancel. Then, repeat Step 1, being sure to click the Photo Album *arrow*, not the Photo album button.

2 Under **Album Layout**, click the **Picture layout arrow**, and then click **2 pictures with title**. Click **Update**. Compare your screen with Figure 6.24 and notice in the Slides/Outline pane that Slides 2, 3, and 4 are reformatted to contain two images. The slide backgrounds are gray because the slides are formatted with the two content layout, which includes a gray background.

Figure 6.24

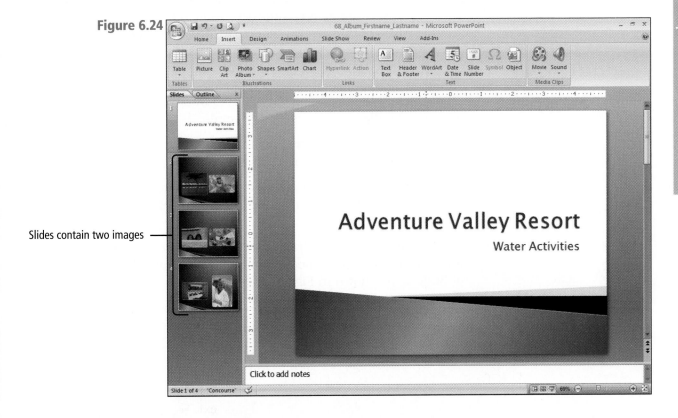

3 Display **Slide 2**. Click in the title placeholder and type **Have Fun in the Pools!** Display **Slide 3**. Click in the title placeholder and type **Make New Friends!** Click **Slide 4**. Click in the title placeholder and type **Relax and Enjoy!**

4 **Save** your presentation.

Objective 3
Share Files with Other Users

Different users can share and modify PowerPoint files by importing Microsoft Office Word 2007 outlines and by exporting PowerPoint slides to Microsoft Office Word 2007. Additionally, a PowerPoint presentation can be saved for viewing on the Web.

Activity 6.11 Importing a Microsoft Word Outline

Recall that the text in the bulleted lists in a PowerPoint presentation are based on an outline in which the bullets are assigned to varying outline levels. An outline that has been created in Microsoft Word using *Word paragraph styles*—built in formats applied to paragraphs and text—can be imported into a PowerPoint presentation. When the outline is imported, the text is converted into slide titles and bullet levels based on the styles in the Word outline. Text formatted with the Heading 1 style is converted to a slide title, and text formatted with a Heading 2 or Heading 3 style is converted to bullet points.

1 If necessary, display **Slide 4**. On the **Home tab**, in the **Slides group**, click the **New Slide arrow**, and then below the gallery, click **Slides from Outline** to display the **Insert Outline** dialog box.

2 Navigate to your student files, click **p06B_Outline**, and then click **Insert**.

The Microsoft Word outline is converted into three new slides, each with a slide title and several bullet points.

3 On the **View tab**, in the **Presentation Views group**, click the **Slide Sorter** button to display all of the slides in the presentation.

Recall that in Slide Sorter view, you can rearrange the order of the slides in your presentation by dragging a selected slide to a new location.

4 Select **Slide 5** and then drag the slide to the left so that the vertical line indicating the new location of the slide is positioned to the right of **Slide 1**, as shown in Figure 6.25.

Selected slide

Figure 6.25

Drag slide to this location

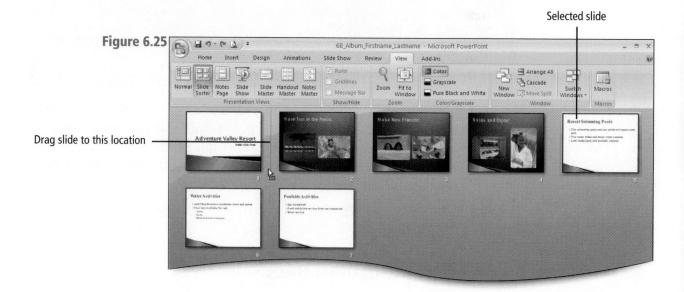

5 Release the mouse button to move the slide. Use the same technique to move **Slide 6** so that it is positioned to the right of **Slide 3**. Select **Slide 7** and drag the slide to position it to the left of **Slide 6**. Compare your screen with Figure 6.26.

Figure 6.26

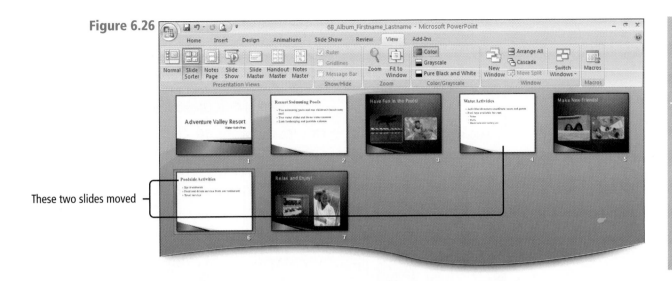

These two slides moved —

6 On the **View tab**, in the **Presentation Views group**, click the **Normal** button to return the presentation to Normal view.

7 **Save** 🖫 the presentation.

Activity 6.12 Exporting a Presentation to Microsoft Word

When you export a presentation to Microsoft Word, you can choose to display the slides in a table with notes or blank lines below or to the right of the image of the slide. For example, you may want to print two slides per page with blank lines to the right of each slide. In PowerPoint, you can either print two slides per page with no lines, or you can print three slides per page with blank lines. By exporting the presentation to Microsoft Word, you can manipulate the layout so that handouts fit the needs of your audience. You can also send the outline version of a presentation to Microsoft Word.

1 From the **Office** menu 🗐 , point to **Publish**, and then click **Create Handouts in Microsoft Office Word**.

The Send To Microsoft Office Word dialog box displays, in which you can specify the layout for the presentation in Word.

2 Click **Blank lines next to slides**. Under **Add slides to Microsoft Office Word document**, click **Paste**, and then compare your screen with Figure 6.27.

The Paste option creates an ***embedded object*** in Microsoft Office Word. An embedded object is one in which a link is established between the object and its source application—in this case, PowerPoint. Thus, while the object displays in Word, you can right-click to display a shortcut menu that includes some of the PowerPoint features. The ***Paste link*** command creates a link in which changes to the slide in the source application, PowerPoint, can be updated in the destination application, Word.

Figure 6.27

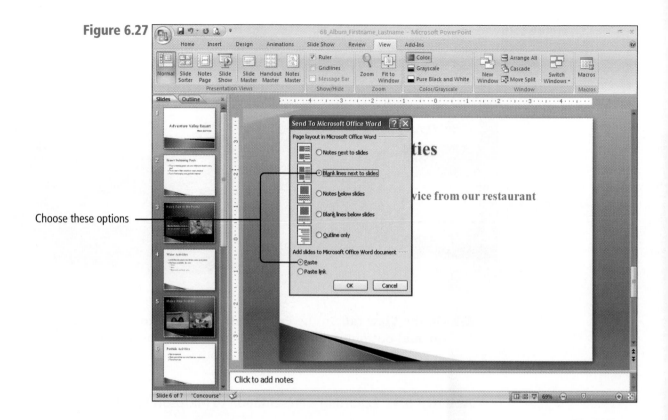

Choose these options

3 Click **OK** to create and display the Microsoft Office Word document. If the document does not display, in the taskbar at the bottom of your window, click the **Document1—Microsoft Word** button.

A three-column table is created in Microsoft Office Word. The first column contains the slide number, the second column contains the slide image, and the third column contains the blank lines. If you are familiar with Microsoft Office Word, you can change the page orientation and margins, modify the table properties, or delete the lines and add text to the third column.

Alert! | **Are the top borders missing from your slides?**

Do not be concerned if the top borders appear to be missing from your slides. When you print the handouts, the borders will print.

4 From the **Office** menu , click **Save As**, and then navigate to your **PowerPoint Chapter 6** folder. In the **File name** box, type **6B_ Handouts_Firsntame_Lastname** and then click **Save** to save your file.

5 On the **Insert tab**, in the **Header & Footer group**, click the **Footer** button. At the bottom of the displayed **Footer gallery**, click **Edit Footer**. On the **Design tab**, in the **Insert group**, click the **Quick Parts** button, and then point to **Field** as shown in Figure 6.28.

Figure 6.28

Quick Parts button

Design tab

Click Field

Footer area

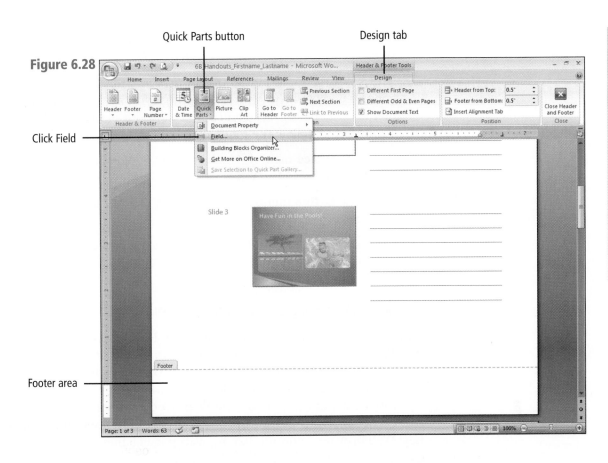

6 Click **Field**, and then in the **Field** dialog box, under **Field names**, locate and click **FileName** as shown in Figure 6.29.

Figure 6.29

Choose the FileName field.

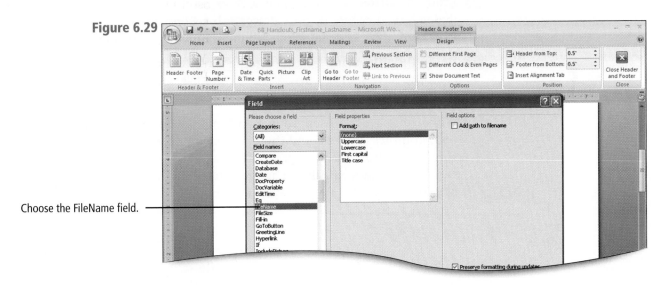

7 Click **OK** to insert a footer with the document file name, and then double-click anywhere in the document to leave the Footer area.

8 On the **Office** menu point to **Print**, and then click **Print Preview** to view how the handouts will print in Word.

Notice that the presentation will print similar to the *Handouts (3 Slides Per Page)* option in PowerPoint, and that the file name displays in the footer.

9 Click the **Close Print Preview** button to return to Microsoft Office Word.

10 Check your *Chapter Assignment Sheet* or your *Course Syllabus* or consult your instructor to determine if you are to submit your assignments on paper or electronically. To submit electronically, go to Step 13, and then follow the instructions provided by your instructor.

11 From the **Office** menu 🔲, click **Print**. At the bottom of the displayed **Print** dialog box, click **OK**.

12 From the **Office** menu 🔲 click **Close**, saving any changes if prompted to do so.

13 At the far right edge of the title bar, click the **Close** button ⊠ to exit the Word program.

Activity 6.13 Saving a Presentation as a Web Page

A presentation created in Microsoft Office PowerPoint 2007 can be saved as a Web page and posted to a company *intranet* or to the World Wide Web. An intranet is an organization's internal network. Recall that information on the World Wide Web is viewed with a browser—software that lets you view and navigate on the Web. Web browsers can read *Hypertext Markup Language* or *HTML*, the language that indicates how Web browsers should display Web page elements.

1 If necessary, **Start** PowerPoint, and then open your file **6B_Album_Firstname_Lastname**.

2 From the **Office** menu 🔲, click **Save As**. In the displayed **Save As** dialog box, navigate to your **PowerPoint Chapter 6** folder. In the **File name** box, type 6B_Web_Album_Firstname_Lastname

3 Below the **File name** box, locate the **Save as type box,** and then click the **Save as type arrow**. Scroll the list, and then click **Single File Web Page** as shown in Figure 6.30.

When you save a presentation as a Single File Web Page, all of the text, graphics, bullets, and theme information are stored within a single file. Thus, the Web page can be sent by email so that others can view the presentation. The file extension for a presentation stored as a Single File Web Page is .mht instead of .pptx.

Figure 6.30

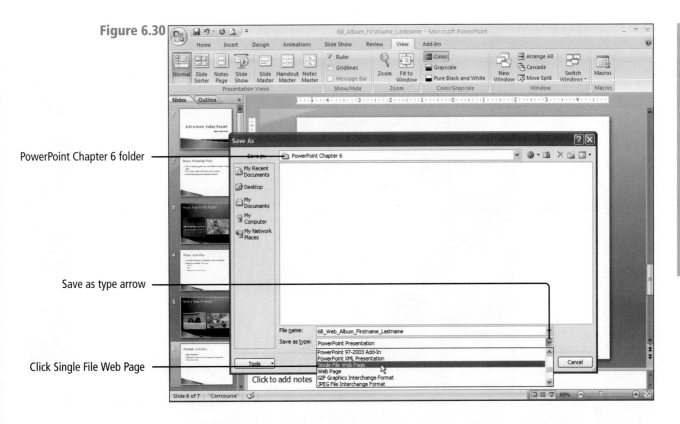

PowerPoint Chapter 6 folder

Save as type arrow

Click Single File Web Page

Click to add notes

4 Below the **Save as type** box, click the **Change Title** button. In the displayed **Set Page Title** dialog box, select the existing text, type **Adventure Valley Resort Water Activities** and then click **OK**.

The text that you type in the Set Page Title dialog box displays in the browser title bar when the Web page is displayed.

5 Click **Publish** to display the **Publish as Web Page** dialog box.

The Publish option creates a copy of the existing presentation so that the original presentation is stored as a PowerPoint file and the copy is stored as a .mht file that can be viewed on the Web.

6 If necessary, under **Publish what?** click the **Complete presentation** option button, and under Browser support, click the Microsoft Internet Explorer 4.0 or later (high fidelity) option button. At the bottom of the **Publish as Web Page** dialog box, click to select the **Open published Web page in browser** check box, and then compare your screen with Figure 6.31.

The *Open published Web page in browser* option displays the presentation in your Web browser after the Publish process is complete.

Figure 6.31

Select these options ————

7 Click **Publish**. A yellow message bar may display near the top of your browser window indicating that your system has restricted ActiveX controls. If necessary, click the yellow bar, click Allow Blocked Content, and then in the displayed message box, click Yes.

After a short time, the presentation opens in your browser. The title bar displays the Page Title that you entered, and a navigation bar with slide numbers and several slide titles displays at the left of the window. The titles of the picture slides do not display. Navigation buttons display below the slide. Compare your screen with Figure 6.32.

Page title

Figure 6.32

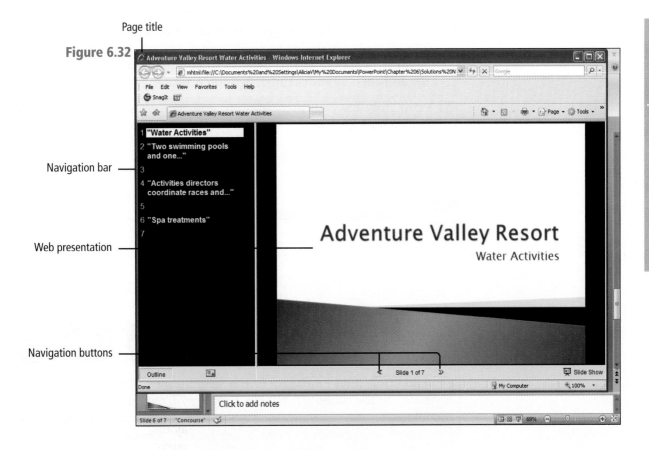

Navigation bar

Web presentation

Navigation buttons

8 In the navigation bar, click the slide numbers to view each slide in the presentation. Alternatively, below the slide, click the ⟪ and ⟫ navigation buttons to display each slide.

9 **Close** ✕ your Web browser to return to your PowerPoint presentation.

10 Create a **Header and Footer** for the **Notes and Handouts**. Include the **Date and time updated automatically**, the **Page number**, and a **Footer** with the file name **6B_Album_Firstname_Lastname**

11 Check your *Chapter Assignment Sheet* or your *Course Syllabus* or consult your instructor to determine if you are to submit your assignments on paper or electronically. To submit electronically, go to Step 13, and then follow the instructions provided by your instructor.

12 **Print Preview** your presentation, and then print **Handouts (4 Slides Per Page)**.

13 **Save** 💾 the changes to your presentation, and then close the presentation.

End **You have completed Project 6B** ─────────

There's More You Can Do!

From My Computer, navigate to the student files that accompany this textbook. In the folder **02_theres_more_you_can_do**, locate and open the folder for this chapter. Open and print the instructions for this project, which are provided to you in Adobe PDF format.

Try IT! 1—Rehearse Presentation Timings

In this Try It! exercise, you will rehearse the timing of a presentation that includes animation and slide transitions.

Content-Based Assessments

Summary

In this chapter, you created a template by formatting slide masters, and then you applied your template to a presentation. You edited a presentation by replacing information and by inserting a photo album. You also practiced using PowerPoint 2007 collaboratively by inserting comments, by importing and exporting presentation information from and to Microsoft Office Word, and by publishing a presentation to the Web.

Key Terms

Content-Based Assessments

Matching

Match each term in the second column with its correct definition in the first column. Write the letter of the term on the blank line in front of the correct definition.

_____ **1.** A slide that holds the information about formatting and text that displays on every slide in a presentation.

_____ **2.** The option that determines the color, position, and transparency values of the gradient fill.

_____ **3.** Notes within a presentation that contain reviewer questions or thoughts.

_____ **4.** The command that enables you to quickly locate all occurrences of specified text and, in its place, enter alternative text.

_____ **5.** A presentation composed of pictures.

_____ **6.** Built-in formats applied to paragraphs and text in Microsoft Office Word.

_____ **7.** The type of list in a presentation that is based on an outline.

_____ **8.** An object in which a link is established between the object and its source application.

_____ **9.** A Paste option that creates a link in which changes to the source application can be updated in the destination application.

_____ **10.** An organization's internal network.

_____ **11.** The software that is used to view a presentation on the Web.

_____ **12.** The save option that stores presentation for Web viewing so that all of the text, graphics, bullets, and theme information are stored within one file.

_____ **13.** The language that indicates how Web browsers should display Web page elements.

_____ **14.** The abbreviation for Hypertext Markup Language.

_____ **15.** A command that creates a copy of a PowerPoint presentation so that it can be viewed on the Web.

A Browser

B Bulleted

C Comments

D Embedded object

E Gradient stop

F HTML

G Hypertext Markup Language

H Intranet

I Paste link

J Photo album

K Publish

L Replace

M Single File Web Page

N Slide master

O Word paragraph styles

Content-Based Assessments

Fill in the Blank

Write the correct word in the space provided.

1. Completed presentations can be shared with many viewers by saving files for viewing on the _____.

2. You can customize a theme by modifying the _____ _____.

3. Within each theme, each _____ _____ includes a slide master that when modified, only affects those slides to which the layout has been applied.

4. Save a presentation as a _____ if you would like to apply the slide master changes to other presentations.

5. The background on individual slide master layouts can be modified to _____ the formatting on the theme slide master.

6. The _____ position determines the location on the slide where the color begins to fade into the next color.

7. The _____ _____ determines the opaqueness of the selected Stop color.

8. To create a duplicate of a selected object positioned down and to the right of the original object, press _____ + _____.

9. In addition to modifying slide master backgrounds and adding objects to a slide master, you can change the size, position, and format of _____.

10. You can use the _____ tab to insert, edit, and delete comments about the presentation.

11. Pictures can be added all at once to your presentation photo album using a _____ _____, scanner, files saved on disk, or a Web camera.

12. A photo album can be formatted by adding captions, templates, textboxes, and _____.

13. By default, the caption includes the _____ _____ of the picture.

14. Different users can share and modify PowerPoint files by _____ a Microsoft Office Word 2007 outline.

15. Text formatted with the Heading 1 style is converted to a _____ _____.

Skills Review

Project 6C — Summer Jobs

In this project, you will apply the skills you practiced from the Objectives in Project 6A.

Objectives: 1. *Create a Template by Modifying Slide Masters;* **2.** *Edit a Presentation.*

In the following Skills Review, you will create a template and presentation that the Recruiting Director for Adventure Valley Amusement Park is developing to inform college students of the summer employment opportunities at the resort. Your completed presentation will look similar to the one shown in Figure 6.33.

For Project 6C, you will need the following files:

New blank PowerPoint presentation
p06C_Logo
p06C_Summer_Jobs

You will save your presentation as
6C_Summer_Jobs_Firstname_Lastname

Figure 6.33

(Project 6C–Summer Jobs continues on the next page)

Content-Based Assessments

(Project 6C–Summer Jobs continued)

1. **Start** PowerPoint and begin a new blank presentation. On the **View tab**, in the **Presentation Views group**, click the **Slide Master** button. Click the first slide master—**Office Theme Slide Master: used by slide(s) 1** so that it displays in the slide pane. On the **Slide Master tab**, in the **Background group**, click the **Background Styles** button, and then click **Style 2** to change the background for all of the slide master layouts.

2. Click in the title placeholder, and then on the **Home tab**, in the **Font group**, click the **Font button arrow**. Click **Arial**. In the content placeholder, click in the first bullet point—*Click to edit Master text styles*. On the **Home tab**, in the **Font group**, click the **Font button arrow**, and then click **Corbel**.

3. From the **Office** menu, click **Save As**. At the bottom of the **Save As** dialog box, click the **Save as type arrow**, and then click **PowerPoint Template**. Navigate to your **PowerPoint Chapter 6** folder. In the **File name box**, type 6C_Template_Firstname_Lastname and then click **Save**.

4. Click the second slide master—**Title Slide Layout: used by slide(s) 1**. On the **Slide Master tab**, in the **Background group**, click the **Background Styles** button, and then click **Format Background**. Under **Fill**, click **Gradient fill**. If necessary, change the **Type** to **Linear**. Click the **Direction arrow**, and then in the first row, click the fifth option—**Linear Left**.

5. Under **Gradient Stops**, click the **Stop 1 arrow** to display the three gradient stops. Click **Stop 3**, and then click **Remove** to remove Stop 3 from the gradient fill and to display the settings for Stop 2. With **Stop 2** displayed, click the **Color button arrow** to display the **Theme Colors gallery**.

Under **Theme Colors**, in the seventh column, click the fourth color—**Olive Green, Accent 3, Lighter 40%**.

6. Click the **Stop 2 arrow**, and then click **Stop 1**. Click the **Color button arrow**. Under **Theme Colors**, in the first column click the first color—**White, Background 1**, and then click **Close** to apply the gradient fill to the slide.

7. On the **Insert tab**, in the **Illustrations group**, click the **Shapes button**, and then under **Rectangles**, click the first shape—**Rectangle**. Position the ⊞ pointer in the upper left corner of the slide, and then drag to the right and down to draw a rectangle that extends to **3 inches before zero on the horizontal ruler** and to the bottom of the slide.

8. On the **Format tab**, in the **Shape Styles group**, click the **More** button. In the displayed **Shapes Styles gallery**, in the fourth column, click the fifth style—**Moderate Effect Accent 3**. In the **Size group**, click in the **Width box**, type **1.75** and then press Enter to resize the rectangle.

9. On the **Insert tab**, in the **Illustrations group**, click the **Picture** button. Navigate to the location where your student files are stored, click **p06C_Logo**, and then click **Insert**. On the **Format tab**, in the **Size group**, click in the **Height box**, type **2** and then press Enter to resize the picture. Drag the picture up and to the left so that its upper left corner aligns with the upper left corner of the slide.

10. With the picture selected, hold down Ctrl and press D. Drag the new picture down and to the left so that its top edge aligns at **1 inch above zero on the vertical ruler** and its left edge aligns with the left

(Project 6C–Summer Jobs continues on the next page)

(Project 6C–Summer Jobs continued)

edge of the slide. Hold down Ctrl and press D to create another picture. If necessary, drag the new picture so that its lower left corner aligns with the lower left corner of the slide.

11. Hold down ⇧ Shift, and then select the top and middle pictures so that all three pictures are selected. On the **Format tab**, in the **Picture Styles group**, click the **Picture Effects** button, and then point to **Soft Edges**. Click **25 Point**.

12. Point to the outer edge of the title placeholder to display the ⊹ pointer, and then drag to the right so that the right edge of the placeholder touches the right edge of the slide. On the **Home tab**, in the **Paragraph group**, click the **Align Text Right** button to change the alignment of the title placeholder.

13. Point to the outer edge of the subtitle placeholder to display the ⊹ pointer, and then drag to the right so that the right edge of the placeholder touches the right edge of the slide. On the **Home tab**, in the **Paragraph group**, click the **Align Text Right** button to change the alignment of the title placeholder. Change the **Font Color** to **Black, Text 1**.

14. Display the third slide master—**Title and Content Layout: used by no slides**. On the **Insert tab**, in the **Illustrations group**, click **Shapes**. Under **Rectangles**, click the second shape—**Rounded Rectangle**. Position the pointer on the left edge of the slide at **2 inches above zero**, and then drag up and to the right so that the top edge of the rectangle touches the bottom of the title placeholder and extends to the right edge of the slide.

15. On the **Format tab**, in the **Shape Styles group**, click the **More** button, and then in the fourth column of the **Shapes Styles gallery**, click the last style—**Intense Effect-Accent 3**. With the rectangle selected, hold down Ctrl and press D to create another rectangle. On the **Format tab**, in the **Size group**, click in the **Height box**. Type **0.1** and then click in the **Width box**. Type **7** and then press Enter to size the rectangle.

16. On the **Format tab**, in the **Arrange group**, click the **Rotate** button, and then click **Rotate Right 90°** so that the two rectangles are intersecting. Drag the rectangle down and to the left so it aligns with the left edge of the title and content placeholders and its lower edge aligns with the lower edge of the slide.

17. With the **Title and Content Layout** slide master displayed, click in the content placeholder. On the **Format tab**, in the **Size group**, click in the **Height box**. Type **4.5** and then click in the **Width box**. Type **8.5** and then press Enter to resize the placeholder.

18. Point to the outer edge of the placeholder to display the ⊹ pointer, and then drag the placeholder down and to the right so that its top edge aligns at **1.5 inches above zero on the vertical ruler** and its right edge aligns with the right edge of the title placeholder.

19. On the **Format tab**, in the **Shape Styles group**, click the **More** button. In the displayed **Shapes Styles gallery**, in the first row, click the fourth style—**Colored Outline-Accent 3**. With the content placeholder selected, on the **Format tab**, in the **Shape Styles group**, click **Shape Effects**.

(Project 6C–Summer Jobs continues on the next page)

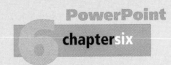

Skills Review

(Project 6C–Summer Jobs continued)

Point to **Glow**, and then below the **Glow Variations gallery**, click **More Glow Colors**. In the first row, click the second color—**Black, Text 1** to add a slight black glow effect to the outside of the placeholder.

20. Click anywhere in the first line of the content placeholder—*Click to edit Master text styles*. On the **Home tab**, in the **Paragraph group**, click the **Bullets button arrow**. Below the **Bullets gallery**, click **Bullets and Numbering**. In the displayed **Bullets and Numbering** dialog box, in the second row, click **Star Bullets**. In the **Size** box, select **100** and then type **75** to change the bullets to 75% of the size of the text. Click **OK** to apply the bullet formatting.

21. Formatting for the template is complete. **Save** and close the presentation template. If necessary start PowerPoint. From your student files, open the file **p06C_Summer_Jobs**. From the **Office** menu, click **Save As**, and then navigate to your **PowerPoint Chapter 6** folder. In the **File name** box, type **6C_Summer_Jobs_Firstname_Lastname** and then click **Save** to save your file.

22. On the **Design tab**, in the **Themes group**, click the **More** button, and then below the **Themes gallery**, click **Browse for Themes**. Navigate to your **PowerPoint Chapter 6** folder, and then click **6C_Template_Firstname_Lastname**. Click **Apply** to format the presentation with the template that you created.

23. Display **Slide 1**. On the **Review tab**, in the **Comments group**, click **New Comment**. Type **Please change the word Winter to**

Summer throughout the presentation. Click anywhere on the slide to close the comment.

24. On the **Home tab**, in the **Editing group**, click the **Replace** button. In the **Replace** dialog box, click in the **Find what** box. Type **Winter** and then in the **Replace with** box, type **Summer** In the **Find and Replace** dialog box, click the **Replace All** button. Click **OK** to close the message box, and then in the **Replace** dialog box, click the **Close** button.

25. Create a **Header and Footer** for the **Notes and Handouts**. Include the **Date and time updated automatically**, the **Page number**, and a **Footer** with the file name **6C_Summer_Jobs_Firstname_Lastname**

26. Check your *Chapter Assignment Sheet* or your *Course Syllabus* or consult your instructor to determine if you are to submit your assignments on paper or electronically. To submit electronically, go to Step 29, and then follow the instructions provided by your instructor.

27. **Print Preview** your presentation, and then in the **Page Setup group**, click the **Print What arrow**. Click **Handouts (4 Slides Per Page)**, and then in the **Preview group**, click **Next Page** to display the text of the comment inserted on Slide 1.

28. Print **Handouts (4 Slides Per Page)**.

29. **Save** the changes to your presentation, and then close the presentation.

 You have completed Project 6C

Content-Based Assessments

Project 6D — Rides

In this project, you will apply the skills you practiced from the Objectives in Project 6B.

Objectives: 1. *Create a Photo Album;* **2.** *Share Files with Other Users.*

In the following Skills Review, you will create a photo album presentation for Web viewing that showcases some of the rides at Adventure Valley Park. Your completed presentation will look similar to the one shown in Figure 6.34.

For Project 6D, you will need the following files:

New blank PowerPoint presentation
p06D_Ride_Outline
p06D_Ride1
p06D_Ride2
p06D_Ride3
p06D_Ride4
p06D_Ride5
p06D_Ride6
p06D_Ride7

You will save your presentation, your Web page, and your document as
6D_Rides_Firstname_Lastname,
6D_Web_Rides_Firstname_Lastname, and
6D_Handouts_Firstname_Lastname

Figure 6.34

(Project 6D–Rides continues on the next page)

Content-Based Assessments

(Project 6D–Rides continued)

1. **Start** PowerPoint and begin a new blank presentation. On the **Insert tab**, in the **Illustrations group**, click the **Photo Album** button. Under **Insert picture from**, click the **File/Disk** button to open the **Insert New Pictures** dialog box. Navigate to your student files, and then click **p06D_Ride1**. Hold down ⇧Shift, and then click **p06D_Ride7** so that seven pictures are selected. Click **Insert**.

2. Click **p06D_Ride7**. Below the **Pictures in album list**, click the **Remove** button to delete the picture from the list. Click **p06D_Ride4**. Below the **Pictures in album** box, click the down arrow *two* times so that **p06D_Ride4** is the last picture in the list.

3. Under **Album Layout**, click the **Picture layout arrow**, and then click **1 picture**. Click the **Frame shape arrow**, and then click **Rounded Rectangle**. Click the **Browse** button, and then in the **Choose Theme** dialog box, click **Equity**, and then click **Select**. In the **Photo Album** dialog box, click **Create** to insert the photo album.

4. Replace the title text—*Photo Album*—with **Adventure Valley Park** and then replace the subtitle text with **Hold On and Enjoy the Rides!**

5. From the **Office** menu, click **Save As**, and then navigate to your **PowerPoint Chapter 6** folder. In the **File name** box, type **6D_Rides_Firstname_Lastname** and then click **Save** to save your file.

6. On the **Insert tab**, in the **Illustrations group**, click the **Photo Album arrow**, and then click **Edit Photo Album**. Under **Album Layout**, click the **Picture layout arrow**, and then click **2 pictures with title**. Click **Update**.

7. Display **Slide 2**. Click in the title placeholder and type **Spin in the Day!** and then **Center** the title. Display **Slide 3**. Click in the title placeholder and type **Enjoy an Evening of Lights!** and then **Center** the title. Display **Slide 4**. Click in the title placeholder and type **Ride Both of Our Ferris Wheels!** and then **Center** the title.

8. On the **Home tab**, in the **Slides group**, click the **New Slide arrow**, and then below the gallery, click **Slides from Outline** to display the **Insert Outline** dialog box. Navigate to your student files, click **p06D_Ride_Outline**, and then click **Insert**.

9. On the **View tab**, in the **Presentation Views group**, click the **Slide Sorter** button to display all of the slides in the presentation. Select **Slide 5** and then drag the slide to the left so that the vertical line indicating the new location of the slide is positioned to the right of **Slide 1**. Release the mouse button to move the slide so that it is the second slide in the presentation. Use the same technique to move **Slide 6** so that it is positioned to the left of **Slide 4**.

10. On the **View tab**, in the **Presentation Views group**, click the **Normal** button to return the presentation to Normal view. **Save** the presentation.

11. From the **Office** menu, point to **Publish**, and then click **Create Handouts in Microsoft Office Word**. Click **Blank lines next to slides**. Under **Add slides to Microsoft Office Word document**, click **Paste**, and then click **OK** to export the presentation to Microsoft Office Word. If necessary, in the taskbar at the bottom of your window, click the **Document1 - Microsoft Word** button to display the Word document.

(Project 6D–Rides continues on the next page)

(Project 6D–Rides continued)

12. From the **Office** menu, click **Save As**, and then navigate to your **PowerPoint Chapter 6** folder. In the **File name** box, type **6D_Handouts_Firstname_Lastname** and then click **Save** to save your file.

13. On the **Insert tab**, in the **Header & Footer group**, click the **Footer** button. At the bottom of the displayed **Footer gallery**, click **Edit Footer**. On the **Design tab**, in the **Insert group**, click the **Quick Parts** button, and then click **Field**. In the **Field** dialog box, under **Field names**, locate and click **FileName**. Click **OK** to insert a footer with the document file name, and then double-click anywhere in the document to leave the Footer area.

14. Check your *Chapter Assignment Sheet* or your *Course Syllabus* or consult your instructor to determine if you are to submit your assignments on paper or electronically. To submit electronically, go to Step 16, and then follow the instructions provided by your instructor.

15. From the **Office** menu, click **Print**. At the bottom of the displayed **Print** dialog box, click **OK**. From the **Office** menu, click **Close**, saving any changes if prompted to do so.

16. At the far right edge of the title bar, click the **Close** button to exit the Word program. If necessary, start PowerPoint, and then open your file **6D_Rides_Firstname_ Lastname**.

17. From the **Office** menu, click **Save As**. In the displayed **Save As** dialog box, navigate to your **PowerPoint Chapter 6** folder. In the **File name** box, type **6D_Web_Rides_ Firstname_Lastname** and then below the **File name** box, locate the **Save as type** box, and click the **Save as type arrow**. Scroll the list, and then click **Single File Web Page**.

18. Below the **Save as type** box, click the **Change Title** button. In the displayed **Set Page Title** dialog box, select the existing text, type **Adventure Valley Rides** and then click **OK**. Click **Publish** to display the **Publish as Web Page** dialog box.

19. If necessary, under **Publish what?** click the **Complete presentation** option button, and under **Browser support**, click the **Microsoft Internet Explorer 4.0 or later (high fidelity)** option button. At the bottom of the **Publish as Web Page** dialog box, select the **Open published Web page in browser** check box. Click **Publish**.

20. A yellow message bar may display near the top of your browser window indicating that your system has restricted ActiveX controls. If necessary, click the yellow bar, click Allow Blocked Content, and then in the displayed message box, click Yes.

21. In the navigation bar, click the slide titles to view each slide in the presentation. Then, close your Web browser to return to your PowerPoint presentation.

22. Create a **Header and Footer** for the **Notes and Handouts**. Include the **Date and time updated automatically**, the **Page number**, and a **Footer** with the file name **6D_Rides_Firstname_Lastname**

23. Check your *Chapter Assignment Sheet* or your *Course Syllabus* or consult your instructor to determine if you are to submit your assignments on paper or electronically. To submit electronically, go to Step 25, and then follow the instructions provided by your instructor.

24. Print Preview your presentation, and then print **Handouts (6 Slides Per Page)**.

25. Save the changes to your presentation, and then close the presentation.

End **You have completed Project 6D**

Content-Based Assessments

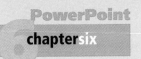

Mastering PowerPoint

Project 6E—Commitment

In this project, you will apply the skills you practiced from the Objectives in Project 6A.

Objectives: 1. *Create a Template by Modifying Slide Masters;* **2.** *Edit a Presentation.*

In the following Mastering PowerPoint project, you will create a presentation that the Human Resources Director uses during staff orientations that details the Adventure Valley Park's mission statement and commitment to staff training and safety. Your completed presentation will look similar to the one shown in Figure 6.35.

For Project 6E, you will need the following files:

New blank PowerPoint presentation
p06E_Commitment
p06E_Wheel

You will save your presentation as
6E_Commitment_Firstname_Lastname

Figure 6.35

(Project 6E–Commitment continues on the next page)

PowerPoint

chaptersix

Mastering PowerPoint

(Project 6E–Commitment continued)

1. **Start** PowerPoint and begin a new blank presentation. Display the **Slide Master**. Display the **Office Theme Slide Master: used by slide(s) 1** layout. On the **Slide Master tab**, in the **Edit Theme group**, click the **Colors** button, and then click **Solstice**. Change the **Background Style** to **Style 10**.

2. Change the title **Font Color** to the last color in the seventh row—**Red, Accent 3, Darker 50%**. Select the content place-holder so that its border displays as a solid line, and then change the **Font** to **Corbel**. Save the file as a **PowerPoint Template** in your **PowerPoint Chapter 6** folder with the file name 6E_Template_ Firstname_Lastname

3. Display the second slide master—**Title Slide Layout: used by slide(s) 1**. In the subtitle placeholder, change the **Font Color** to **Black, Text 1**. Display the **Format Background** dialog box, and then under **Fill**, click **Gradient fill**. Change the **Type** to **Linear**, and then change the **Direction** to the third option—**Linear Diagonal**. If necessary, change the angle to **135** and then close the **Format Background** dialog box.

4. Insert a rectangle shape. Position the ⊞ pointer at the top edge of the slide at **4.5 inches before zero on the horizontal ruler**, and then drag down and to the right to draw a rectangle that extends to **4 inches before zero on the horizontal ruler** and to the bottom of the slide.

5. With the rectangle selected, in the **Shape Styles group**, click the **Shape Fill** button, and then in the seventh column, click the fifth color—**Red, Accent 3, Darker 25%**. Apply the same color to the shape outline. Change the **Width** of the rectangle to **.15**.

6. Duplicate the rectangle, and then drag the new rectangle to the middle of the slide. **Rotate** the new rectangle to the **Right 90°**, and then drag the rectangle down and to the left so it is aligned with the left edge of the slide at **3 inches below zero on the vertical ruler**. Size the rectangle so that it extends from the left edge to the right edge of the slide.

7. From your student files, insert the **Picture p06E_Wheel**. Format the picture by changing the **Picture Shape** to a **Rounded Rectangle**. Apply a **Glow Picture Effect** by displaying **More Glow Colors**. In the **Theme Colors gallery**, in the first row, apply the fourth color—**Brown, Text 2**. Drag the picture down and to the left and position it at the intersection of the two rectangles as shown in Figure 6.34 at the beginning of this project.

8. Display the third slide master—**Title and Content Layout: used by no slides**. Insert a rectangle shape. Position the ⊞ pointer at **zero on the horizontal ruler**, and at **3 inches below zero on the verti-cal ruler**. Drag down and to the right to draw a narrow rectangle that extends to the right edge of the slide. Size the rectan-gle by changing the **Height** to **.2**.

9. With the rectangle selected, in the **Shape Styles group**, click the **Shape Fill** button, and then in the seventh column, click the fifth color—**Red, Accent 3, Darker 25%**. Apply a **5 Point Soft Edges Shape Effect**.

10. Duplicate the rectangle, and then **Rotate** the new rectangle to the **Right 90°** so that the two rectangles are intersecting. Drag the rectangle up and to the right so that its left edge is aligned with the right edge of the content placeholder and its lower edge is aligned with the lower edge of the slide.

(Project 6E–Commitment continues on the next page)

Content-Based Assessments

(Project 6E–Commitment continued)

11. Display the second slide master layout— **Title Slide Layout: used by slide(s) 1**. Select the picture, and then on the **Home tab**, click **Copy**. Display the third slide master layout—**Title and Content Layout: used by no slides**, and then **Paste** the picture. Size the picture by changing its **Height** to **.75** and then drag the picture to the right so that its left edge aligns at **4 inches after zero on the horizontal ruler** and its bottom edge aligns at **3.5 inches below zero on the vertical ruler**.

12. Click anywhere in the first line of the content placeholder—*Click to edit Master text styles*. Display the **Bullets and Numbering** dialog box, and then in the first row, click **Filled Square Bullets**. Change the color to the last color in the seventh column—**Red, Accent 3, Darker 50%**.

13. Formatting for the template is complete. **Save** and close the presentation template. If necessary, start PowerPoint. From your student files, open the file **p06E_Commitment**, and then save the file in your **PowerPoint Chapter 6** folder as 6E_Commitment_Firstname_Lastname

14. Display the **Themes gallery**, and then click **Browse for Themes**. Navigate to your

PowerPoint Chapter 6 folder, and then apply the template that you created— **6E_Template_Firstname_Lastname**.

15. Display **Slide 1**, and then insert the following **Comment: Please change the word Park to Resort throughout the presentation**. Click anywhere on the slide to close the comment, and then use the **Replace** command to replace all occurrences of the word **Park** with **Resort**

16. Create a **Header and Footer** for the **Notes and Handouts**. Include the **Date and time updated automatically**, the **Page number**, and a **Footer** with the file name 6E_Commitment_Firstname_Lastname

17. Check your *Chapter Assignment Sheet* or your *Course Syllabus* or consult your instructor to determine if you are to submit your assignments on paper or electronically. To submit electronically, go to Step 19, and then follow the instructions provided by your instructor.

18. **Print Preview** your presentation, and then print **Handouts (6 Slides Per Page)**.

19. **Save** the changes to your presentation, and then close the presentation.

End **You have completed Project 6E**

chaptersix | Mastering PowerPoint

Project 6F — Restaurants

In this project, you will apply the skills you practiced from the Objectives in Project 6B.

Objectives: 3. *Create a Photo Album;* **4.** *Share Files with Other Users.*

In the following Mastering PowerPoint Assessment, you will create a photo album presentation that includes information about the Adventure Valley Resort restaurants. Your completed presentation will look similar to the one shown in Figure 6.36.

For Project 6F, you will need the following files:

New blank PowerPoint presentation
p06F_Restaurant_Outline
p06F_Restaurant1
p06F_Restaurant2
p06F_Restaurant3
p06F_Restaurant4
p06F_Restaurant5
p06F_Restaurant6
p06F_Restaurant7

**You will save your presentation, Web page, and document as
6F_Restaurants_Firstname_Lastname,
6F_Web_Restaurants_Firstname_Lastname, and
6F_Handouts_Firstname_Lastname**

Figure 6.36

(Project 6F–Restaurants continues on the next page)

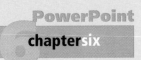

(Project 6F–Restaurants continued)

1. **Start** PowerPoint, begin a new blank presentation, and insert a new **Photo Album**. Insert the seven pictures for this project—**p06F_Restaurant1** though **p06F_Restaurant7**. Remove **p06F_Restaurant5** from the list, and then move the pictures as necessary so that they are in the following order: **p06F_Restaurant1**, **p06F_Restaurant2**, **p06F_Restaurant3**, **p06F_Restaurant7**, **p06F_Restaurant4**, and **p06F_Restaurant6**.

2. Modify the album layout by changing the picture layout to **2 pictures with title**, the frame shape to **Compound Frame**, **Black** and the theme to **Civic**. On the first slide, change the title to **Adventure Valley Resort** and then change the subtitle to **A Little Taste of Our Restaurants**

3. Display **Slide 2**, and then change the title to **Take a Seat!** Display **Slide 3**, and then change the title to **Meet Some Guests and the Management Team** Display **Slide 4** and then change the title to **Sample Our Selection! Save** the presentation in your **PowerPoint Chapter 6** folder as **6F_Restaurants_Firstname_Lastname**

4. With **Slide 4** displayed, from your student files, insert the slides from the Microsoft Office Word outline **p06F_Restaurant_Outline**, and then display the presentation in **Slide Sorter** view. Move **Slide 5** so that it becomes **Slide 2**, move **Slide 6** so that it becomes **Slide 4**, and then move **Slide 7** so that it becomes **Slide 6**. Return the presentation to **Normal** view, display **Slide 7**, and then insert a new slide with the **Section Header** layout. In the title placeholder, type **Join Us for Food and Fun** and then in the subtitle placeholder, type **At Adventure Valley Resort**

5. **Save** the presentation, and then publish the presentation and create handouts in

   Microsoft Office Word with blank lines next to slides. If necessary, display the Word document by clicking its button in the taskbar. **Save** the Word document in your **PowerPoint Chapter 6** folder as **6F_Handouts_Firstname_Lastname** and then insert a footer using the **FileName Field**. After you have created the footer, double-click anywhere in the document to leave the Footer area.

6. Check your *Chapter Assignment Sheet* or your *Course Syllabus* or consult your instructor to determine if you are to submit your assignments on paper or electronically. To submit electronically, go to Step 9, and then follow the instructions provided by your instructor.

7. From the **Office** menu, click **Print**. At the bottom of the displayed **Print** dialog box, click **OK**. From the **Office** menu, click **Close**, saving any changes if prompted to do so.

8. At the far right edge of the title bar, click the **Close** button to exit the Word program. If necessary, Start PowerPoint, and then open your file **6F_Restaurants_Firstname_Lastname**.

9. **Save** your presentation in your **PowerPoint Chapter 6** folder as a **Single File Web Page** with the File name **6F_Web_Restaurants_Firstname_Lastname** Click the **Change Title** button, and then in the **Set Page Title** dialog box, type **Adventure Valley Restaurants** and then click **OK**. Click **Publish** to display the **Publish as Web Page** dialog box. Publish the complete presentation using the **Microsoft Internet Explorer 4.0 or later (high fidelity)** option. At the bottom of the **Publish as Web Page** dialog box, select the **Open published Web page in browser** check box.

(Project 6F–Restaurants continues on the next page)

Content-Based Assessments

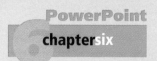
(Project 6F–Restaurants continued)

Click **Publish**, and if necessary, Allow Blocked Content. View each slide, and then close your Web browser to return to your PowerPoint presentation.

10. Create a **Header and Footer** for the **Notes and Handouts**. Include the **Date and time updated automatically**, the **Page number**, and a **Footer** with the file name 6F_Restaurants_Firstname_Lastname

11. Check your *Chapter Assignment Sheet* or your *Course Syllabus* or consult your

instructor to determine if you are to submit your assignments on paper or electronically. To submit electronically, go to Step 13, and then follow the instructions provided by your instructor.

12. **Print Preview** your presentation, and then print **Handouts (4 Slides Per Page)**.

13. **Save** the changes to your presentation, and then close the presentation.

End **You have completed Project 6F** _____

Content-Based Assessments

Mastering PowerPoint

Project 6G—Orientation

In this project, you will apply the skills you practiced from the Objectives in Projects 6A and 6B.

Objectives: 1. *Create a Template by Modifying Slide Masters;* **2.** *Edit a Presentation;* **4.** *Share Files with Other Users.*

In the following Mastering PowerPoint Assessment, you will create a template and single file Web page presentation that is used for the new employee orientation program at Adventure Valley Resort. Your completed presentation will look similar to the one shown in Figure 6.37.

For Project 6G, you will need the following files:

New blank PowerPoint presentation

p06G_Orientation_Outline

p06G_Logo

You will save your presentation and your Web page as 6G_Orientation_Firstname_Lastname and 6G_Web_Orientation_Firstname_Lastname

Figure 6.37

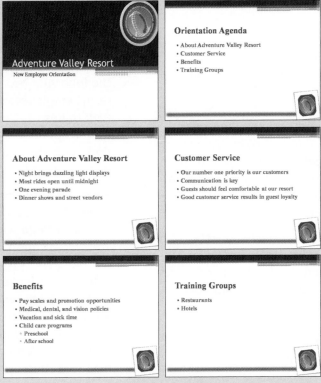

(Project 6G–Orientation continues on the next page)

(Project 6G–Orientation continued)

1. **Start** PowerPoint and begin a new blank presentation. Apply the **Urban Theme**, and then display the **Slide Master**. **Save** the file as a **PowerPoint Template** in your **PowerPoint Chapter 6** folder with the file name **6G_Template_Firstname_Lastname**

2. Display the second slide master—**Title Slide Layout: used by slide(s) 1**. From your student files, insert the **Picture p06G_Logo**, and then recolor the picture by applying **Light Variation—Accent color 2 Light**. Change the **Height** of the picture to **2.75** and then drag the picture to the upper right corner of the slide. Apply the last **Picture Style—Metal Oval**.

3. Display the third master—**Title and Content Layout: used by no slides**. Select the content placeholder and then drag the center bottom sizing handle up so that the bottom of the placeholder is aligned at **3 inches below zero on the vertical ruler**.

4. Insert a **Rectangle** shape. Position the ⊞ pointer at the left edge of the slide and at **3 inches below zero on the vertical ruler**, and then drag down and to the right to draw a rectangle that extends to **3.5 inches below zero on the vertical ruler** and to the right edge of the slide. Display the **Shape Styles gallery**, and then in the second row, apply the third style—**Colored Fill-Accent 2**. Apply a **Shape Effect—Soft Edges, 10 Point**.

5. Display the second slide master—**Title Slide Layout: used by slide(s) 1**. **Copy** the picture, and then display the third master—**Title and Content Layout: used by no slides**. **Paste** the picture. Change the **Height** of the picture to **1.5** and then apply **Picture Style Rotated, White**. (Hint: The style is the tilted, white bordered style.) Drag the picture down to the

lower right corner of the slide. **Save** and close the template.

6. If necessary, start PowerPoint and begin a new blank presentation. In the title placeholder type **Adventure Valley Resort** and in the subtitle placeholder type **New Employee Orientation**

7. From your student files, insert the Microsoft Office Word Outline **p06G_Orientation_Outline**, and then save the presentation in your **PowerPoint Chapter 6** folder with the file name **6G_Orientation_Firstname_Lastname**

8. From your student files, apply the template that you created—**6G_Template_Firstname_Lastname** (Hint: Display the Themes gallery, and then Browse for Themes.) In the **Slides/Outline pane**, select **Slide 2**, hold down ⇧ Shift and select **Slide 6** so that Slides 2 through 6 are selected. Change the layout to **Title and Content** so that the slide master layout that you created is applied to the slides.

9. On **Slide 1**, insert a **New Comment** with the following text: **This orientation is for resort employees so please change the word Park to Resort.** Close the comment, and then **Replace** all instances of the word *Park* with the word *Resort.* **Save** the presentation.

10. Save your presentation in your **PowerPoint Chapter 6** folder as a **Single File Web Page** with the File name **6G_Web_Orientation_Firstname_Lastname** In the **Set Page Title** dialog box, type **New Employee Orientation** and then publish the **Complete presentation** using the **Microsoft Internet Explorer 4.0 or later (high fidelity)** option. Select the **Open published Web page in browser** check box, and then view each slide in your

(Project 6G–Orientation continues on the next page)

Content-Based Assessments

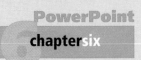
(Project 6G–Orientation continued)

browser window. If necessary, Allow Blocked Content. Close your Web browser to return to your PowerPoint presentation.

11. Create a **Header and Footer** for the **Notes and Handouts**. Include the **Date and time updated automatically**, the **Page number**, and a **Footer** with the file name 6G_Orientation_Firstname_Lastname

12. Check your *Chapter Assignment Sheet* or your *Course Syllabus* or consult your

instructor to determine if you are to submit your assignments on paper or electronically. To submit electronically, go to Step 14, and then follow the instructions provided by your instructor.

13. **Print Preview** your presentation, and then print **Handouts (6 Slides Per Page)**.

14. **Save** the changes to your presentation, and then close the presentation.

End **You have completed Project 6G** _____

Content-Based Assessments

Mastering PowerPoint

Project 6H—Rafting Trip

In this project, you will apply the skills you practiced from the Objectives in Projects 6A and 6B.

Objectives: 1. *Create a Template by Modifying Slide Masters;* **3.** *Create a Photo Album;* **4.** *Share Files with Other Users.*

In the following Mastering PowerPoint Assessment, you will create a photo album presentation with pictures of an employee river rafting trip sponsored by the Human Resources Department at Adventure Valley Park. Your completed presentation will look similar to the one shown in Figure 6.38.

For Project 6H, you will need the following files:

New blank PowerPoint presentation
p06H_Raft1
p06H_Raft2
p06H_Raft3
p06H_Raft4
p06H_Raft5
p06H_Raft6

You will save your presentation and your document as 6H_Rafting_Trip_Firstname_Lastname and 6H_Handouts_Firstname_Lastname

Figure 6.38

(Project 6H–Rafting Trip continues on the next page)

(Project 6H–Rafting Trip continued)

1. **Start** PowerPoint, begin a new blank presentation, and insert **a Photo Album**. From your student files, select **p06H_Raft1**, hold down ⇧Shift, and then click **p06H_Raft6** and then insert the six selected pictures. Remove **p06H_Raft3** from the list. Rearrange the list of pictures as necessary so that they are in the following order: p06H_Raft4, p06H_Raft6, p06H_Raft1, p06H_Raft5, p06H_Raft2.

2. Modify the album layout by changing the picture layout to **1 picture with title**, the **Frame Shape** to **Center Shadow Rectangle**, and the **Theme** to **Paper**. On the first slide, change the title to **Employee Rafting Trip** and then change the subtitle to **Adventure Valley Park**

3. Display **Slide 2**. Change the title to **Getting Ready for the Day!** Display **Slide 3**. Change the title to **Whitewater Ahead!** Display **Slide 4**. Change the title to **Hold On Tight!** Display **Slide 5**. Change the title to **Don't Fall In!** Display **Slide 6**. Change the title to **You Survived!**

4. **Save** the presentation in your **PowerPoint Chapter 6** folder as **6H_Rafting_Trip_Firstname_Lastname**

5. Display the **Slide Master**, and then select the first slide master layout—**Paper Slide Master: used by slide(s) 1-6**. In the **Edit Theme group**, change the colors to **Flow**, and then change the background style to **Style 7**.

6. Select the title placeholder, and then **Center** the title and change the **Font** to **Arial Black**. On the **Home tab**, in the **Paragraph group**, click the **Align Text** button, and then click **Middle** so that the text is centered vertically within the placeholder. With the title placeholder still selected, display the **Shape Styles gallery**,

and then in the last row, apply the fourth style—**Intense Effect-Accent 3**.

7. Display the second slide master layout—**Title Slide Layout: used by slides(s) 1**. In the title placeholder, change the **Align Text** option to **Middle**. In the subtitle placeholder, change the **Font Size** to **28**. Return the presentation to **Normal** view, and then notice that the changes applied to the slide master were applied to all of the slides in the presentation. **Save** the presentation.

8. **Publish** the presentation and **Create Handouts in Microsoft Office Word** with **Blank lines next to slides**. If necessary, display the Word document, and then **Save** the Word document in your **PowerPoint Chapter 6** folder as **6H_Handouts_Firstname_Lastname** Insert a **Footer** using the **FileName Field**. After you have created the footer, double-click anywhere in the document to leave the Footer area.

9. Check your *Chapter Assignment Sheet* or your *Course Syllabus* or consult your instructor to determine if you are to submit your assignments on paper or electronically. To submit electronically, go to Step 11, and then follow the instructions provided by your instructor.

10. From the **Office** menu, click **Print**. At the bottom of the displayed **Print** dialog box, click **OK**. From the **Office** menu, click **Close**, saving any changes if prompted to do so.

11. At the far right edge of the title bar, click the **Close** button to exit the Word program. If necessary, start PowerPoint, and then open your file **6H_Rafting_Trip_Firstname_Lastname**.

(Project 6H–Rafting Trip continues on the next page)

Mastering PowerPoint

(Project 6H–Rafting Trip continued)

12. Create a **Header and Footer** for the **Notes and Handouts**. Include the **Date and time updated automatically**, the **Page number**, and a **Footer** with the file name 6H_Rafting_Trip_Firstname_Lastname

13. Check your *Chapter Assignment Sheet* or your *Course Syllabus* or consult your instructor to determine if you are to submit your assignments on paper or electronically.

To submit electronically, go to Step 15, and then follow the instructions provided by your instructor.

14. **Print Preview** your presentation, and then print **Handouts (6 Slides Per Page)**.

15. **Save** the changes to your presentation, and then close the presentation.

End **You have completed Project 6H**

Content-Based Assessments

Mastering PowerPoint

Project 6I — Carnival

In this project, you will apply the skills you practiced from all of the Objectives in Projects 6A and 6B.

Objectives: 1. *Create a Template by Modifying Slide Masters;* **2.** *Edit a Presentation;* **3.** *Create a Photo Album;* **4.** *Share Files with Other Users.*

In the following Mastering PowerPoint Assessment, you will create a template and a photo album illustrating Carnival Days at Adventure Valley Resort that the Public Relations department will post on the Adventure Valley Resort Web site. Your completed presentation will look similar to the one shown in Figure 6.39.

For Project 6I, you will need the following files:

New blank PowerPoint presentation
p06I_Carnival1
p06I_Carnival2
p06I_Carnival3
p06I_Carnival4
p06I_Carnival5
p06I_Carnival6
p06I_Carnival7
p06I_Fireworks
p06I_Carnival_Outline

You will save your presentation and your Web page as
6I_Carnival_Firstname_Lastname and
6I_Web_Carnival_Firstname_Lastname

Figure 6.39

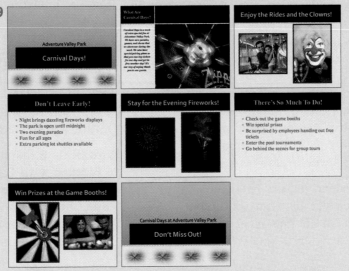

(Project 6I–Carnival continues on the next page)

Content-Based Assessments

(Project 6I–Carnival continued)

1. **Start** PowerPoint and begin a new blank presentation. Apply the **Module Theme**, and then display the **Slide Master**. Select the first slide master layout—**Module Slide Master: used by slide(s) 1**, and then change the background style to **Style 9**. **Save** the file as a **PowerPoint Template** in your **PowerPoint Chapter 6** folder with the file name 6I_Template_Firstname_Lastname

2. Display the second slide master layout—**Title Slide Layout: used by slide(s) 1**. Click in the upper black area of the slide to select the large black rectangle. Display the **Shape Styles gallery**, and then in the last row, apply the second style—**Intense Effect-Accent 1**.

3. Click in the title placeholder, and then display the **Shape Styles gallery**. In the last row, apply the first style—**Intense Effect-Dark 1**. **Center** the title text, and then change the **Line Spacing** to **2.0**.

4. Click in the subtitle placeholder, and then change the **Font Color** to **Black, Text 1**. **Center** the subtitle text, and then change the font size to **32**.

5. From your student files, insert the **Picture p06I_Fireworks**, and then drag the picture so that its lower left corner aligns with the lower left corner of the slide. Duplicate the picture using Ctrl+D, and then drag the duplicated picture up and to the right so that the tops of the two pictures align and the left edge of the duplicated picture touches the right edge of the original picture. The pictures will be side by side.

6. Duplicate the second picture two times. The four pictures will align across the bottom of the slide. Do not be concerned if the fourth picture extends slightly off the

edge of the slide. Select all four pictures. (Hint: Use ⇧ Shift), and then apply a **50 Point Soft Edges Picture Effect.**) **Save** and close the template.

7. **Start** PowerPoint, begin a new blank presentation, and insert a **Photo Album**. From your student files, select **p06I_Carnival1**, hold down ⇧ Shift, click **p06I_Carnival7,** and then insert the seven selected pictures. **Remove p06I_Carnival1** from the list, and then if necessary, move **p06I_Carnival7** so that it is the last picture in the list.

8. Change the picture layout to **2 pictures with title**, and the frame shape to **Compound Frame, Black**. To apply the template that you created, click the **Browse** button, navigate to your **PowerPoint Chapter 6** folder, click **6I_Template_Firstname_Lastname**, and then click **Select**. **Create** the photo album.

9. On **Slide 1**, change the presentation title to **Fiesta Days!** Change the subtitle to **Adventure Valley Park** and then save the presentation in your **PowerPoint Chapter 6** folder as 6I_Carnival_Firstname_Lastname

10. Type the following titles on **Slides 2**, **3**, and **4**:
    Enjoy the Rides and the Clowns!
    Stay for the Evening Fireworks!
    Win Prizes at the Game Booths!

11. With **Slide 4** displayed, from your student files, insert the Microsoft Office Word Outline—**p06I_Carnival_Outline**.

12. With **Slide 5** displayed, change the **Layout** to **Picture with Caption**. Select the title and change the **Font Size** to **28**, and the **Font Color** to the fifth color in the first row—**Gold, Accent 1**. Select the caption paragraph, and then change the **Font Size**

(Project 6I–Carnival continues on the next page)

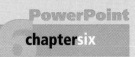

Mastering PowerPoint

(Project 6I–Carnival continued)

to **20**. **Center** the caption, and then apply **Italic**. In the picture placeholder, from your student files, insert **p06I_Carnival1**.

13. Display the presentation in **Slide Sorter** view, and then move **Slide 5** so that it becomes **Slide 2**. Move **Slide 6** so that it becomes **Slide 4**, and then move **Slide 7** so that it becomes **Slide 6**. Return the presentation to **Normal** view.

14. On **Slides 4** and **6**, change the title **Font Color** to **Gold, Accent 1**, and then **Center** the titles on both slides.

15. Display **Slide 7** and then add a **New Slide** with the **Title Slide** layout. In the title placeholder type **Don't Miss Out!** and in the subtitle placeholder type **Fiesta Days at Adventure Valley Park**

16. On **Slide 1**, insert a comment with the text **Please replace all instances of Fiesta with Carnival**. Close the comment, and then **Replace** all instances of the word *Fiesta* with *Carnival*. **Save** your presentation.

17. **Save** your presentation in your **PowerPoint Chapter 6** folder as a **Single File Web Page** with the File name

6I_Web_Carnival_Firstname_Lastname and then publish the **Complete presentation** using the **Microsoft Internet Explorer 4.0 or later (high fidelity)** option. Select the **Open published Web page in browser** check box, and if necessary, Allow Blocked Content. View each slide in your browser window. Close your Web browser to return to your PowerPoint presentation.

18. Create a **Header and Footer** for the **Notes and Handouts**. Include the **Date and time updated automatically**, the **Page number**, and a **Footer** with the file name 6I_Carnival_Firstname_Lastname

19. Check your *Chapter Assignment Sheet* or your *Course Syllabus* or consult your instructor to determine if you are to submit your assignments on paper or electronically. To submit electronically, go to Step 21, and then follow the instructions provided by your instructor.

20. **Print Preview** your presentation, and then print **Handouts (3 Slides Per Page)**.

21. **Save** the changes to your presentation, and then close the presentation.

End You have completed Project 6I

Content-Based Assessments

Business Running Case

Project 6J—Business_Running_Case

In this project, you will apply the skills you practiced from all the Objectives in Projects 6A and 6B.

From My Computer, navigate to the student files that accompany this textbook. In the folder **03_business_running_case**, locate and open the folder for this chapter. Open and print the instructions for this project, which are provided to you in Adobe PDF format. Follow the instructions and use the skills you have gained thus far to assist Jennifer Nelson in meeting the challenges of owning and running her business.

PowerPoint
chaptersix

Rubric

The following outcomes-based assessments are *open-ended assessments*. That is, there is no specific correct result; your result will depend on your approach to the information provided. Make *professional quality* your goal. Use the following scoring rubric to guide you in *how* to approach the problem and then to evaluate *how well* your approach solves the problem.

The *criteria*—Software Mastery, Content, Format and Layout, and Process—represent the knowledge and skills you have gained that you can apply to solving the problem. The *levels of performance*—Professional Quality, Approaching Professional Quality, or Needs Quality Improvement—help you and your instructor evaluate your result.

	Your completed project is of Professional Quality if you:	Your completed project is Approaching Professional Quality if you:	Your completed project Needs Quality Improvements if you:
1-Software Mastery	Choose and apply the most appropriate skills, tools, and features and identify efficient methods to solve the problem.	Choose and apply some appropriate skills, tools, and features, but not in the most efficient manner.	Choose inappropriate skills, tools, or features, or are inefficient in solving the problem.
2-Content	Construct a solution that is clear and well organized, contains content that is accurate, appropriate to the audience and purpose, and is complete. Provide a solution that contains no errors of spelling, grammar, or style.	Construct a solution in which some components are unclear, poorly organized, inconsistent, or incomplete. Misjudge the needs of the audience. Have some errors in spelling, grammar, or style, but the errors do not detract from comprehension.	Construct a solution that is unclear, incomplete, or poorly organized, containing some inaccurate or inappropriate content; and contains many errors of spelling, grammar, or style. Do not solve the problem.
3-Format and Layout	Format and arrange all elements to communicate information and ideas, clarify function, illustrate relationships, and indicate relative importance.	Apply appropriate format and layout features to some elements, but not others. Overuse features, causing minor distraction.	Apply format and layout that does not communicate information or ideas clearly. Do not use format and layout features to clarify function, illustrate relationships, or indicate relative importance. Use available features excessively, causing distraction.
4-Process	Use an organized approach that integrates planning, development, self-assessment, revision, and reflection.	Demonstrate an organized approach in some areas, but not others; or, use an insufficient process of organization throughout.	Do not use an organized approach to solve the problem.

Outcomes-Based Assessments

Problem Solving

Project 6K — Coasters

In this project, you will construct a solution by applying any combination of the Objectives found in Projects 6A and 6B.

For Project 6K, you will need the following file:

New blank PowerPoint presentation

**You will save your presentation as
6K_Coasters_Firstname_Lastname**

Adventure Valley Resort is participating in a travel fair and the resort director would like to have a photo album presentation for the fair that showcases the roller coasters at the park. Create a photo album presentation with pictures that you have, or follow the instructions in the following Note for ideas on finding images using the Clip Art feature in PowerPoint. Apply appropriate slide titles, a theme, transitions and animation, and include at least two slides that describe the roller coasters in the pictures that you have chosen. Add the file name and page number to the Notes and Handouts footer and check the presentation for spelling errors. Save the presentation as **6K_Coasters_Profile_Firstname_Lastname** and then submit it as directed.

Note: You can find many appropriate images available to Microsoft Office users. To access these images, click the Insert tab, and then from the Illustrations group, click the Clip Art button. In the Clip Art task pane, type a key word—such as *roller coaster*—in the *Search for* box. You can specify the image type (clip art or photographs) and where to search. The largest variety of photographs can be found by including Web Collections in the *Search in* box. You can also use images from earlier projects in this chapter, or images from your personal collection. After you insert the pictures, save each picture as a JPEG so that you can insert it in the photo album.

End **You have completed Project 6K** ————————————

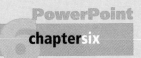

Problem Solving

Project 6L — Child Care

In this project, you will construct a solution by applying any combination of the Objectives found in Projects 6A and 6B.

For Project 6L, you will need the following file:

New blank PowerPoint presentation

**You will save your presentation as
6L_Child_Care_Firstname_Lastname**

Many of the employees at Adventure Valley Resort are the primary care-givers for their young children. The management at Adventure Valley Resort is committed to helping their employees achieve a balance between their work and personal lives and have decided to add a child care program as a benefit for resort employees. The Human Resources director has developed a plan for two programs—an all day program for children under 5 years of age and an after school program for children in Kindergarten through 8th grade. In the preschool program, there will be four children for every teacher, and there will be reading programs, free play, field trips, arts and crafts, and music. Employees may enroll their children in an all day program for $75 per week or in a morning or after-noon program for $50 per week. The after school program will include organized sports and tutors that can assist children with homework. Vacation camps will be available during school breaks and vacations. The cost is $50 per week for the after school program and $100 per week for the vacation camp program. The child care director has a Masters degree in Child Development and 15 years of experience in preschool and ele-mentary school teaching. At the minimum, each teacher has an Associates degree in Child Development and is CPR certified.

Create and save a template that can be applied to a presentation about the day care program. Then, using the information in the previous para-graph, create a presentation that the Human Resources director can show at an upcoming staff meeting to inform employees of the program. Apply the template to the presentation, and insert images, shapes, or tables to appropriately reflect the information. See the note at the end of project 6K for information on finding images for this project. Add the file name and page number to the Notes and Handouts footer and check for spelling errors. Save the presentation as **6L_Child_Care_Firstname_Lastname** and then submit it as directed.

End You have completed Project 6L

Problem Solving

Project 6M — Finance

In this project, you will construct a solution by applying any combination of the Objectives found in Projects 6A and 6B.

For Project 6M, you will need the following files:

New blank PowerPoint presentation
p06M_Finance_Outline
p06M_Logo

**You will save your presentation as
6M_Finance_Firstname_Lastname**

The Finance director of Adventure Valley Resort has requested that you create a presentation that can be shown at an upcoming board of directors meeting highlighting the financial, attendance, and guest information about the resort. Create a template for the presentation and include in the template a gradient fill background and the Adventure Valley Resort logo found in your student files—**p06M_Logo**. Recolor, size, and apply effects as necessary to the picture so that it blends with the template that you create. Save the template, and then start a new presentation. From your student files, insert the Microsoft Office Word outline—**p06M_Finance_Outline**, and then apply the template. Apply slide transitions and animation. Add the file name and page number to the Notes and Handouts footer and check for spelling errors. Save the presentation as **6M_Finance_Firstname_Lastname** and then submit it as directed.

End **You have completed Project 6M**————————

Problem Solving

Project 6N—Guests

In this project, you will construct a solution by applying any combination of the Objectives found in Projects 6A and 6B.

For Project 6N, you will need the following files:

New blank PowerPoint presentation
p06N_Guests1
p06N_Guests2
p06N_Guests3
p06N_Guests4
p06N_Guests5

You will save your presentation, document, and Web page as 6N_Guests_Firstname_Lastname, 6N_Handouts_Firstname_Lastname, and 6N_Web_Guests_Firstname_Lastname

---

The Adventure Valley Resort Public Relations Department is developing a presentation for viewing on the Web that highlights guests who are enjoying themselves at the resort. From your student files, use the pictures **p06N_Guests1** through **p06N_Guests5** to create a photo album presentation with one picture and a title on each slide. Save the presentation as **6N_Guests_Firstname_Lastname** Choose an appropriate theme, create and format a title slide, and insert appropriate slide titles. Add the file name and page number to the Notes and Handouts footer and check for spelling errors. Create handouts in Microsoft Office Word, and then save the Word document as **6N_Handouts_Firstname_Lastname** Add the FileName field to the footer, and then save and close Microsoft Office Word. Open the presentation again in PowerPoint, and then publish the presentation as a single file Web page with the file name **6N_Web_Guests_ Firstname_Lastname** Submit the presentation as directed.

End You have completed Project 6N ——————————————

Outcomes-Based Assessments

Problem Solving

Project 6O—Employee News

In this project, you will construct a solution by applying any combination of the Objectives found in Projects 6A and 6B.

> **For Project 6O, you will need the following files:**
>
> New blank PowerPoint presentation
> p06O_Employee_News_Outline

You will save your presentation and Web page as 6O_Employee_News_Firstname_Lastname and 6O_Web_Employee_News_Firstname_Lastname

The Public Relations Department of Adventure Valley Resort publishes to the resort's intranet a monthly presentation that highlights the achievements of three employees who have achieved outstanding customer service reviews from resort guests. Create and save a template that includes a picture that is either representative of an amusement park or of the concept of good customer service. See the note at the end of Project 6K for information on finding an image for this project. After you have created and saved the template, start a new blank presentation. From your student files, insert the Microsoft Word outline—**p06O_Employee_News_Outline**. Apply the template that you created, and then publish the presentation as a Web page with the File name **6O_Web_Employee_News_Firstname_Lastname** Add the file name to the Notes and Handouts footer and check for spelling errors. Save the presentation as **6O_Employee_News_Firstname_Lastname** and then submit it as directed.

End **You have completed Project 6O** ——————————

PowerPoint
chaptersix

 You and *GO!*

Project 6P—You and *GO!*

In this project, you will construct a solution by applying any combination of the skills you practiced from the Objectives in Projects 6A and 6B.

From My Computer, navigate to the student files that accompany this textbook. In the folder **04_you_and_go**, locate and open the folder for this chapter. Open and print the instructions for this project, which are provided to you in Adobe PDF format. Follow the instructions to create a presentation describing an amusement park that you would like to visit.

End **You have completed Project 6P** ——————————

GO! with Help

Project 6Q—You and *GO!*

You can create a self-running presentation that can be viewed at a kiosk or on the Web. Use Microsoft Office Help to learn about self-running presentations.

1 **Start** PowerPoint. At the far right end of the Ribbon, click the **Microsoft Office PowerPoint Help** button.

2 In the **Type words to search for** box, type **Self-running presentations** and then press ⏎.

3 Click the **Create a self-running presentation** link, and then read the information and steps. When you are through, close the Help window, and then **Exit** PowerPoint.

 End **You have completed Project 6Q** ——————————

Glossary

Action button A type of hyperlink created using an AutoShape.

Angle A gradient fill option that determines the progression of colors from one area of the slide to another.

Animation effects A command that introduces individual slide elements so that the slide can be displayed one element at a time.

Annotate The action of writing notes on the slide while the slide show is running.

AutoFit A feature that widens the column to accommodate the longest cell entry in the column.

Background style A slide background fill variation that combines theme colors in different intensities.

Black slide A slide that displays at the end of a slide presentation indicating the end of the slide show.

Body font A font that is applied to all slide text except titles.

Browser Software that lets you view and navigate on the Web.

Bulleted levels Outline levels identified by a symbol.

Category labels Chart elements that display along the bottom of the chart to identify the categories of data.

Cell The intersection of a column and row.

Cell reference A combination of the column letter and row number identifying a cell.

Chart A graphic representation of numeric data.

Chart Area The area surrounding a chart.

Chart layout The combination of displayed chart elements, including the title, legend, and data labels.

Clip Art Drawings, movies, sounds, or photographic images that are included with Microsoft Office or downloaded from the Web.

Column chart A type of chart used to compare data.

Comments Notes within a presentation that contain reviewer questions or thoughts.

Contextual tabs Specialized tools for working with a selected object and that appear as additional tabs in the Ribbon.

Contextual tools Tools that enable you to perform specific commands related to the selected object, and display one or more contextual tabs that contain related groups of commands that you will need when working with the type of object that is selected.

Copy A command that duplicates a selection and places it on the Clipboard.

Cropping The action of trimming a picture to remove unwanted vertical or horizontal edges.

Crosshair pointer The pointer that indicates that you can draw a shape.

Custom animation list A list that indicates the animation effect applied to slide items.

Custom show A presentation within a presentation in which you group several slides to be shown to a particular audience.

Cut A command that removes selected text or graphics from your presentation and moves the selection to the Clipboard.

Data labels Labels that identify pie slices and that indicate the percentage of the total or a value that each slice represents.

Data marker A column, bar, area, dot, pie slice, or other symbol in a chart that represents a single data point.

Data point A chart value that originates in a worksheet cell.

Data series A group of related data points.

Deselect The action of canceling a selection.

Direction A gradient fill option that determines the progression of colors from one area of the slide to another.

Drag-and-drop The action of moving a selection by dragging it to a new location.

Dragging The technique of holding down the left mouse button and moving over an area of text in order to select it.

Editing The process of adding, deleting, or changing the contents of a slide.

Effect options Animation options that include changing the direction of an effect and playing a sound when an animation takes place.

Embedded object An object in which a link is established between the object and its source application.

Emphasis effect An animation effect that draws attention to a slide element that is currently displayed.

Entrance effects Animations that bring a slide element onto the screen.

Eraser A feature that merges cells by deleting existing borders.

Exit effects Animations that move a slide element off the screen.

Explode A method of emphasizing a slice of a pie chart by pulling the slice out of the pie.

Fill color The inside color of text or an object.

Font A set of characters with the same design and shape.

Font styles Font formatting that emphasizes text, including bold, italic, and underline.

Font theme A theme that determines the font applied to two types of slide text—headings and body.

Footer Text that displays at the bottom of every slide or that prints at the bottom of a sheet of slide handouts or notes pages.

Format Painter A feature that copies formatting from one selection of text to another, thus ensuring formatting consistency in your presentation.

Formatting Changing the appearance of the text, layout, and design of a slide.

Gallery A visual representation of a command's options.

Gradient fill A color combination in which one color fades into another.

Gradient stop A gradient fill option that determines the color, position, and transparency values of the gradient fill. Each color used in the gradient fill must be included as a gradient stop.

Group Several objects treated as one unit.

Guides Vertical and horizontal lines that display in the rulers to give you a visual indication of where the crosshair pointer is positioned so that you can draw a shape.

Header Text that displays at the top of every slide or that prints at the top of a sheet of slide handouts or notes pages.

Headings font The font that is applied to slide titles.

Hidden slide A slide that displays when the action button to which it is linked is clicked during an onscreen presentation.

HTML The abbreviation for Hypertext Markup Language.

Hyperlink A button, text, or image that when selected, activates another information resource.

Hypertext Markup Language The language that indicates how Web browsers should display Web page elements.

Insertion point A blinking vertical line that indicates where text will be inserted.

Intranet An organization's internal network.

Layout The placement and arrangement of the text and graphic elements on a slide.

Leader lines Lines that connect a pie slice to its corresponding data label.

Legend A chart element that identifies the patterns or colors that are assigned to the categories in the chart.

Line chart A type of chart that show trends over time.

Live preview A technology that shows the results of applying an editing or formatting change as you move your pointer over the results presented in the gallery.

Merge cells A feature that combines selected cells into one cell.

Mini toolbar A small toolbar containing frequently used formatting commands, and sometimes accompanied by a shortcut menu of other frequently used commands, which displays as a result of right-clicking a selection or of selecting text.

Navigation tools Buttons used during a slide show to move to display slides in any order.

Normal view The view in which the PowerPoint window is divided into three areas: the Slides/Outline pane, the Slide pane, and the Notes pane.

Notes pages Printouts that contain the slide image in the top half of the page and speaker's notes in the lower half of the page.

Nudge The action of moving objects in small increments using the directional arrow keys.

Office Clipboard A temporary storage area maintained by your Microsoft Office program.

Paste The action of placing text or objects that have been copied or moved from one location to another location.

Paste link A Paste option that creates a link in which change to a source application can be updated in the destination application.

Photo album A presentation composed of pictures.

Pie chart A type of chart that is used to illustrate percentages or proportions and that includes only one series of data.

Placeholder A slide element that reserves a portion of a slide and serves as a container for text, graphics, and other slide elements.

Points A unit of measure that describes the size of a font.

Presentation graphics software A program used to effectively present information to an audience.

Preset colors Built-in gradient fill color options.

Print Preview A feature that displays your presentation as it will print based on the options that you select.

Rotation handle A feature used to rotate an object in any direction in any increment.

Shape Style A combination of formatting effects that includes 3-D, glow, and bevel effects and shadows.

Shapes Drawing objects including lines, arrows, stars and banners, and ovals and rectangles that are used to help convey a message by showing process and by containing text.

Shortcut menu A context-sensitive menu that displays commands and options relevant to the selected object.

Sizing handles White circles or squares that surround an image and are used to size the image.

Slide handouts Printed images of more than one slide on a sheet of paper.

Slide master A slide that holds the information about formatting and text that displays on every slide in a presentation, including placeholder positions, background design, theme formatting, bullets, and fonts styles.

Slide Sorter View A view useful for rearranging slides in which all of the slides in the presentation display as thumbnails.

SmartArt graphic A designer-quality visual representation of your information that you can create by choosing from among many different layouts to effectively community your message or ideas.

SmartArt Styles Combinations of formatting effects that are applied to diagrams.

Split cells A feature that divides a selected cell into the number of specified cells.

Synonyms Words with the same meaning as a selected word.

Table A format for information that organizes and presents text and data in columns and rows.

Table style Formatting applied to an entire table so that it is consistent with the presentation theme.

Task pane A window within a Microsoft Office application that allows you to enter options for completing a command.

Template A model on which a presentation is based that may include text, graphics, and color schemes.

Text Alignment The horizontal placement of text within a placeholder.

Text box An object that is used to position text anywhere on the slide.

Thesaurus A research tool that provides a list of synonyms.

Thumbnails Miniature images of each slide.

Toggle buttons Buttons that are clicked once to turn them on and then clicked again to turn them off.

Transition The way that a slide appears or disappears during an onscreen slide show.

Type There are five types of gradient fills—linear, radial, rectangular, path, and shade from title. The types determine the angle and directions from which the gradient fill is applied.

URL The acronym for Uniform Resource Locator.

Word styles Built-in formats applied to paragraphs and text in Microsoft Office Word.

WordArt A feature that applies combinations of decorative formatting to text, including shadows, reflections, and 3-D effects, as well as changing the line and fill color of text.

Index

Draw Table, border, 249–251
Draw Table feature, 249–253
duplicating objects, 101–104

E

editing data after closing Excel, 194
editing text
    slides, 11–12
    using thesaurus, 18
effect options, 175
embedded object, 411
entrance and emphasis effects, 268–269
Eraser, 249
Excel
    column, widening, 259–262
    editing data after closing, 194
existing presentation, inserting slides from, 36–37
exit effects, 269–270

F

file names, 10
finding and replacing text, 401–402
Fly in effect, 268
folder, 9–11
fonts, 246
    slide master, 387
Format Painter, 89–90
formatting
    chart elements, 263–265
    font and font size, changing, 20–22
    font styles, applying, 22–23
    grouped objects, 331–332
    rotating picture, 320–324
    slide layout, modifying, 24–25
    slide masters, 389
    text, clearing, 114
    text alignment and line spacing, 23–24
    text box, 96
    theme, changing, 25–27
forward, bringing object, 327
front, bringing object to, 327

G

gallery, 12
glow variations, 396
gradient fill, 99
    templates, formatting with, 389–391
gradient stops, 390–391
graphics, 39, 90. *See also* animation
    adding and removing shapes in diagram,
      118–119
    cells, filling, 256–257
    changing diagram type and size, 120–122
    changing size and shape of picture, 92–93
    clip art, 40–42
    compressing, ● CD 5–6
    cropping, 324–326
    deleting shapes containing text, 119
    duplicating and aligning objects, 101–104
    grouping objects, 329–331
    inserting and recoloring, 318–320
    inserting using Content Layout, 91
    moving, sizing, and formatting grouped objects,
      331–332
    moving and sizing images, 42–44

order, changing, 327–329
picture, saving group as, 332–335
rotating, 320–324
style, applying, 44–45
styles, applying, 99–101
templates, adding to, 392–396
text box, inserting and positioning, 93–96
grayscale, 31
Group buttons, 5
grouping objects, 329–331
    saving as picture, 332–335
guides, 96

H

handouts
    creating in Word, 411
    headers and footers, 27–29
    printing, 413–414
headers and footers, 27–29, 257
Help, 45–46
hidden slides, 342–343
Hierarchy graphic, 115
Home tab
    Drawing group, 98
    Font group, 21, 22, 99
    Paragraph group, 23–24, 85
    Slides group, 24
hyperlinks
    action button, 340–342
    to another slide, 339–342
    custom shows, 345–347
    hidden slides, 342–343
    Web page, 337–338
Hypertext Markup Language (HTML), 414

I

Illustrations group, 404
images. *See* animation; graphics
inserting
    graphics, 318–320
    placeholders, 398
    slide, 12–14
    table, 238–239
    tables on Title Only slide, 247–249
insertion point, 93
Insert tab, 116
    Illustrations group, 404
Internet file transfer programs, 10
intranet, 414

L

labels, pie chart, 262–263
landscape orientation, slides, ● CD 1–2
layout, 12
    changing, 247
    charts, modifying, 262–263
leader lines, 263
legend, 191. *See also* data labels
light variations, pictures, 319
lines, wrapping text, 244
line spacing, 23–24
List graphic, 115
list levels, increasing and decreasing,
    14–16
Live Preview, 21